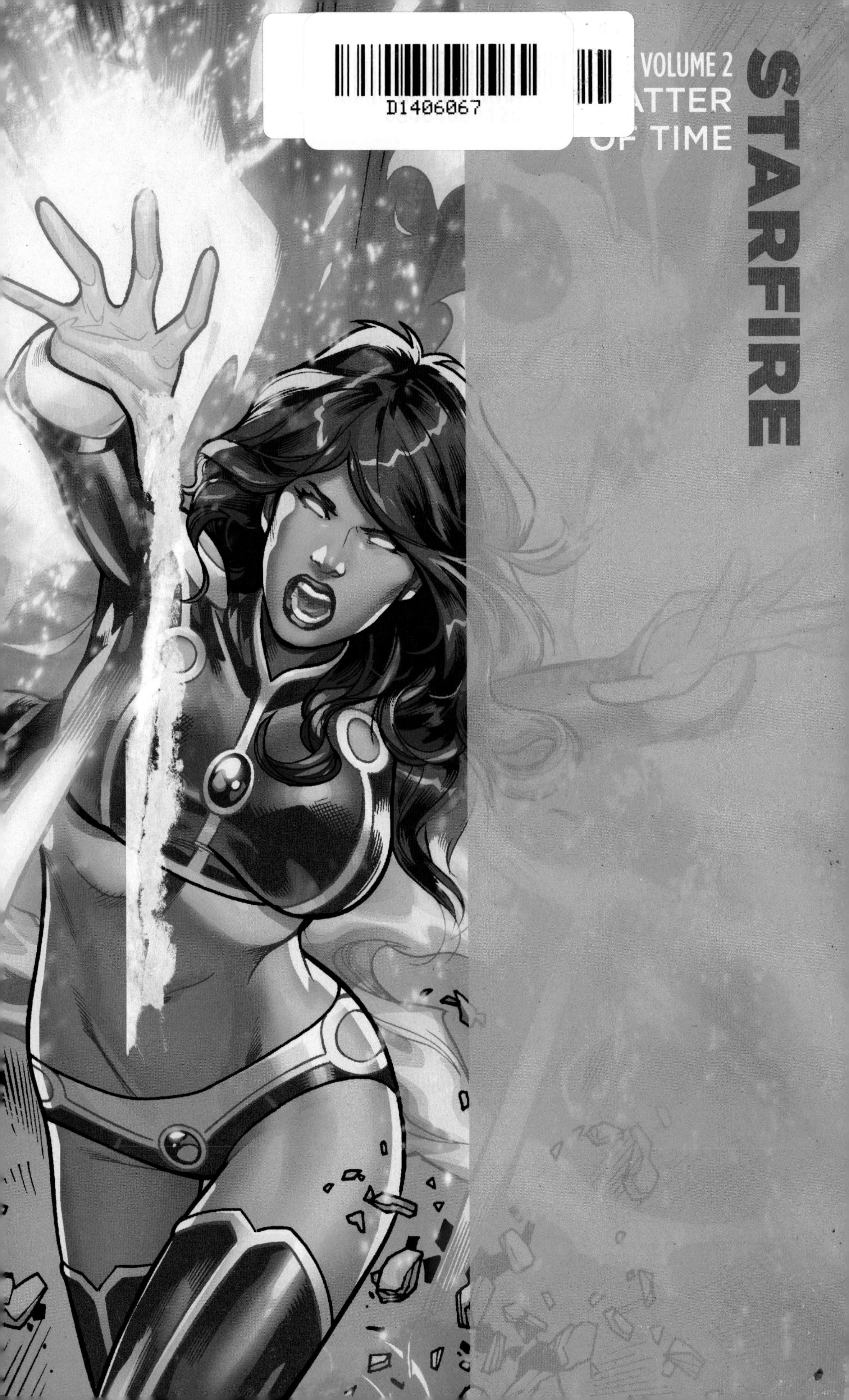
VOLUME 2
ATTER
OF TIME
STARFIRE

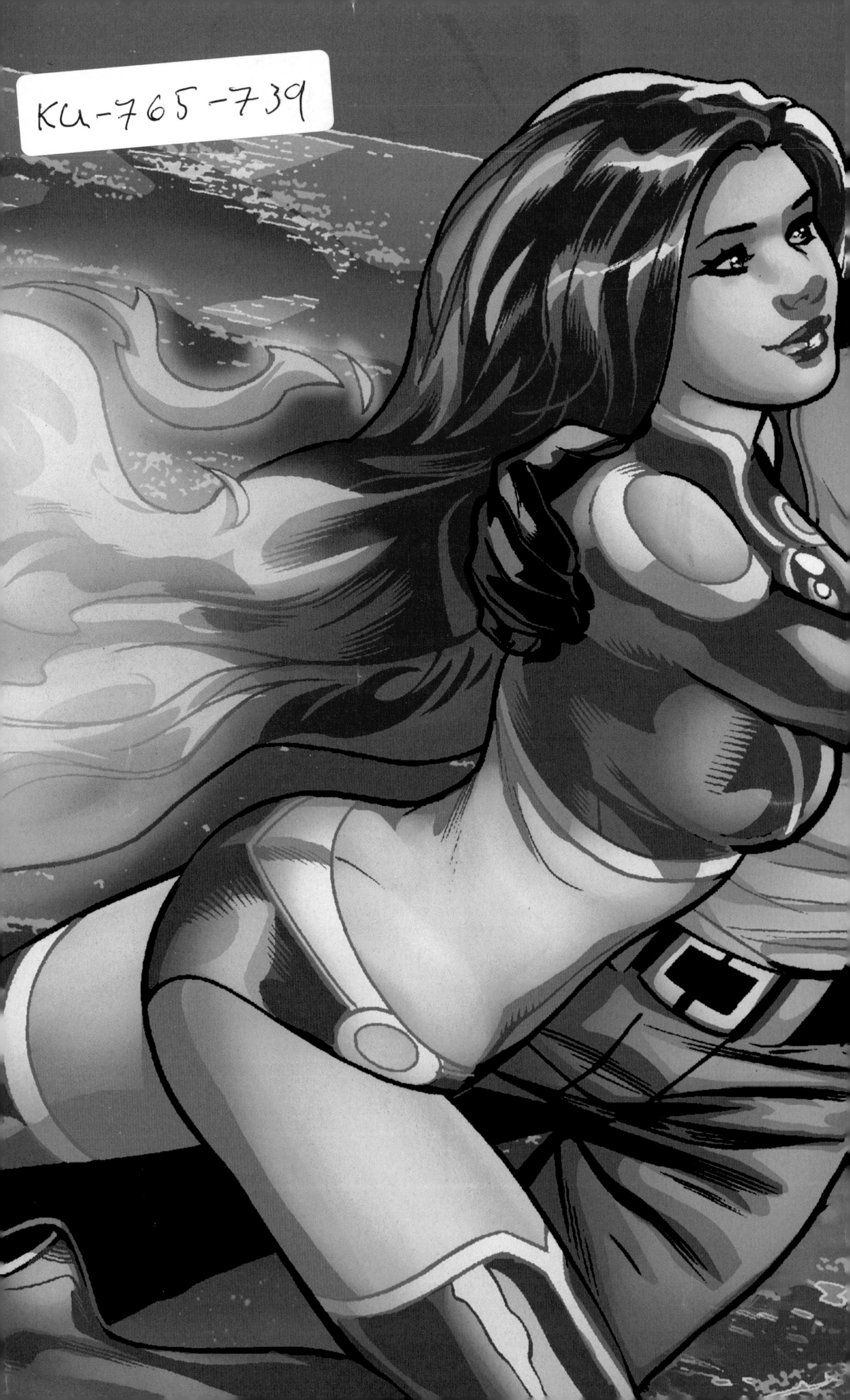

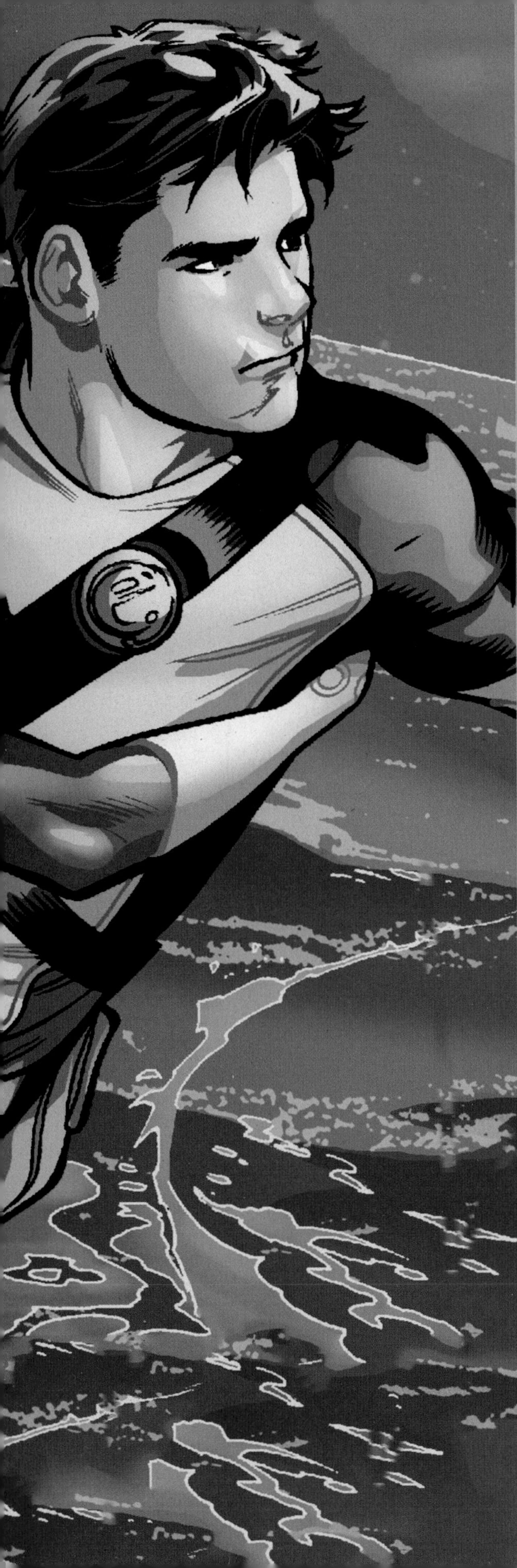

STARFIRE

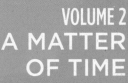

VOLUME 2
A MATTER OF TIME

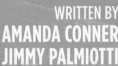

WRITTEN BY
AMANDA CONNER
JIMMY PALMIOTTI

PENCILS BY
ELSA CHARRETIER
EMANUELA LUPACCHINO
MIRCO PIERFEDERICI
RAY McCARTHY
SEAN PARSONS

COLOR BY
HI-FI

LETTERS BY
TOM NAPOLITANO
ROB LEIGH
COREY BREEN

ORIGINAL SERIES &
COLLECTION COVER ART BY
AMANDA CONNER &
PAUL MOUNTS

STARFIRE CREATED BY
MARV WOLFMAN AND
GEORGE PÉREZ

SUPERMAN CREATED BY
JERRY SIEGEL AND
JOE SHUSTER

BY SPECIAL ARRANGEMENT WITH
THE JERRY SIEGEL FAMILY

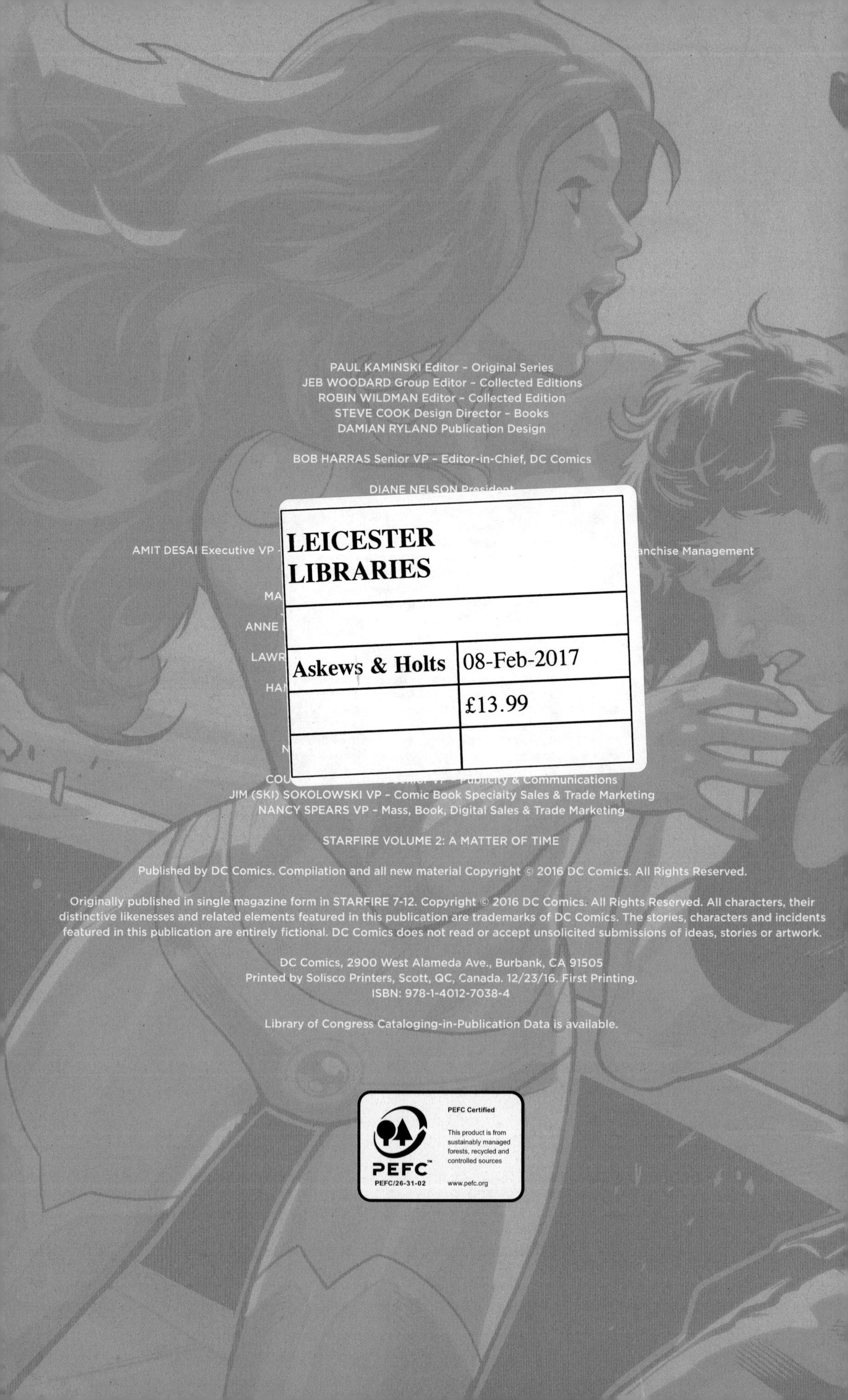

PAUL KAMINSKI Editor – Original Series
JEB WOODARD Group Editor – Collected Editions
ROBIN WILDMAN Editor – Collected Edition
STEVE COOK Design Director – Books
DAMIAN RYLAND Publication Design

BOB HARRAS Senior VP – Editor-in-Chief, DC Comics

DIANE NELSON President

AMIT DESAI Executive VP – [...] [...]anchise Management

MA[...]

ANNE [...]

LAWR[...]

HA[...]

N[...]

COU[...] Senior VP – Publicity & Communications
JIM (SKI) SOKOLOWSKI VP – Comic Book Specialty Sales & Trade Marketing
NANCY SPEARS VP – Mass, Book, Digital Sales & Trade Marketing

STARFIRE VOLUME 2: A MATTER OF TIME

Published by DC Comics. Compilation and all new material Copyright © 2016 DC Comics. All Rights Reserved.

Originally published in single magazine form in STARFIRE 7-12. Copyright © 2016 DC Comics. All Rights Reserved. All characters, their distinctive likenesses and related elements featured in this publication are trademarks of DC Comics. The stories, characters and incidents featured in this publication are entirely fictional. DC Comics does not read or accept unsolicited submissions of ideas, stories or artwork.

DC Comics, 2900 West Alameda Ave., Burbank, CA 91505
Printed by Solisco Printers, Scott, QC, Canada. 12/23/16. First Printing.
ISBN: 978-1-4012-7038-4

Library of Congress Cataloging-in-Publication Data is available.

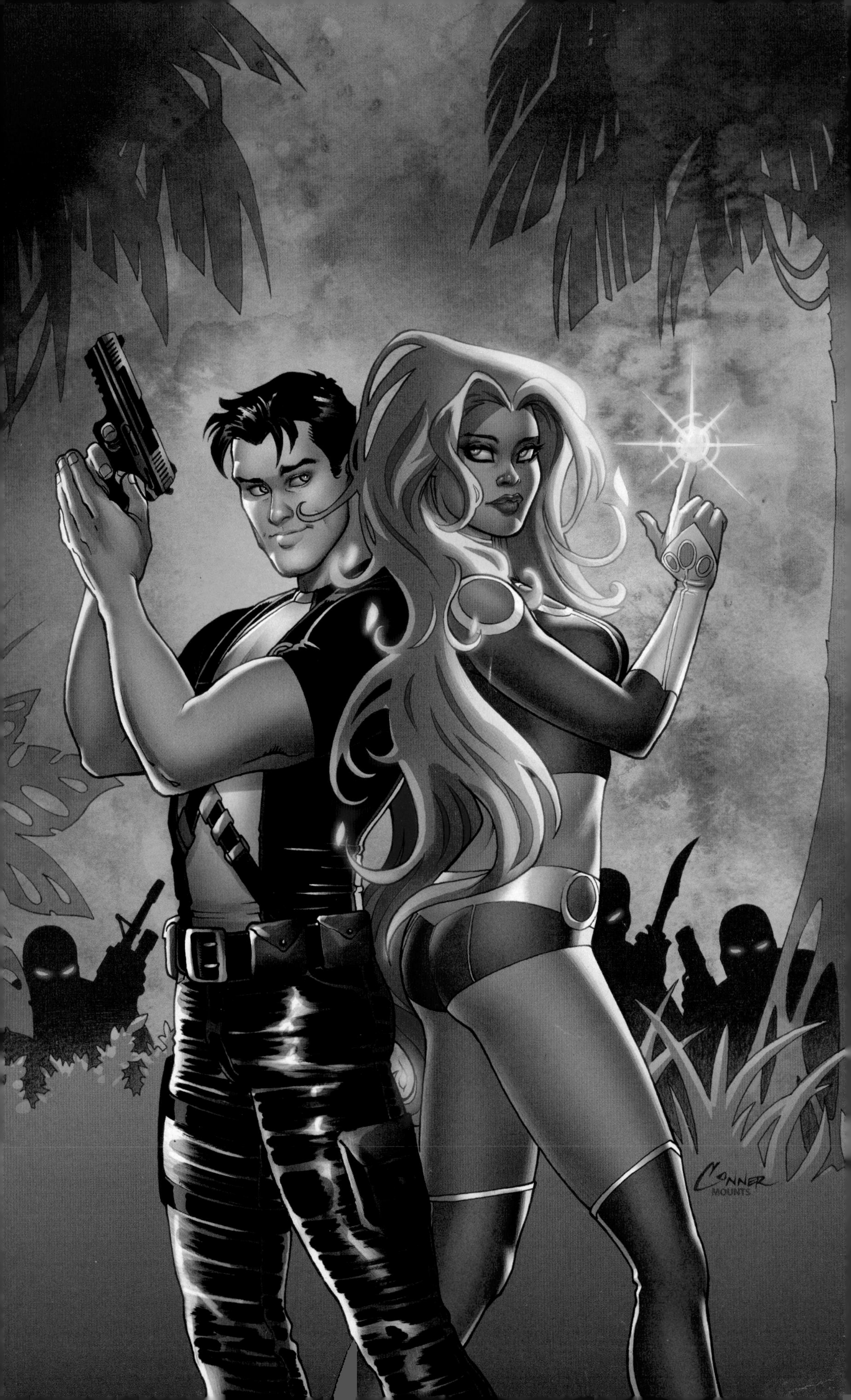
CONNER
MOUNTS

SURRENDER

AMANDA CONNER & JIMMY PALMIOTTI writers EMANUELA LUPACCHINO pencils MIRCO PIERFEDERICI pencil assists
RAY McCARTHY & SEAN PARSONS inks HI-FI colors TOM NAPOLITANO letters

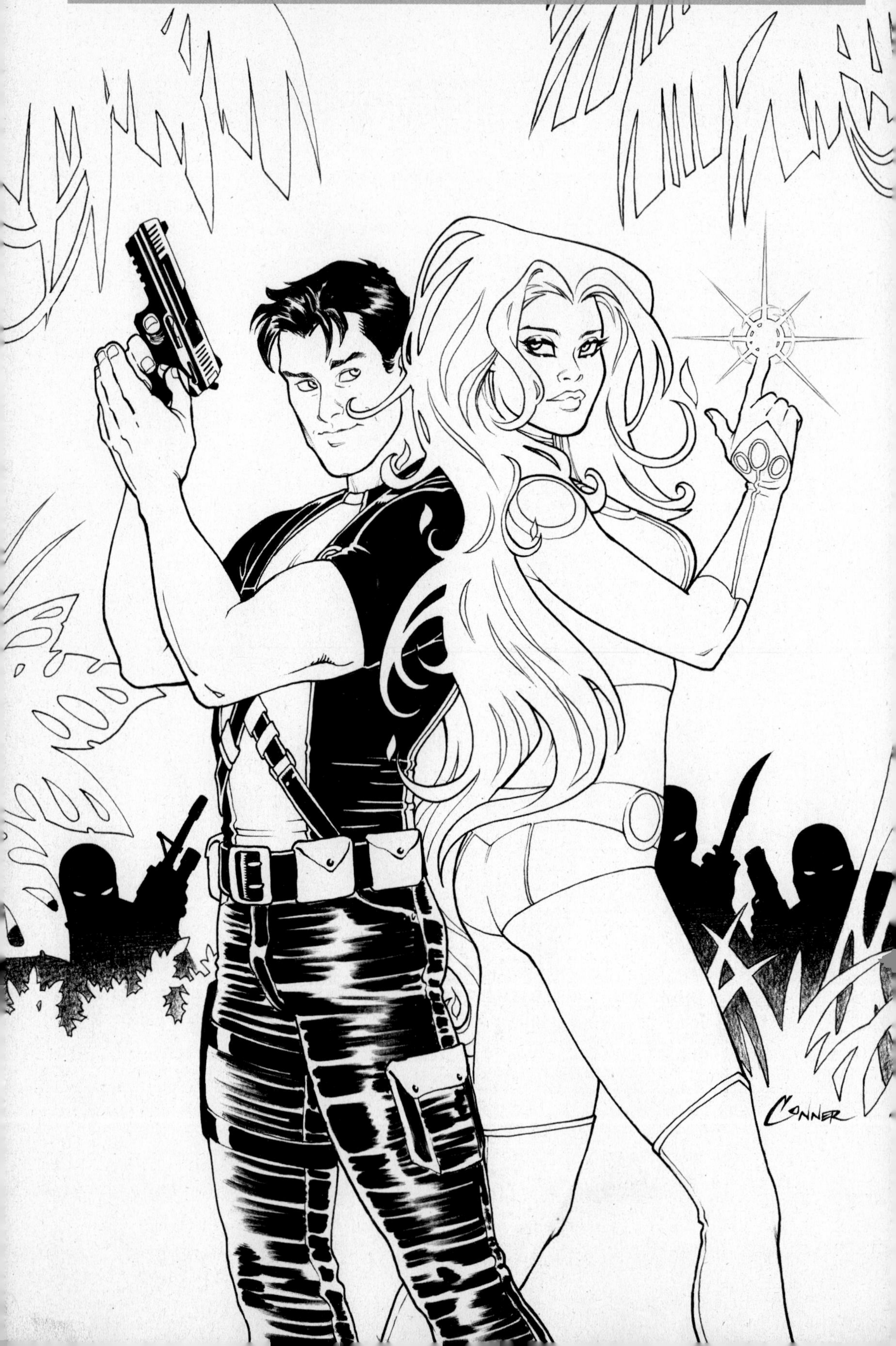
CONNER

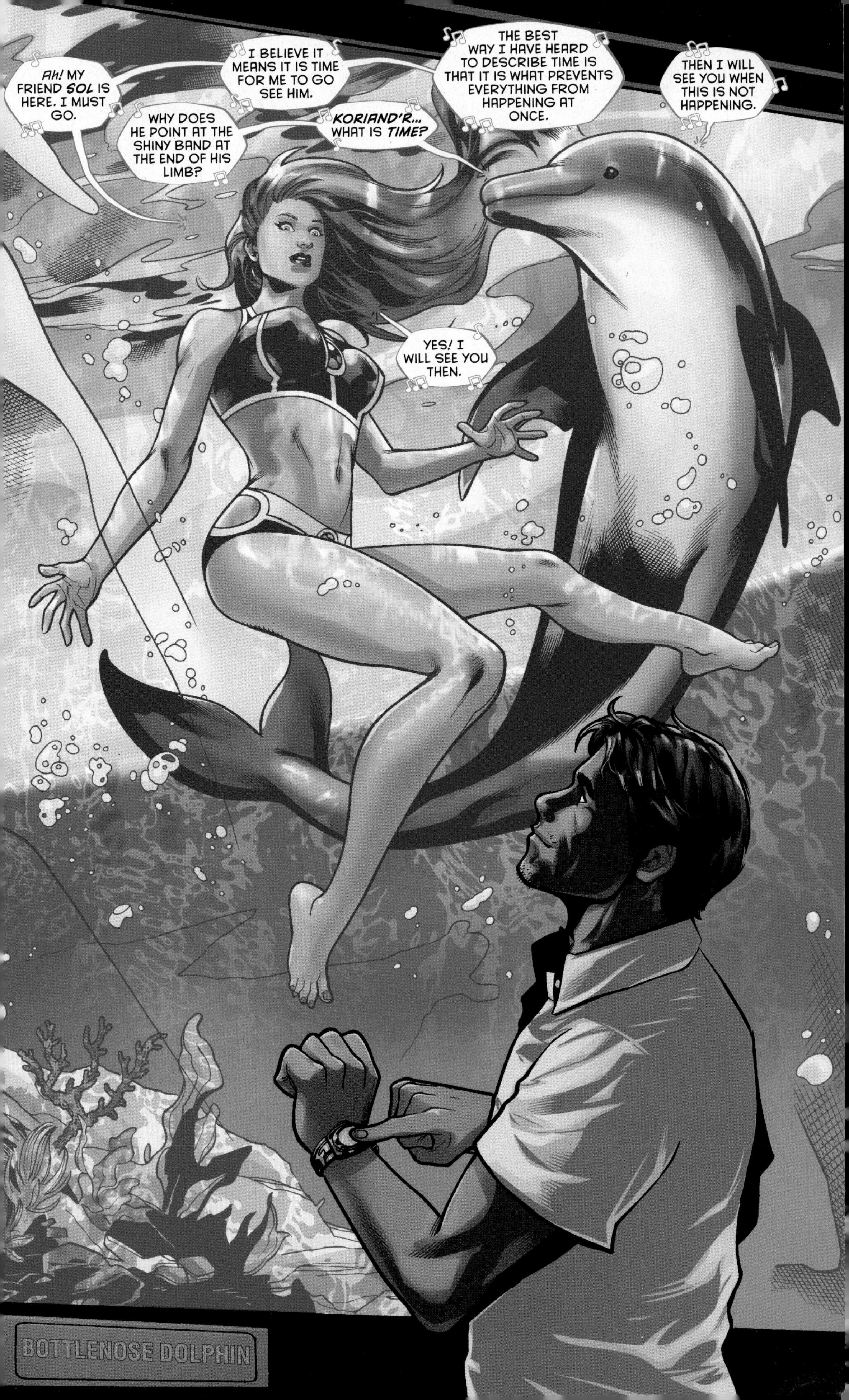
AH! MY FRIEND SOL IS HERE. I MUST GO.
WHY DOES HE POINT AT THE SHINY BAND AT THE END OF HIS LIMB?
I BELIEVE IT MEANS IT IS TIME FOR ME TO GO SEE HIM.
KORIAND'R... WHAT IS TIME?
THE BEST WAY I HAVE HEARD TO DESCRIBE TIME IS THAT IT IS WHAT PREVENTS EVERYTHING FROM HAPPENING AT ONCE.
THEN I WILL SEE YOU WHEN THIS IS NOT HAPPENING.
YES! I WILL SEE YOU THEN.
BOTTLENOSE DOLPHIN

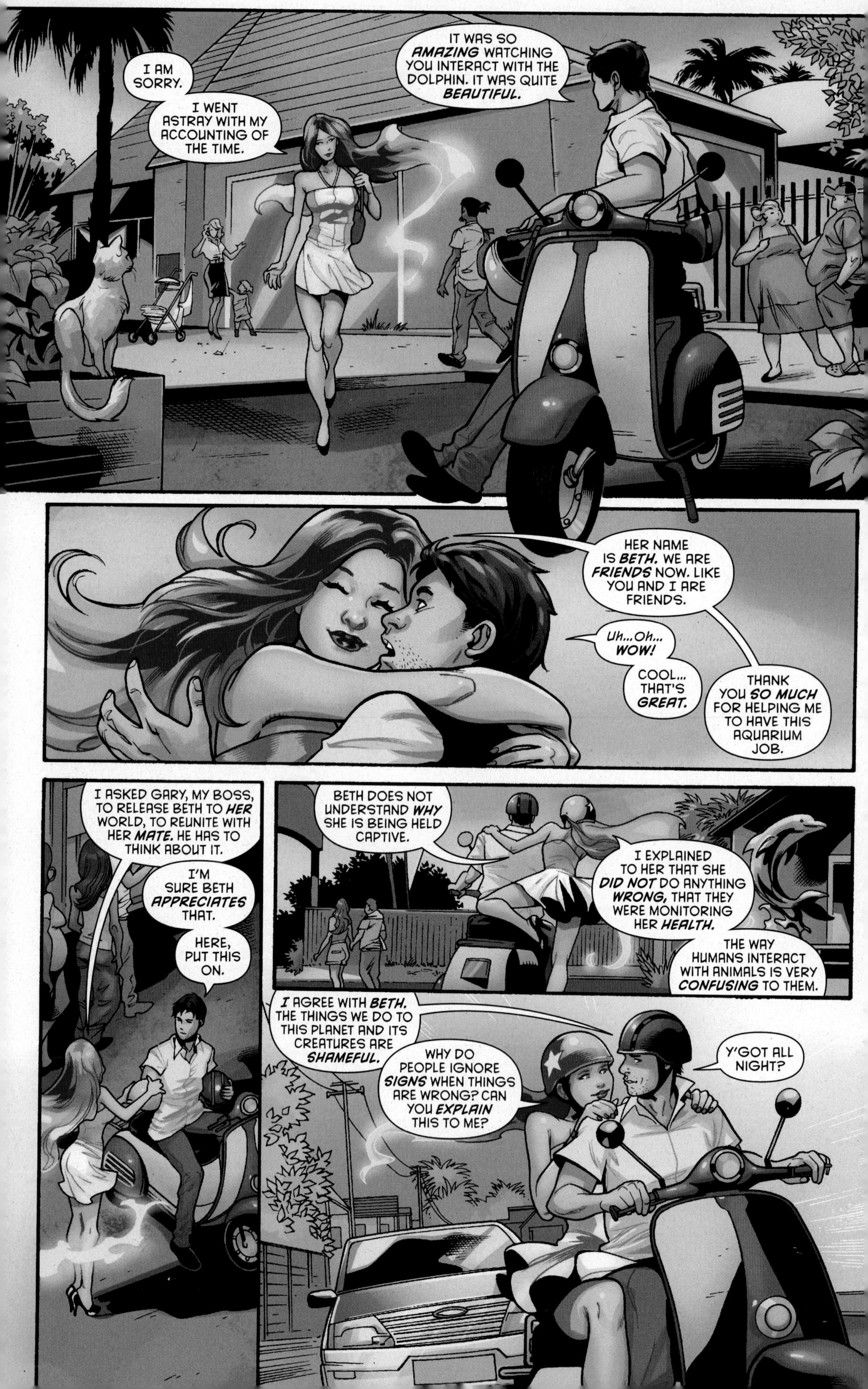
I AM SORRY.
I WENT ASTRAY WITH MY ACCOUNTING OF THE TIME.
IT WAS SO AMAZING WATCHING YOU INTERACT WITH THE DOLPHIN. IT WAS QUITE BEAUTIFUL.
HER NAME IS BETH. WE ARE FRIENDS NOW. LIKE YOU AND I ARE FRIENDS.
Uh...Oh... WOW!
COOL... THAT'S GREAT.
THANK YOU SO MUCH FOR HELPING ME TO HAVE THIS AQUARIUM JOB.
I ASKED GARY, MY BOSS, TO RELEASE BETH TO HER WORLD, TO REUNITE WITH HER MATE. HE HAS TO THINK ABOUT IT.
I'M SURE BETH APPRECIATES THAT.
HERE, PUT THIS ON.
BETH DOES NOT UNDERSTAND WHY SHE IS BEING HELD CAPTIVE.
I EXPLAINED TO HER THAT SHE DID NOT DO ANYTHING WRONG, THAT THEY WERE MONITORING HER HEALTH.
THE WAY HUMANS INTERACT WITH ANIMALS IS VERY CONFUSING TO THEM.
I AGREE WITH BETH. THE THINGS WE DO TO THIS PLANET AND ITS CREATURES ARE SHAMEFUL.
WHY DO PEOPLE IGNORE SIGNS WHEN THINGS ARE WRONG? CAN YOU EXPLAIN THIS TO ME?
Y'GOT ALL NIGHT?

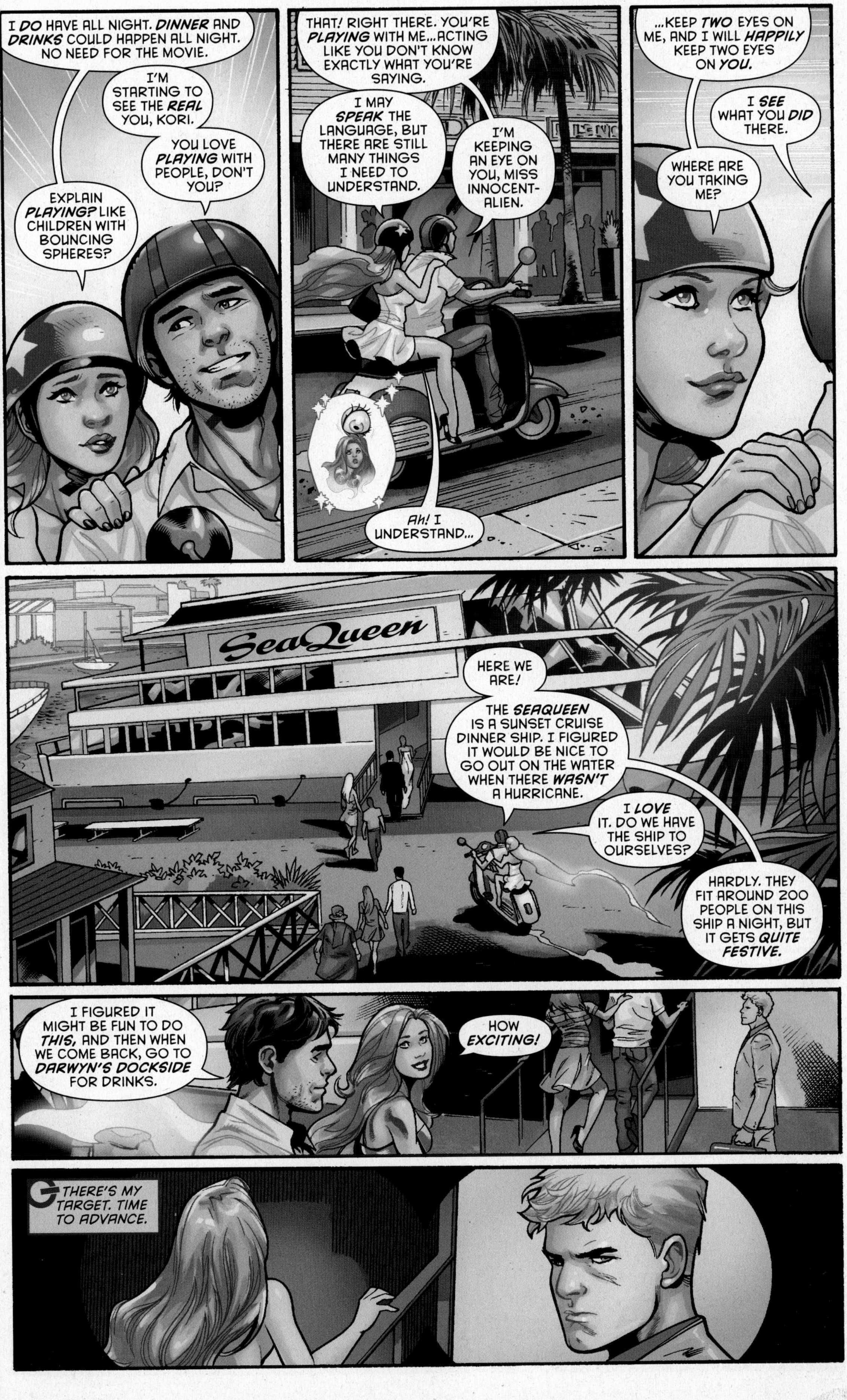

I DO HAVE ALL NIGHT. DINNER AND DRINKS COULD HAPPEN ALL NIGHT. NO NEED FOR THE MOVIE.
I'M STARTING TO SEE THE REAL YOU, KORI.
YOU LOVE PLAYING WITH PEOPLE, DON'T YOU?
EXPLAIN PLAYING? LIKE CHILDREN WITH BOUNCING SPHERES?
THAT! RIGHT THERE. YOU'RE PLAYING WITH ME...ACTING LIKE YOU DON'T KNOW EXACTLY WHAT YOU'RE SAYING.
I MAY SPEAK THE LANGUAGE, BUT THERE ARE STILL MANY THINGS I NEED TO UNDERSTAND.
I'M KEEPING AN EYE ON YOU, MISS INNOCENT-ALIEN.
AH! I UNDERSTAND...
...KEEP TWO EYES ON ME, AND I WILL HAPPILY KEEP TWO EYES ON YOU.
I SEE WHAT YOU DID THERE.
WHERE ARE YOU TAKING ME?
SeaQueen
HERE WE ARE!
THE SEAQUEEN IS A SUNSET CRUISE DINNER SHIP. I FIGURED IT WOULD BE NICE TO GO OUT ON THE WATER WHEN THERE WASN'T A HURRICANE.
I LOVE IT. DO WE HAVE THE SHIP TO OURSELVES?
HARDLY. THEY FIT AROUND 200 PEOPLE ON THIS SHIP A NIGHT, BUT IT GETS QUITE FESTIVE.
I FIGURED IT MIGHT BE FUN TO DO THIS, AND THEN WHEN WE COME BACK, GO TO DARWYN'S DOCKSIDE FOR DRINKS.
HOW EXCITING!
THERE'S MY TARGET. TIME TO ADVANCE.

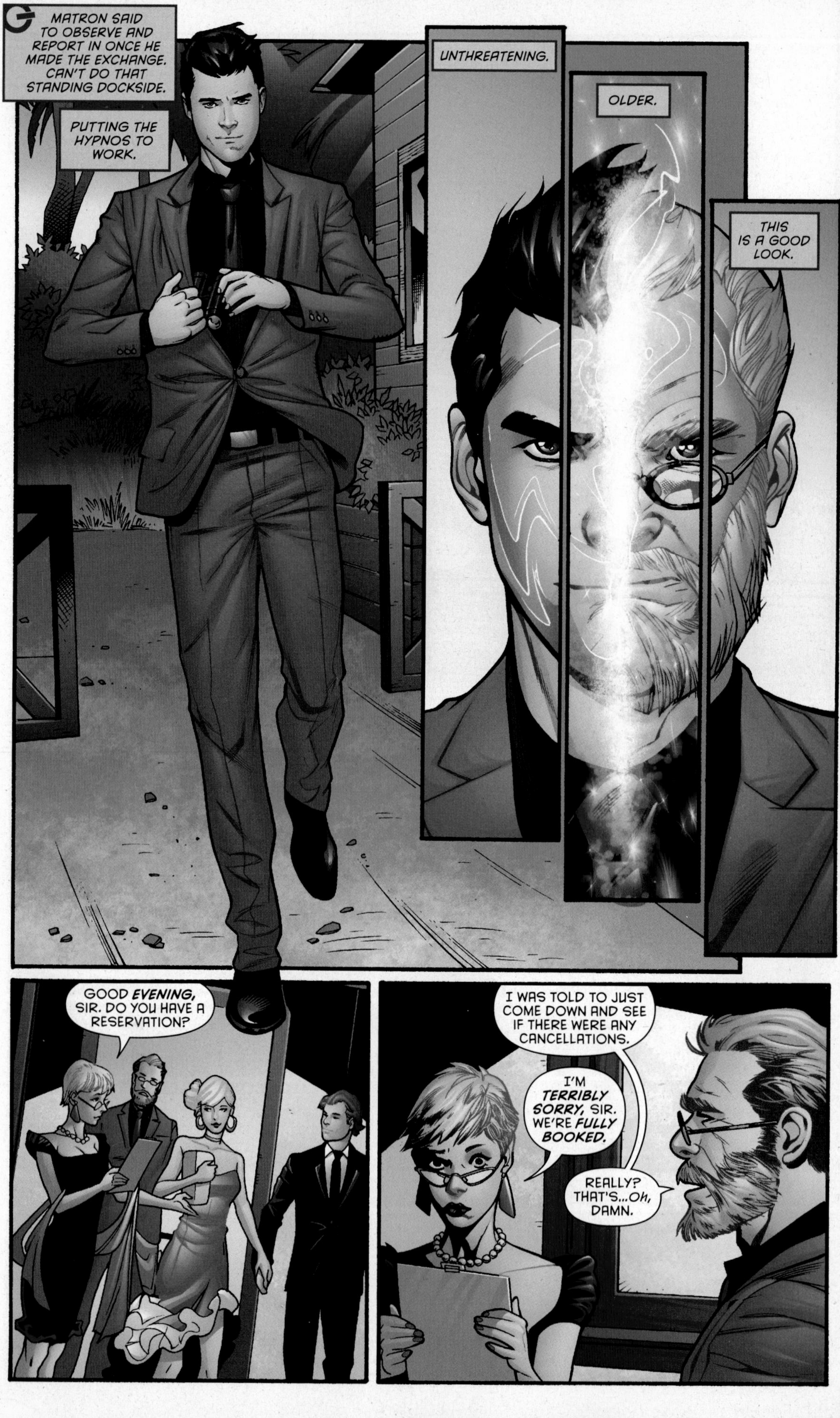

MATRON SAID TO OBSERVE AND REPORT IN ONCE HE MADE THE EXCHANGE. CAN'T DO THAT STANDING DOCKSIDE.
PUTTING THE HYPNOS TO WORK.
UNTHREATENING.
OLDER.
THIS IS A GOOD LOOK.
GOOD *EVENING*, SIR. DO YOU HAVE A RESERVATION?
I WAS TOLD TO JUST COME DOWN AND SEE IF THERE WERE ANY CANCELLATIONS.
I'M *TERRIBLY SORRY*, SIR. WE'RE *FULLY BOOKED*.
REALLY? THAT'S...OH, DAMN.

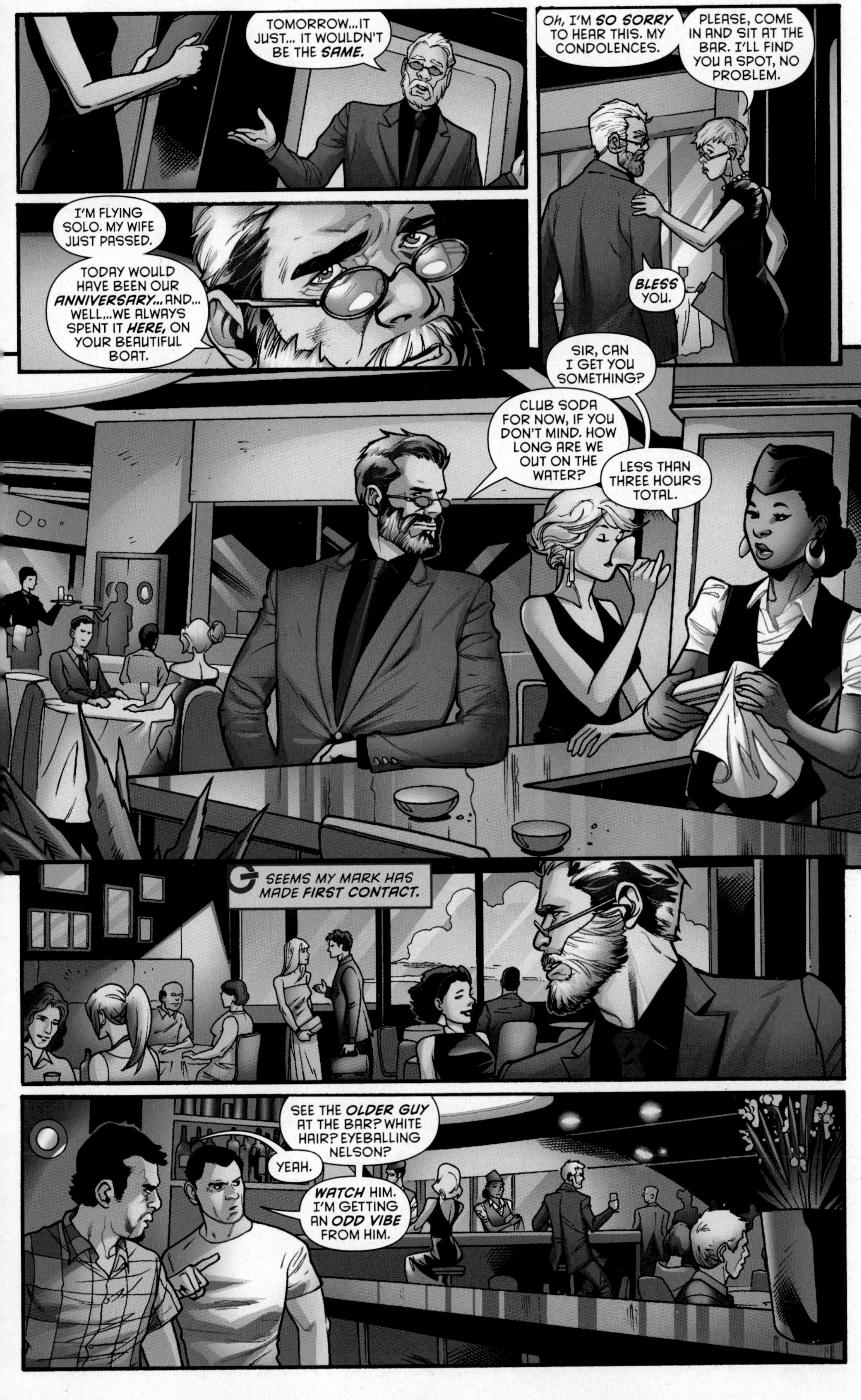
TOMORROW...IT JUST... IT WOULDN'T BE THE SAME.
Oh, I'M SO SORRY TO HEAR THIS. MY CONDOLENCES.
PLEASE, COME IN AND SIT AT THE BAR. I'LL FIND YOU A SPOT, NO PROBLEM.
I'M FLYING SOLO. MY WIFE JUST PASSED.
TODAY WOULD HAVE BEEN OUR ANNIVERSARY... AND... WELL... WE ALWAYS SPENT IT HERE, ON YOUR BEAUTIFUL BOAT.
BLESS YOU.
SIR, CAN I GET YOU SOMETHING?
CLUB SODA FOR NOW, IF YOU DON'T MIND. HOW LONG ARE WE OUT ON THE WATER?
LESS THAN THREE HOURS TOTAL.
SEEMS MY MARK HAS MADE FIRST CONTACT.
SEE THE OLDER GUY AT THE BAR? WHITE HAIR? EYEBALLING NELSON?
YEAH.
WATCH HIM. I'M GETTING AN ODD VIBE FROM HIM.

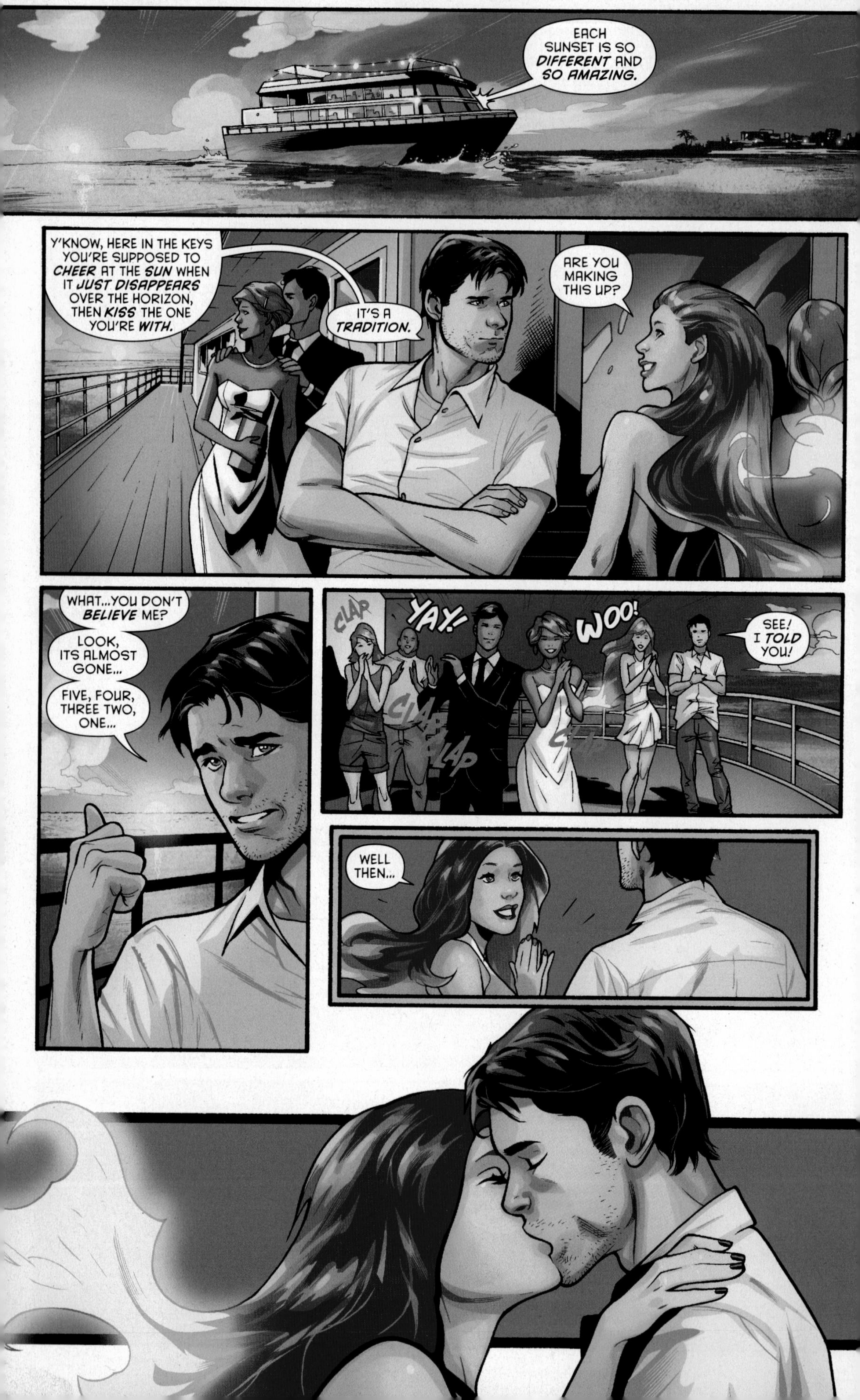

EACH SUNSET IS SO DIFFERENT AND SO AMAZING.
Y'KNOW, HERE IN THE KEYS YOU'RE SUPPOSED TO CHEER AT THE SUN WHEN IT JUST DISAPPEARS OVER THE HORIZON, THEN KISS THE ONE YOU'RE WITH.
IT'S A TRADITION.
ARE YOU MAKING THIS UP?
WHAT...YOU DON'T BELIEVE ME?
LOOK, ITS ALMOST GONE...
FIVE, FOUR, THREE TWO, ONE...
CLAP
YAY!
WOO!
CLAP
CLAP
CLAP
CLAP
SEE! I TOLD YOU!
WELL THEN...

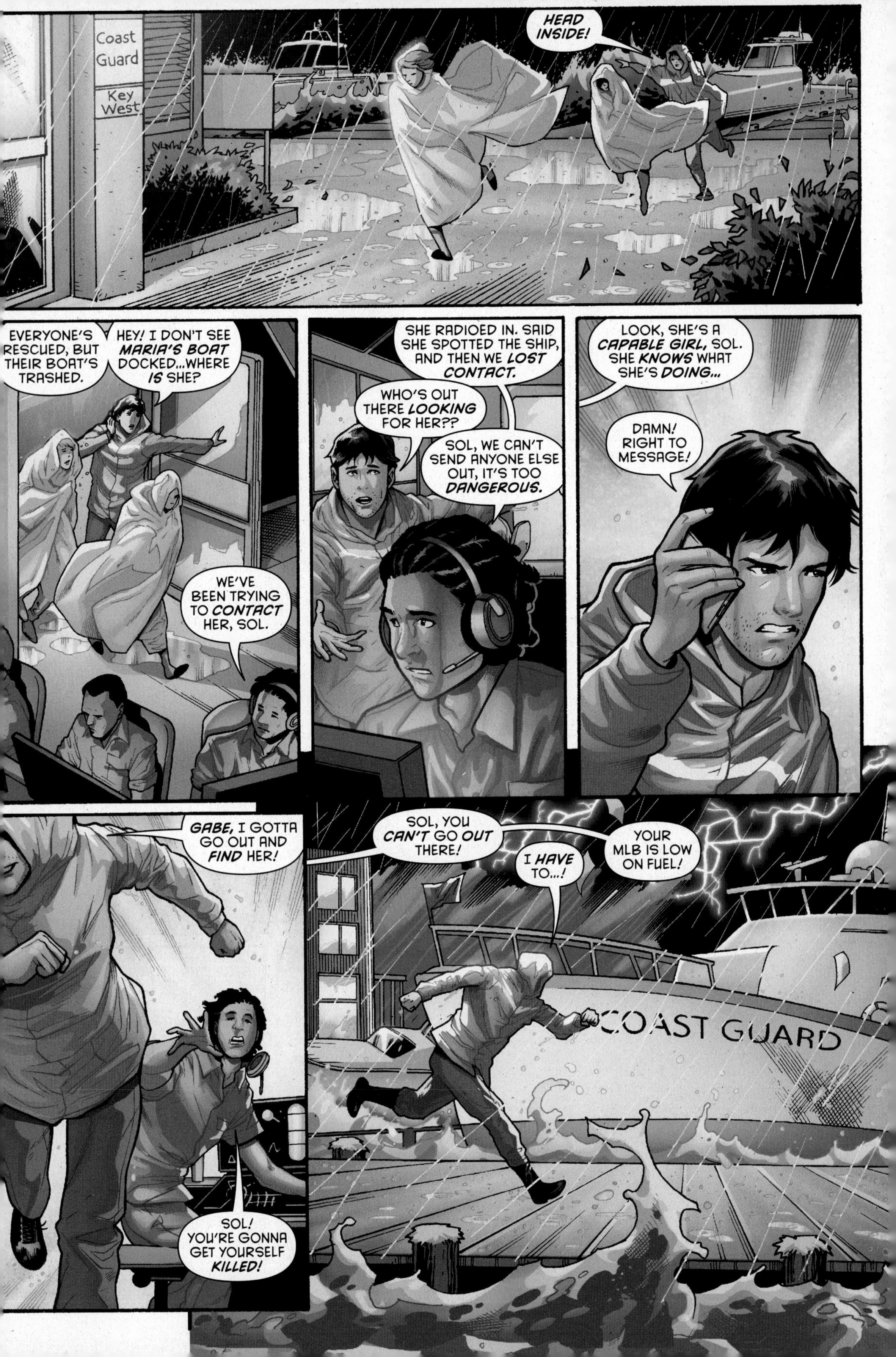
Coast Guard
Key West
HEAD INSIDE!
EVERYONE'S RESCUED, BUT THEIR BOAT'S TRASHED.
HEY! I DON'T SEE MARIA'S BOAT DOCKED...WHERE IS SHE?
WE'VE BEEN TRYING TO CONTACT HER, SOL.
SHE RADIOED IN. SAID SHE SPOTTED THE SHIP, AND THEN WE LOST CONTACT.
WHO'S OUT THERE LOOKING FOR HER??
SOL, WE CAN'T SEND ANYONE ELSE OUT, IT'S TOO DANGEROUS.
LOOK, SHE'S A CAPABLE GIRL, SOL. SHE KNOWS WHAT SHE'S DOING...
DAMN! RIGHT TO MESSAGE!
GABE, I GOTTA GO OUT AND FIND HER!
SOL! YOU'RE GONNA GET YOURSELF KILLED!
SOL, YOU CAN'T GO OUT THERE!
YOUR MLB IS LOW ON FUEL!
I HAVE TO...!
COAST GUARD

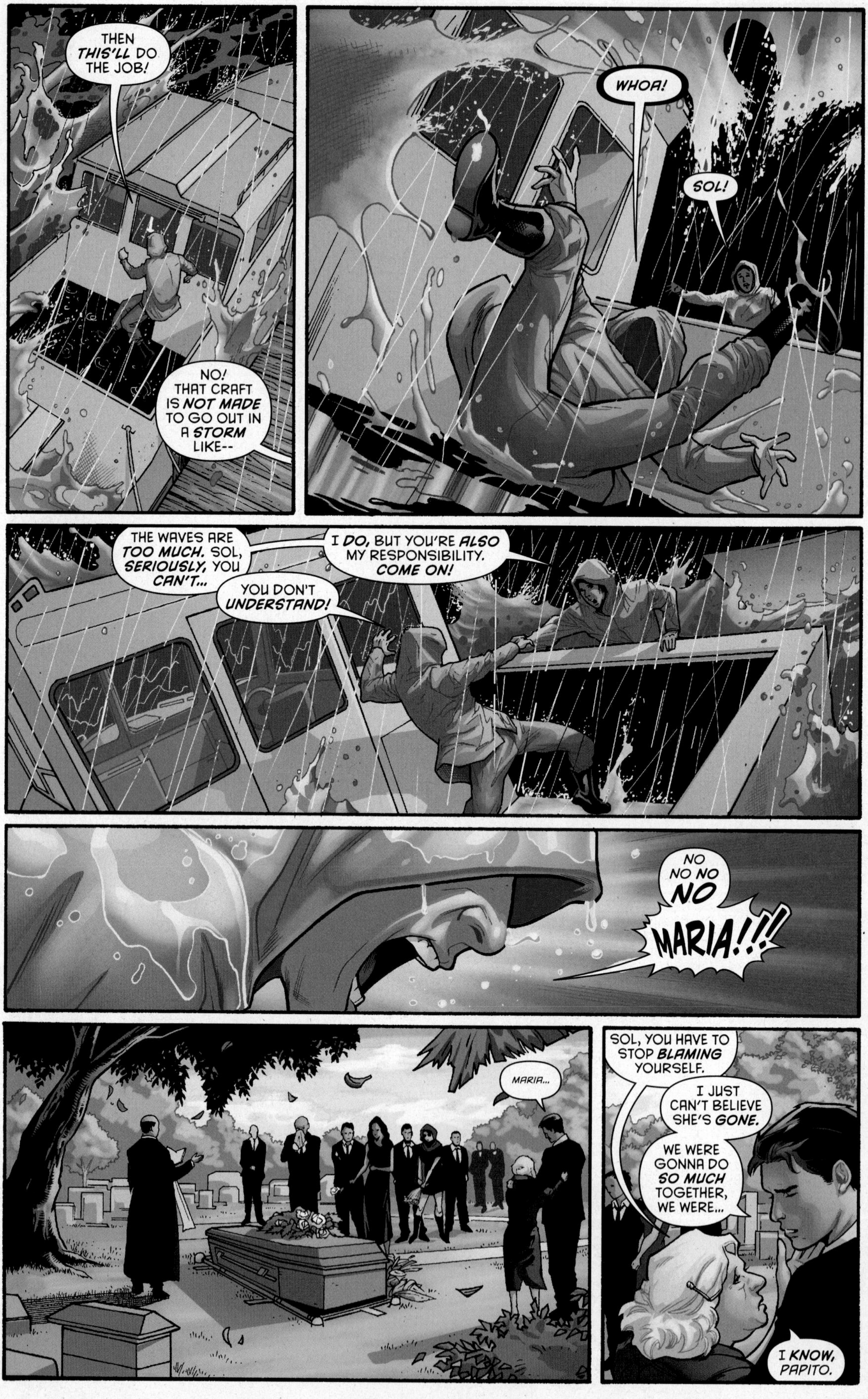
THEN *THIS'LL* DO THE JOB!
NO! THAT CRAFT IS *NOT MADE* TO GO OUT IN A *STORM* LIKE--
WHOA!
SOL!
THE WAVES ARE *TOO MUCH.* SOL, *SERIOUSLY,* YOU *CAN'T...*
YOU DON'T *UNDERSTAND!*
I *DO,* BUT YOU'RE *ALSO* MY RESPONSIBILITY. *COME ON!*
NO NO NO *NO*
MARIA!!!
MARIA...
SOL, YOU HAVE TO STOP *BLAMING* YOURSELF.
I JUST CAN'T BELIEVE SHE'S *GONE.*
WE WERE GONNA DO *SO MUCH* TOGETHER, WE WERE...
I KNOW, PAPITO.

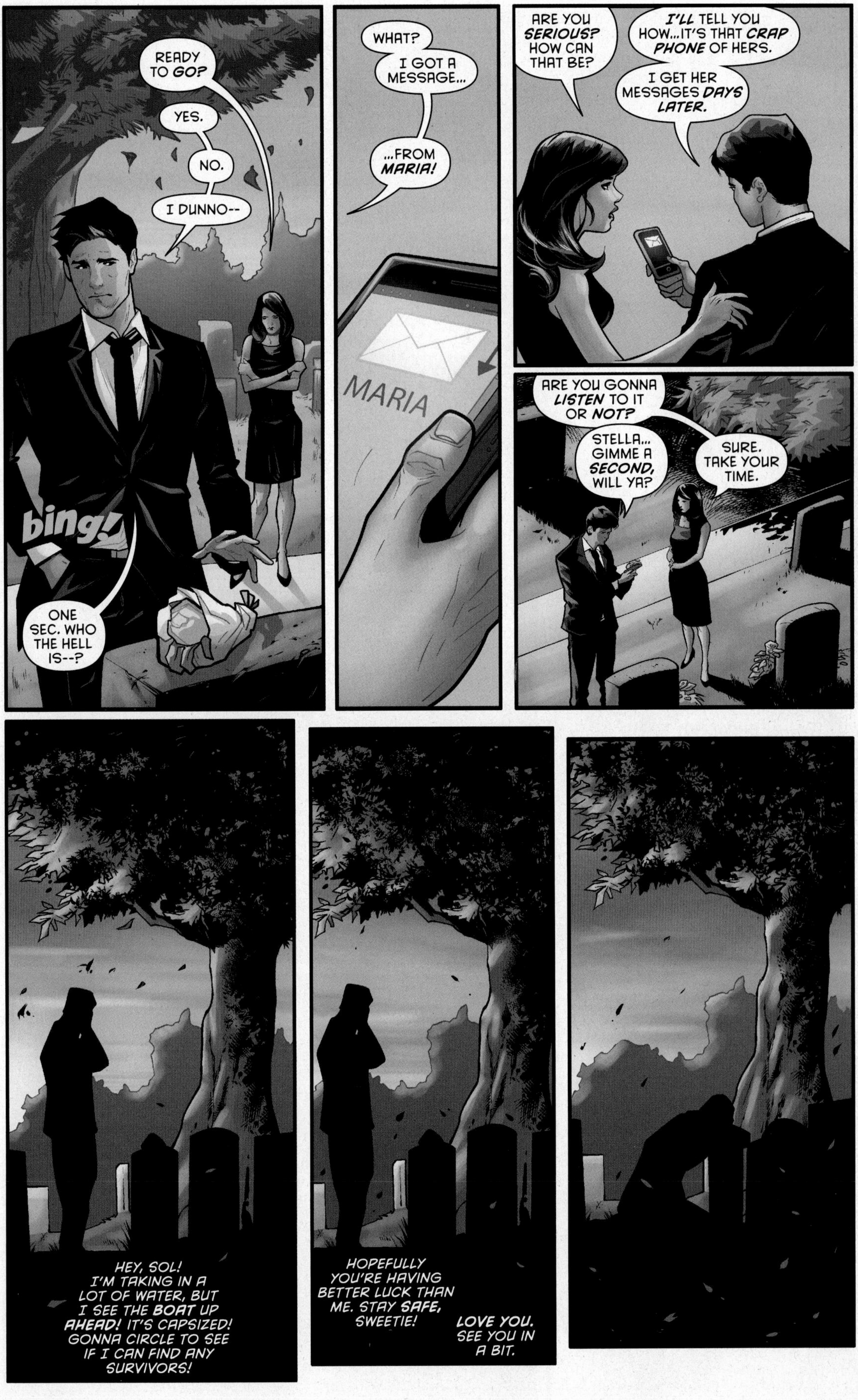
READY TO GO?
YES.
NO.
I DUNNO--
bing!
ONE SEC. WHO THE HELL IS--?
WHAT?
I GOT A MESSAGE...
...FROM MARIA!
MARIA
ARE YOU SERIOUS? HOW CAN THAT BE?
I'LL TELL YOU HOW...IT'S THAT CRAP PHONE OF HERS.
I GET HER MESSAGES DAYS LATER.
ARE YOU GONNA LISTEN TO IT OR NOT?
STELLA... GIMME A SECOND, WILL YA?
SURE. TAKE YOUR TIME.
HEY, SOL! I'M TAKING IN A LOT OF WATER, BUT I SEE THE BOAT UP AHEAD! IT'S CAPSIZED! GONNA CIRCLE TO SEE IF I CAN FIND ANY SURVIVORS!
HOPEFULLY YOU'RE HAVING BETTER LUCK THAN ME. STAY SAFE, SWEETIE!
LOVE YOU. SEE YOU IN A BIT.

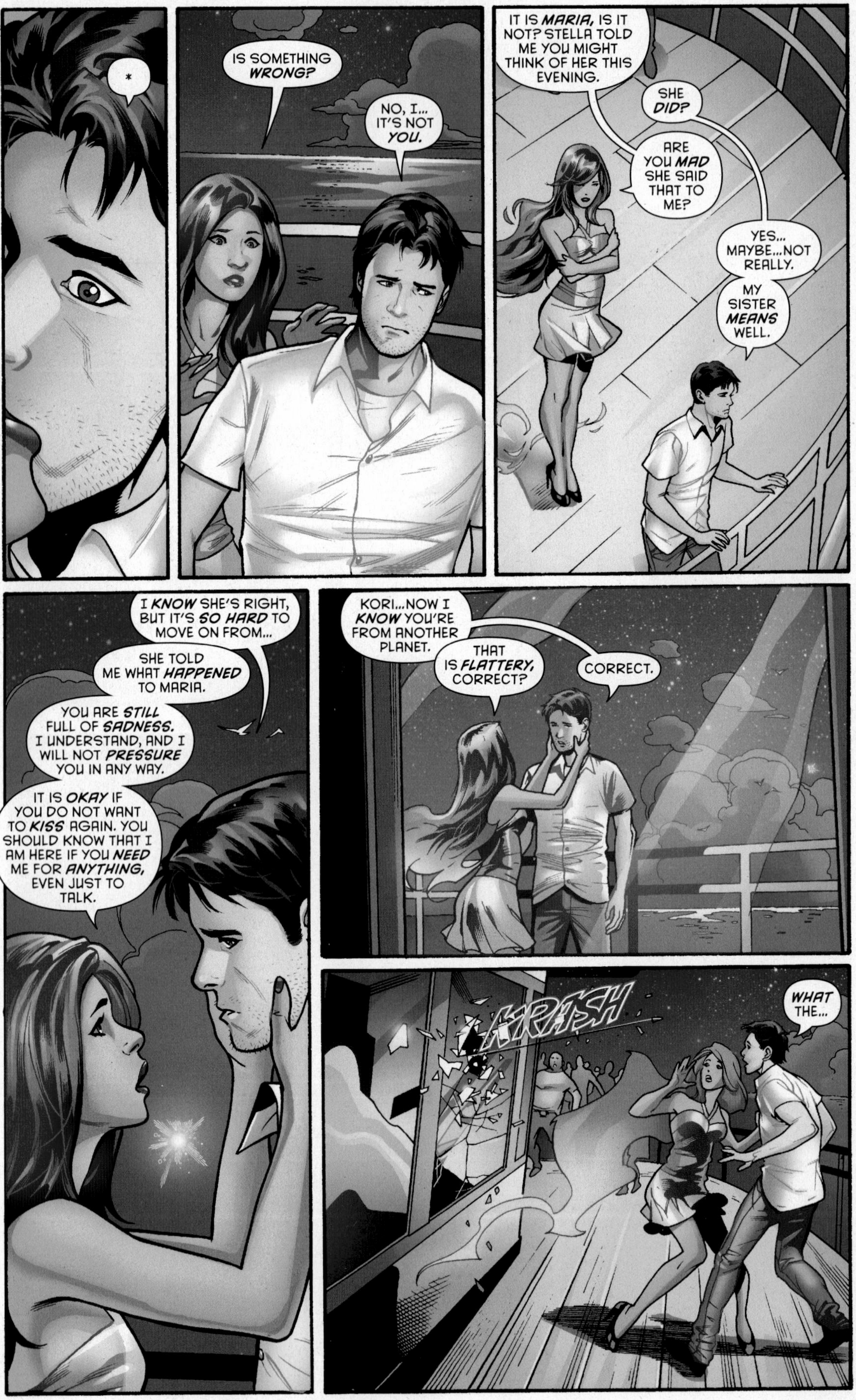
*
IS SOMETHING WRONG?
NO, I... IT'S NOT YOU.
IT IS MARIA, IS IT NOT? STELLA TOLD ME YOU MIGHT THINK OF HER THIS EVENING.
SHE DID?
ARE YOU MAD SHE SAID THAT TO ME?
YES... MAYBE...NOT REALLY.
MY SISTER MEANS WELL.
I KNOW SHE'S RIGHT, BUT IT'S SO HARD TO MOVE ON FROM...
SHE TOLD ME WHAT HAPPENED TO MARIA.
YOU ARE STILL FULL OF SADNESS. I UNDERSTAND, AND I WILL NOT PRESSURE YOU IN ANY WAY.
IT IS OKAY IF YOU DO NOT WANT TO KISS AGAIN. YOU SHOULD KNOW THAT I AM HERE IF YOU NEED ME FOR ANYTHING, EVEN JUST TO TALK.
KORI...NOW I KNOW YOU'RE FROM ANOTHER PLANET.
THAT IS FLATTERY, CORRECT?
CORRECT.
KRASH
WHAT THE...

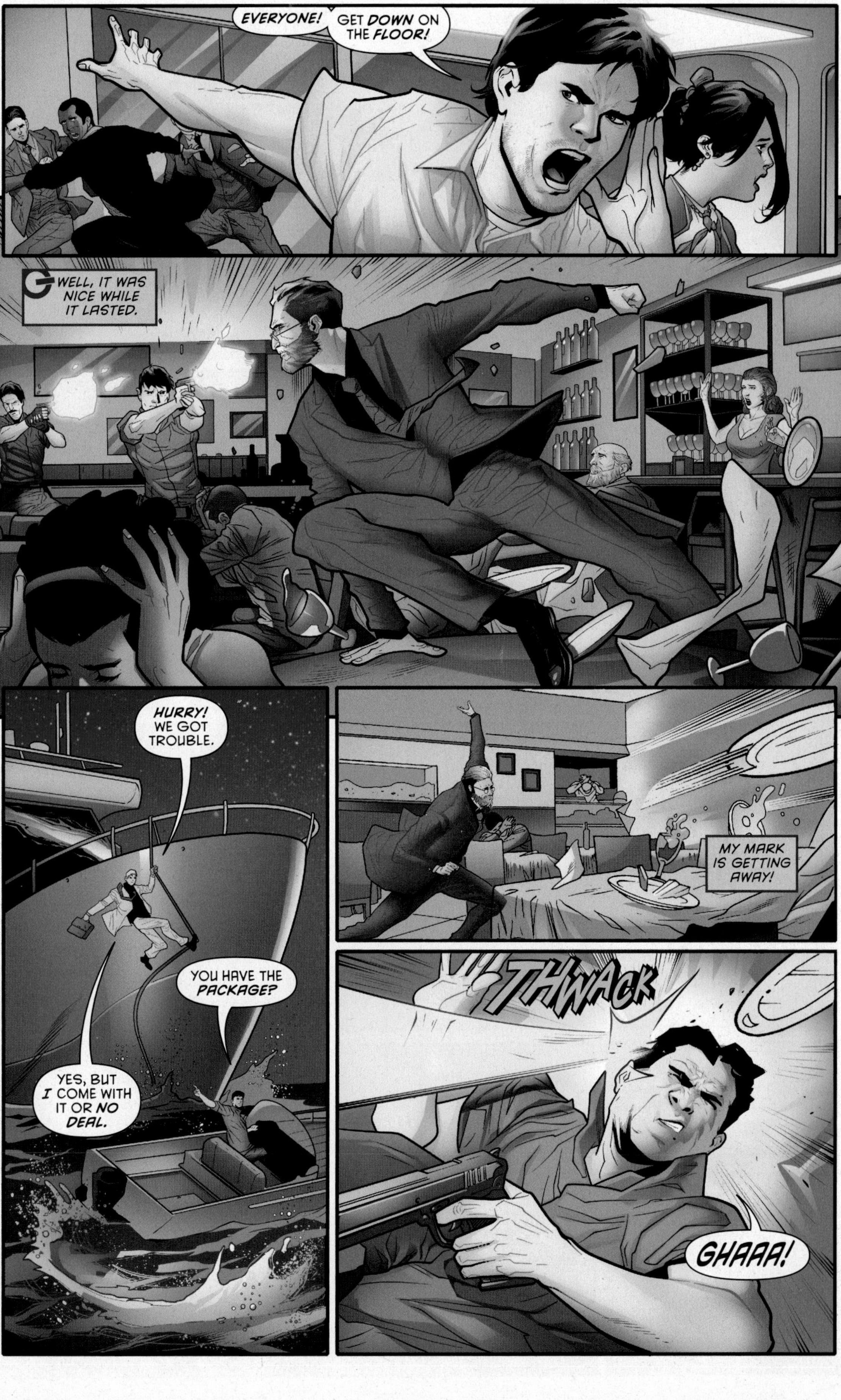
EVERYONE!
GET DOWN ON THE FLOOR!
WELL, IT WAS NICE WHILE IT LASTED.
HURRY! WE GOT TROUBLE.
YOU HAVE THE PACKAGE?
YES, BUT I COME WITH IT OR NO DEAL.
MY MARK IS GETTING AWAY!
THWACK
GHAAA!

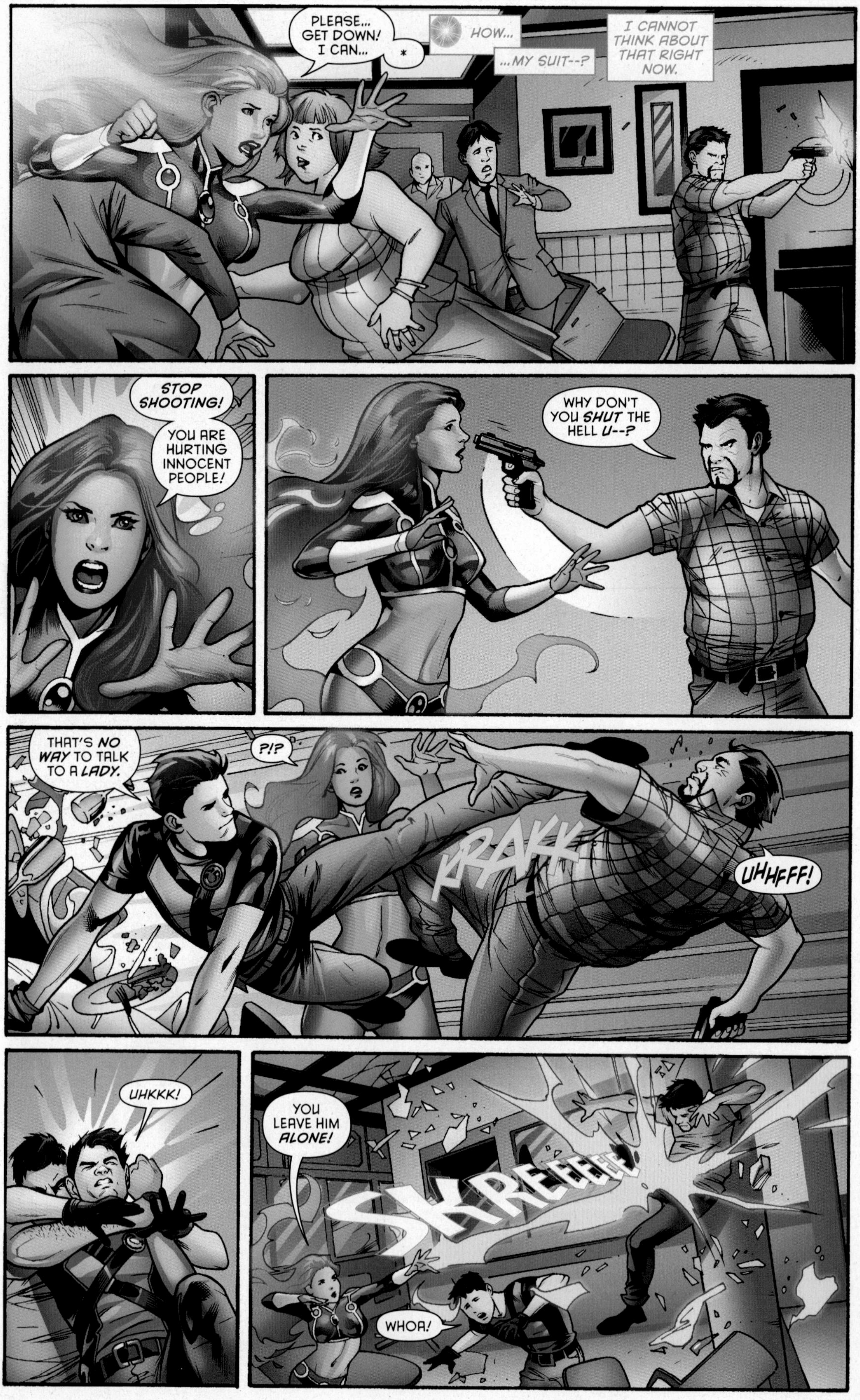
PLEASE... GET DOWN! I CAN...
HOW...
...MY SUIT--?
I CANNOT THINK ABOUT THAT RIGHT NOW.
STOP SHOOTING!
YOU ARE HURTING INNOCENT PEOPLE!
WHY DON'T YOU SHUT THE HELL U--?
THAT'S NO WAY TO TALK TO A LADY.
?!?
KRAKK
UHHFFF!
UHKKK!
YOU LEAVE HIM ALONE!
SKREEEEE
WHOA!

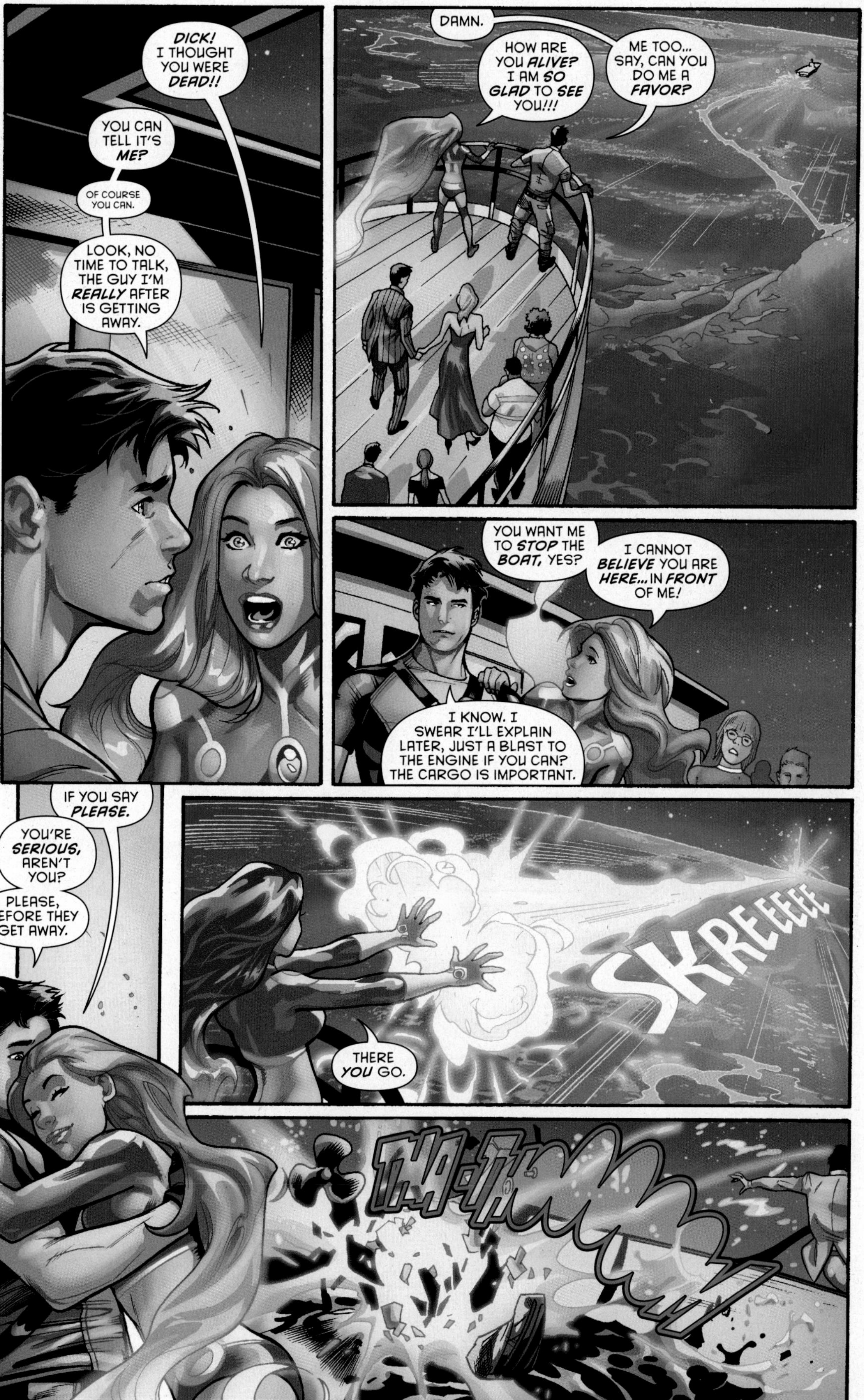
DICK! I THOUGHT YOU WERE DEAD!!
YOU CAN TELL IT'S ME?
OF COURSE YOU CAN.
LOOK, NO TIME TO TALK, THE GUY I'M REALLY AFTER IS GETTING AWAY.
DAMN.
HOW ARE YOU ALIVE? I AM SO GLAD TO SEE YOU!!!
ME TOO... SAY, CAN YOU DO ME A FAVOR?
YOU WANT ME TO STOP THE BOAT, YES?
I CANNOT BELIEVE YOU ARE HERE... IN FRONT OF ME!
I KNOW. I SWEAR I'LL EXPLAIN LATER, JUST A BLAST TO THE ENGINE IF YOU CAN? THE CARGO IS IMPORTANT.
IF YOU SAY PLEASE.
YOU'RE SERIOUS, AREN'T YOU?
PLEASE, BEFORE THEY GET AWAY.
SKREEEEE
THERE YOU GO.

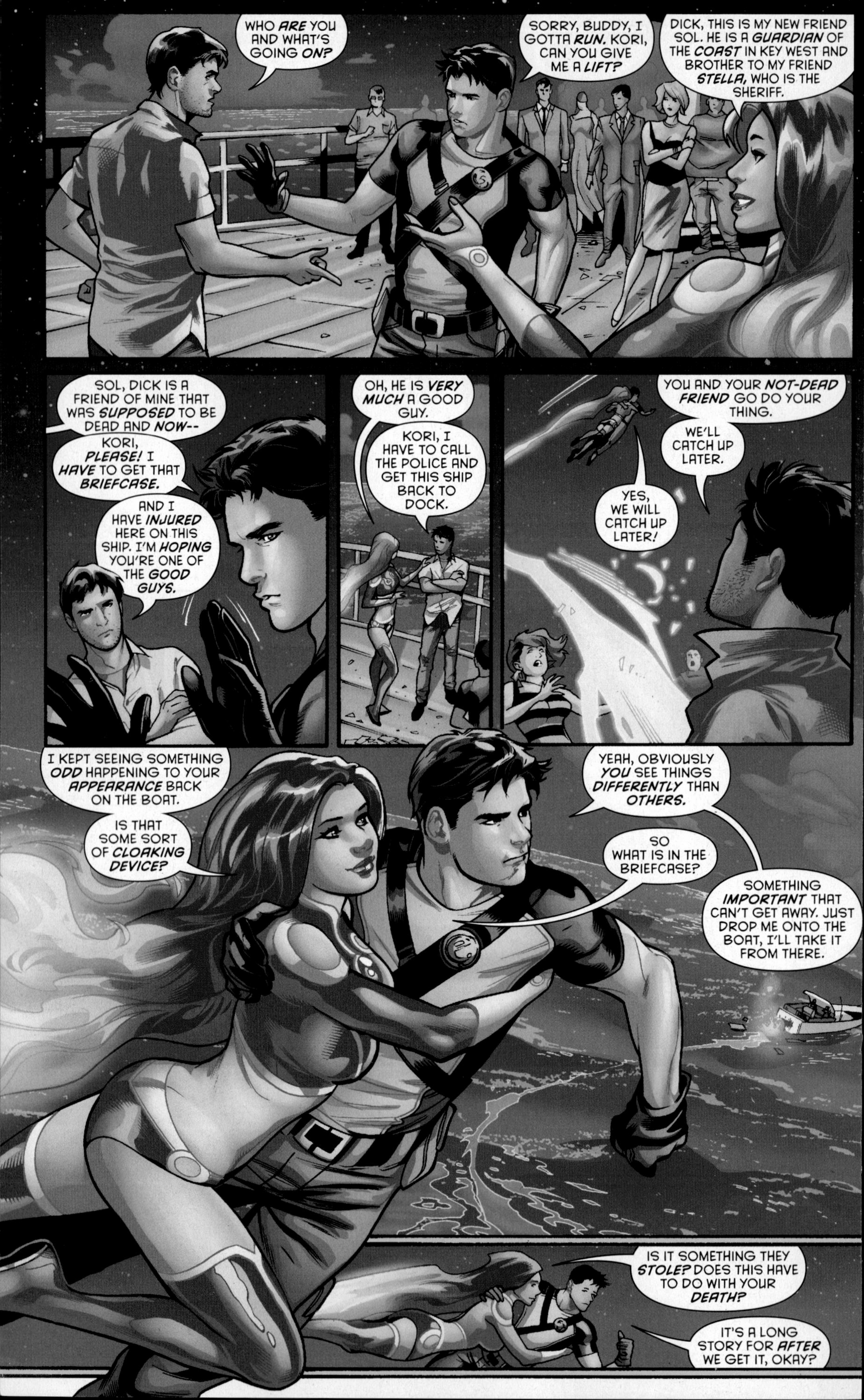
WHO ARE YOU AND WHAT'S GOING ON?
SORRY, BUDDY, I GOTTA RUN. KORI, CAN YOU GIVE ME A LIFT?
DICK, THIS IS MY NEW FRIEND SOL. HE IS A GUARDIAN OF THE COAST IN KEY WEST AND BROTHER TO MY FRIEND STELLA, WHO IS THE SHERIFF.
SOL, DICK IS A FRIEND OF MINE THAT WAS SUPPOSED TO BE DEAD AND NOW--
KORI, PLEASE! I HAVE TO GET THAT BRIEFCASE.
AND I HAVE INJURED HERE ON THIS SHIP. I'M HOPING YOU'RE ONE OF THE GOOD GUYS.
OH, HE IS VERY MUCH A GOOD GUY.
KORI, I HAVE TO CALL THE POLICE AND GET THIS SHIP BACK TO DOCK.
YOU AND YOUR NOT-DEAD FRIEND GO DO YOUR THING.
WE'LL CATCH UP LATER.
YES, WE WILL CATCH UP LATER!
I KEPT SEEING SOMETHING ODD HAPPENING TO YOUR APPEARANCE BACK ON THE BOAT.
IS THAT SOME SORT OF CLOAKING DEVICE?
YEAH, OBVIOUSLY YOU SEE THINGS DIFFERENTLY THAN OTHERS.
SO WHAT IS IN THE BRIEFCASE?
SOMETHING IMPORTANT THAT CAN'T GET AWAY. JUST DROP ME ONTO THE BOAT, I'LL TAKE IT FROM THERE.
IS IT SOMETHING THEY STOLE? DOES THIS HAVE TO DO WITH YOUR DEATH?
IT'S A LONG STORY FOR AFTER WE GET IT, OKAY?

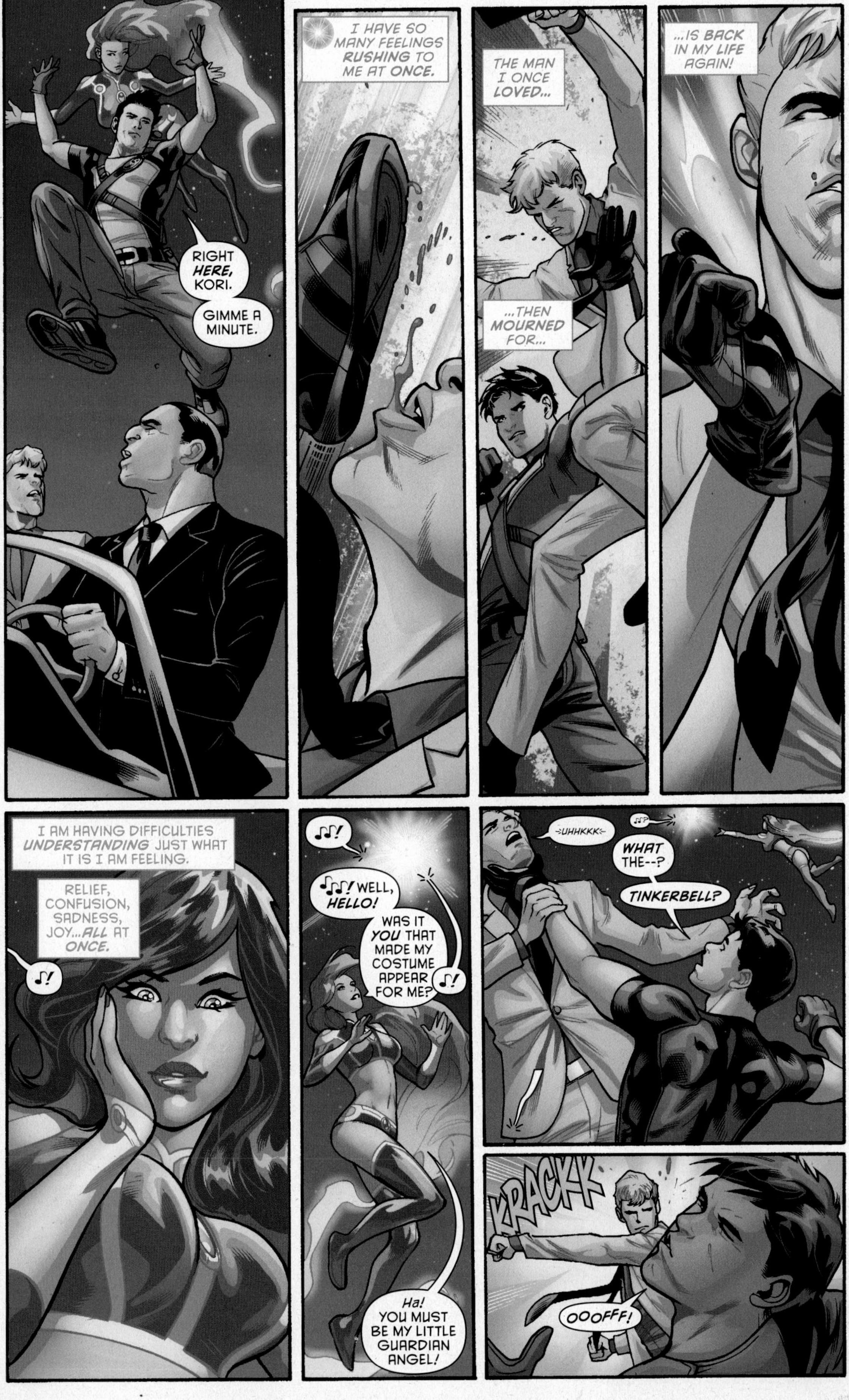
RIGHT HERE, KORI.
GIMME A MINUTE.
I HAVE SO MANY FEELINGS RUSHING TO ME AT ONCE.
THE MAN I ONCE LOVED...
...THEN MOURNED FOR...
...IS BACK IN MY LIFE AGAIN!
I AM HAVING DIFFICULTIES UNDERSTANDING JUST WHAT IT IS I AM FEELING.
RELIEF, CONFUSION, SADNESS, JOY...ALL AT ONCE.
♪!
♫!
♫! WELL, HELLO!
WAS IT YOU THAT MADE MY COSTUME APPEAR FOR ME?
♪!
Ha! YOU MUST BE MY LITTLE GUARDIAN ANGEL!
UHHKKK
♫?
WHAT THE--?
TINKERBELL?
KRACKK
OOOFFF!

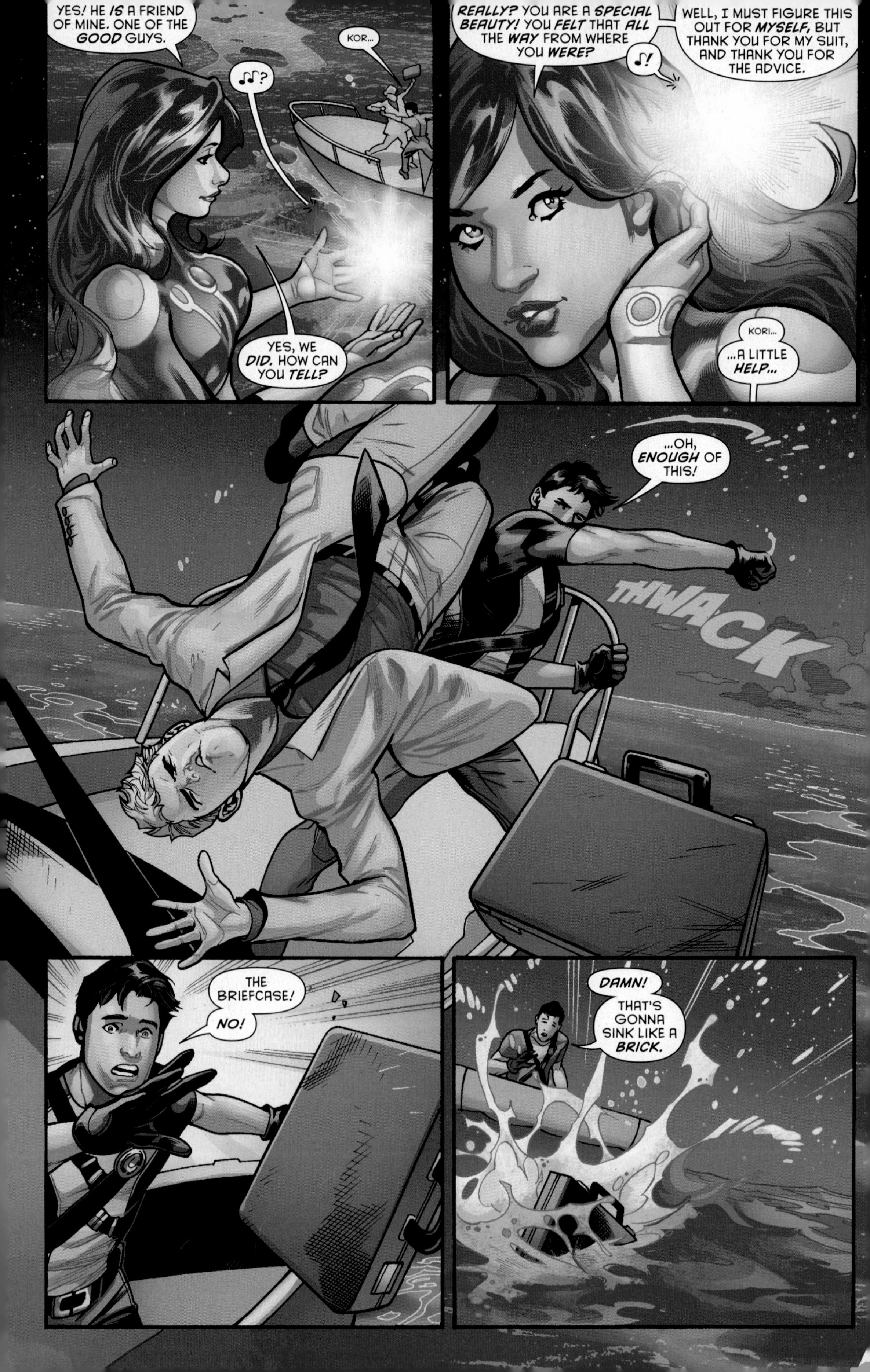
YES! HE IS A FRIEND OF MINE. ONE OF THE GOOD GUYS.
KOR...
♫♫?
YES, WE DID. HOW CAN YOU TELL?
REALLY? YOU ARE A SPECIAL BEAUTY! YOU FELT THAT ALL THE WAY FROM WHERE YOU WERE?
♫!
WELL, I MUST FIGURE THIS OUT FOR MYSELF, BUT THANK YOU FOR MY SUIT, AND THANK YOU FOR THE ADVICE.
KORI...
...A LITTLE HELP...
...OH, ENOUGH OF THIS!
THWACK
THE BRIEFCASE!
NO!
DAMN!
THAT'S GONNA SINK LIKE A BRICK.

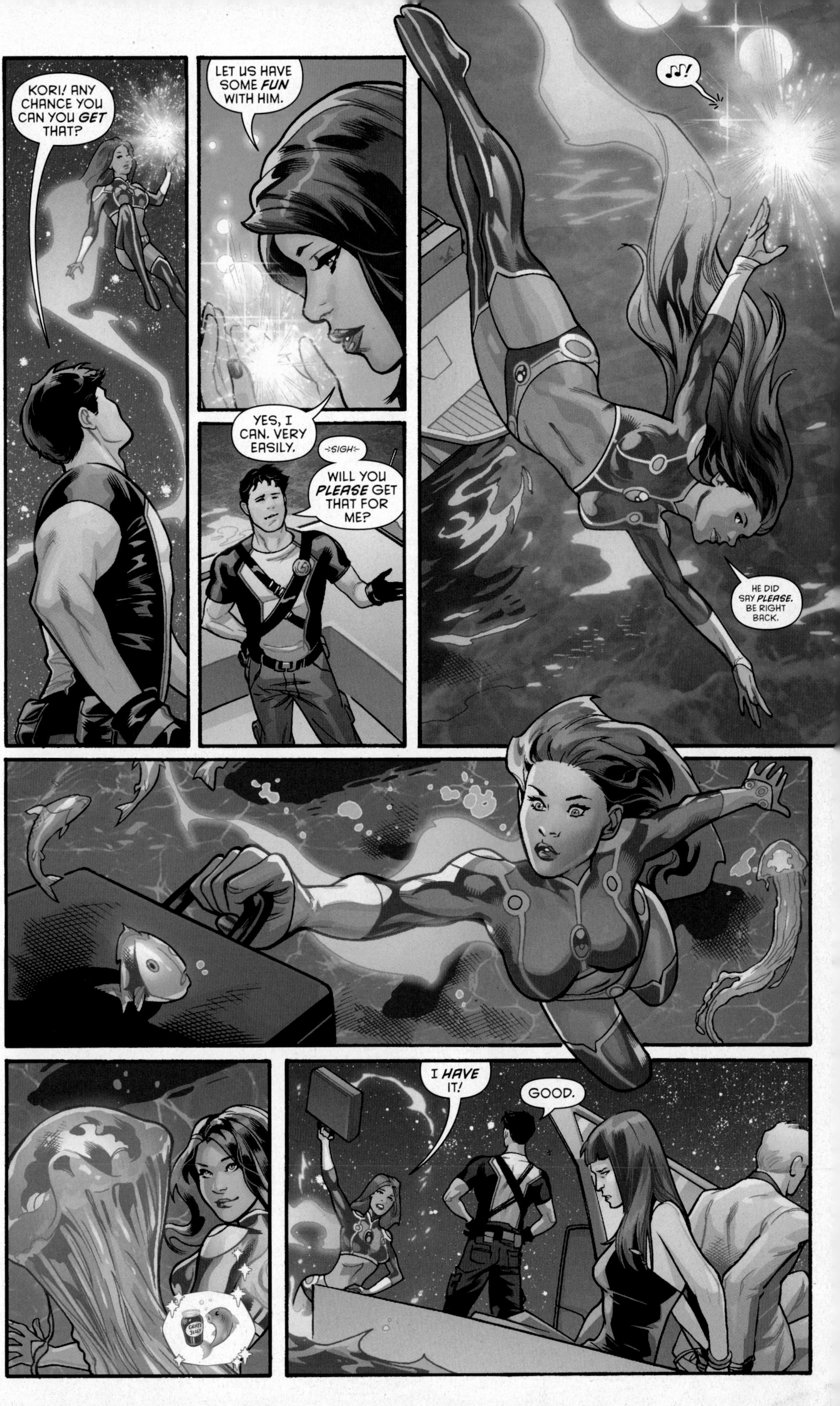
KORI! ANY CHANCE YOU CAN YOU GET THAT?
LET US HAVE SOME FUN WITH HIM.
YES, I CAN. VERY EASILY.
SIGH
WILL YOU PLEASE GET THAT FOR ME?
♫!
HE DID SAY PLEASE. BE RIGHT BACK.
I HAVE IT!
GOOD.

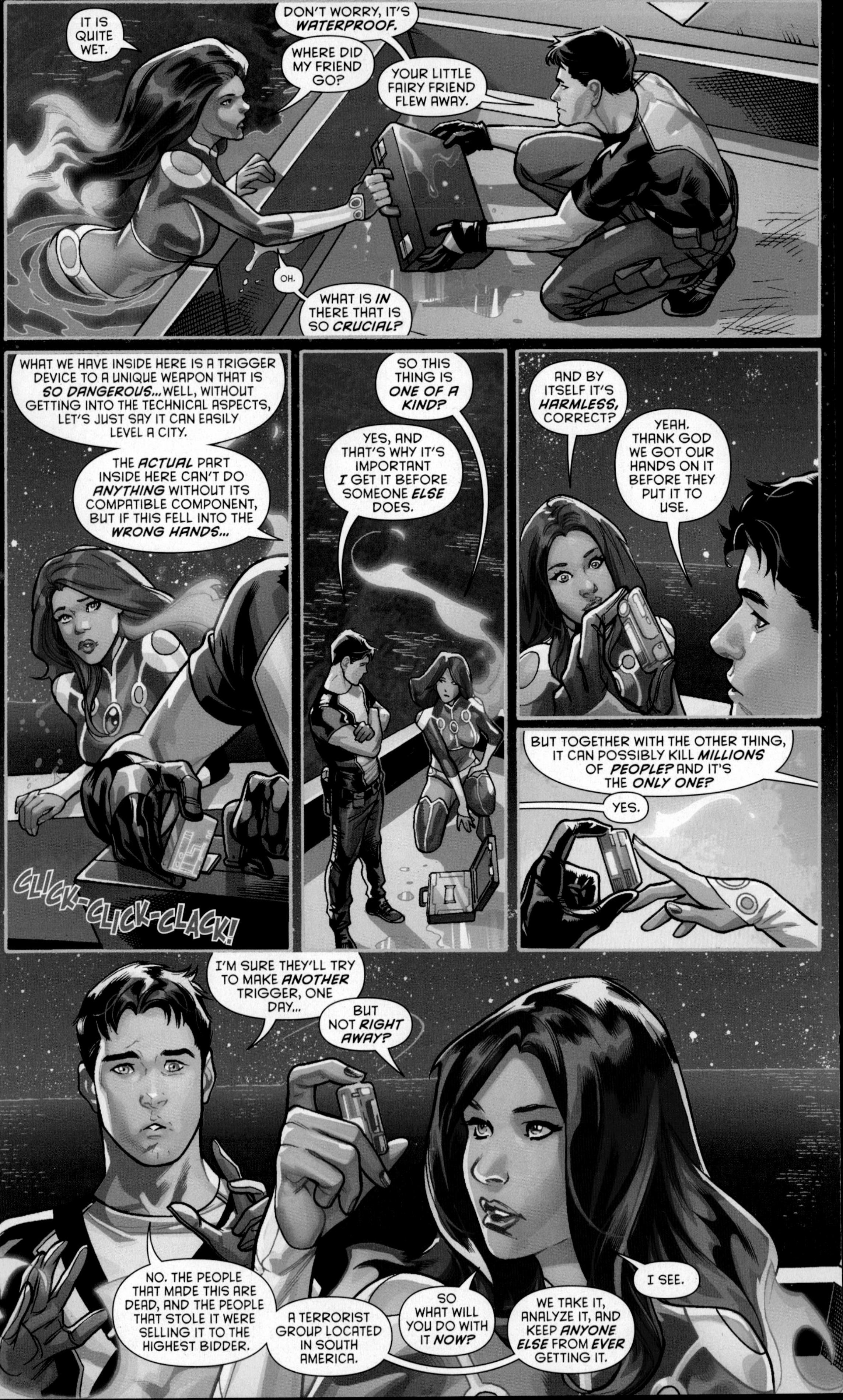
IT IS QUITE WET.
DON'T WORRY, IT'S WATERPROOF.
WHERE DID MY FRIEND GO?
YOUR LITTLE FAIRY FRIEND FLEW AWAY.
OH.
WHAT IS IN THERE THAT IS SO CRUCIAL?
WHAT WE HAVE INSIDE HERE IS A TRIGGER DEVICE TO A UNIQUE WEAPON THAT IS SO DANGEROUS... WELL, WITHOUT GETTING INTO THE TECHNICAL ASPECTS, LET'S JUST SAY IT CAN EASILY LEVEL A CITY.
THE ACTUAL PART INSIDE HERE CAN'T DO ANYTHING WITHOUT ITS COMPATIBLE COMPONENT, BUT IF THIS FELL INTO THE WRONG HANDS...
CLICK-CLICK-CLACK!
SO THIS THING IS ONE OF A KIND?
YES, AND THAT'S WHY IT'S IMPORTANT I GET IT BEFORE SOMEONE ELSE DOES.
AND BY ITSELF IT'S HARMLESS, CORRECT?
YEAH. THANK GOD WE GOT OUR HANDS ON IT BEFORE THEY PUT IT TO USE.
BUT TOGETHER WITH THE OTHER THING, IT CAN POSSIBLY KILL MILLIONS OF PEOPLE? AND IT'S THE ONLY ONE?
YES.
I'M SURE THEY'LL TRY TO MAKE ANOTHER TRIGGER, ONE DAY...
BUT NOT RIGHT AWAY?
NO. THE PEOPLE THAT MADE THIS ARE DEAD, AND THE PEOPLE THAT STOLE IT WERE SELLING IT TO THE HIGHEST BIDDER.
A TERRORIST GROUP LOCATED IN SOUTH AMERICA.
SO WHAT WILL YOU DO WITH IT NOW?
WE TAKE IT, ANALYZE IT, AND KEEP ANYONE ELSE FROM EVER GETTING IT.
I SEE.

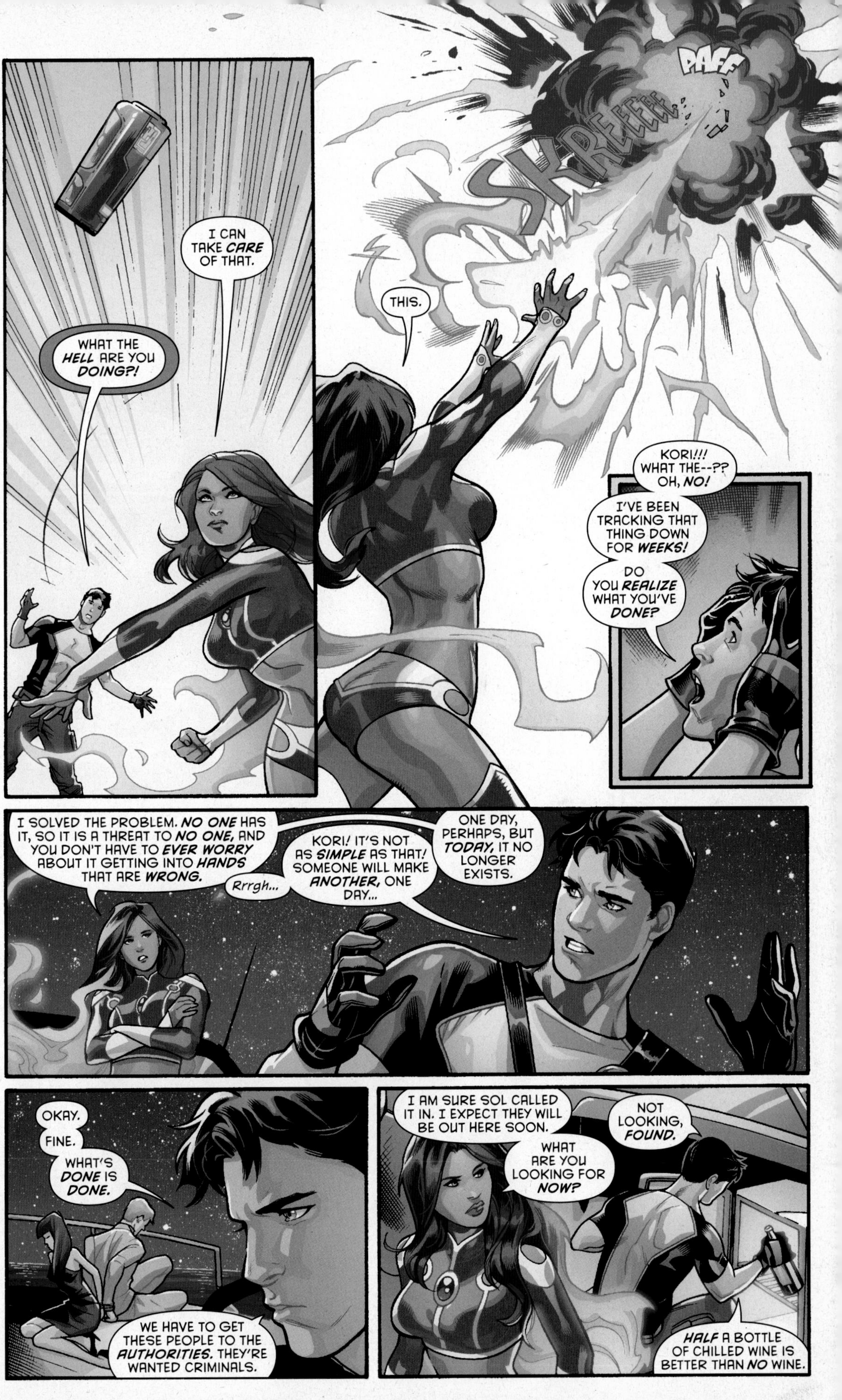

I CAN TAKE CARE OF THAT.
WHAT THE HELL ARE YOU DOING?!
THIS.
SKREEEEE
PAFF
KORI!!! WHAT THE--?? OH, NO!
I'VE BEEN TRACKING THAT THING DOWN FOR WEEKS!
DO YOU REALIZE WHAT YOU'VE DONE?
I SOLVED THE PROBLEM. NO ONE HAS IT, SO IT IS A THREAT TO NO ONE, AND YOU DON'T HAVE TO EVER WORRY ABOUT IT GETTING INTO HANDS THAT ARE WRONG.
Rrrgh...
KORI! IT'S NOT AS SIMPLE AS THAT! SOMEONE WILL MAKE ANOTHER, ONE DAY...
ONE DAY, PERHAPS, BUT TODAY, IT NO LONGER EXISTS.
OKAY.
FINE.
WHAT'S DONE IS DONE.
WE HAVE TO GET THESE PEOPLE TO THE AUTHORITIES. THEY'RE WANTED CRIMINALS.
I AM SURE SOL CALLED IT IN. I EXPECT THEY WILL BE OUT HERE SOON.
WHAT ARE YOU LOOKING FOR NOW?
NOT LOOKING, FOUND.
HALF A BOTTLE OF CHILLED WINE IS BETTER THAN NO WINE.

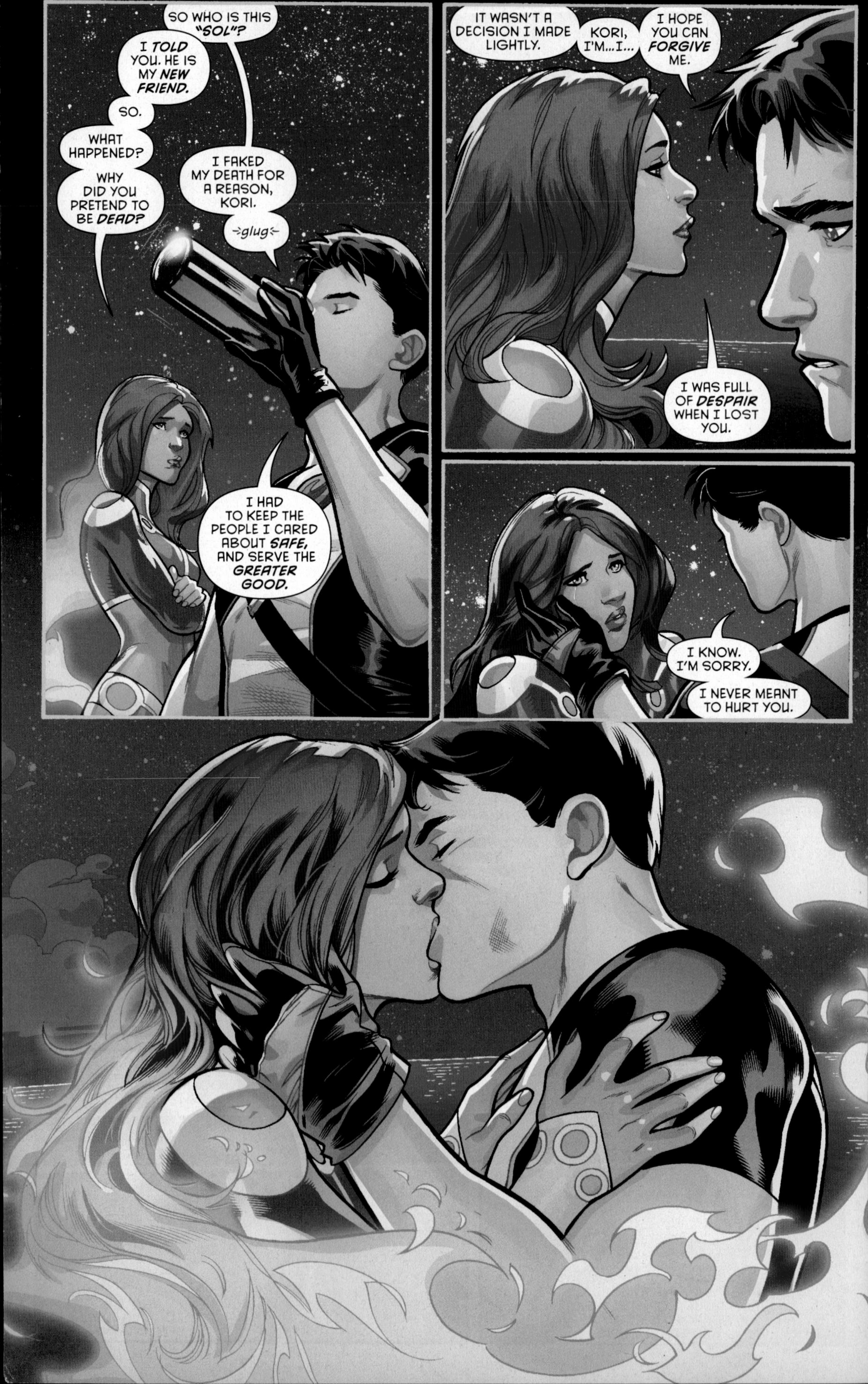

SO WHO IS THIS "SOL"?
I TOLD YOU. HE IS MY NEW FRIEND.
SO.
WHAT HAPPENED?
WHY DID YOU PRETEND TO BE DEAD?
I FAKED MY DEATH FOR A REASON, KORI.
glug
I HAD TO KEEP THE PEOPLE I CARED ABOUT SAFE, AND SERVE THE GREATER GOOD.
IT WASN'T A DECISION I MADE LIGHTLY.
KORI, I'M...I...
I HOPE YOU CAN FORGIVE ME.
I WAS FULL OF DESPAIR WHEN I LOST YOU.
I KNOW. I'M SORRY.
I NEVER MEANT TO HURT YOU.

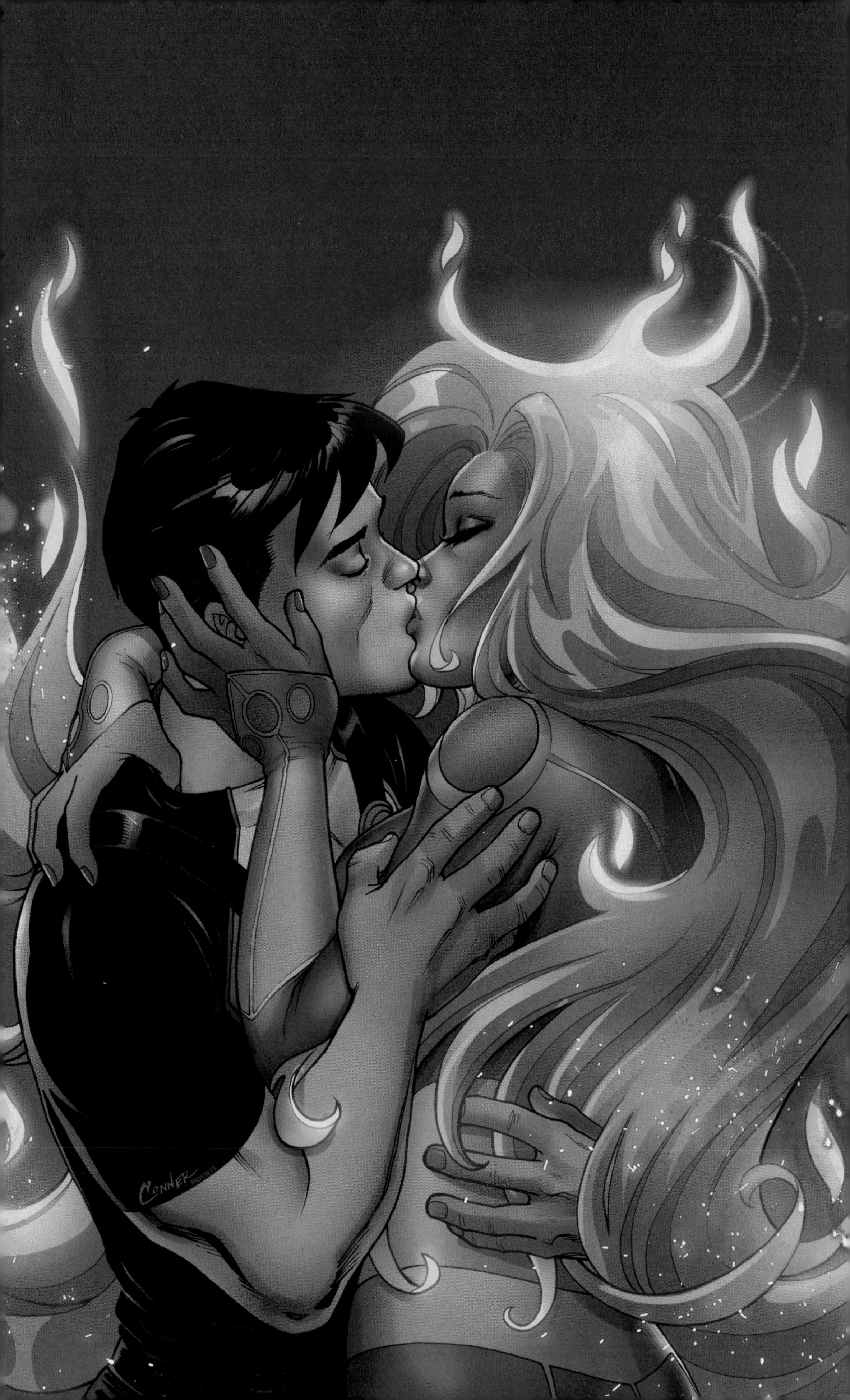
CONNER
MOUNTS

LOVERS AND OTHER DANGERS

AMANDA CONNER & JIMMY PALMIOTTI writers EMANUELA LUPACCHINO pencils MIRCO PIERFEDERICI pencil assists RAY McCARTHY inks HI-FI colors TOM NAPOLITANO letters

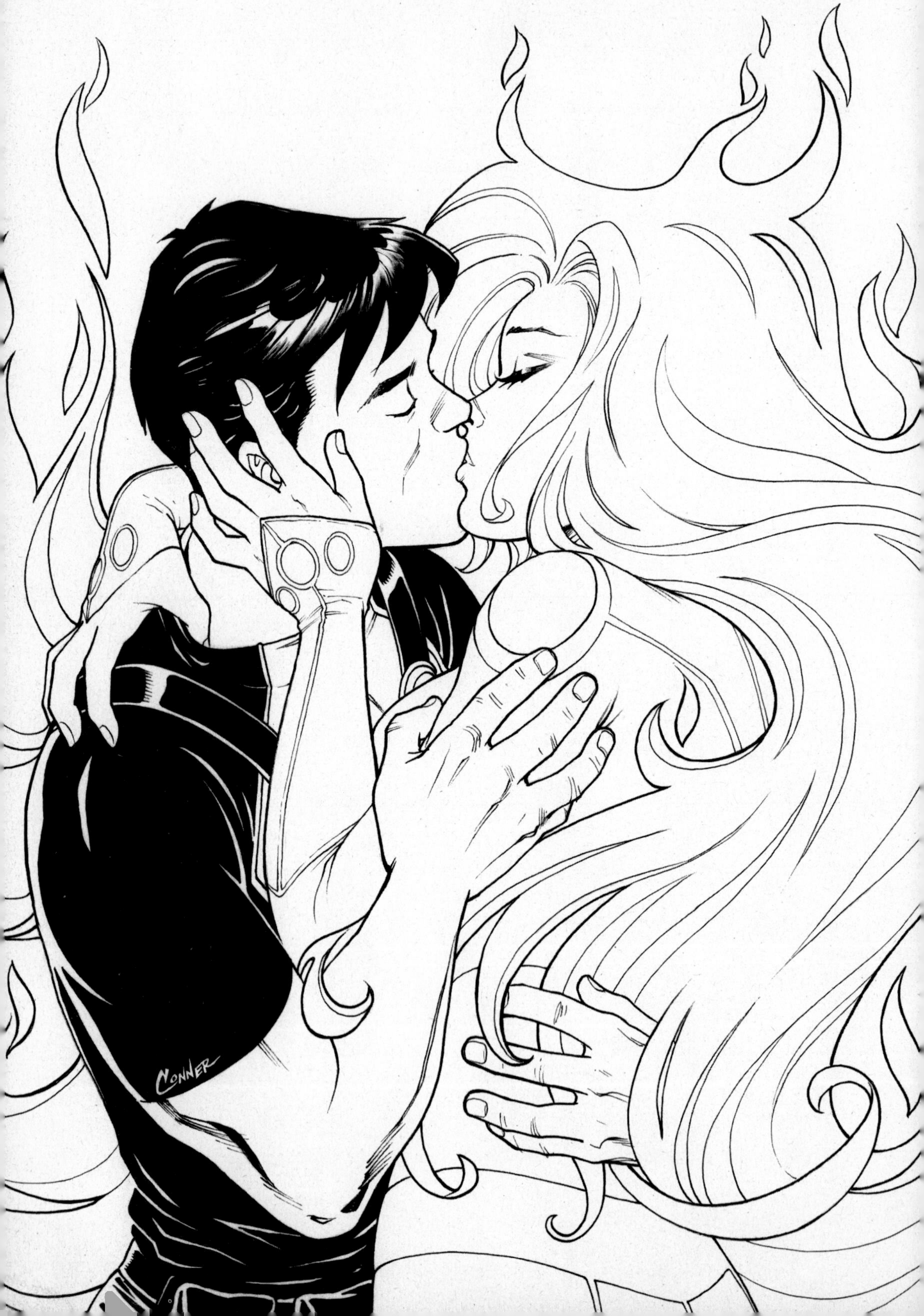
CONNER

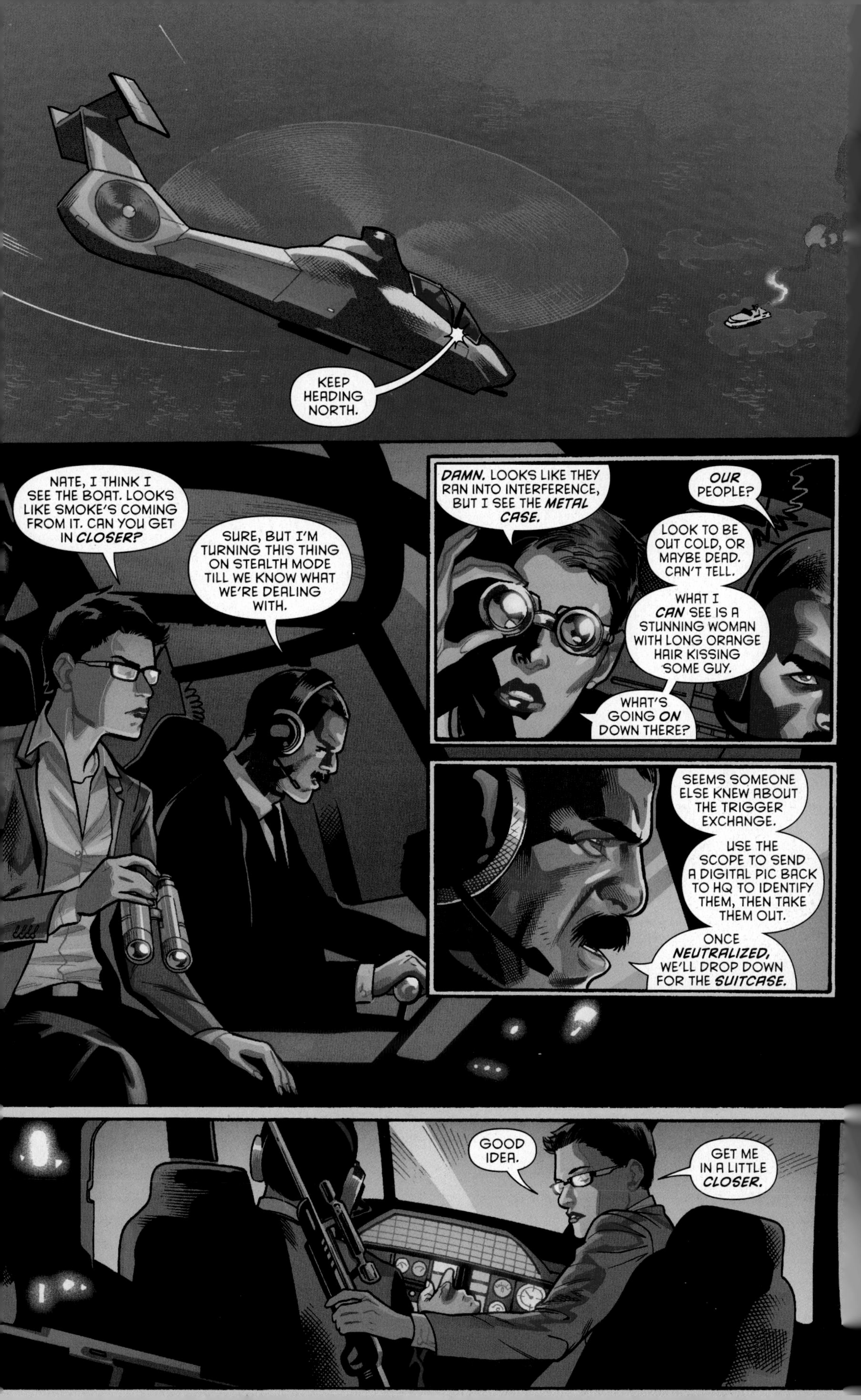
KEEP HEADING NORTH.
NATE, I THINK I SEE THE BOAT. LOOKS LIKE SMOKE'S COMING FROM IT. CAN YOU GET IN CLOSER?
SURE, BUT I'M TURNING THIS THING ON STEALTH MODE TILL WE KNOW WHAT WE'RE DEALING WITH.
DAMN. LOOKS LIKE THEY RAN INTO INTERFERENCE, BUT I SEE THE METAL CASE.
OUR PEOPLE?
LOOK TO BE OUT COLD, OR MAYBE DEAD. CAN'T TELL.
WHAT I CAN SEE IS A STUNNING WOMAN WITH LONG ORANGE HAIR KISSING SOME GUY.
WHAT'S GOING ON DOWN THERE?
SEEMS SOMEONE ELSE KNEW ABOUT THE TRIGGER EXCHANGE.
USE THE SCOPE TO SEND A DIGITAL PIC BACK TO HQ TO IDENTIFY THEM, THEN TAKE THEM OUT.
ONCE NEUTRALIZED, WE'LL DROP DOWN FOR THE SUITCASE.
GOOD IDEA.
GET ME IN A LITTLE CLOSER.

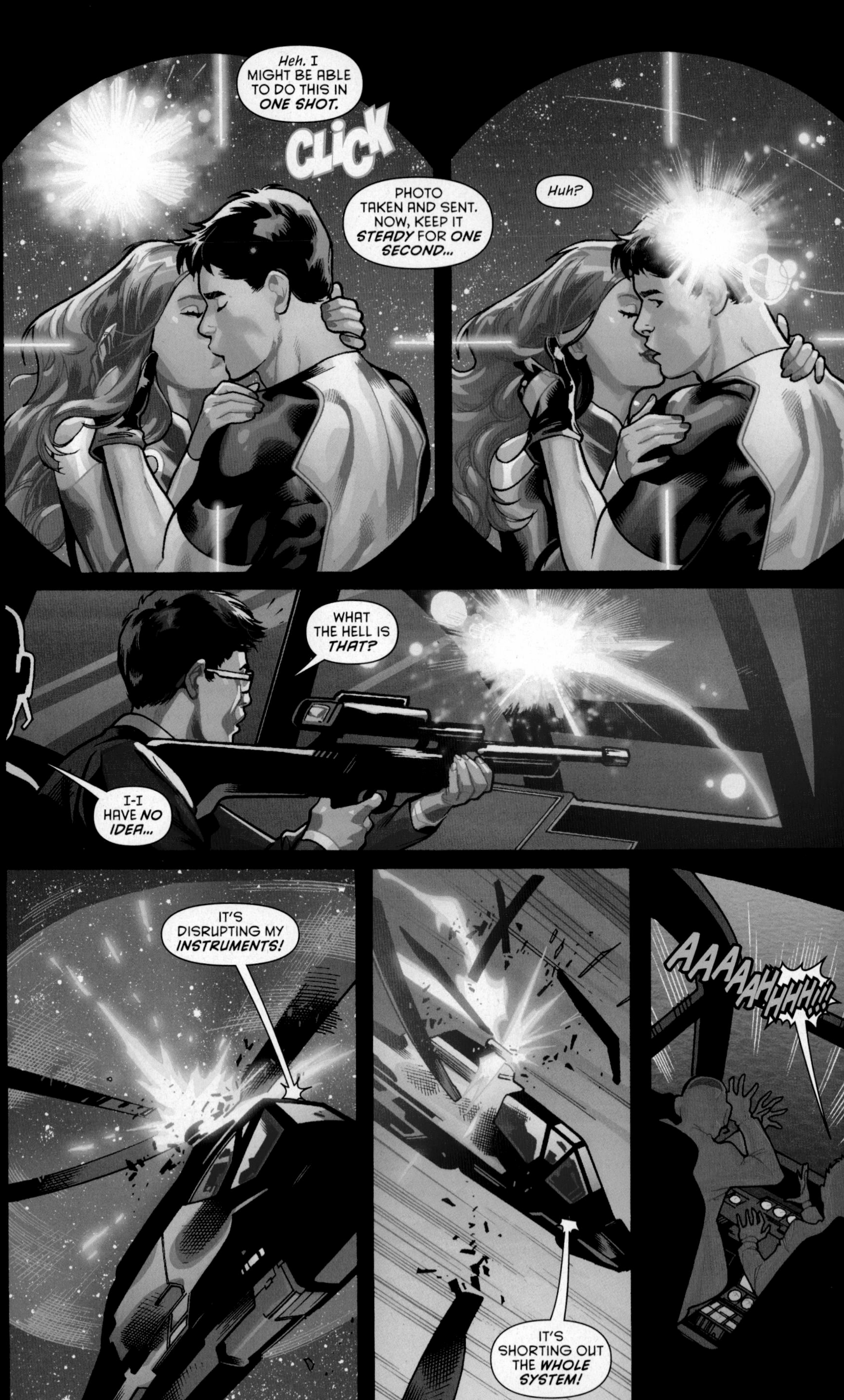
Heh. I MIGHT BE ABLE TO DO THIS IN ONE SHOT.
CLICK
PHOTO TAKEN AND SENT. NOW, KEEP IT STEADY FOR ONE SECOND...
Huh?
WHAT THE HELL IS THAT?
I-I HAVE NO IDEA...
IT'S DISRUPTING MY INSTRUMENTS!
IT'S SHORTING OUT THE WHOLE SYSTEM!
AAAAAHHHH!!!

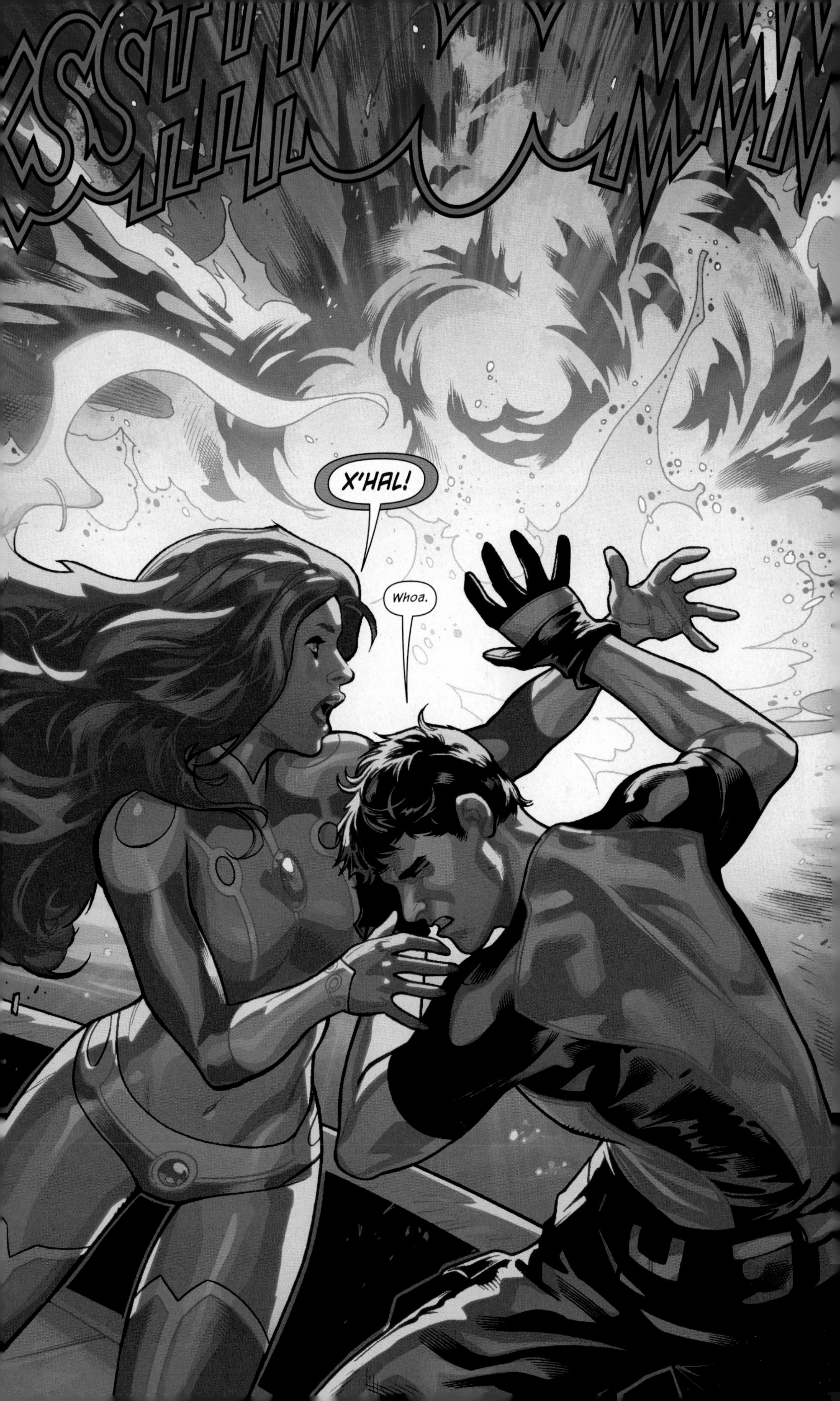
X'HAL!
Whoa.

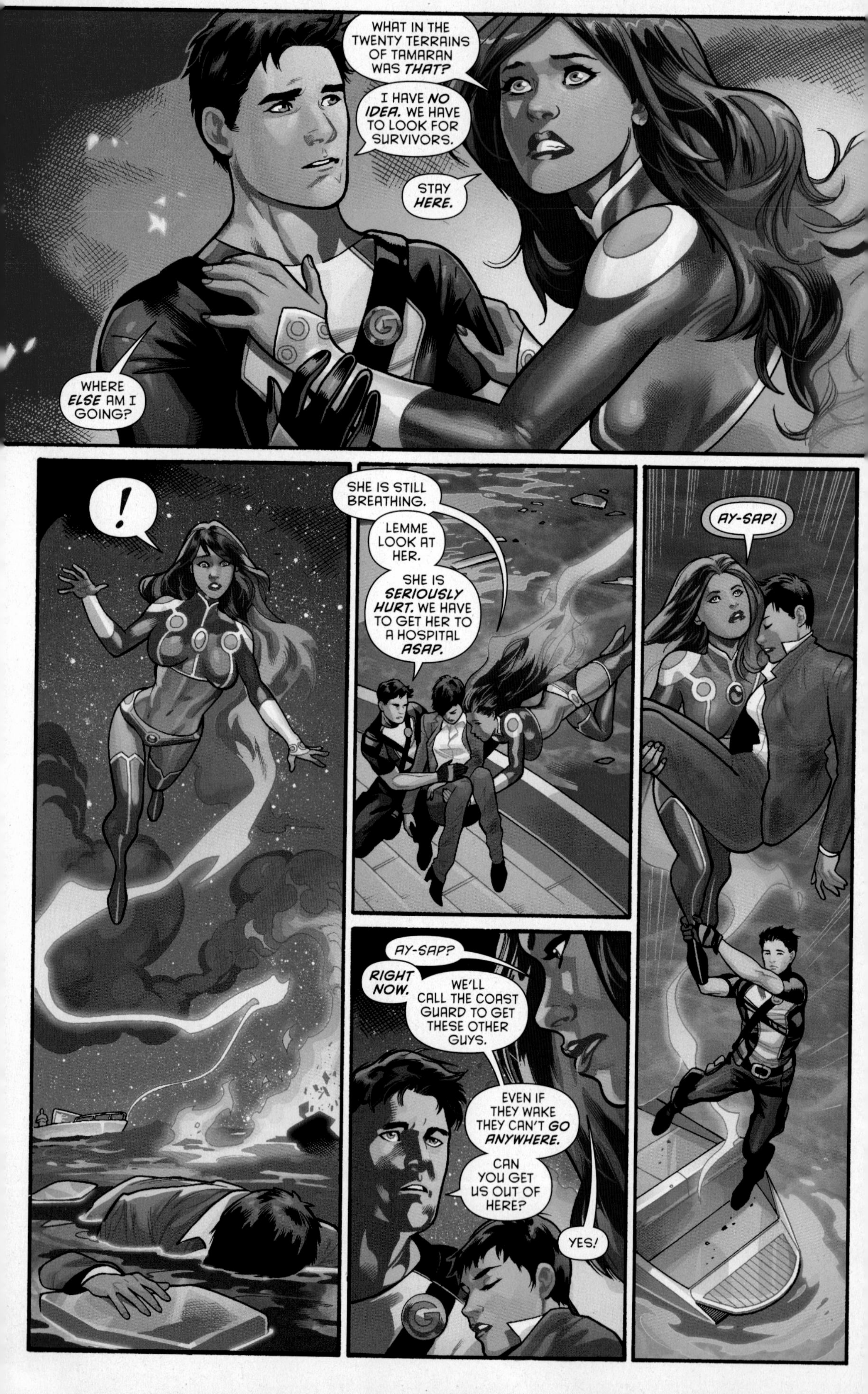
WHAT IN THE TWENTY TERRAINS OF TAMARAN WAS *THAT?*
I HAVE *NO IDEA.* WE HAVE TO LOOK FOR SURVIVORS.
STAY *HERE.*
WHERE *ELSE* AM I GOING?
!
SHE IS STILL BREATHING.
LEMME LOOK AT HER.
SHE IS *SERIOUSLY HURT.* WE HAVE TO GET HER TO A HOSPITAL *ASAP.*
AY-SAP?
RIGHT NOW.
WE'LL CALL THE COAST GUARD TO GET THESE OTHER GUYS.
EVEN IF THEY WAKE THEY CAN'T *GO ANYWHERE.*
CAN YOU GET US OUT OF HERE?
YES!
AY-SAP!

ALMOST THERE.

COMING UP RIGHT AHEAD.

SO WERE YOU GUYS ON AN ACTUAL *DATE*, OR JUST GRABBING DINNER?

SORT OF A *FIRST DATE* THAT WENT *HORRIBLY WRONG.* DO ME A FAVOR AND MAKE SURE THAT LINE TO THEIR VESSEL IS SECURE. WE'RE GONNA TOW THEIR BOAT IN.

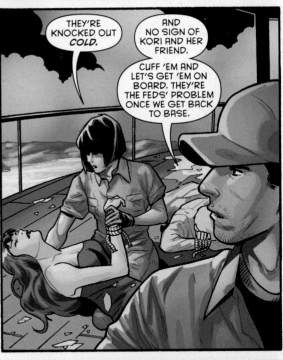

THEY'RE KNOCKED OUT *COLD.*

AND NO SIGN OF KORI AND HER FRIEND.

CUFF 'EM AND LET'S GET 'EM ON BOARD. THEY'RE THE FEDS' PROBLEM ONCE WE GET BACK TO BASE.

LET'S *GO*, RAVE. WE GOTTA HEAD BACK.

SOL, ONE SECOND. LET'S JUST WAIT TILL THE SUN COMES UP. *PLEASE.*

YOU KNOW I'M *NEVER* ON DUTY THIS EARLY.

SURE.

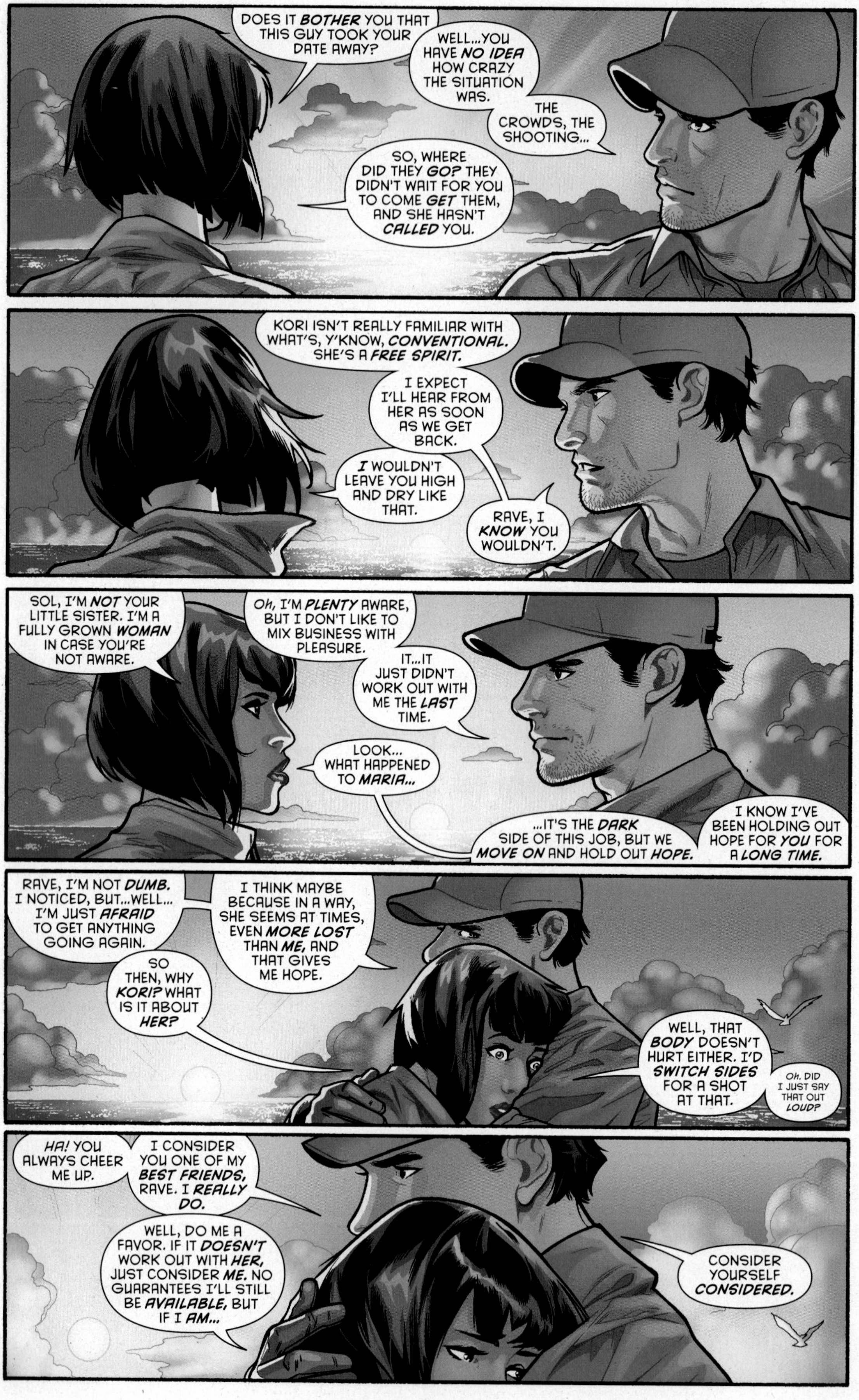
DOES IT BOTHER YOU THAT THIS GUY TOOK YOUR DATE AWAY?
WELL...YOU HAVE NO IDEA HOW CRAZY THE SITUATION WAS.
THE CROWDS, THE SHOOTING...
SO, WHERE DID THEY GO? THEY DIDN'T WAIT FOR YOU TO COME GET THEM, AND SHE HASN'T CALLED YOU.
KORI ISN'T REALLY FAMILIAR WITH WHAT'S, Y'KNOW, CONVENTIONAL. SHE'S A FREE SPIRIT.
I EXPECT I'LL HEAR FROM HER AS SOON AS WE GET BACK.
I WOULDN'T LEAVE YOU HIGH AND DRY LIKE THAT.
RAVE, I KNOW YOU WOULDN'T.
SOL, I'M NOT YOUR LITTLE SISTER. I'M A FULLY GROWN WOMAN IN CASE YOU'RE NOT AWARE.
Oh, I'M PLENTY AWARE, BUT I DON'T LIKE TO MIX BUSINESS WITH PLEASURE.
IT...IT JUST DIDN'T WORK OUT WITH ME THE LAST TIME.
LOOK... WHAT HAPPENED TO MARIA...
...IT'S THE DARK SIDE OF THIS JOB, BUT WE MOVE ON AND HOLD OUT HOPE.
I KNOW I'VE BEEN HOLDING OUT HOPE FOR YOU FOR A LONG TIME.
RAVE, I'M NOT DUMB. I NOTICED, BUT...WELL... I'M JUST AFRAID TO GET ANYTHING GOING AGAIN.
SO THEN, WHY KORI? WHAT IS IT ABOUT HER?
I THINK MAYBE BECAUSE IN A WAY, SHE SEEMS AT TIMES, EVEN MORE LOST THAN ME, AND THAT GIVES ME HOPE.
WELL, THAT BODY DOESN'T HURT EITHER. I'D SWITCH SIDES FOR A SHOT AT THAT.
Oh. DID I JUST SAY THAT OUT LOUD?
HA! YOU ALWAYS CHEER ME UP.
I CONSIDER YOU ONE OF MY BEST FRIENDS, RAVE. I REALLY DO.
WELL, DO ME A FAVOR. IF IT DOESN'T WORK OUT WITH HER, JUST CONSIDER ME. NO GUARANTEES I'LL STILL BE AVAILABLE, BUT IF I AM...
CONSIDER YOURSELF CONSIDERED.

Time Off for Good Behavior.

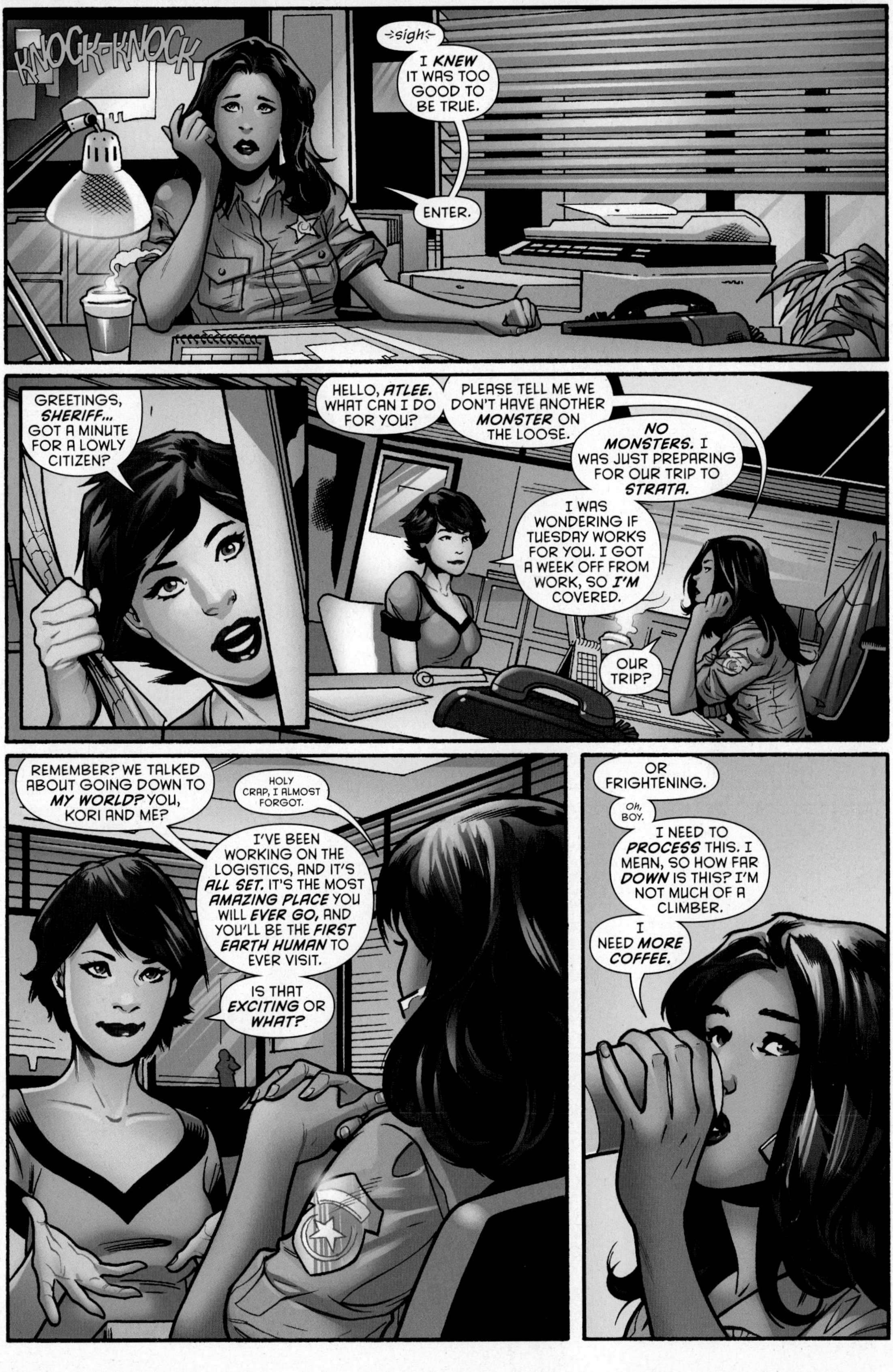
KNOCK-KNOCK
-sigh-
I KNEW IT WAS TOO GOOD TO BE TRUE.
ENTER.
GREETINGS, SHERIFF... GOT A MINUTE FOR A LOWLY CITIZEN?
HELLO, ATLEE. WHAT CAN I DO FOR YOU?
PLEASE TELL ME WE DON'T HAVE ANOTHER MONSTER ON THE LOOSE.
NO MONSTERS. I WAS JUST PREPARING FOR OUR TRIP TO STRATA.
I WAS WONDERING IF TUESDAY WORKS FOR YOU. I GOT A WEEK OFF FROM WORK, SO I'M COVERED.
OUR TRIP?
REMEMBER? WE TALKED ABOUT GOING DOWN TO MY WORLD? YOU, KORI AND ME?
HOLY CRAP, I ALMOST FORGOT.
I'VE BEEN WORKING ON THE LOGISTICS, AND IT'S ALL SET. IT'S THE MOST AMAZING PLACE YOU WILL EVER GO, AND YOU'LL BE THE FIRST EARTH HUMAN TO EVER VISIT.
IS THAT EXCITING OR WHAT?
OR FRIGHTENING.
Oh, BOY.
I NEED TO PROCESS THIS. I MEAN, SO HOW FAR DOWN IS THIS? I'M NOT MUCH OF A CLIMBER.
I NEED MORE COFFEE.

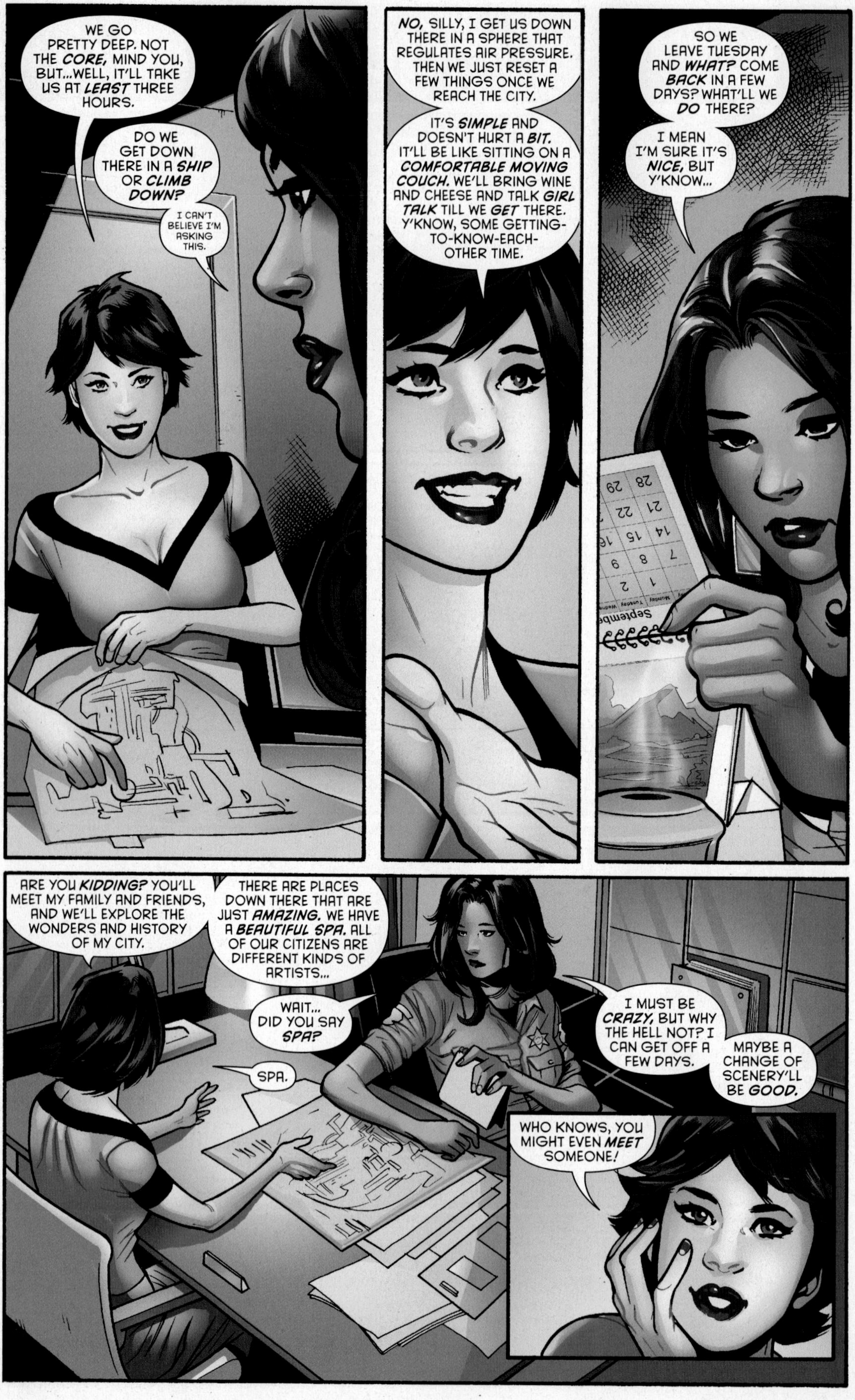

WE GO PRETTY DEEP. NOT THE CORE, MIND YOU, BUT...WELL, IT'LL TAKE US AT LEAST THREE HOURS.
DO WE GET DOWN THERE IN A SHIP OR CLIMB DOWN?
I CAN'T BELIEVE I'M ASKING THIS.
NO, SILLY, I GET US DOWN THERE IN A SPHERE THAT REGULATES AIR PRESSURE. THEN WE JUST RESET A FEW THINGS ONCE WE REACH THE CITY.
IT'S SIMPLE AND DOESN'T HURT A BIT. IT'LL BE LIKE SITTING ON A COMFORTABLE MOVING COUCH. WE'LL BRING WINE AND CHEESE AND TALK GIRL TALK TILL WE GET THERE. Y'KNOW, SOME GETTING-TO-KNOW-EACH-OTHER TIME.
SO WE LEAVE TUESDAY AND WHAT? COME BACK IN A FEW DAYS? WHAT'LL WE DO THERE?
I MEAN I'M SURE IT'S NICE, BUT Y'KNOW...
ARE YOU KIDDING? YOU'LL MEET MY FAMILY AND FRIENDS, AND WE'LL EXPLORE THE WONDERS AND HISTORY OF MY CITY.
THERE ARE PLACES DOWN THERE THAT ARE JUST AMAZING. WE HAVE A BEAUTIFUL SPA. ALL OF OUR CITIZENS ARE DIFFERENT KINDS OF ARTISTS...
WAIT... DID YOU SAY SPA?
SPA.
I MUST BE CRAZY, BUT WHY THE HELL NOT? I CAN GET OFF A FEW DAYS.
MAYBE A CHANGE OF SCENERY'LL BE GOOD.
WHO KNOWS, YOU MIGHT EVEN MEET SOMEONE!

Hello, Goodbye, Hope You Don't Die. Again.

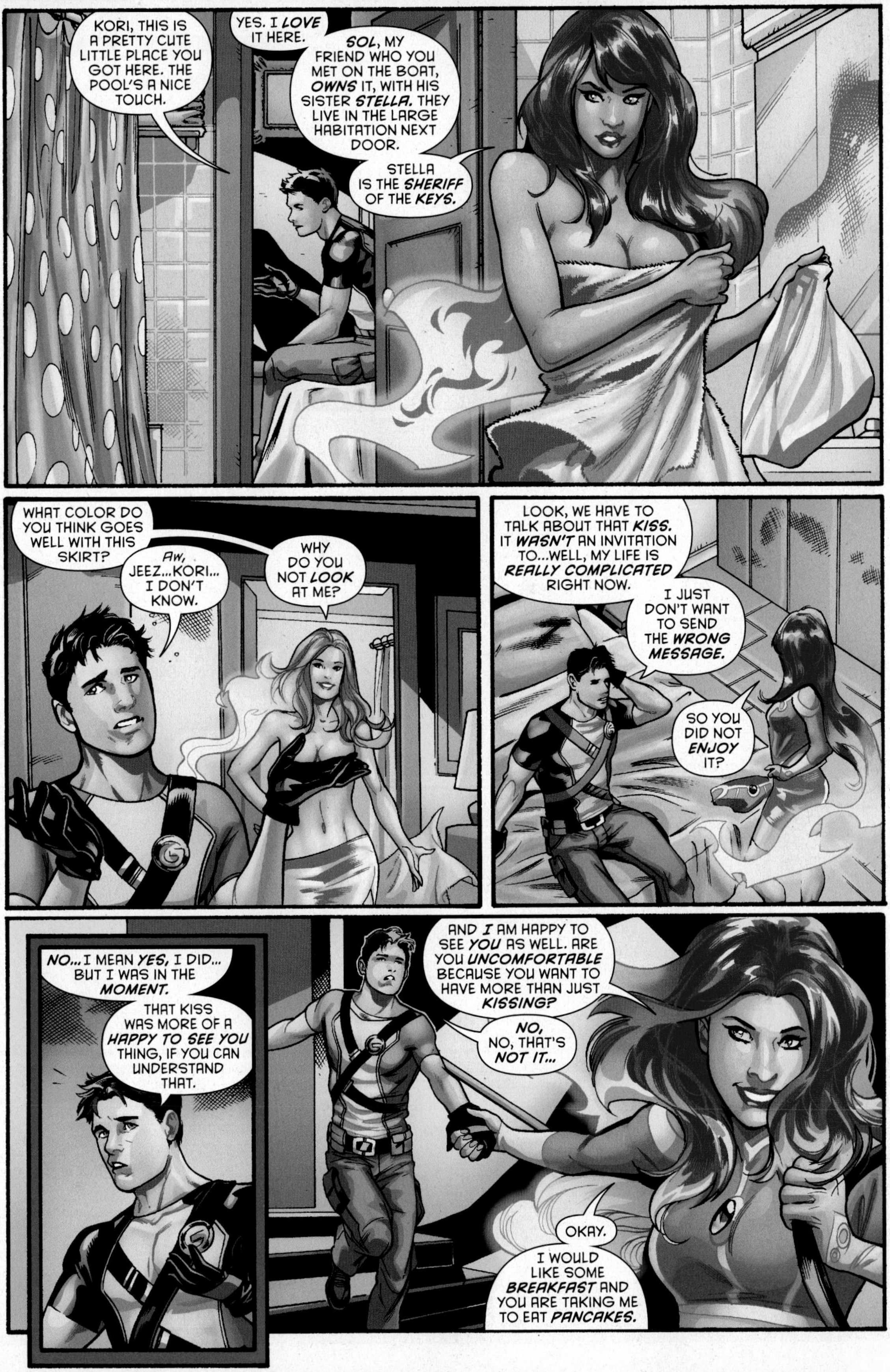
KORI, THIS IS A PRETTY CUTE LITTLE PLACE YOU GOT HERE. THE POOL'S A NICE TOUCH.
YES. I LOVE IT HERE.
SOL, MY FRIEND WHO YOU MET ON THE BOAT, OWNS IT, WITH HIS SISTER STELLA. THEY LIVE IN THE LARGE HABITATION NEXT DOOR.
STELLA IS THE SHERIFF OF THE KEYS.
WHAT COLOR DO YOU THINK GOES WELL WITH THIS SKIRT?
AW, JEEZ...KORI... I DON'T KNOW.
WHY DO YOU NOT LOOK AT ME?
LOOK, WE HAVE TO TALK ABOUT THAT KISS. IT WASN'T AN INVITATION TO...WELL, MY LIFE IS REALLY COMPLICATED RIGHT NOW.
I JUST DON'T WANT TO SEND THE WRONG MESSAGE.
SO YOU DID NOT ENJOY IT?
NO...I MEAN YES, I DID... BUT I WAS IN THE MOMENT.
THAT KISS WAS MORE OF A HAPPY TO SEE YOU THING, IF YOU CAN UNDERSTAND THAT.
AND I AM HAPPY TO SEE YOU AS WELL. ARE YOU UNCOMFORTABLE BECAUSE YOU WANT TO HAVE MORE THAN JUST KISSING?
NO, NO, THAT'S NOT IT...
OKAY.
I WOULD LIKE SOME BREAKFAST AND YOU ARE TAKING ME TO EAT PANCAKES.

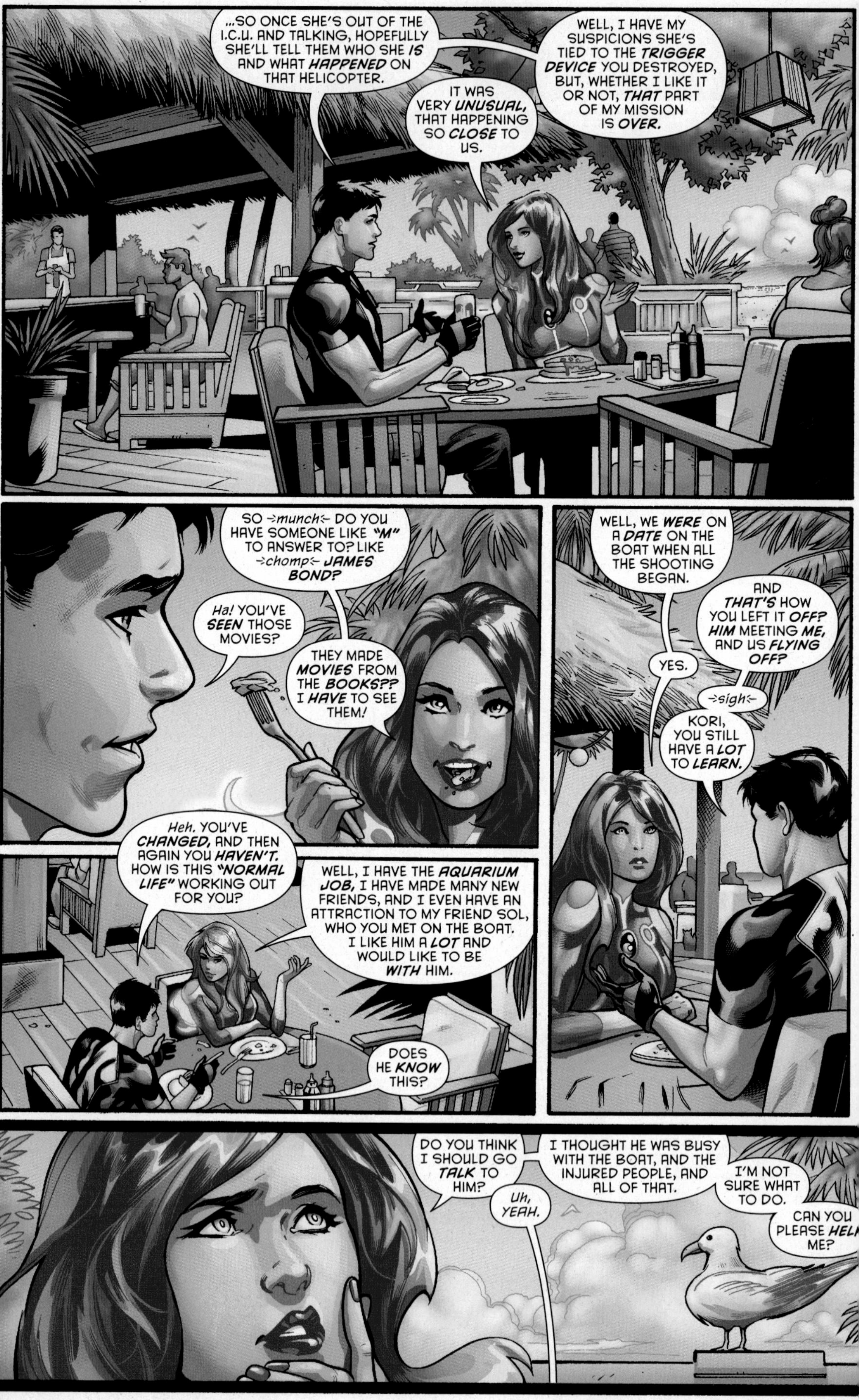
...SO ONCE SHE'S OUT OF THE I.C.U. AND TALKING, HOPEFULLY SHE'LL TELL THEM WHO SHE *IS* AND WHAT *HAPPENED* ON THAT HELICOPTER.
WELL, I HAVE MY SUSPICIONS SHE'S TIED TO THE *TRIGGER DEVICE* YOU DESTROYED, BUT, WHETHER I LIKE IT OR NOT, *THAT* PART OF MY MISSION IS *OVER.*
IT WAS VERY *UNUSUAL,* THAT HAPPENING SO *CLOSE* TO US.
SO ~munch~ DO YOU HAVE SOMEONE LIKE *"M"* TO ANSWER TO? LIKE ~chomp~ *JAMES BOND?*
Ha! YOU'VE *SEEN* THOSE MOVIES?
THEY MADE *MOVIES* FROM THE *BOOKS??* I *HAVE* TO SEE THEM!
Heh. YOU'VE *CHANGED,* AND THEN AGAIN YOU *HAVEN'T.* HOW IS THIS *"NORMAL LIFE"* WORKING OUT FOR YOU?
WELL, I HAVE THE *AQUARIUM JOB,* I HAVE MADE MANY NEW FRIENDS, AND I EVEN HAVE AN ATTRACTION TO MY FRIEND SOL, WHO YOU MET ON THE BOAT. I LIKE HIM A *LOT* AND WOULD LIKE TO BE *WITH* HIM.
DOES HE *KNOW* THIS?
WELL, WE *WERE* ON A *DATE* ON THE BOAT WHEN ALL THE SHOOTING BEGAN.
AND *THAT'S* HOW YOU LEFT IT *OFF? HIM* MEETING *ME,* AND US *FLYING OFF?*
YES.
~sigh~
KORI, YOU STILL HAVE A *LOT* TO *LEARN.*
I THOUGHT HE WAS BUSY WITH THE BOAT, AND THE INJURED PEOPLE, AND ALL OF THAT.
DO YOU THINK I SHOULD GO *TALK* TO HIM?
Uh, YEAH.
I'M NOT SURE WHAT TO DO.
CAN YOU PLEASE *HELP* ME?

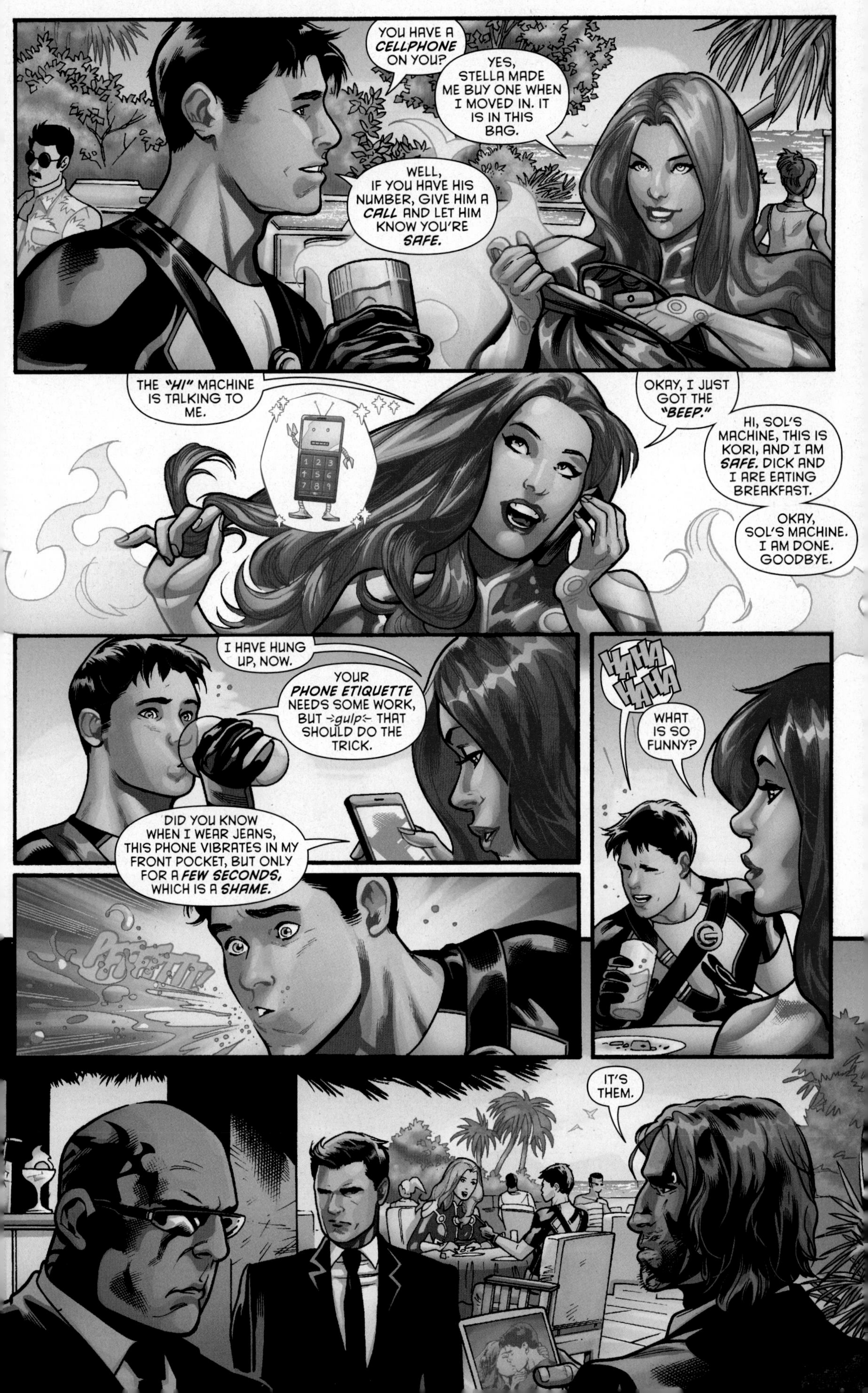

YOU HAVE A CELLPHONE ON YOU?
YES, STELLA MADE ME BUY ONE WHEN I MOVED IN. IT IS IN THIS BAG.
WELL, IF YOU HAVE HIS NUMBER, GIVE HIM A CALL AND LET HIM KNOW YOU'RE SAFE.
THE "HI" MACHINE IS TALKING TO ME.
OKAY, I JUST GOT THE "BEEP."
HI, SOL'S MACHINE, THIS IS KORI, AND I AM SAFE. DICK AND I ARE EATING BREAKFAST.
OKAY, SOL'S MACHINE. I AM DONE. GOODBYE.
I HAVE HUNG UP, NOW.
YOUR PHONE ETIQUETTE NEEDS SOME WORK, BUT ->gulp<- THAT SHOULD DO THE TRICK.
DID YOU KNOW WHEN I WEAR JEANS, THIS PHONE VIBRATES IN MY FRONT POCKET, BUT ONLY FOR A FEW SECONDS, WHICH IS A SHAME.
PFFFFTTT!
HAHA HAHA
WHAT IS SO FUNNY?
IT'S THEM.

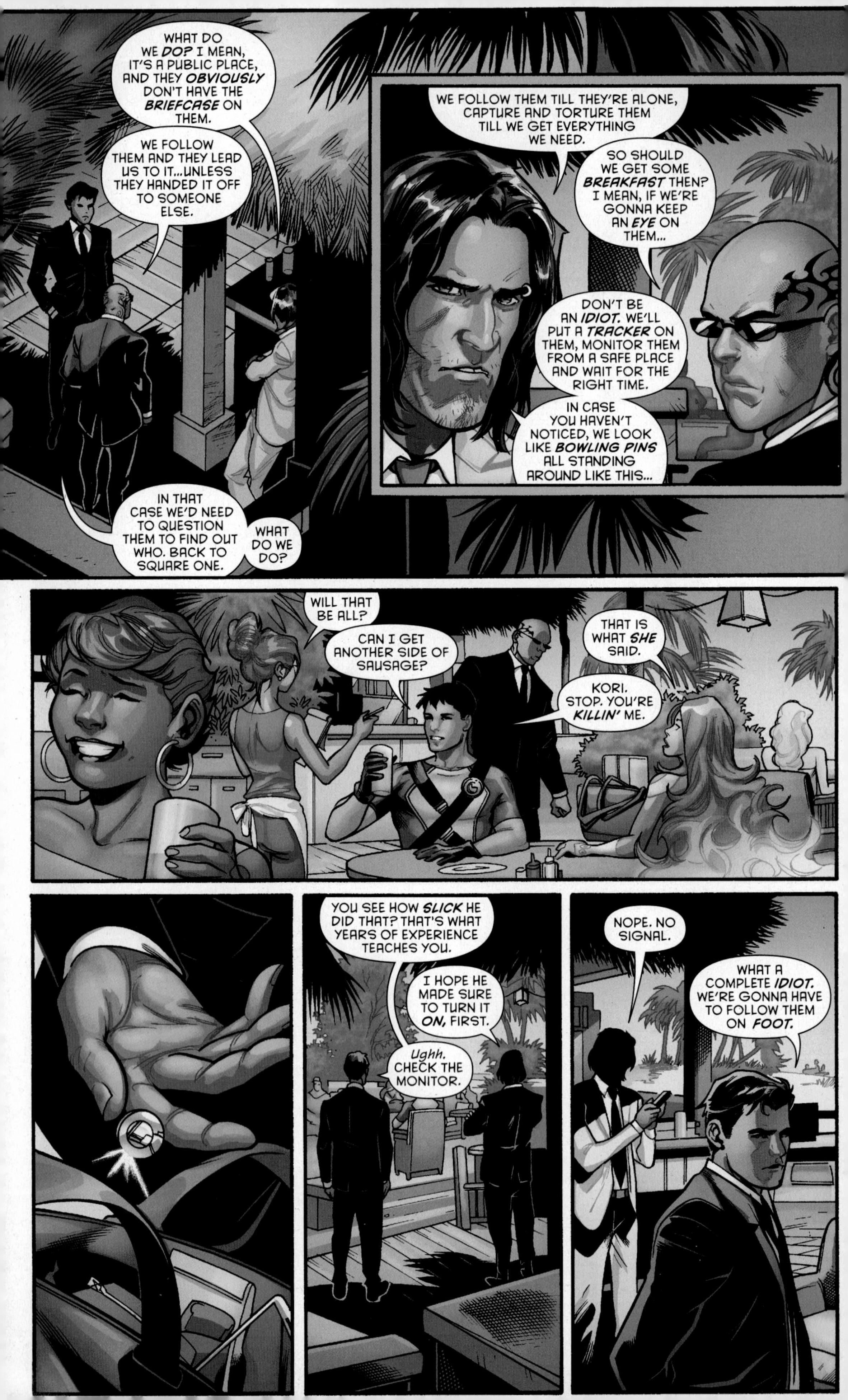
WHAT DO WE DO? I MEAN, IT'S A PUBLIC PLACE, AND THEY OBVIOUSLY DON'T HAVE THE BRIEFCASE ON THEM.
WE FOLLOW THEM AND THEY LEAD US TO IT...UNLESS THEY HANDED IT OFF TO SOMEONE ELSE.
IN THAT CASE WE'D NEED TO QUESTION THEM TO FIND OUT WHO. BACK TO SQUARE ONE.
WHAT DO WE DO?
WE FOLLOW THEM TILL THEY'RE ALONE, CAPTURE AND TORTURE THEM TILL WE GET EVERYTHING WE NEED.
SO SHOULD WE GET SOME BREAKFAST THEN? I MEAN, IF WE'RE GONNA KEEP AN EYE ON THEM...
DON'T BE AN IDIOT. WE'LL PUT A TRACKER ON THEM, MONITOR THEM FROM A SAFE PLACE AND WAIT FOR THE RIGHT TIME.
IN CASE YOU HAVEN'T NOTICED, WE LOOK LIKE BOWLING PINS ALL STANDING AROUND LIKE THIS...
WILL THAT BE ALL?
CAN I GET ANOTHER SIDE OF SAUSAGE?
THAT IS WHAT SHE SAID.
KORI. STOP. YOU'RE KILLIN' ME.
YOU SEE HOW SLICK HE DID THAT? THAT'S WHAT YEARS OF EXPERIENCE TEACHES YOU.
I HOPE HE MADE SURE TO TURN IT ON, FIRST.
Ughh. CHECK THE MONITOR.
NOPE. NO SIGNAL.
WHAT A COMPLETE IDIOT. WE'RE GONNA HAVE TO FOLLOW THEM ON FOOT.

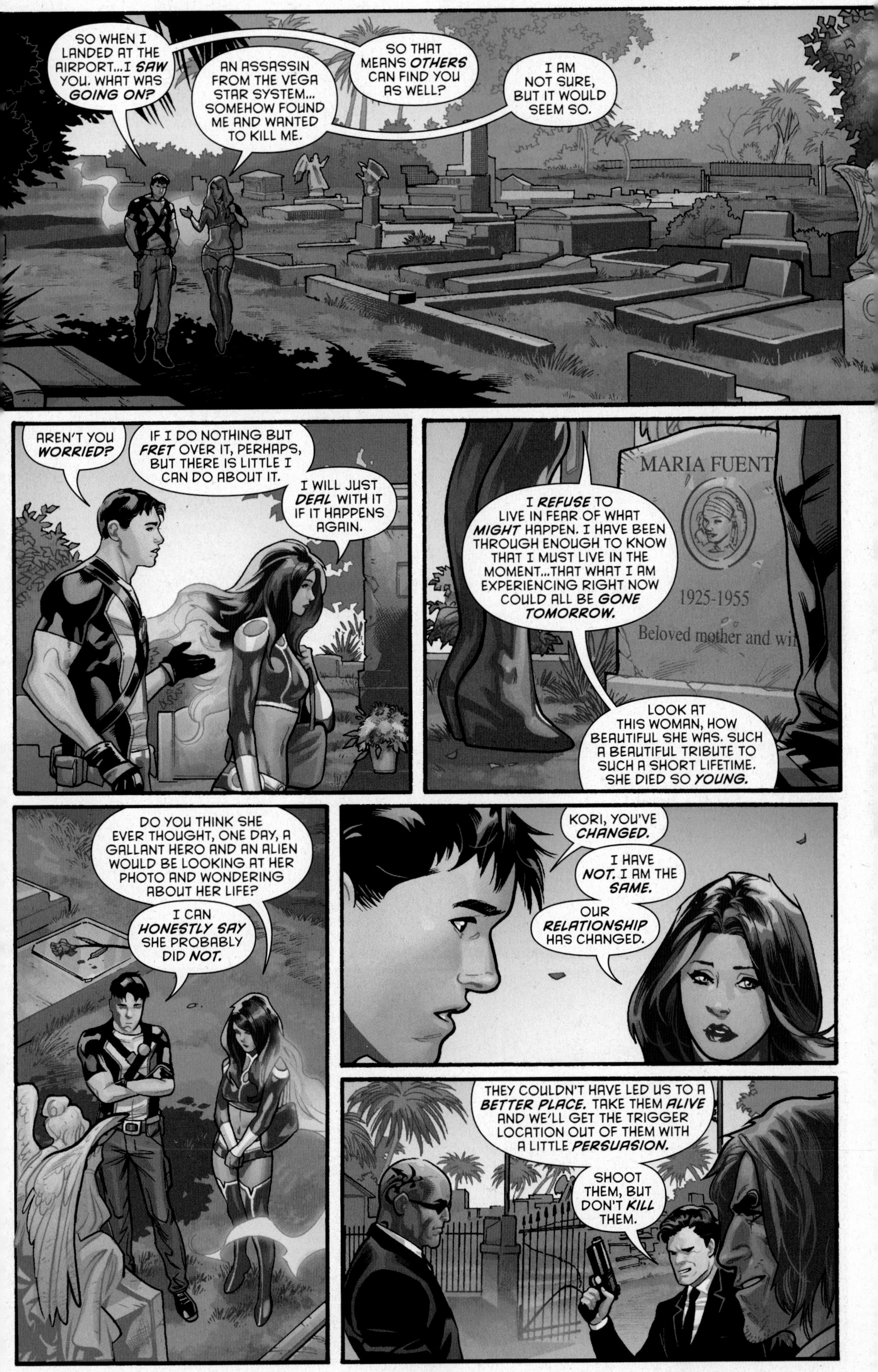

SO WHEN I LANDED AT THE AIRPORT...I SAW YOU. WHAT WAS GOING ON?
AN ASSASSIN FROM THE VEGA STAR SYSTEM... SOMEHOW FOUND ME AND WANTED TO KILL ME.
SO THAT MEANS OTHERS CAN FIND YOU AS WELL?
I AM NOT SURE, BUT IT WOULD SEEM SO.
AREN'T YOU WORRIED?
IF I DO NOTHING BUT FRET OVER IT, PERHAPS, BUT THERE IS LITTLE I CAN DO ABOUT IT.
I WILL JUST DEAL WITH IT IF IT HAPPENS AGAIN.
I REFUSE TO LIVE IN FEAR OF WHAT MIGHT HAPPEN. I HAVE BEEN THROUGH ENOUGH TO KNOW THAT I MUST LIVE IN THE MOMENT...THAT WHAT I AM EXPERIENCING RIGHT NOW COULD ALL BE GONE TOMORROW.
MARIA FUENT
1925-1955
Beloved mother and wi
LOOK AT THIS WOMAN, HOW BEAUTIFUL SHE WAS. SUCH A BEAUTIFUL TRIBUTE TO SUCH A SHORT LIFETIME. SHE DIED SO YOUNG.
DO YOU THINK SHE EVER THOUGHT, ONE DAY, A GALLANT HERO AND AN ALIEN WOULD BE LOOKING AT HER PHOTO AND WONDERING ABOUT HER LIFE?
I CAN HONESTLY SAY SHE PROBABLY DID NOT.
KORI, YOU'VE CHANGED.
I HAVE NOT. I AM THE SAME.
OUR RELATIONSHIP HAS CHANGED.
THEY COULDN'T HAVE LED US TO A BETTER PLACE. TAKE THEM ALIVE AND WE'LL GET THE TRIGGER LOCATION OUT OF THEM WITH A LITTLE PERSUASION.
SHOOT THEM, BUT DON'T KILL THEM.

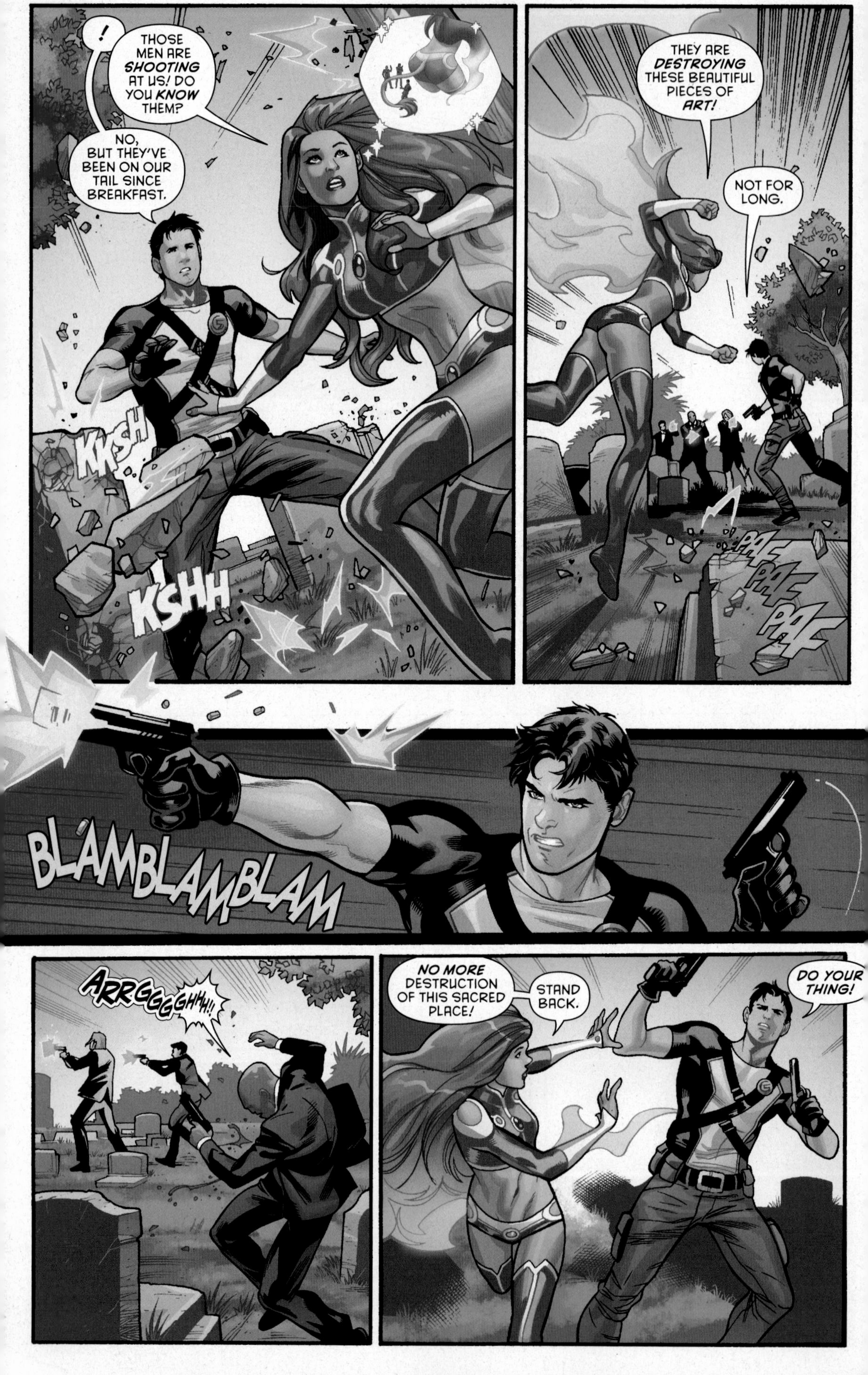
!
THOSE MEN ARE SHOOTING AT US! DO YOU KNOW THEM?
NO, BUT THEY'VE BEEN ON OUR TAIL SINCE BREAKFAST.
KKSH
KSHH
THEY ARE DESTROYING THESE BEAUTIFUL PIECES OF ART!
NOT FOR LONG.
PAF PAF PAF
BLAMBLAMBLAM
ARRGGGGHHH!!
NO MORE DESTRUCTION OF THIS SACRED PLACE!
STAND BACK.
DO YOUR THING!

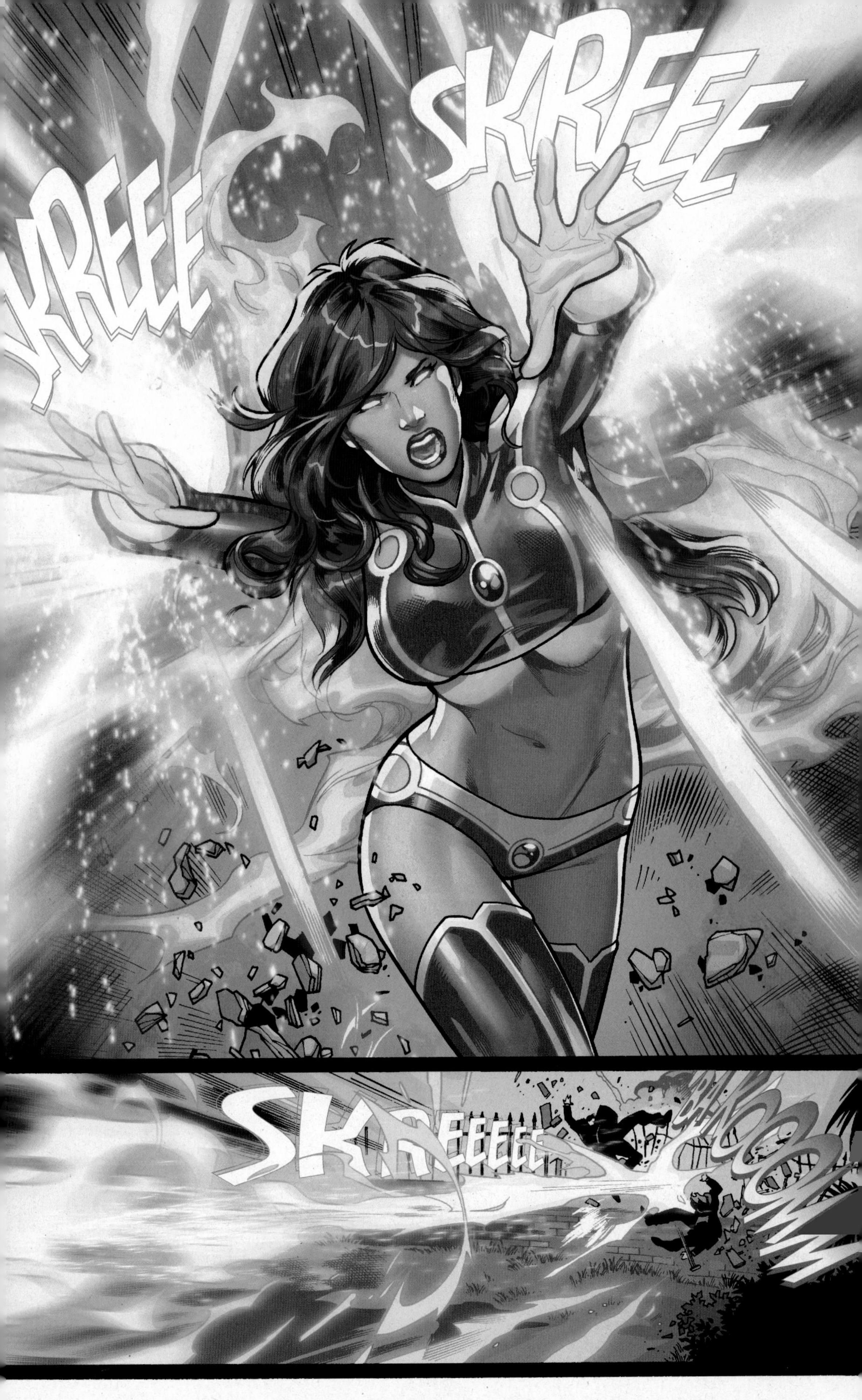
KREEE
SKREEE

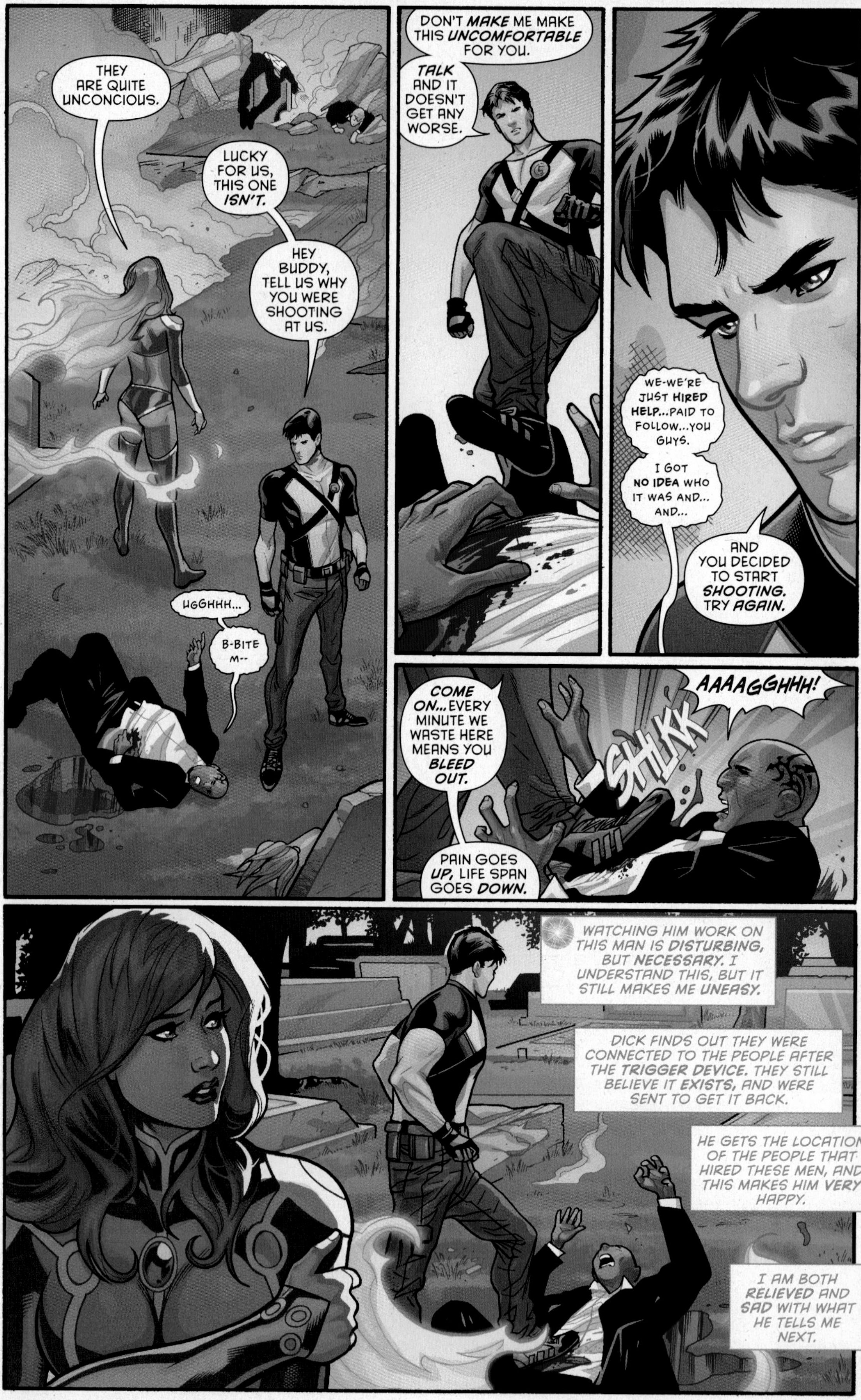
THEY ARE QUITE UNCONCIOUS.
LUCKY FOR US, THIS ONE ISN'T.
HEY BUDDY, TELL US WHY YOU WERE SHOOTING AT US.
UGGHHH...
B-BITE M--
DON'T MAKE ME MAKE THIS UNCOMFORTABLE FOR YOU.
TALK AND IT DOESN'T GET ANY WORSE.
WE-WE'RE JUST HIRED HELP...PAID TO FOLLOW...YOU GUYS.
I GOT NO IDEA WHO IT WAS AND... AND...
AND YOU DECIDED TO START SHOOTING. TRY AGAIN.
COME ON...EVERY MINUTE WE WASTE HERE MEANS YOU BLEED OUT.
SHUKK
AAAAGGHHH!
PAIN GOES UP, LIFE SPAN GOES DOWN.
WATCHING HIM WORK ON THIS MAN IS DISTURBING, BUT NECESSARY. I UNDERSTAND THIS, BUT IT STILL MAKES ME UNEASY.
DICK FINDS OUT THEY WERE CONNECTED TO THE PEOPLE AFTER THE TRIGGER DEVICE. THEY STILL BELIEVE IT EXISTS, AND WERE SENT TO GET IT BACK.
HE GETS THE LOCATION OF THE PEOPLE THAT HIRED THESE MEN, AND THIS MAKES HIM VERY HAPPY.
I AM BOTH RELIEVED AND SAD WITH WHAT HE TELLS ME NEXT.

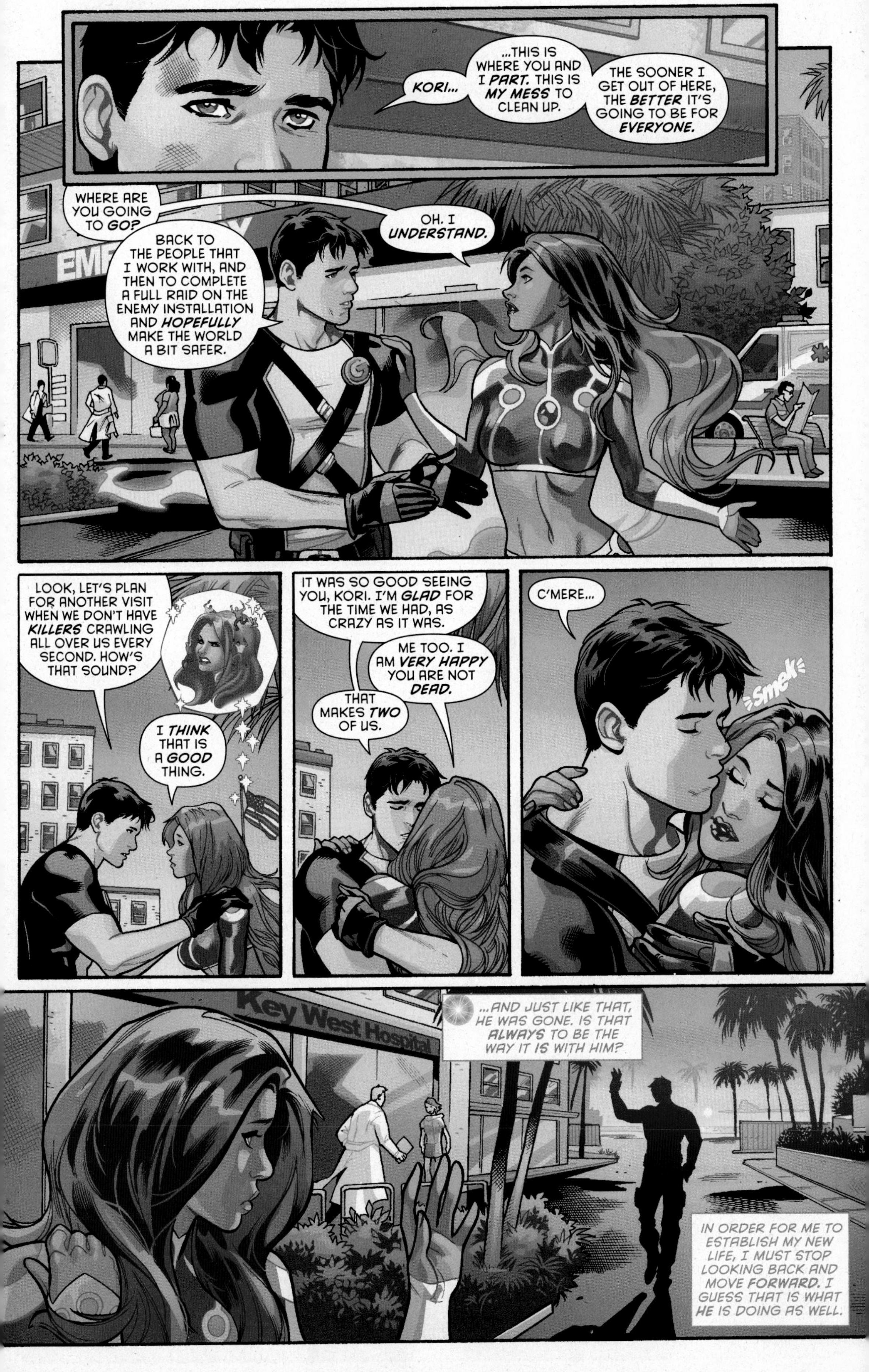
KORI...
...THIS IS WHERE YOU AND I PART. THIS IS MY MESS TO CLEAN UP.
THE SOONER I GET OUT OF HERE, THE BETTER IT'S GOING TO BE FOR EVERYONE.
WHERE ARE YOU GOING TO GO?
OH. I UNDERSTAND.
BACK TO THE PEOPLE THAT I WORK WITH, AND THEN TO COMPLETE A FULL RAID ON THE ENEMY INSTALLATION AND HOPEFULLY MAKE THE WORLD A BIT SAFER.
LOOK, LET'S PLAN FOR ANOTHER VISIT WHEN WE DON'T HAVE KILLERS CRAWLING ALL OVER US EVERY SECOND. HOW'S THAT SOUND?
I THINK THAT IS A GOOD THING.
IT WAS SO GOOD SEEING YOU, KORI. I'M GLAD FOR THE TIME WE HAD, AS CRAZY AS IT WAS.
ME TOO. I AM VERY HAPPY YOU ARE NOT DEAD.
THAT MAKES TWO OF US.
C'MERE...
Smek
Key West Hospital
...AND JUST LIKE THAT, HE WAS GONE. IS THAT ALWAYS TO BE THE WAY IT IS WITH HIM?
IN ORDER FOR ME TO ESTABLISH MY NEW LIFE, I MUST STOP LOOKING BACK AND MOVE FORWARD. I GUESS THAT IS WHAT HE IS DOING AS WELL.

Meta-Metamorphisis...

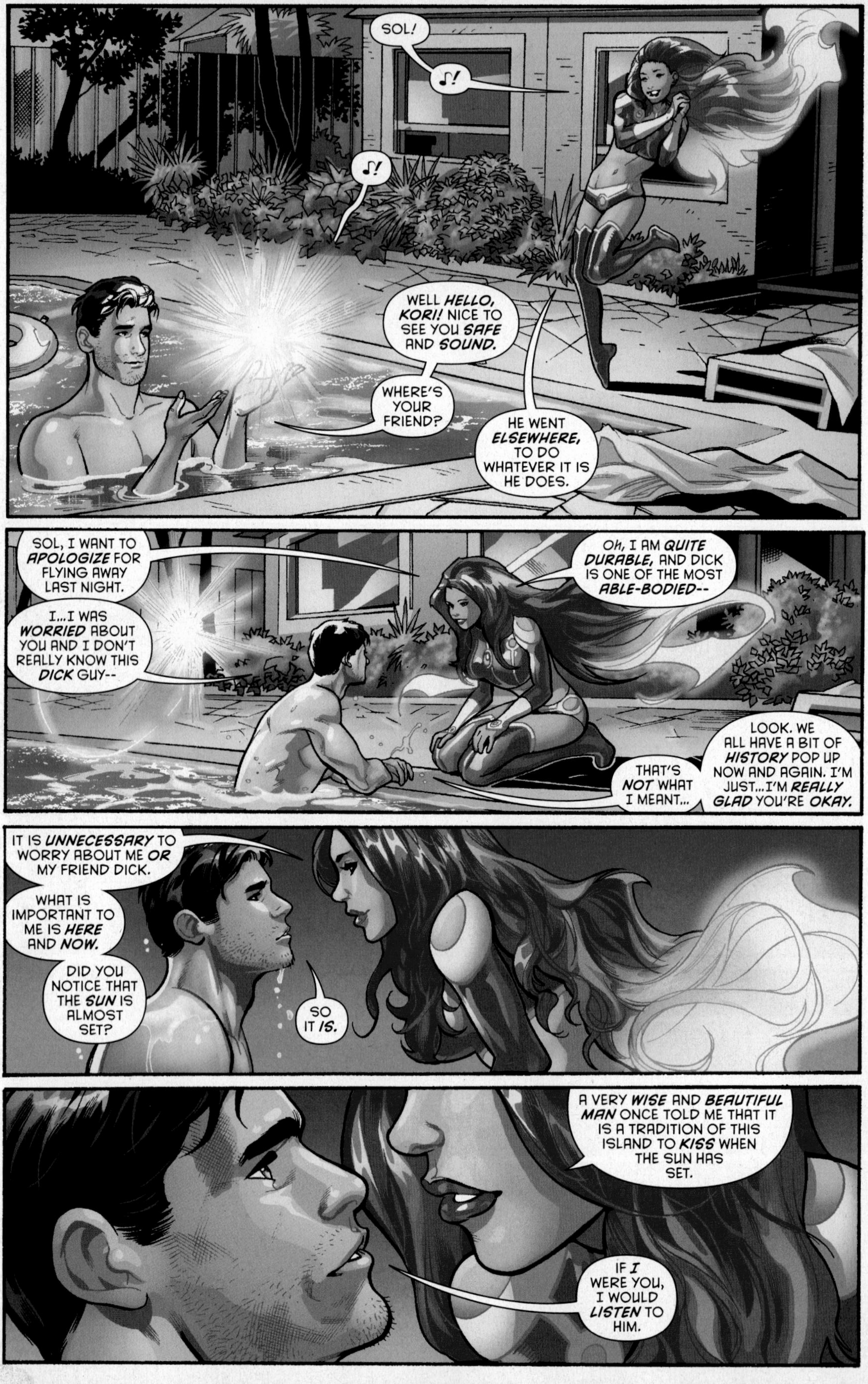
SOL!
♫!
♫!
WELL HELLO, KORI! NICE TO SEE YOU SAFE AND SOUND.
WHERE'S YOUR FRIEND?
HE WENT ELSEWHERE, TO DO WHATEVER IT IS HE DOES.
SOL, I WANT TO APOLOGIZE FOR FLYING AWAY LAST NIGHT.
I...I WAS WORRIED ABOUT YOU AND I DON'T REALLY KNOW THIS DICK GUY--
Oh, I AM QUITE DURABLE, AND DICK IS ONE OF THE MOST ABLE-BODIED--
THAT'S NOT WHAT I MEANT...
LOOK. WE ALL HAVE A BIT OF HISTORY POP UP NOW AND AGAIN. I'M JUST...I'M REALLY GLAD YOU'RE OKAY.
IT IS UNNECESSARY TO WORRY ABOUT ME OR MY FRIEND DICK.
WHAT IS IMPORTANT TO ME IS HERE AND NOW.
DID YOU NOTICE THAT THE SUN IS ALMOST SET?
SO IT IS.
A VERY WISE AND BEAUTIFUL MAN ONCE TOLD ME THAT IT IS A TRADITION OF THIS ISLAND TO KISS WHEN THE SUN HAS SET.
IF I WERE YOU, I WOULD LISTEN TO HIM.

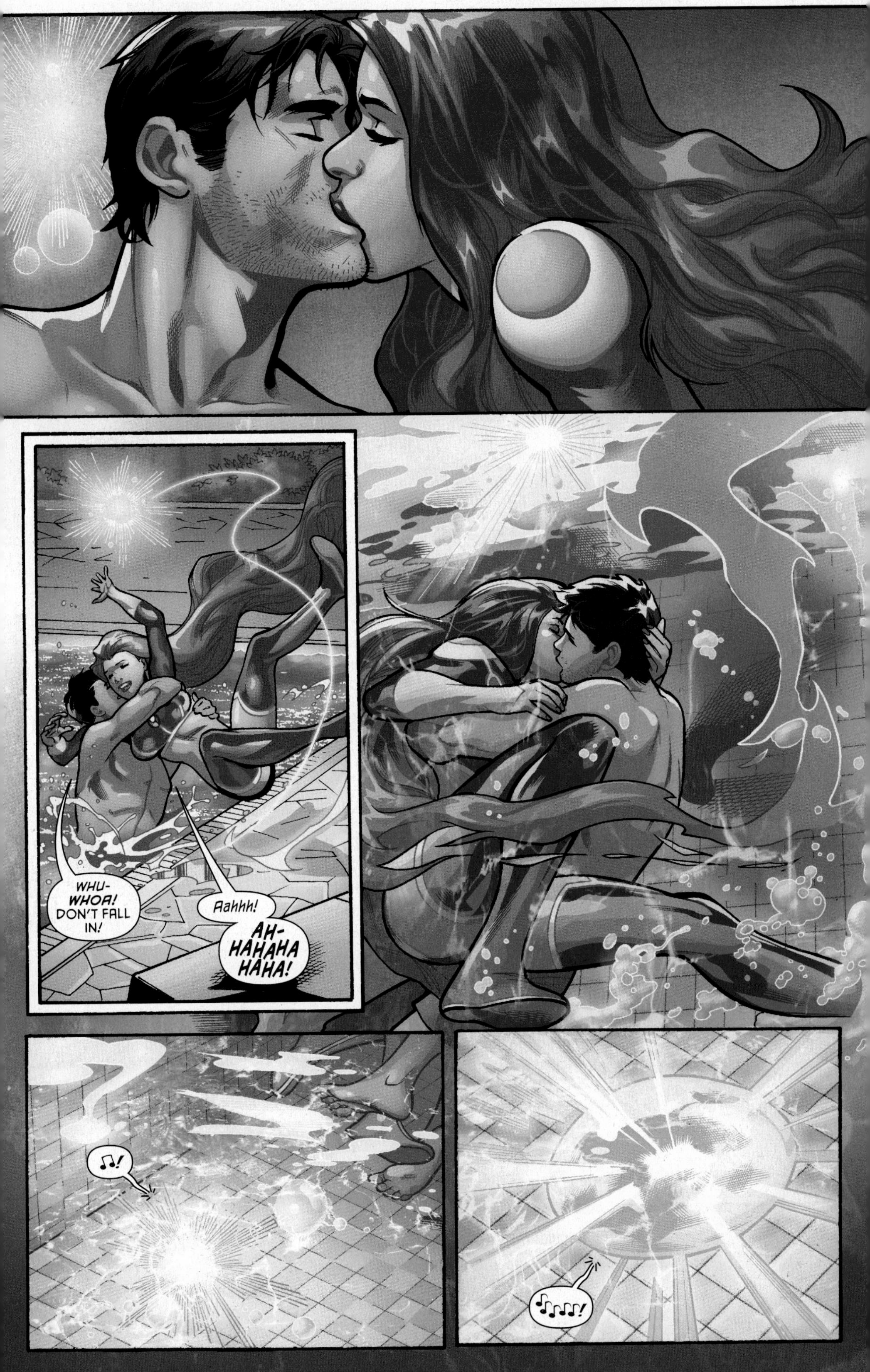
WHU-WHOA! DON'T FALL IN!
Aahhh!
AH-HAHAHA HAHA!
♫!
♫♫♫!

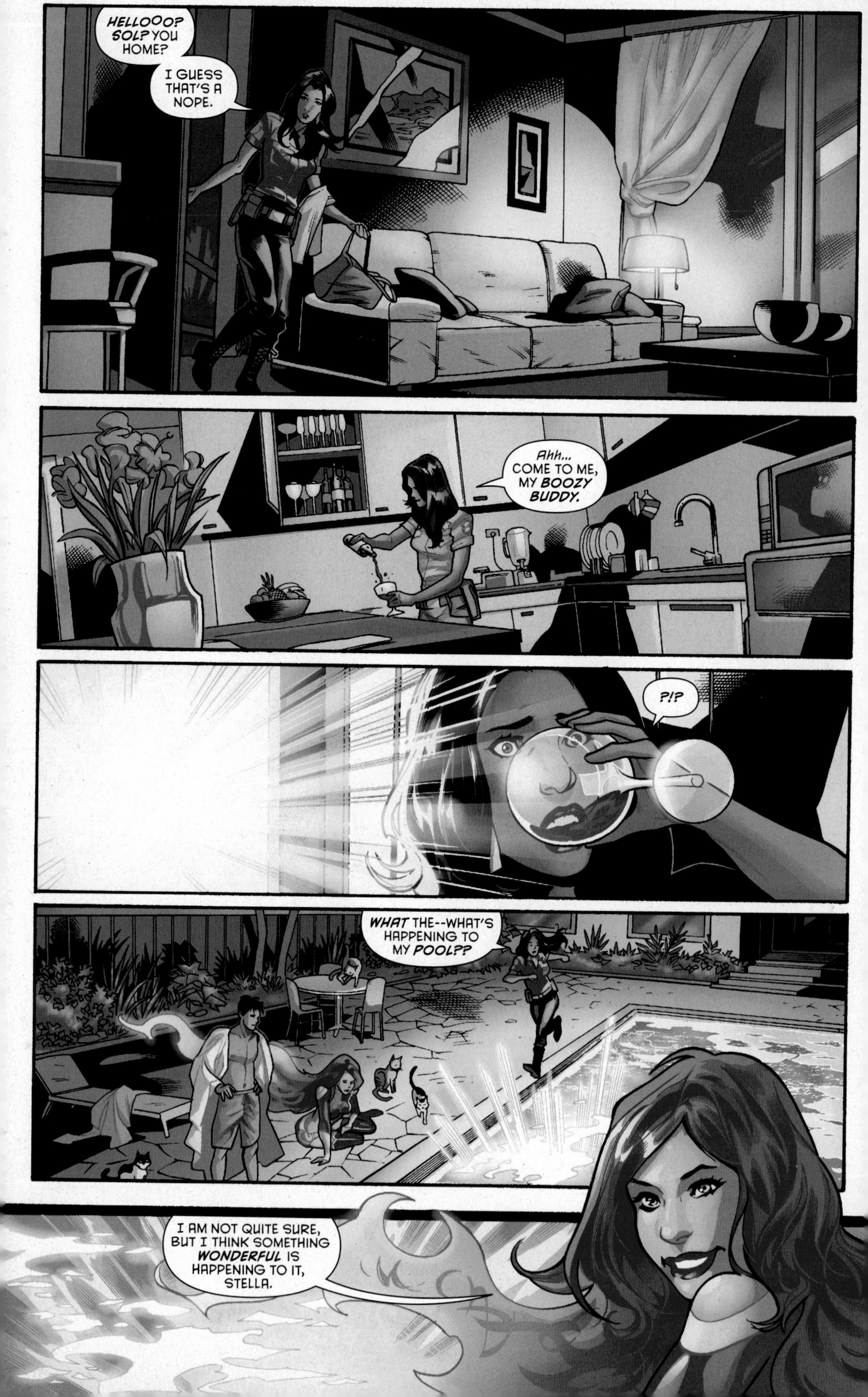
HELLOOO? SOL? YOU HOME?
I GUESS THAT'S A NOPE.
Ahh... COME TO ME, MY BOOZY BUDDY.
?!?
WHAT THE--WHAT'S HAPPENING TO MY POOL??
I AM NOT QUITE SURE, BUT I THINK SOMETHING WONDERFUL IS HAPPENING TO IT, STELLA.

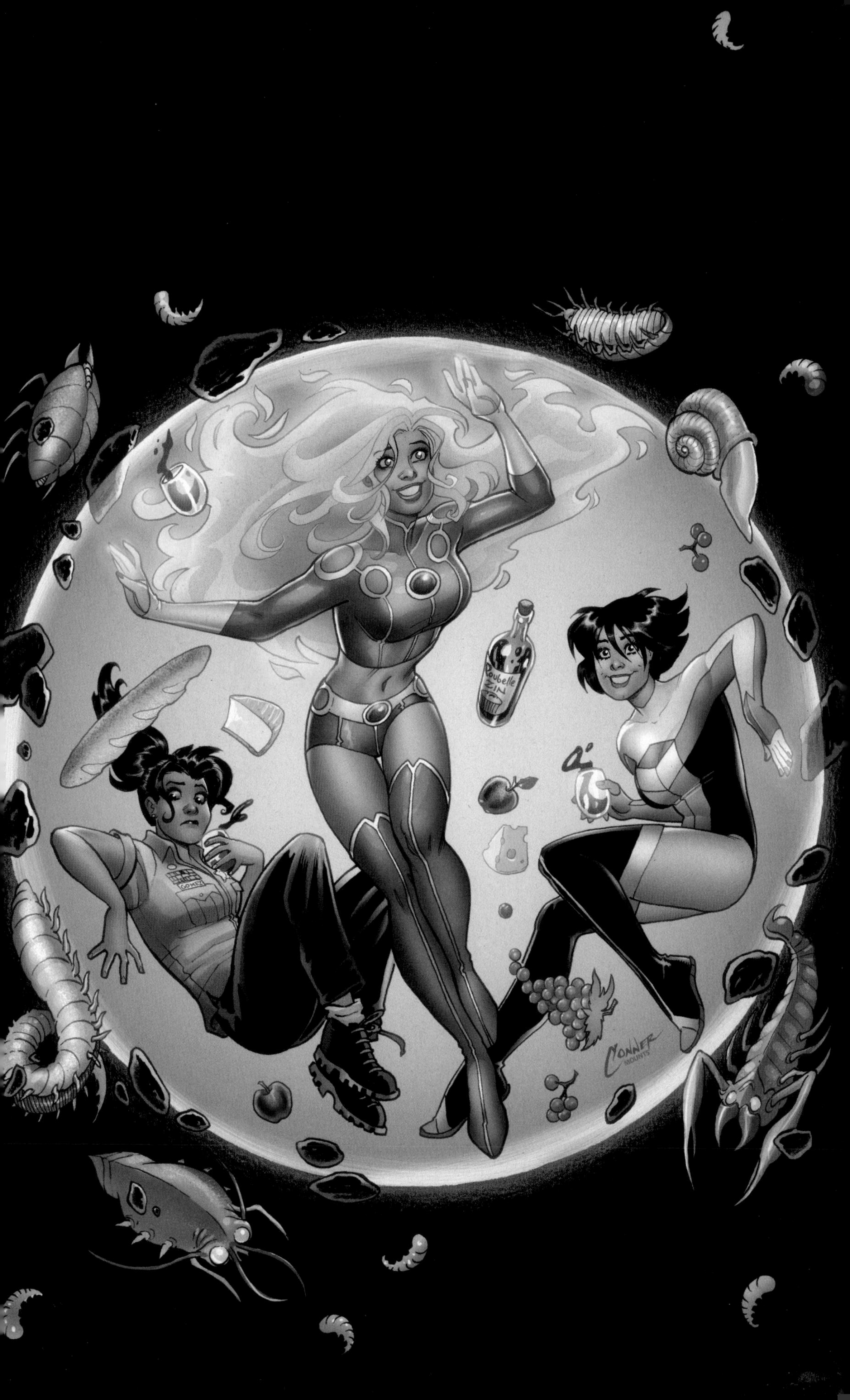
Poubelle ZIN
CONNER
MOUNTS

APPROACHING THE ABYSS

AMANDA CONNER & JIMMY PALMIOTTI writers ELSA CHARRETIER art HI-FI colors TOM NAPOLITANO letters

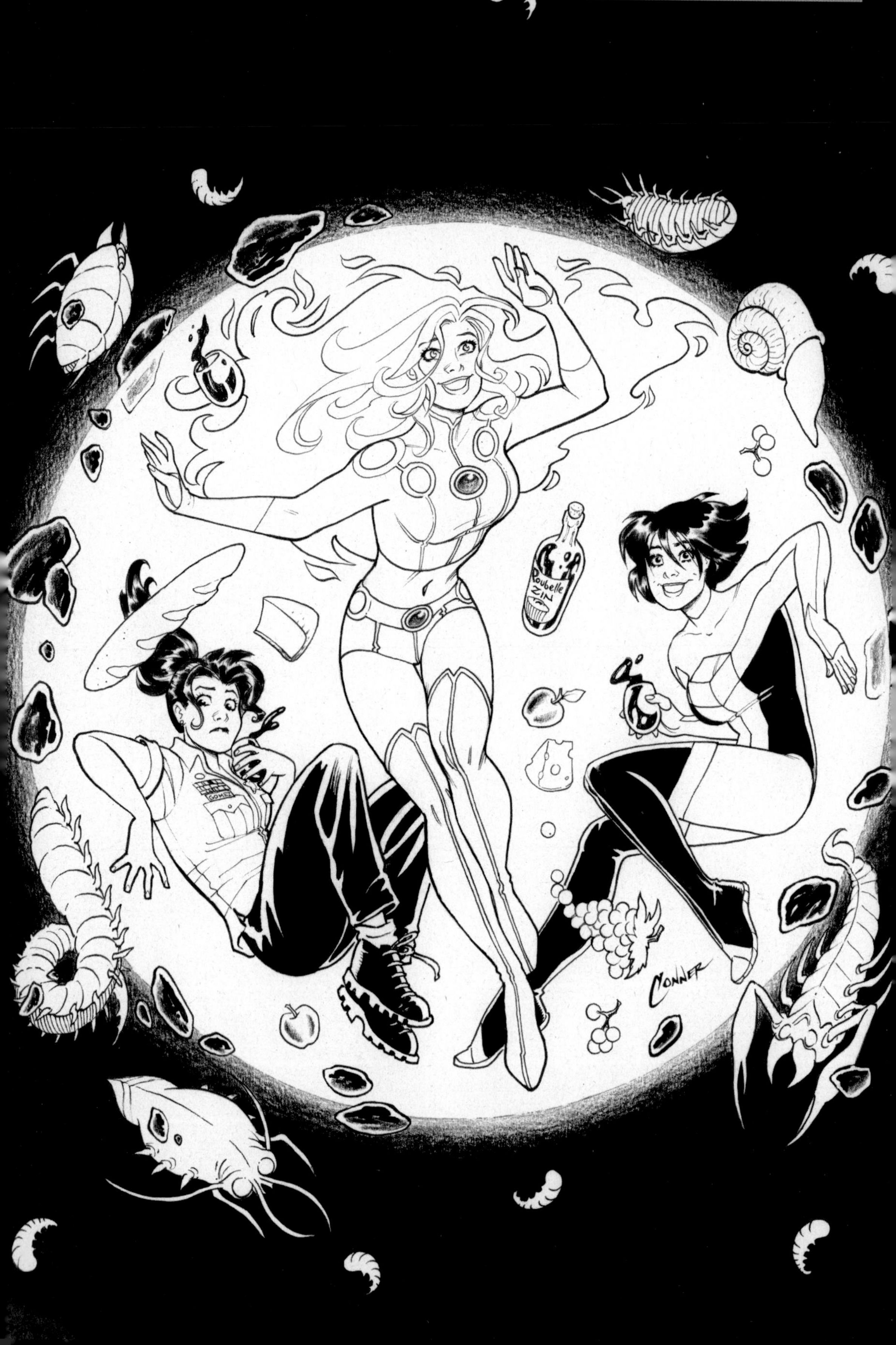

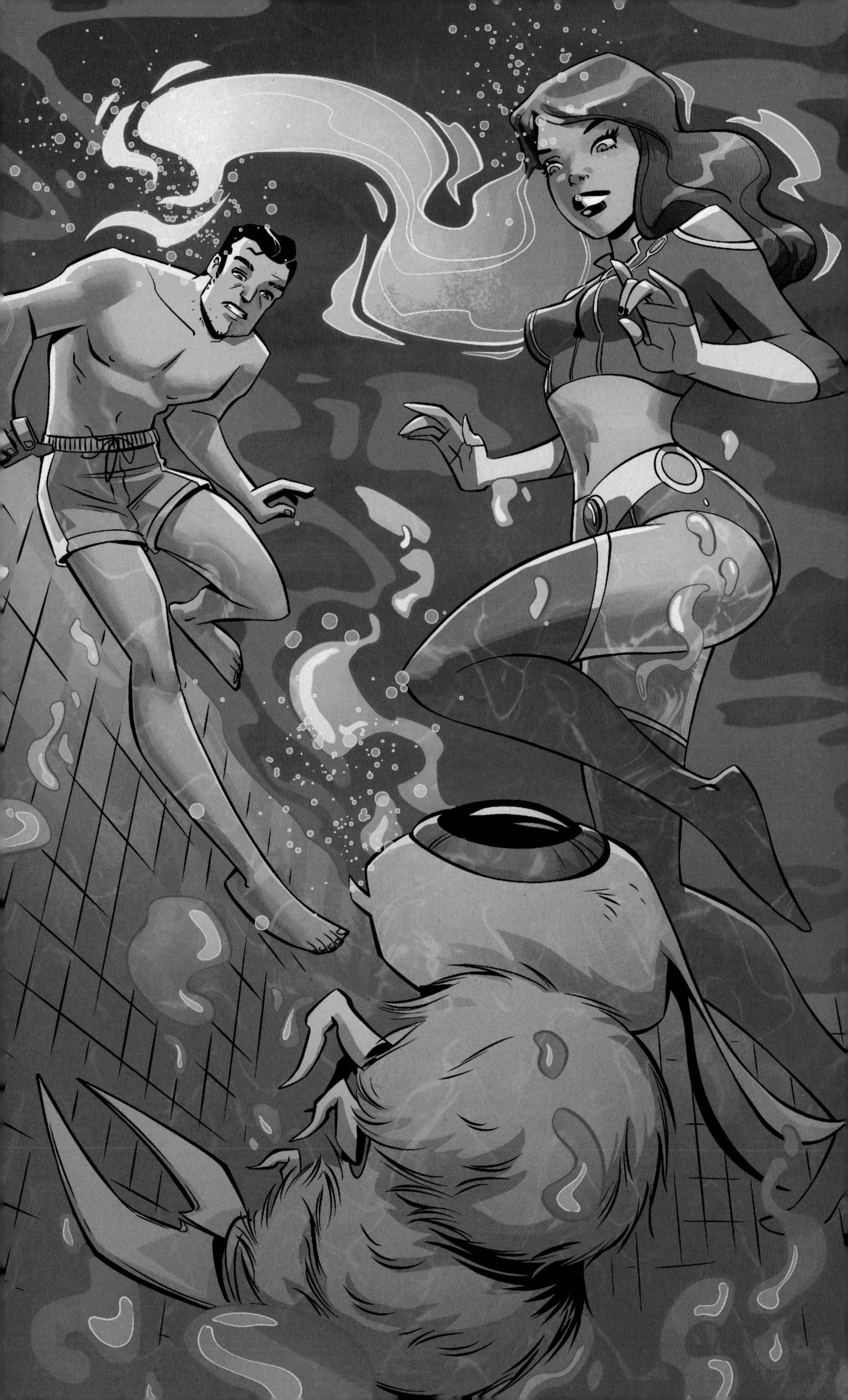

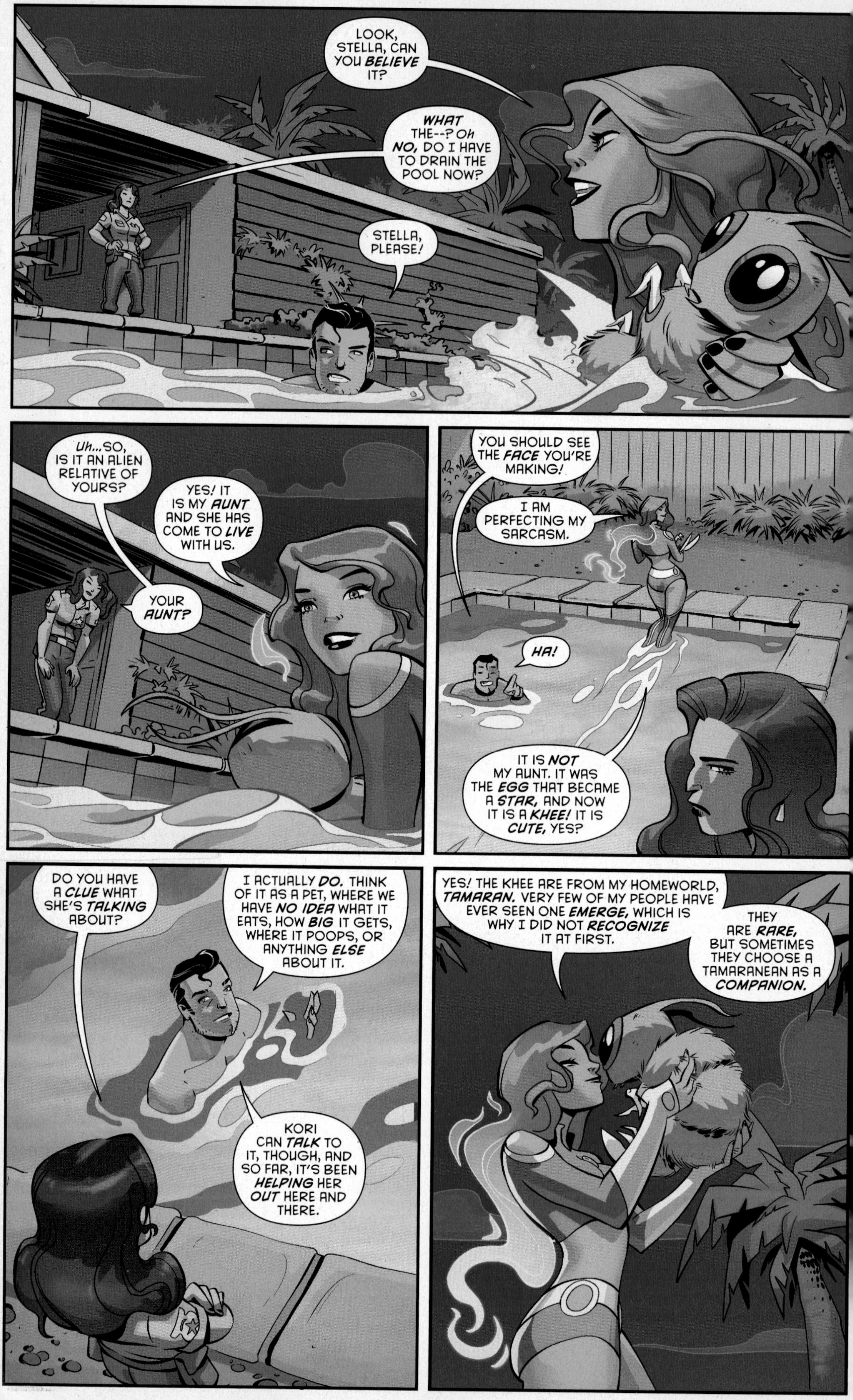
LOOK, STELLA, CAN YOU BELIEVE IT?
WHAT THE--? Oh NO, DO I HAVE TO DRAIN THE POOL NOW?
STELLA, PLEASE!
Uh...SO, IS IT AN ALIEN RELATIVE OF YOURS?
YES! IT IS MY AUNT AND SHE HAS COME TO LIVE WITH US.
YOUR AUNT?
YOU SHOULD SEE THE FACE YOU'RE MAKING!
I AM PERFECTING MY SARCASM.
HA!
IT IS NOT MY AUNT. IT WAS THE EGG THAT BECAME A STAR, AND NOW IT IS A KHEE! IT IS CUTE, YES?
DO YOU HAVE A CLUE WHAT SHE'S TALKING ABOUT?
I ACTUALLY DO. THINK OF IT AS A PET, WHERE WE HAVE NO IDEA WHAT IT EATS, HOW BIG IT GETS, WHERE IT POOPS, OR ANYTHING ELSE ABOUT IT.
KORI CAN TALK TO IT, THOUGH, AND SO FAR, IT'S BEEN HELPING HER OUT HERE AND THERE.
YES! THE KHEE ARE FROM MY HOMEWORLD, TAMARAN. VERY FEW OF MY PEOPLE HAVE EVER SEEN ONE EMERGE, WHICH IS WHY I DID NOT RECOGNIZE IT AT FIRST.
THEY ARE RARE, BUT SOMETIMES THEY CHOOSE A TAMARANEAN AS A COMPANION.

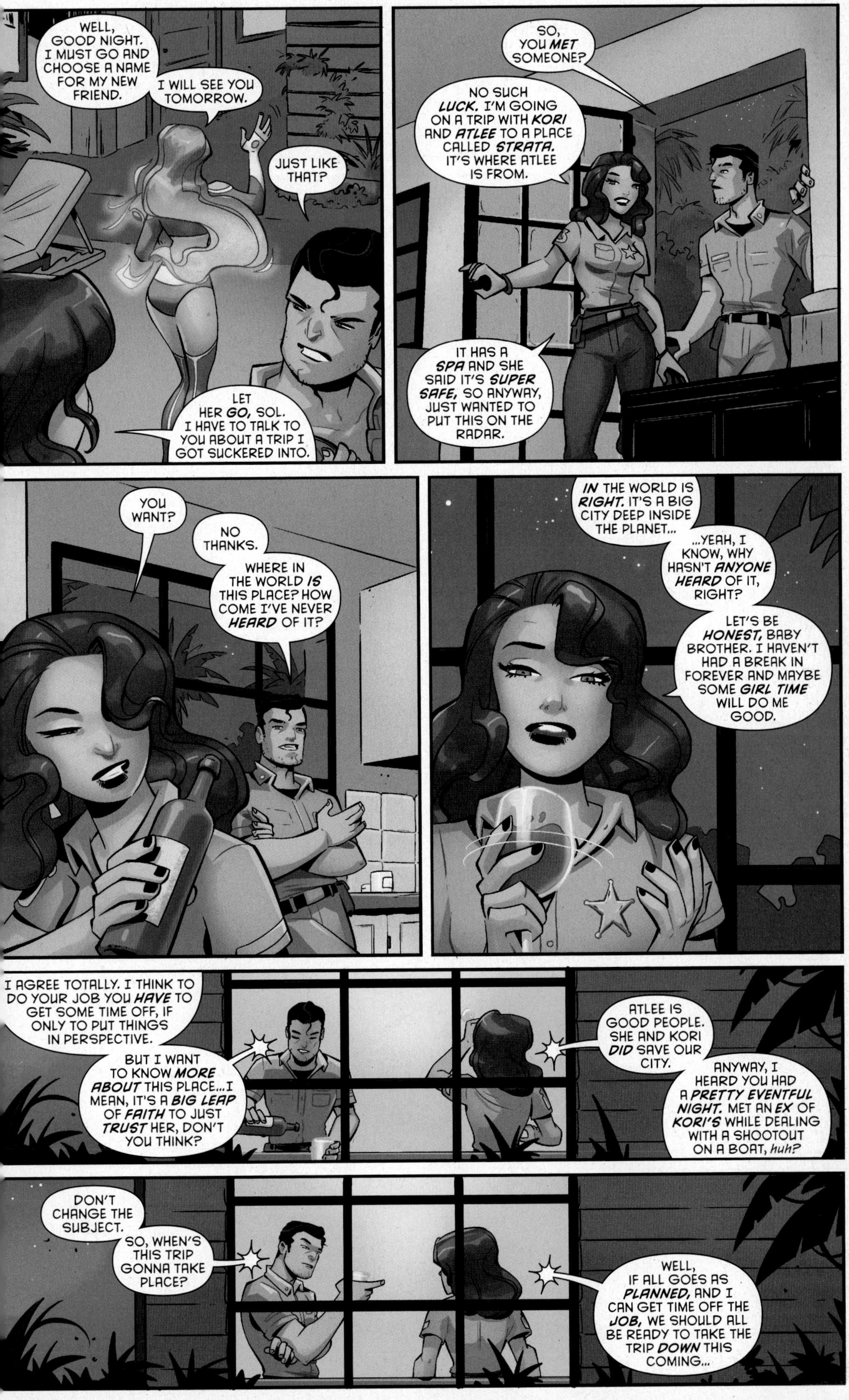
WELL, GOOD NIGHT. I MUST GO AND CHOOSE A NAME FOR MY NEW FRIEND.
I WILL SEE YOU TOMORROW.
JUST LIKE THAT?
LET HER GO, SOL. I HAVE TO TALK TO YOU ABOUT A TRIP I GOT SUCKERED INTO.
SO, YOU MET SOMEONE?
NO SUCH LUCK. I'M GOING ON A TRIP WITH KORI AND ATLEE TO A PLACE CALLED STRATA. IT'S WHERE ATLEE IS FROM.
IT HAS A SPA AND SHE SAID IT'S SUPER SAFE, SO ANYWAY, JUST WANTED TO PUT THIS ON THE RADAR.
YOU WANT?
NO THANKS.
WHERE IN THE WORLD IS THIS PLACE? HOW COME I'VE NEVER HEARD OF IT?
IN THE WORLD IS RIGHT. IT'S A BIG CITY DEEP INSIDE THE PLANET...
...YEAH, I KNOW, WHY HASN'T ANYONE HEARD OF IT, RIGHT?
LET'S BE HONEST, BABY BROTHER. I HAVEN'T HAD A BREAK IN FOREVER AND MAYBE SOME GIRL TIME WILL DO ME GOOD.
I AGREE TOTALLY. I THINK TO DO YOUR JOB YOU HAVE TO GET SOME TIME OFF, IF ONLY TO PUT THINGS IN PERSPECTIVE.
BUT I WANT TO KNOW MORE ABOUT THIS PLACE...I MEAN, IT'S A BIG LEAP OF FAITH TO JUST TRUST HER, DON'T YOU THINK?
ATLEE IS GOOD PEOPLE. SHE AND KORI DID SAVE OUR CITY.
ANYWAY, I HEARD YOU HAD A PRETTY EVENTFUL NIGHT. MET AN EX OF KORI'S WHILE DEALING WITH A SHOOTOUT ON A BOAT, huh?
DON'T CHANGE THE SUBJECT.
SO, WHEN'S THIS TRIP GONNA TAKE PLACE?
WELL, IF ALL GOES AS PLANNED, AND I CAN GET TIME OFF THE JOB, WE SHOULD ALL BE READY TO TAKE THE TRIP DOWN THIS COMING...

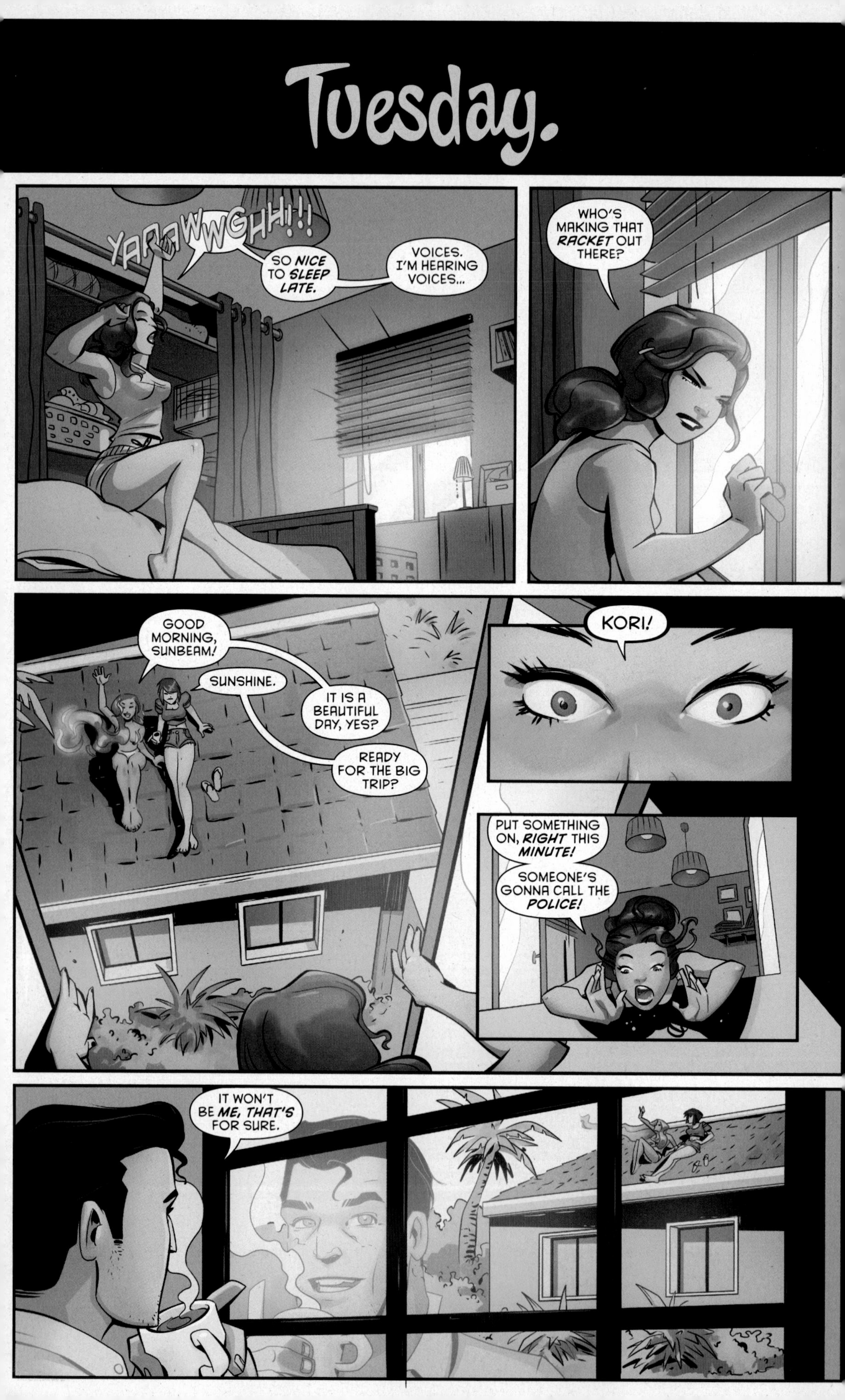
Tuesday.
YARAWWGHH!!!
SO NICE TO SLEEP LATE.
VOICES. I'M HEARING VOICES...
WHO'S MAKING THAT RACKET OUT THERE?
GOOD MORNING, SUNBEAM!
SUNSHINE.
IT IS A BEAUTIFUL DAY, YES?
READY FOR THE BIG TRIP?
KORI!
PUT SOMETHING ON, RIGHT THIS MINUTE!
SOMEONE'S GONNA CALL THE POLICE!
IT WON'T BE ME, THAT'S FOR SURE.

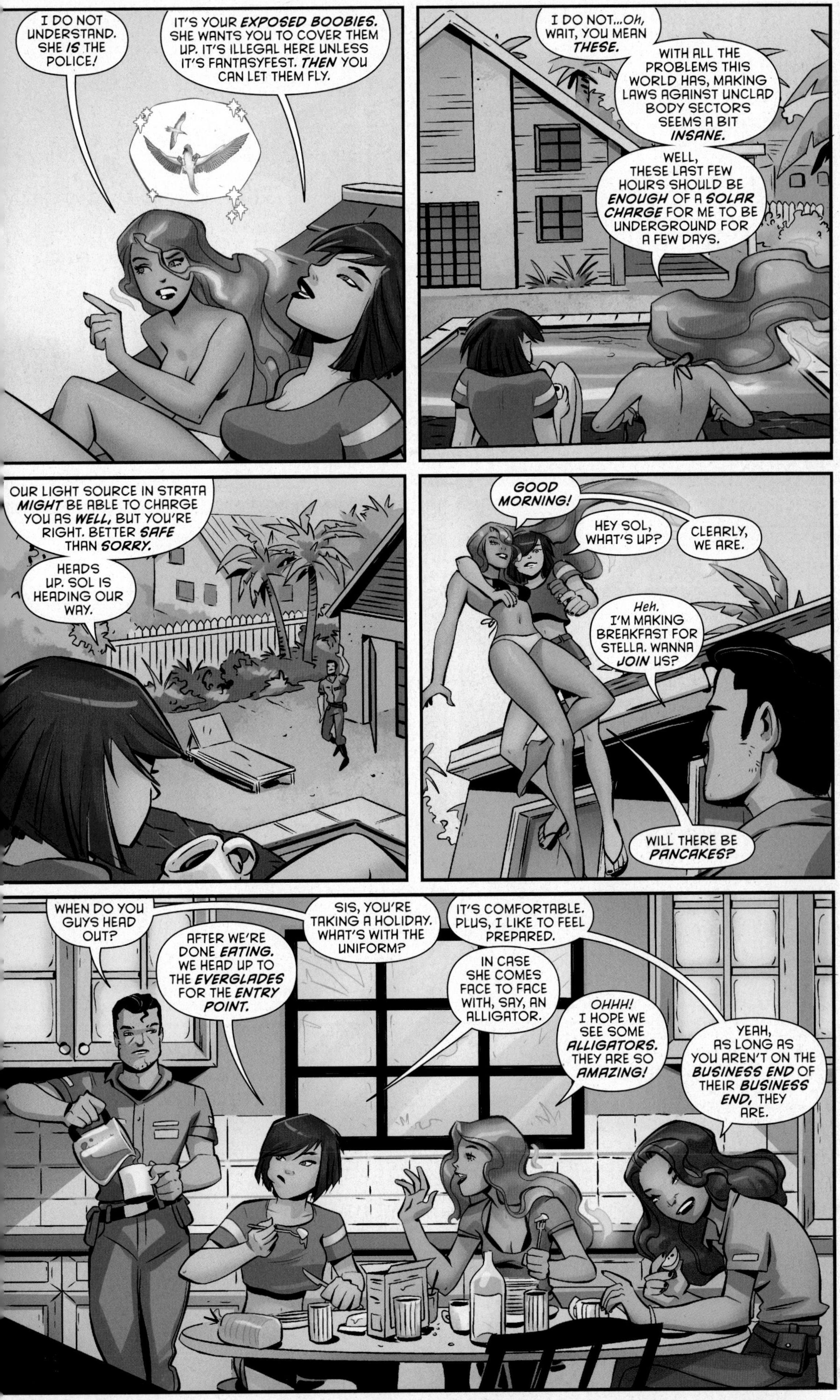

I DO NOT UNDERSTAND. SHE IS THE POLICE!
IT'S YOUR EXPOSED BOOBIES. SHE WANTS YOU TO COVER THEM UP. IT'S ILLEGAL HERE UNLESS IT'S FANTASYFEST. THEN YOU CAN LET THEM FLY.
I DO NOT...Oh, WAIT, YOU MEAN THESE.
WITH ALL THE PROBLEMS THIS WORLD HAS, MAKING LAWS AGAINST UNCLAD BODY SECTORS SEEMS A BIT INSANE.
WELL, THESE LAST FEW HOURS SHOULD BE ENOUGH OF A SOLAR CHARGE FOR ME TO BE UNDERGROUND FOR A FEW DAYS.
OUR LIGHT SOURCE IN STRATA MIGHT BE ABLE TO CHARGE YOU AS WELL, BUT YOU'RE RIGHT. BETTER SAFE THAN SORRY.
HEADS UP. SOL IS HEADING OUR WAY.
GOOD MORNING!
HEY SOL, WHAT'S UP?
CLEARLY, WE ARE.
Heh. I'M MAKING BREAKFAST FOR STELLA. WANNA JOIN US?
WILL THERE BE PANCAKES?
WHEN DO YOU GUYS HEAD OUT?
AFTER WE'RE DONE EATING. WE HEAD UP TO THE EVERGLADES FOR THE ENTRY POINT.
SIS, YOU'RE TAKING A HOLIDAY. WHAT'S WITH THE UNIFORM?
IT'S COMFORTABLE. PLUS, I LIKE TO FEEL PREPARED.
IN CASE SHE COMES FACE TO FACE WITH, SAY, AN ALLIGATOR.
OHHH! I HOPE WE SEE SOME ALLIGATORS. THEY ARE SO AMAZING!
YEAH, AS LONG AS YOU AREN'T ON THE BUSINESS END OF THEIR BUSINESS END, THEY ARE.

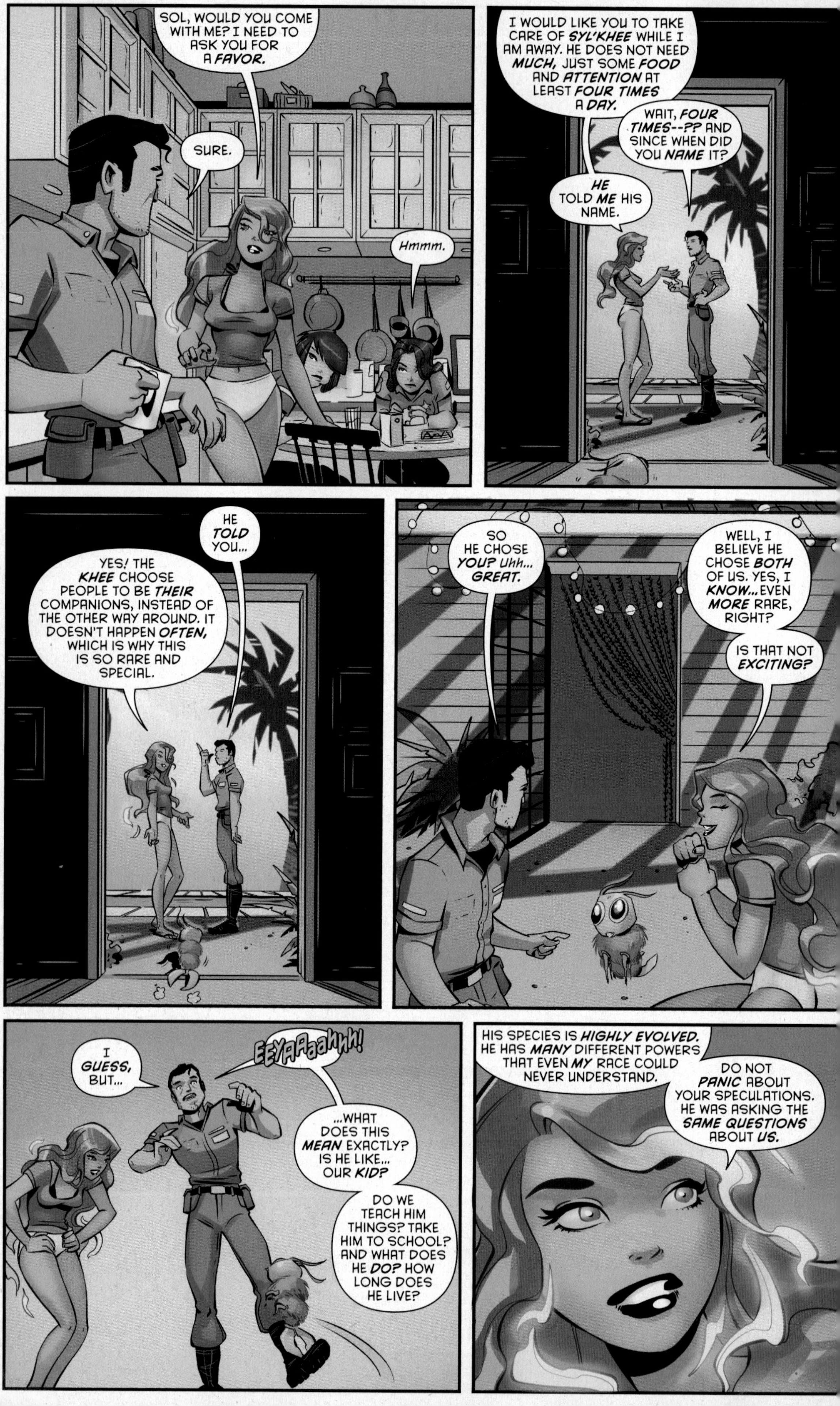
SOL, WOULD YOU COME WITH ME? I NEED TO ASK YOU FOR A FAVOR.
SURE.
Hmmm.
I WOULD LIKE YOU TO TAKE CARE OF SYL'KHEE WHILE I AM AWAY. HE DOES NOT NEED MUCH, JUST SOME FOOD AND ATTENTION AT LEAST FOUR TIMES A DAY.
WAIT, FOUR TIMES--?? AND SINCE WHEN DID YOU NAME IT?
HE TOLD ME HIS NAME.
HE TOLD YOU...
YES! THE KHEE CHOOSE PEOPLE TO BE THEIR COMPANIONS, INSTEAD OF THE OTHER WAY AROUND. IT DOESN'T HAPPEN OFTEN, WHICH IS WHY THIS IS SO RARE AND SPECIAL.
SO HE CHOSE YOU? Uhh... GREAT.
WELL, I BELIEVE HE CHOSE BOTH OF US. YES, I KNOW... EVEN MORE RARE, RIGHT?
IS THAT NOT EXCITING?
I GUESS, BUT...
EEYAAaahhh!
...WHAT DOES THIS MEAN EXACTLY? IS HE LIKE... OUR KID?
DO WE TEACH HIM THINGS? TAKE HIM TO SCHOOL? AND WHAT DOES HE DO? HOW LONG DOES HE LIVE?
HIS SPECIES IS HIGHLY EVOLVED. HE HAS MANY DIFFERENT POWERS THAT EVEN MY RACE COULD NEVER UNDERSTAND.
DO NOT PANIC ABOUT YOUR SPECULATIONS. HE WAS ASKING THE SAME QUESTIONS ABOUT US.

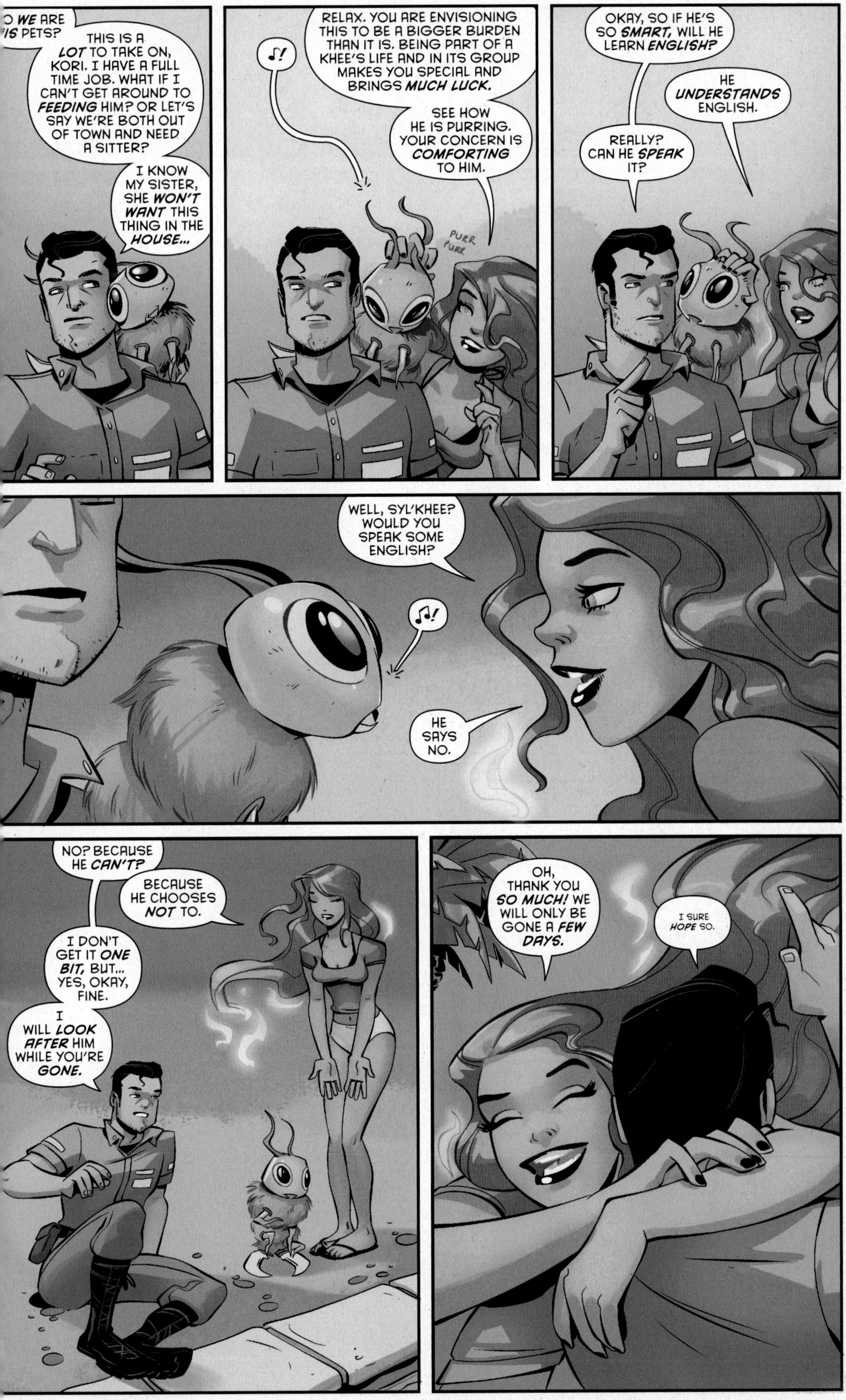
O WE ARE
IS PETS?
THIS IS A LOT TO TAKE ON, KORI. I HAVE A FULL TIME JOB. WHAT IF I CAN'T GET AROUND TO FEEDING HIM? OR LET'S SAY WE'RE BOTH OUT OF TOWN AND NEED A SITTER?
I KNOW MY SISTER, SHE WON'T WANT THIS THING IN THE HOUSE...
♪!
RELAX. YOU ARE ENVISIONING THIS TO BE A BIGGER BURDEN THAN IT IS. BEING PART OF A KHEE'S LIFE AND IN ITS GROUP MAKES YOU SPECIAL AND BRINGS MUCH LUCK.
SEE HOW HE IS PURRING. YOUR CONCERN IS COMFORTING TO HIM.
PURR PURR
OKAY, SO IF HE'S SO SMART, WILL HE LEARN ENGLISH?
HE UNDERSTANDS ENGLISH.
REALLY? CAN HE SPEAK IT?
WELL, SYL'KHEE? WOULD YOU SPEAK SOME ENGLISH?
♪♪!
HE SAYS NO.
NO? BECAUSE HE CAN'T?
BECAUSE HE CHOOSES NOT TO.
I DON'T GET IT ONE BIT, BUT... YES, OKAY, FINE.
I WILL LOOK AFTER HIM WHILE YOU'RE GONE.
OH, THANK YOU SO MUCH! WE WILL ONLY BE GONE A FEW DAYS.
I SURE HOPE SO.

The Business End.

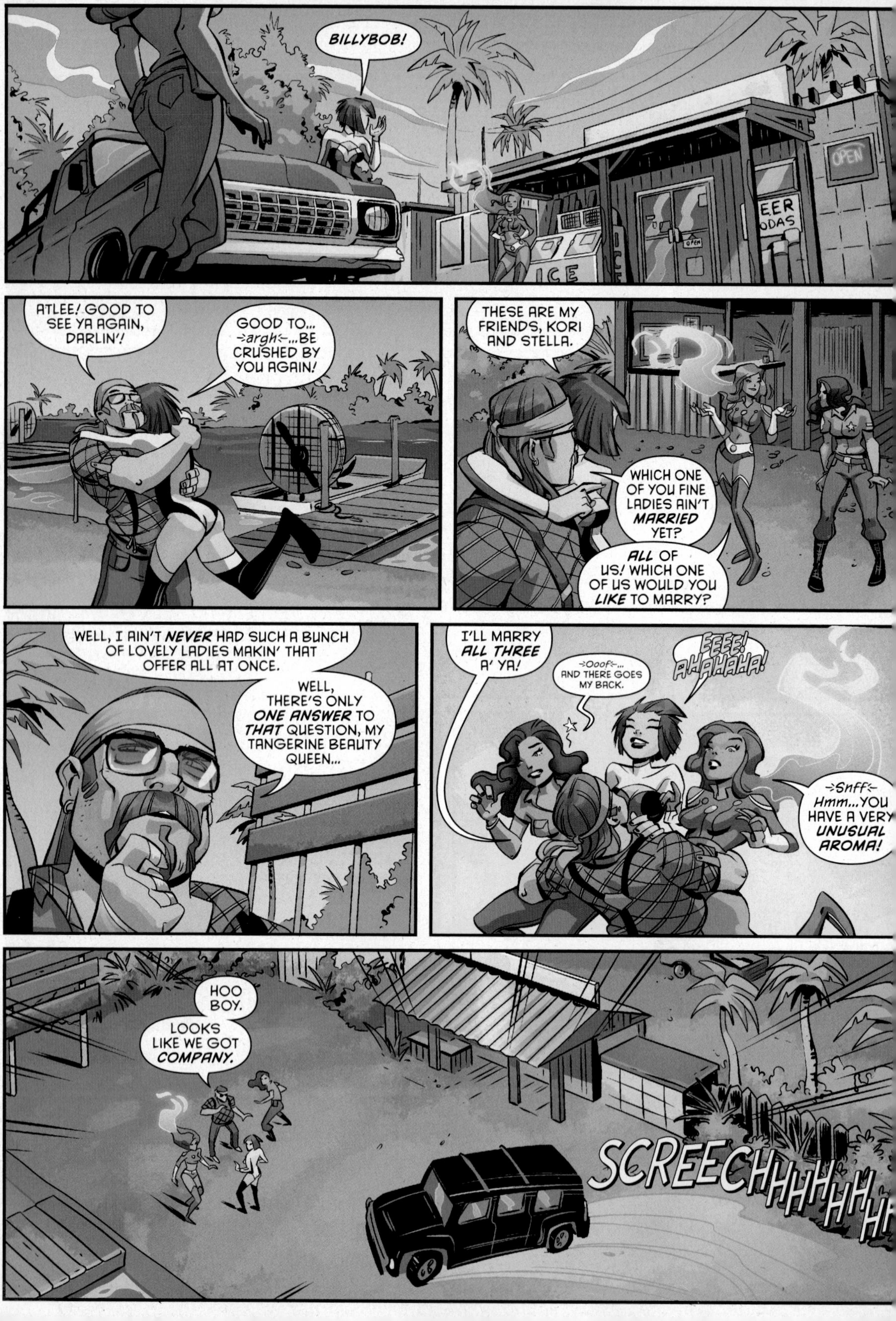
BILLYBOB!
ATLEE! GOOD TO SEE YA AGAIN, DARLIN'!
GOOD TO... ~argh~...BE CRUSHED BY YOU AGAIN!
THESE ARE MY FRIENDS, KORI AND STELLA.
WHICH ONE OF YOU FINE LADIES AIN'T MARRIED YET?
ALL OF US! WHICH ONE OF US WOULD YOU LIKE TO MARRY?
WELL, I AIN'T NEVER HAD SUCH A BUNCH OF LOVELY LADIES MAKIN' THAT OFFER ALL AT ONCE.
WELL, THERE'S ONLY ONE ANSWER TO THAT QUESTION, MY TANGERINE BEAUTY QUEEN...
I'LL MARRY ALL THREE A' YA!
~Ooof~... AND THERE GOES MY BACK.
EEEE! AHAHAHA!
~Snff~ Hmm...YOU HAVE A VERY UNUSUAL AROMA!
HOO BOY.
LOOKS LIKE WE GOT COMPANY.
SCREECHHHHHHH

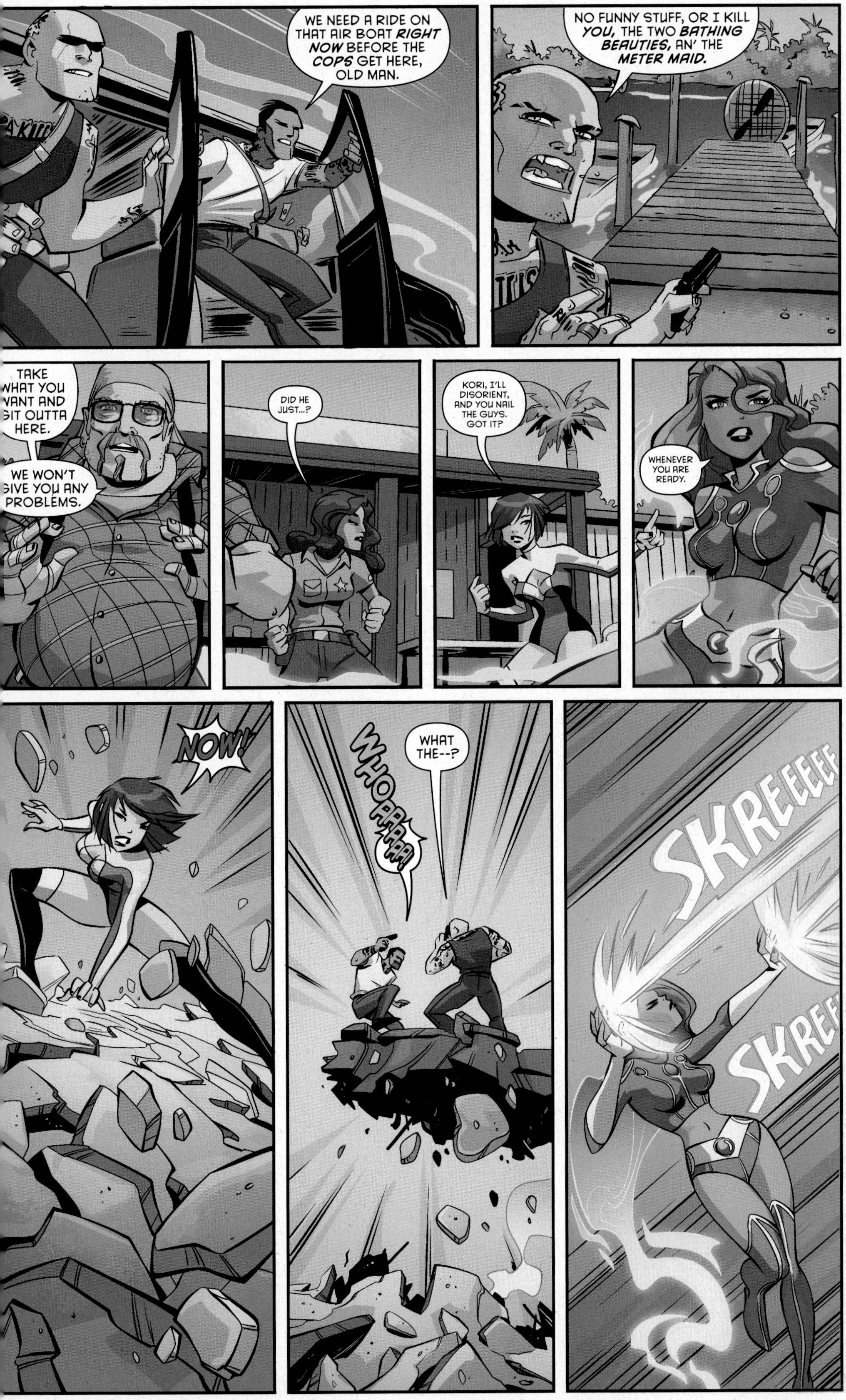

WE NEED A RIDE ON THAT AIR BOAT RIGHT NOW BEFORE THE COPS GET HERE, OLD MAN.
NO FUNNY STUFF, OR I KILL YOU, THE TWO BATHING BEAUTIES, AN' THE METER MAID.
TAKE WHAT YOU WANT AND GIT OUTTA HERE.
WE WON'T GIVE YOU ANY PROBLEMS.
DID HE JUST...?
KORI, I'LL DISORIENT, AND YOU NAIL THE GUYS. GOT IT?
WHENEVER YOU ARE READY.
NOW!
WHOAAAA!
WHAT THE--?
SKREEEEE
SKREE

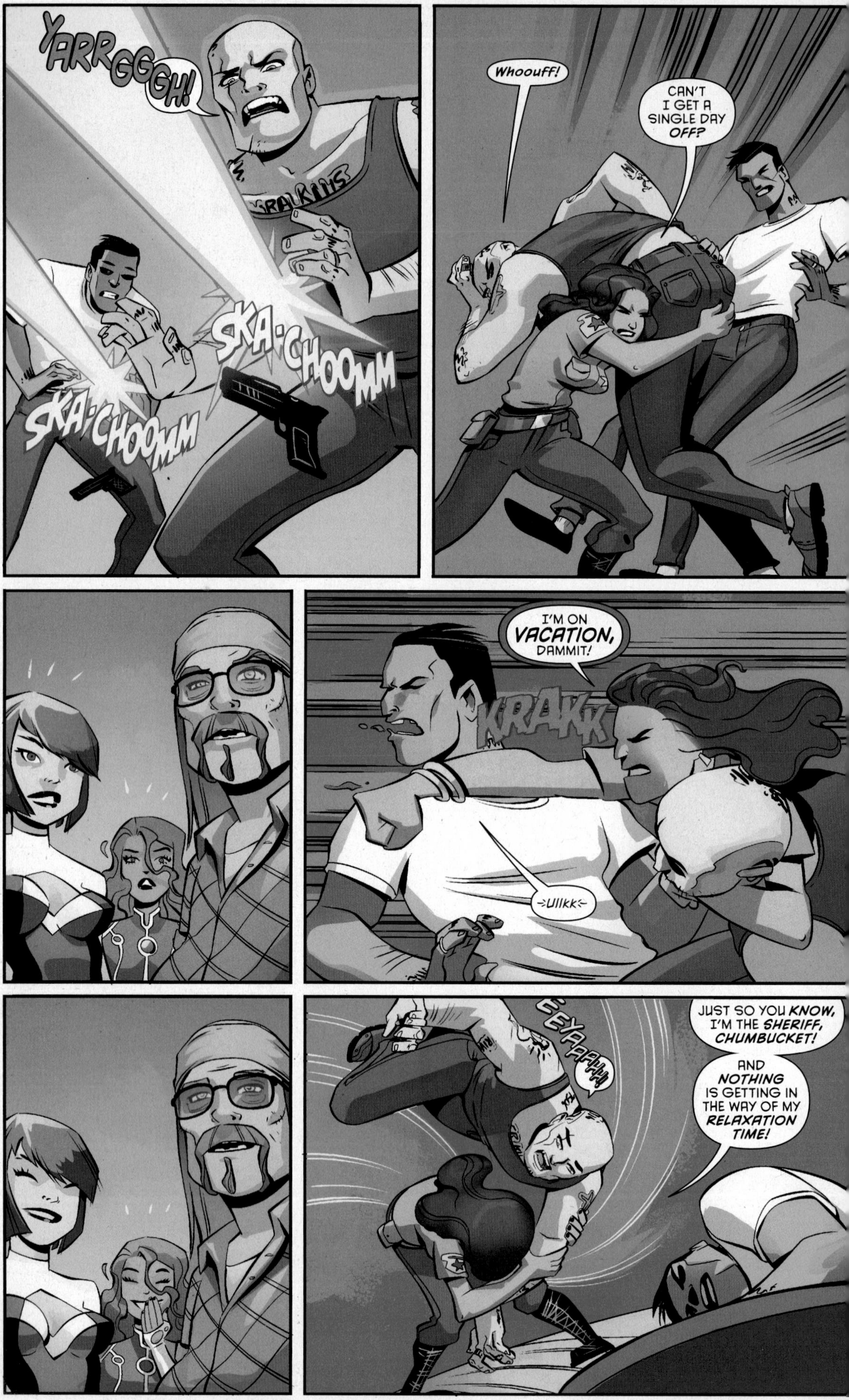
YARRGGGH!
SKA-CHOOMM
SKA-CHOOMM
Whooouff!
CAN'T I GET A SINGLE DAY OFF?
I'M ON VACATION, DAMMIT!
KRAKK
UIIKK
EEYAAHH
JUST SO YOU KNOW, I'M THE SHERIFF, CHUMBUCKET!
AND NOTHING IS GETTING IN THE WAY OF MY RELAXATION TIME!

Foreverglades.

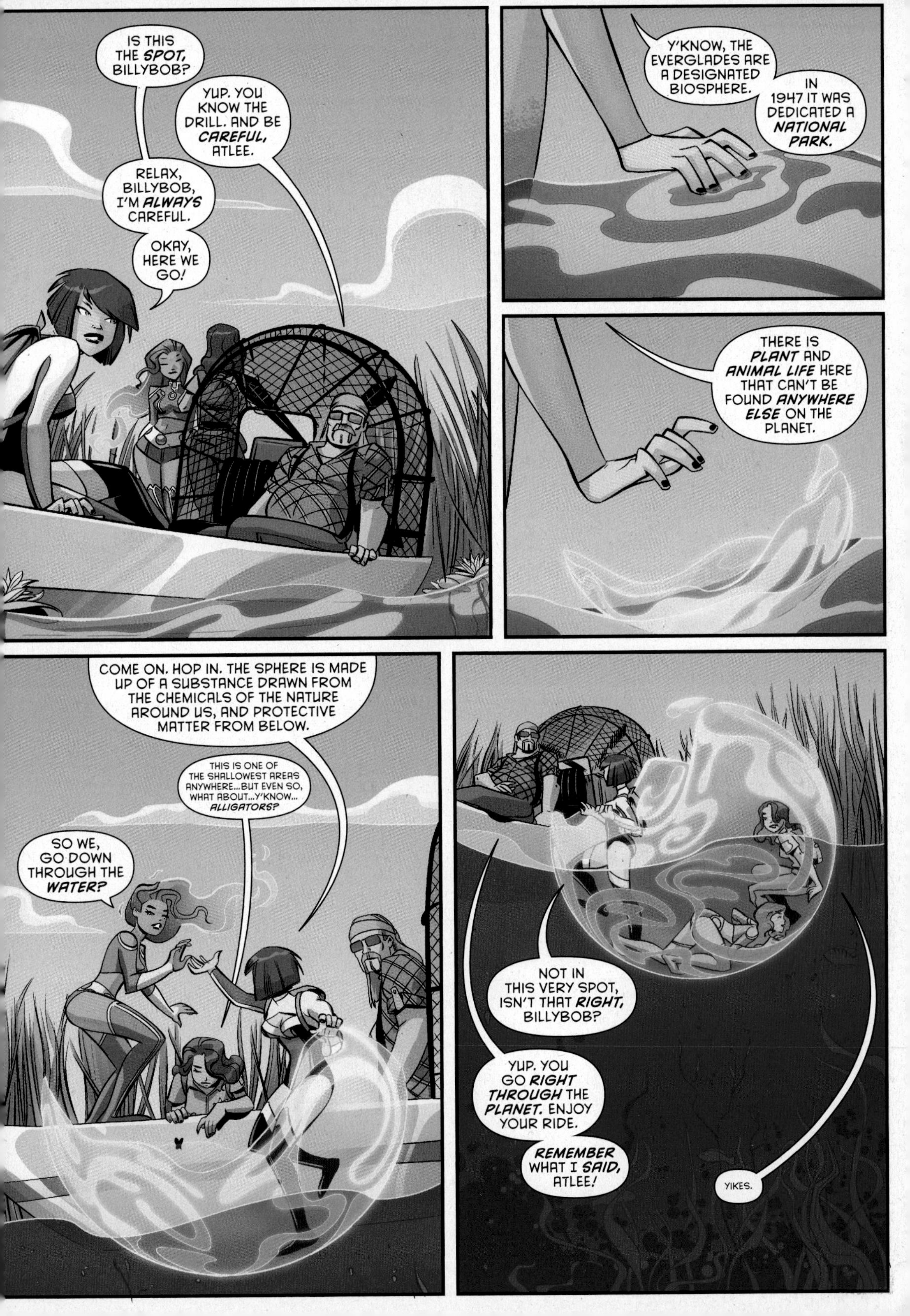
IS THIS THE *SPOT,* BILLYBOB?
YUP. YOU KNOW THE DRILL. AND BE *CAREFUL,* ATLEE.
RELAX, BILLYBOB, I'M *ALWAYS* CAREFUL.
OKAY, HERE WE GO!
Y'KNOW, THE EVERGLADES ARE A DESIGNATED BIOSPHERE.
IN 1947 IT WAS DEDICATED A *NATIONAL PARK.*
THERE IS *PLANT* AND *ANIMAL LIFE* HERE THAT CAN'T BE FOUND *ANYWHERE ELSE* ON THE PLANET.
COME ON. HOP IN. THE SPHERE IS MADE UP OF A SUBSTANCE DRAWN FROM THE CHEMICALS OF THE NATURE AROUND US, AND PROTECTIVE MATTER FROM BELOW.
THIS IS ONE OF THE SHALLOWEST AREAS ANYWHERE...BUT EVEN SO, WHAT ABOUT...Y'KNOW... *ALLIGATORS?*
SO WE, GO DOWN THROUGH THE *WATER?*
NOT IN THIS VERY SPOT, ISN'T THAT *RIGHT,* BILLYBOB?
YUP. YOU GO *RIGHT THROUGH* THE *PLANET.* ENJOY YOUR RIDE.
REMEMBER WHAT I *SAID,* ATLEE!
YIKES.

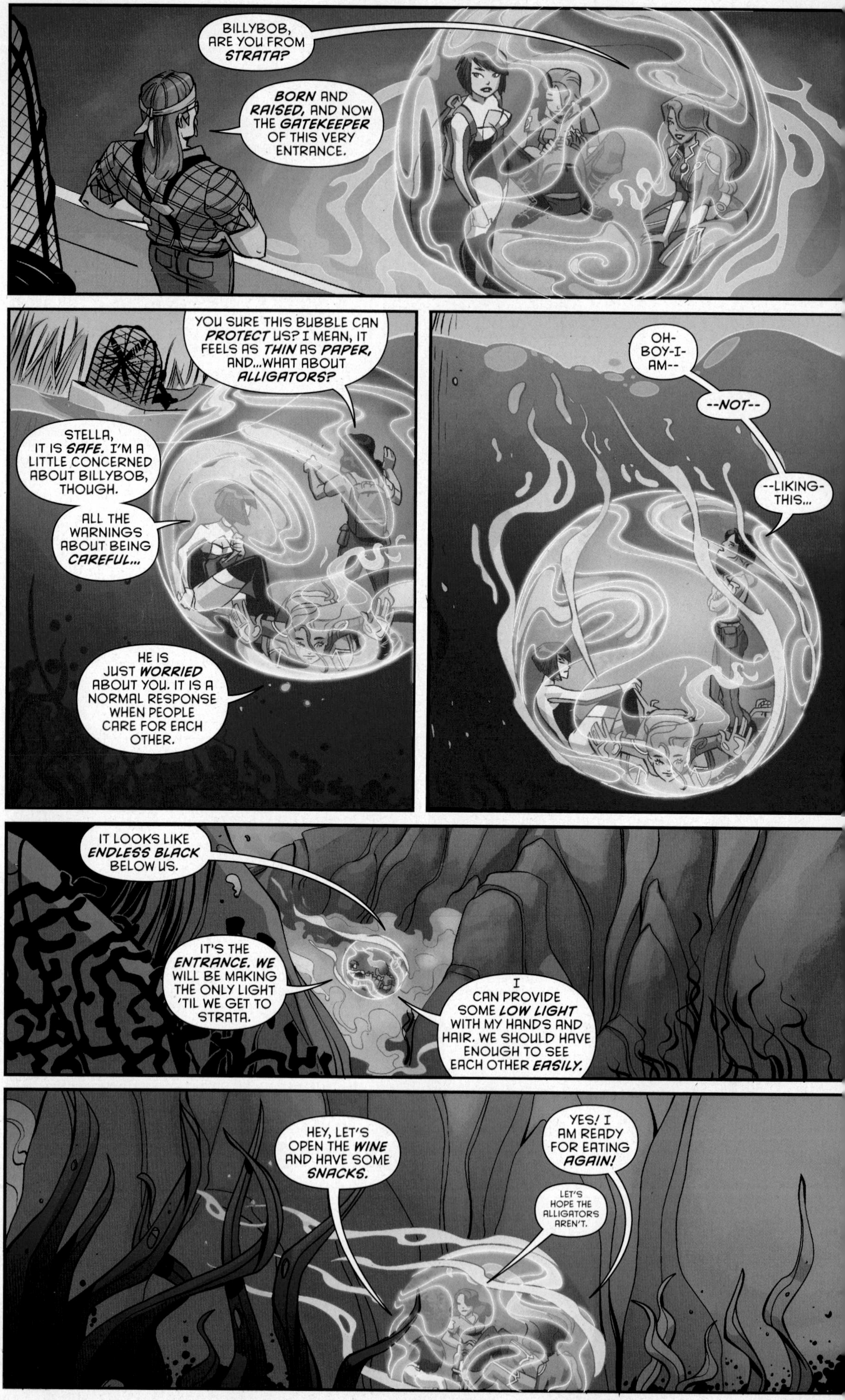
BILLYBOB, ARE YOU FROM STRATA?
BORN AND RAISED, AND NOW THE GATEKEEPER OF THIS VERY ENTRANCE.
YOU SURE THIS BUBBLE CAN PROTECT US? I MEAN, IT FEELS AS THIN AS PAPER, AND...WHAT ABOUT ALLIGATORS?
STELLA, IT IS SAFE. I'M A LITTLE CONCERNED ABOUT BILLYBOB, THOUGH.
ALL THE WARNINGS ABOUT BEING CAREFUL...
HE IS JUST WORRIED ABOUT YOU. IT IS A NORMAL RESPONSE WHEN PEOPLE CARE FOR EACH OTHER.
OH-BOY-I-AM--
--NOT--
--LIKING-THIS...
IT LOOKS LIKE ENDLESS BLACK BELOW US.
IT'S THE ENTRANCE. WE WILL BE MAKING THE ONLY LIGHT 'TIL WE GET TO STRATA.
I CAN PROVIDE SOME LOW LIGHT WITH MY HANDS AND HAIR. WE SHOULD HAVE ENOUGH TO SEE EACH OTHER EASILY.
HEY, LET'S OPEN THE WINE AND HAVE SOME SNACKS.
YES! I AM READY FOR EATING AGAIN!
LET'S HOPE THE ALLIGATORS AREN'T.

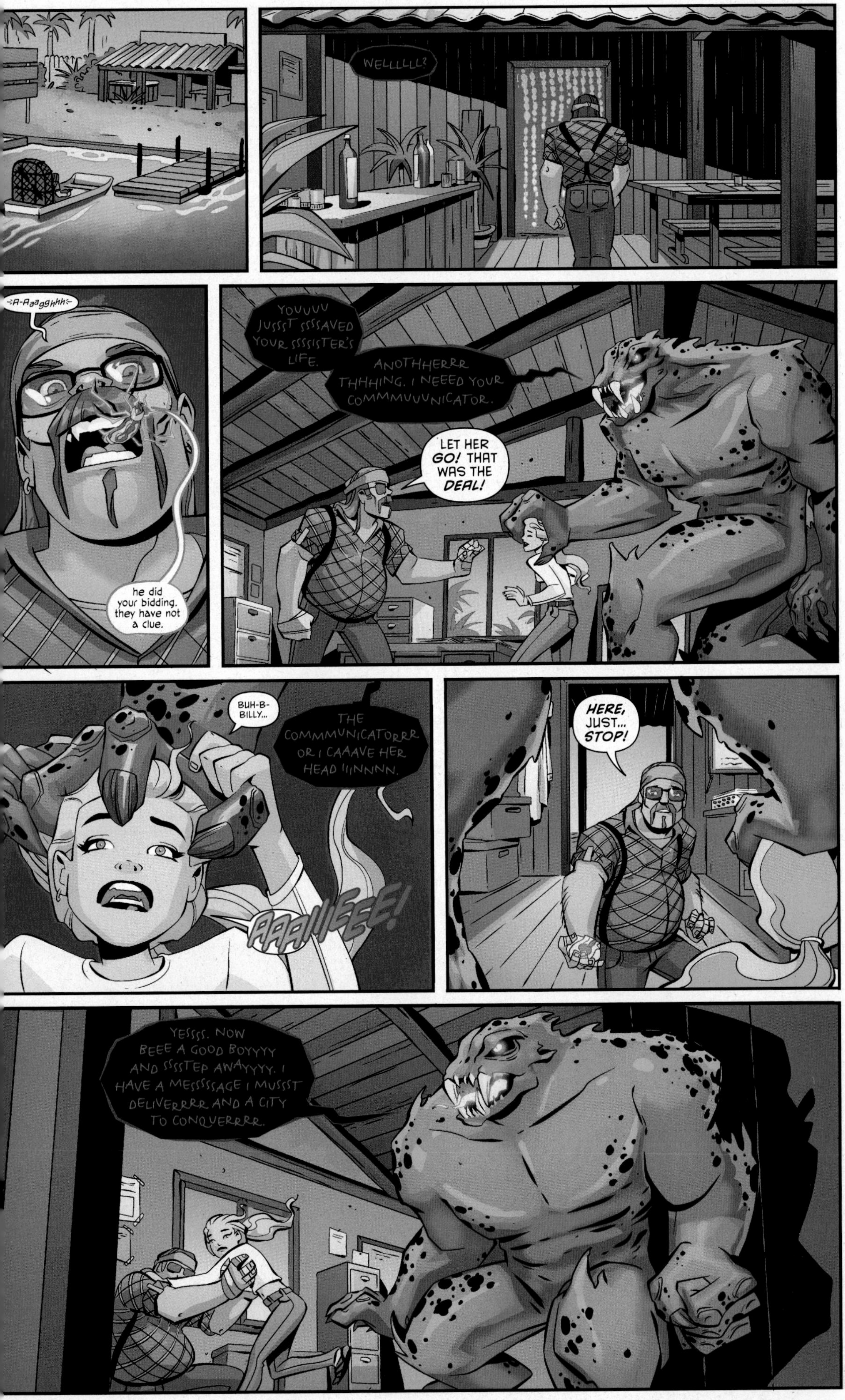
WELLLLLL?
A-Aaagghhh
he did your bidding. they have not a clue.
YOUUUU JUSSST SSSSAVED YOUR SSSSISTER'S LIFE.
ANOTHHERRR THHHING. I NEEED YOUR COMMMUUUNICATOR.
LET HER GO! THAT WAS THE DEAL!
BUH-B-BILLY...
THE COMMMUNICATORRR OR I CAAAVE HER HEAD IIINNNN.
AAAIIIEEEE!
HERE, JUST... STOP!
YESSSS. NOW BEEE A GOOD BOYYYY AND SSSSTEP AWAYYYY. I HAVE A MESSSSSAGE I MUSSST DELIVERRRR AND A CITY TO CONQUERRRR.

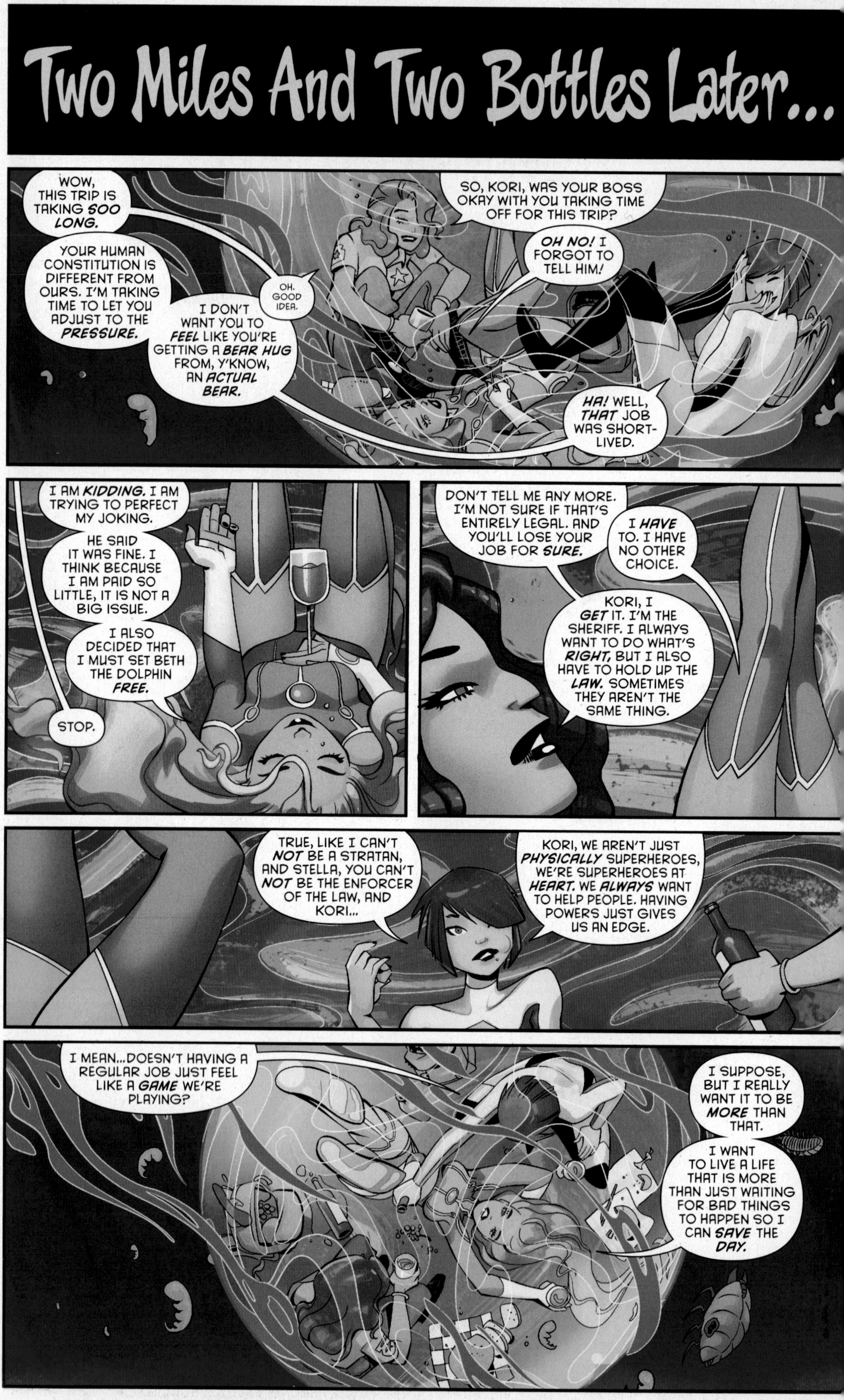
Two Miles And Two Bottles Later...
WOW, THIS TRIP IS TAKING SOO LONG.
YOUR HUMAN CONSTITUTION IS DIFFERENT FROM OURS. I'M TAKING TIME TO LET YOU ADJUST TO THE PRESSURE.
I DON'T WANT YOU TO FEEL LIKE YOU'RE GETTING A BEAR HUG FROM, Y'KNOW, AN ACTUAL BEAR.
OH. GOOD IDEA.
SO, KORI, WAS YOUR BOSS OKAY WITH YOU TAKING TIME OFF FOR THIS TRIP?
OH NO! I FORGOT TO TELL HIM!
HA! WELL, THAT JOB WAS SHORT-LIVED.
I AM KIDDING. I AM TRYING TO PERFECT MY JOKING.
HE SAID IT WAS FINE. I THINK BECAUSE I AM PAID SO LITTLE, IT IS NOT A BIG ISSUE.
I ALSO DECIDED THAT I MUST SET BETH THE DOLPHIN FREE.
STOP.
DON'T TELL ME ANY MORE. I'M NOT SURE IF THAT'S ENTIRELY LEGAL. AND YOU'LL LOSE YOUR JOB FOR SURE.
I HAVE TO. I HAVE NO OTHER CHOICE.
KORI, I GET IT. I'M THE SHERIFF. I ALWAYS WANT TO DO WHAT'S RIGHT, BUT I ALSO HAVE TO HOLD UP THE LAW. SOMETIMES THEY AREN'T THE SAME THING.
TRUE, LIKE I CAN'T NOT BE A STRATAN, AND STELLA, YOU CAN'T NOT BE THE ENFORCER OF THE LAW, AND KORI...
KORI, WE AREN'T JUST PHYSICALLY SUPERHEROES, WE'RE SUPERHEROES AT HEART. WE ALWAYS WANT TO HELP PEOPLE. HAVING POWERS JUST GIVES US AN EDGE.
I MEAN...DOESN'T HAVING A REGULAR JOB JUST FEEL LIKE A GAME WE'RE PLAYING?
I SUPPOSE, BUT I REALLY WANT IT TO BE MORE THAN THAT.
I WANT TO LIVE A LIFE THAT IS MORE THAN JUST WAITING FOR BAD THINGS TO HAPPEN SO I CAN SAVE THE DAY.

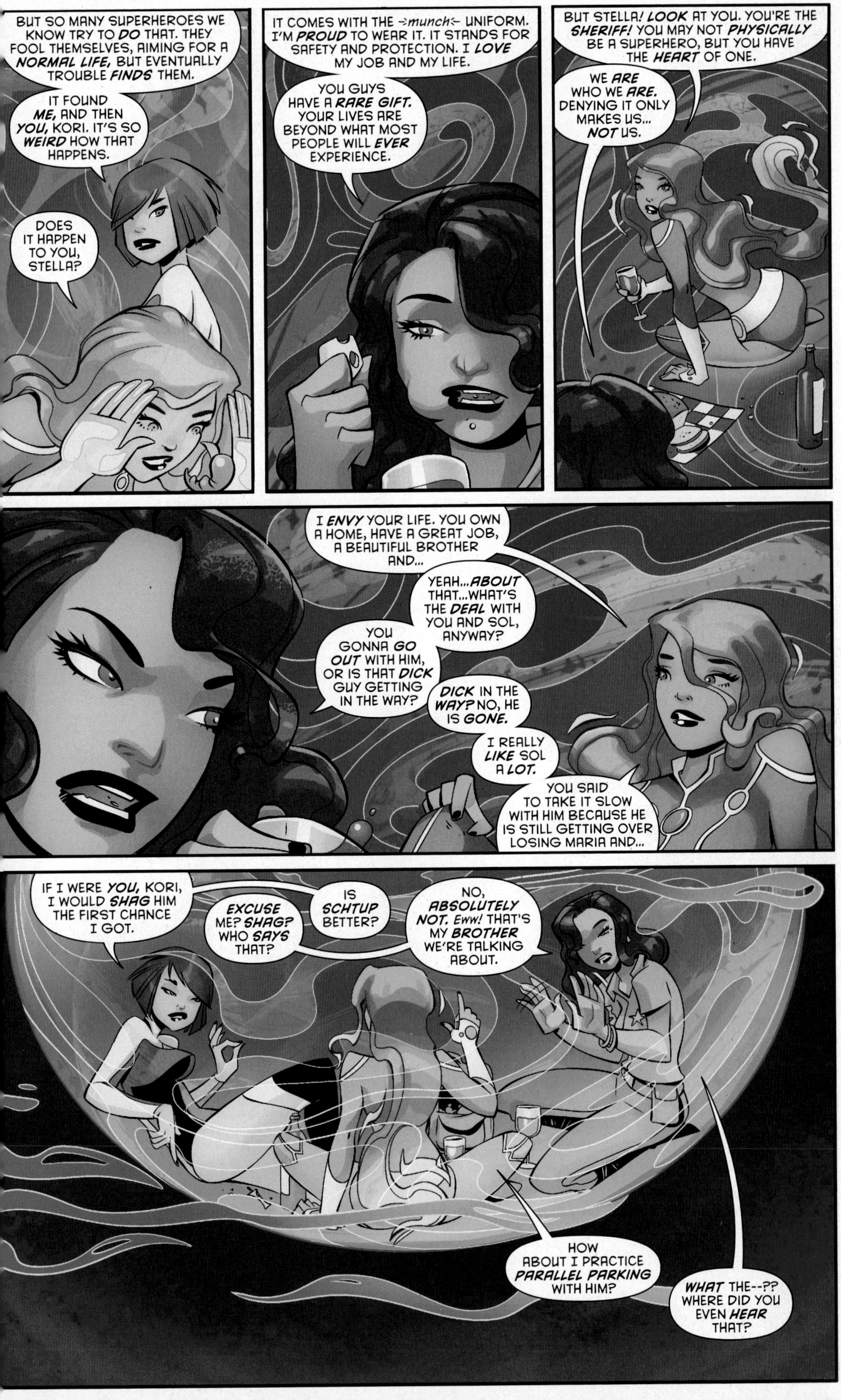
BUT SO MANY SUPERHEROES WE KNOW TRY TO *DO* THAT. THEY FOOL THEMSELVES, AIMING FOR A *NORMAL LIFE*, BUT EVENTUALLY TROUBLE *FINDS* THEM.
IT FOUND *ME,* AND THEN *YOU,* KORI. IT'S SO *WEIRD* HOW THAT HAPPENS.
DOES IT HAPPEN TO YOU, STELLA?
IT COMES WITH THE ⇒*munch*⇐ UNIFORM. I'M *PROUD* TO WEAR IT. IT STANDS FOR SAFETY AND PROTECTION. I *LOVE* MY JOB AND MY LIFE.
YOU GUYS HAVE A *RARE GIFT.* YOUR LIVES ARE BEYOND WHAT MOST PEOPLE WILL *EVER* EXPERIENCE.
BUT STELLA! *LOOK* AT YOU. YOU'RE THE *SHERIFF!* YOU MAY NOT *PHYSICALLY* BE A SUPERHERO, BUT YOU HAVE THE *HEART* OF ONE.
WE *ARE* WHO WE *ARE.* DENYING IT ONLY MAKES US... *NOT* US.
I *ENVY* YOUR LIFE. YOU OWN A HOME, HAVE A GREAT JOB, A BEAUTIFUL BROTHER AND...
YEAH...*ABOUT* THAT...WHAT'S THE *DEAL* WITH YOU AND SOL, ANYWAY?
YOU GONNA *GO OUT* WITH HIM, OR IS THAT *DICK* GUY GETTING IN THE WAY?
DICK IN THE *WAY?* NO, HE IS *GONE.*
I REALLY *LIKE* SOL A *LOT.*
YOU SAID TO TAKE IT SLOW WITH HIM BECAUSE HE IS STILL GETTING OVER LOSING MARIA AND...
IF I WERE *YOU,* KORI, I WOULD *SHAG* HIM THE FIRST CHANCE I GOT.
EXCUSE ME? *SHAG?* WHO *SAYS* THAT?
IS *SCHTUP* BETTER?
NO, *ABSOLUTELY NOT.* *Eww!* THAT'S MY *BROTHER* WE'RE TALKING ABOUT.
HOW ABOUT I PRACTICE *PARALLEL PARKING* WITH HIM?
WHAT THE--?? WHERE DID YOU EVEN *HEAR* THAT?

Shock And Awwwww.

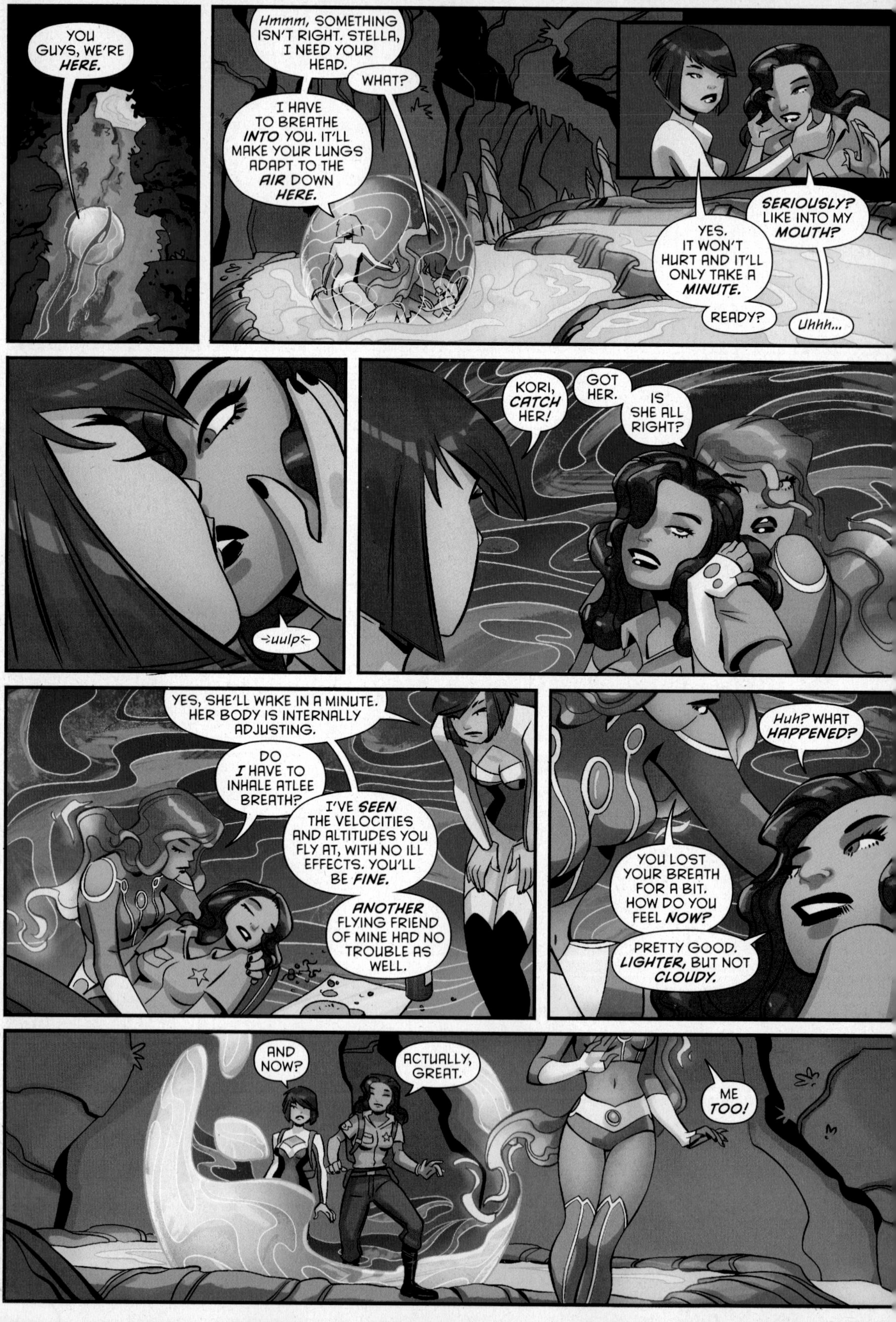

YOU GUYS, WE'RE HERE.
Hmmm, SOMETHING ISN'T RIGHT. STELLA, I NEED YOUR HEAD.
WHAT?
I HAVE TO BREATHE INTO YOU. IT'LL MAKE YOUR LUNGS ADAPT TO THE AIR DOWN HERE.
SERIOUSLY? LIKE INTO MY MOUTH?
YES. IT WON'T HURT AND IT'LL ONLY TAKE A MINUTE.
READY?
Uhhh...
uulp
KORI, CATCH HER!
GOT HER.
IS SHE ALL RIGHT?
YES, SHE'LL WAKE IN A MINUTE. HER BODY IS INTERNALLY ADJUSTING.
DO I HAVE TO INHALE ATLEE BREATH?
I'VE SEEN THE VELOCITIES AND ALTITUDES YOU FLY AT, WITH NO ILL EFFECTS. YOU'LL BE FINE.
ANOTHER FLYING FRIEND OF MINE HAD NO TROUBLE AS WELL.
Huh? WHAT HAPPENED?
YOU LOST YOUR BREATH FOR A BIT. HOW DO YOU FEEL NOW?
PRETTY GOOD. LIGHTER, BUT NOT CLOUDY.
AND NOW?
ACTUALLY, GREAT.
ME TOO!

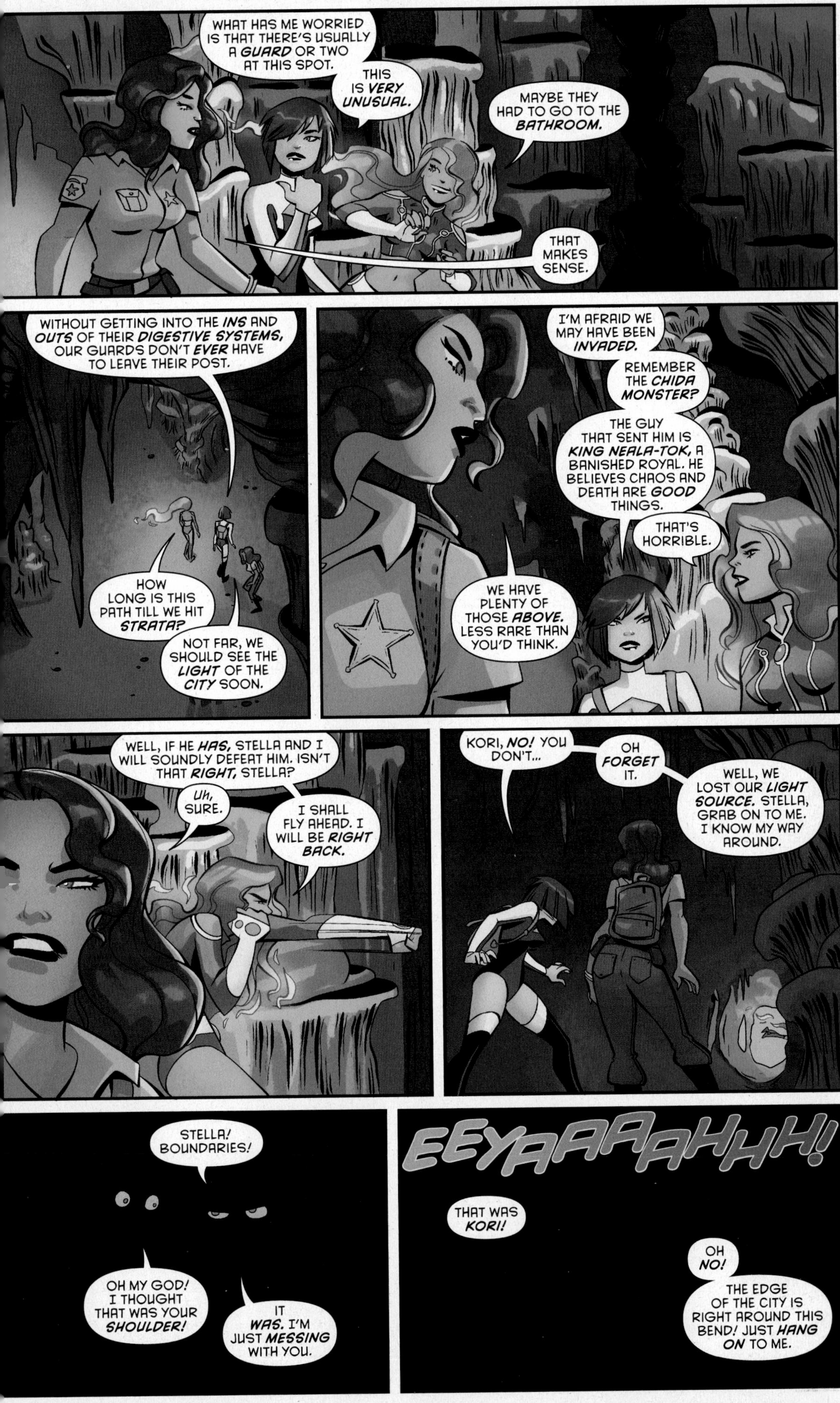
WHAT HAS ME WORRIED IS THAT THERE'S USUALLY A GUARD OR TWO AT THIS SPOT.
THIS IS VERY UNUSUAL.
MAYBE THEY HAD TO GO TO THE BATHROOM.
THAT MAKES SENSE.
WITHOUT GETTING INTO THE INS AND OUTS OF THEIR DIGESTIVE SYSTEMS, OUR GUARDS DON'T EVER HAVE TO LEAVE THEIR POST.
HOW LONG IS THIS PATH TILL WE HIT STRATA?
NOT FAR, WE SHOULD SEE THE LIGHT OF THE CITY SOON.
I'M AFRAID WE MAY HAVE BEEN INVADED.
REMEMBER THE CHIDA MONSTER?
THE GUY THAT SENT HIM IS KING NEALA-TOK, A BANISHED ROYAL. HE BELIEVES CHAOS AND DEATH ARE GOOD THINGS.
THAT'S HORRIBLE.
WE HAVE PLENTY OF THOSE ABOVE. LESS RARE THAN YOU'D THINK.
WELL, IF HE HAS, STELLA AND I WILL SOUNDLY DEFEAT HIM. ISN'T THAT RIGHT, STELLA?
Uh, SURE.
I SHALL FLY AHEAD. I WILL BE RIGHT BACK.
KORI, NO! YOU DON'T...
OH FORGET IT.
WELL, WE LOST OUR LIGHT SOURCE. STELLA, GRAB ON TO ME. I KNOW MY WAY AROUND.
STELLA! BOUNDARIES!
OH MY GOD! I THOUGHT THAT WAS YOUR SHOULDER!
IT WAS. I'M JUST MESSING WITH YOU.
EEYAAAAAHHH!
THAT WAS KORI!
OH NO!
THE EDGE OF THE CITY IS RIGHT AROUND THIS BEND! JUST HANG ON TO ME.

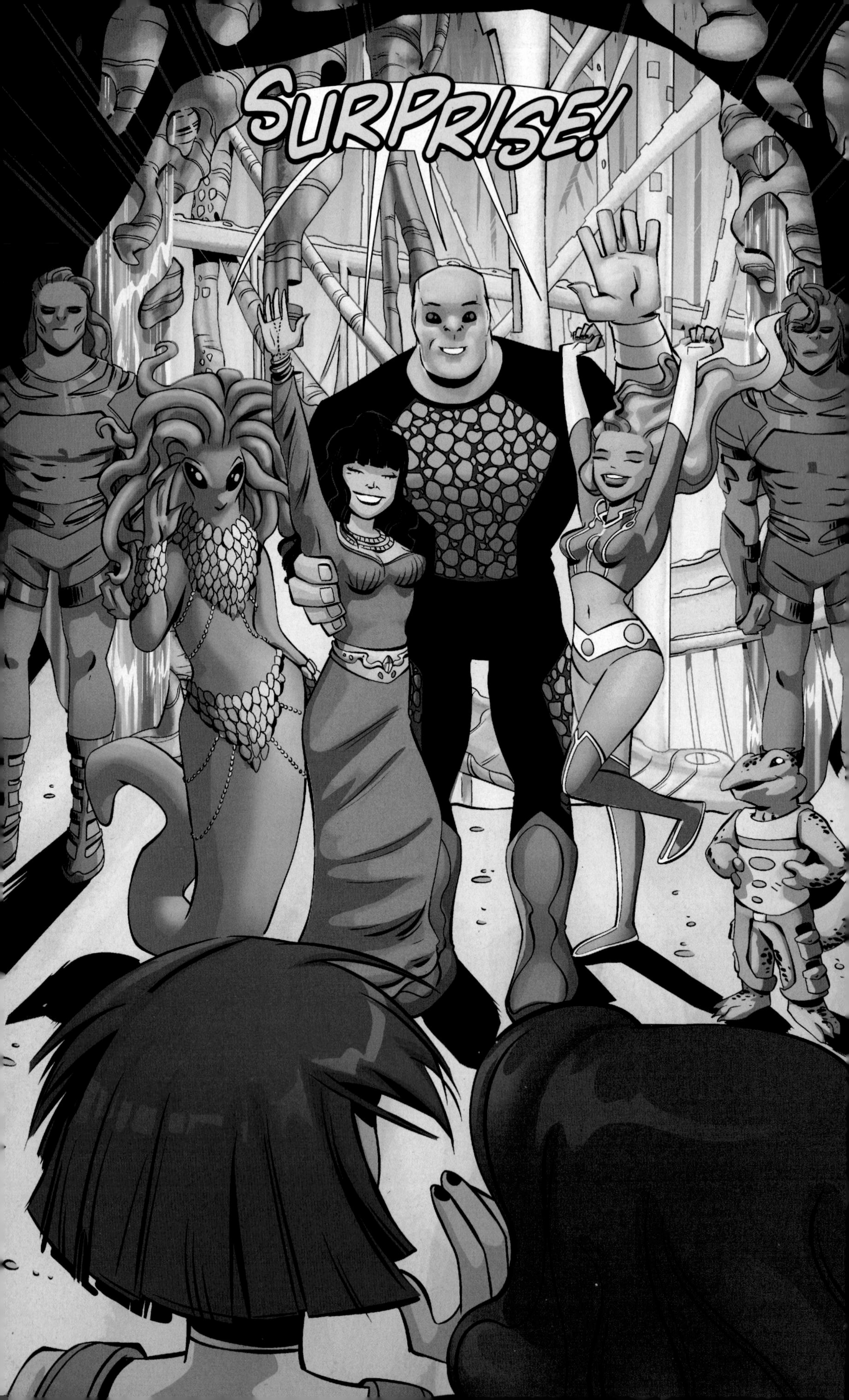
SURPRISE!

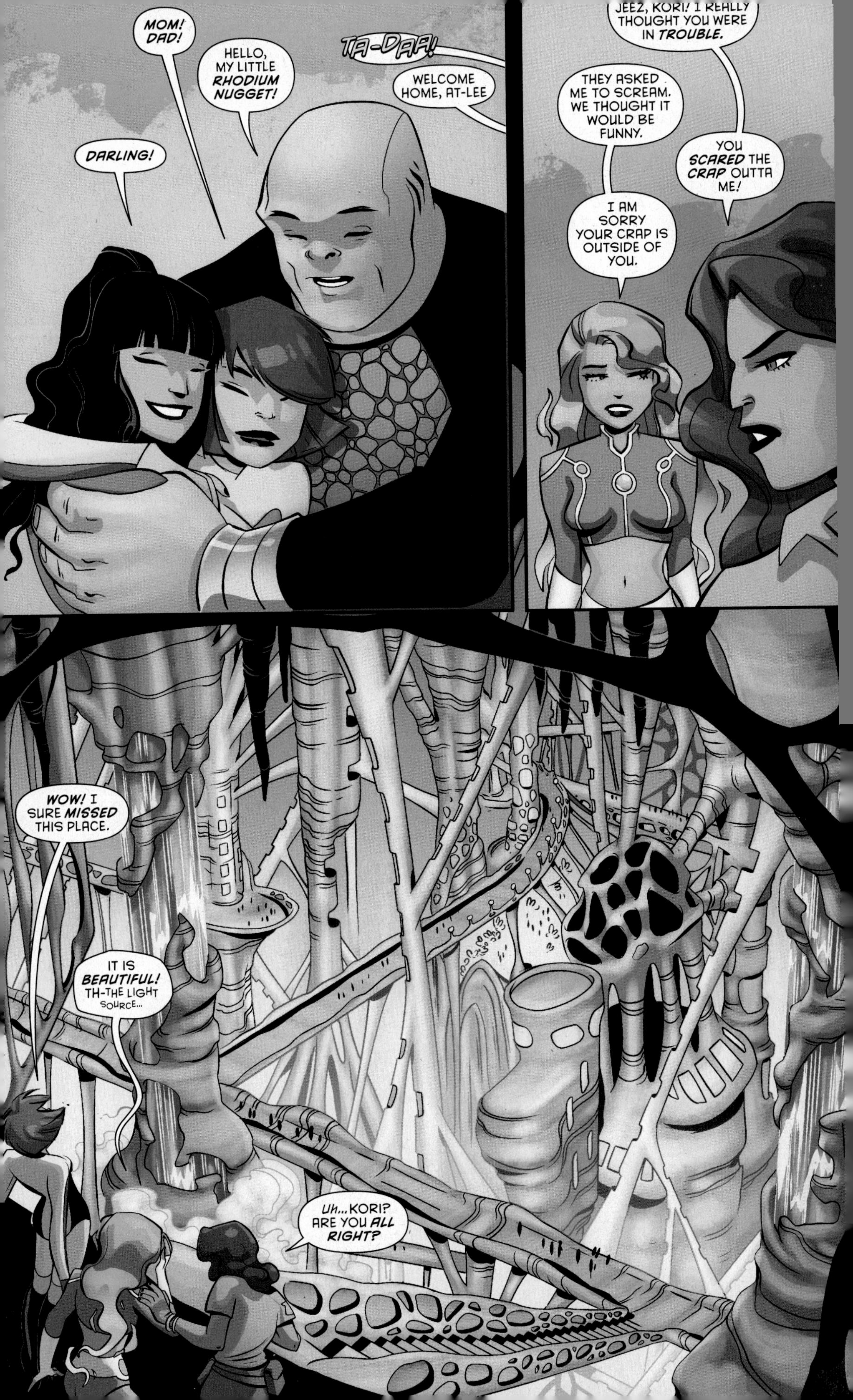
MOM! DAD!
HELLO, MY LITTLE RHODIUM NUGGET!
TA-DAA!
WELCOME HOME, AT-LEE
DARLING!
JEEZ, KORI! I REALLY THOUGHT YOU WERE IN TROUBLE.
THEY ASKED ME TO SCREAM. WE THOUGHT IT WOULD BE FUNNY.
YOU SCARED THE CRAP OUTTA ME!
I AM SORRY YOUR CRAP IS OUTSIDE OF YOU.
WOW! I SURE MISSED THIS PLACE.
IT IS BEAUTIFUL! TH-THE LIGHT SOURCE...
UH...KORI? ARE YOU ALL RIGHT?

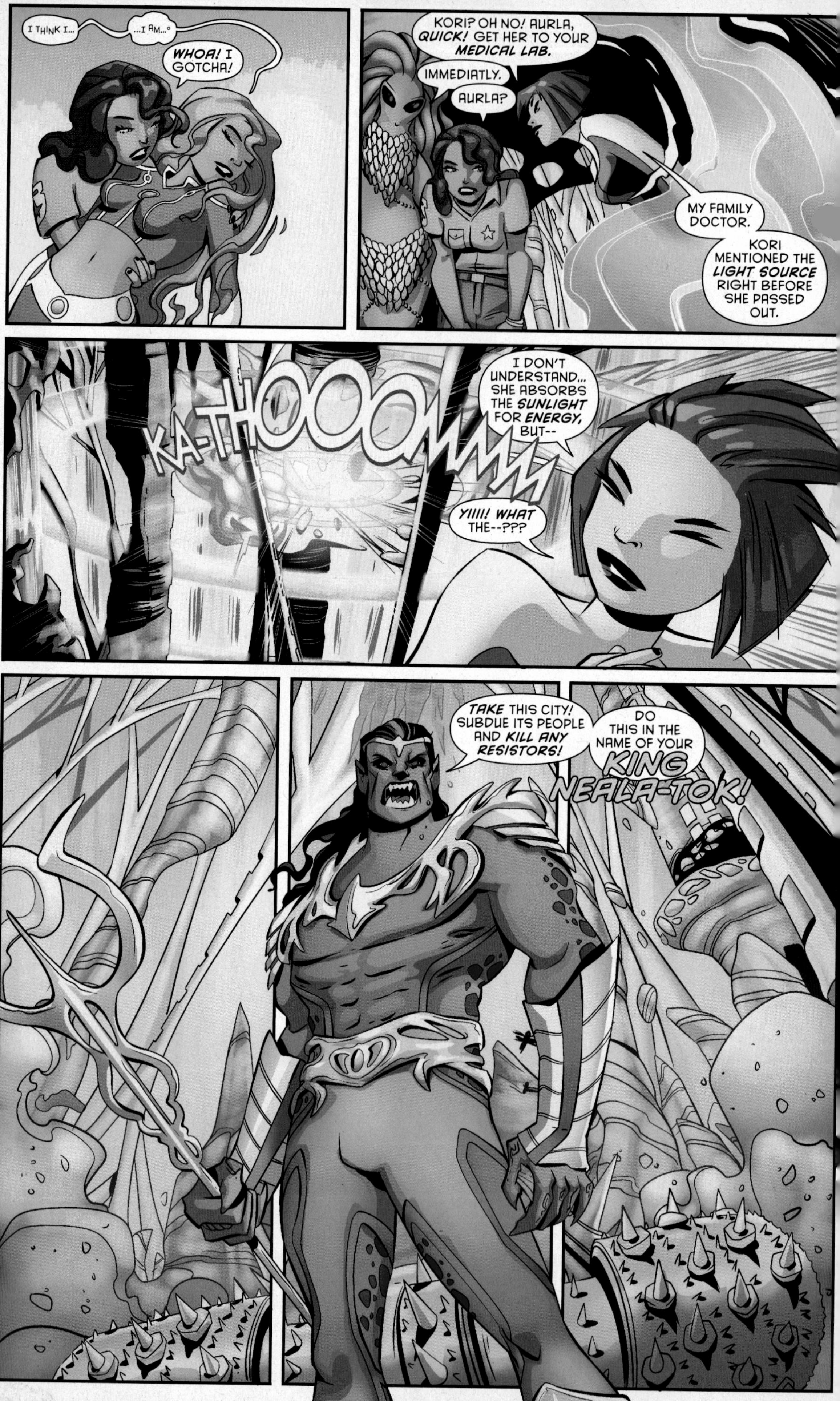

I THINK I...
...I AM...
WHOA! I GOTCHA!
KORI? OH NO! AURLA, QUICK! GET HER TO YOUR MEDICAL LAB.
IMMEDIATLY.
AURLA?
MY FAMILY DOCTOR.
KORI MENTIONED THE LIGHT SOURCE RIGHT BEFORE SHE PASSED OUT.
I DON'T UNDERSTAND... SHE ABSORBS THE SUNLIGHT FOR ENERGY, BUT--
KA-THOOOOMMMM
YIIII! WHAT THE--???
TAKE THIS CITY! SUBDUE ITS PEOPLE AND KILL ANY RESISTORS!
DO THIS IN THE NAME OF YOUR KING NEALA-TOK!

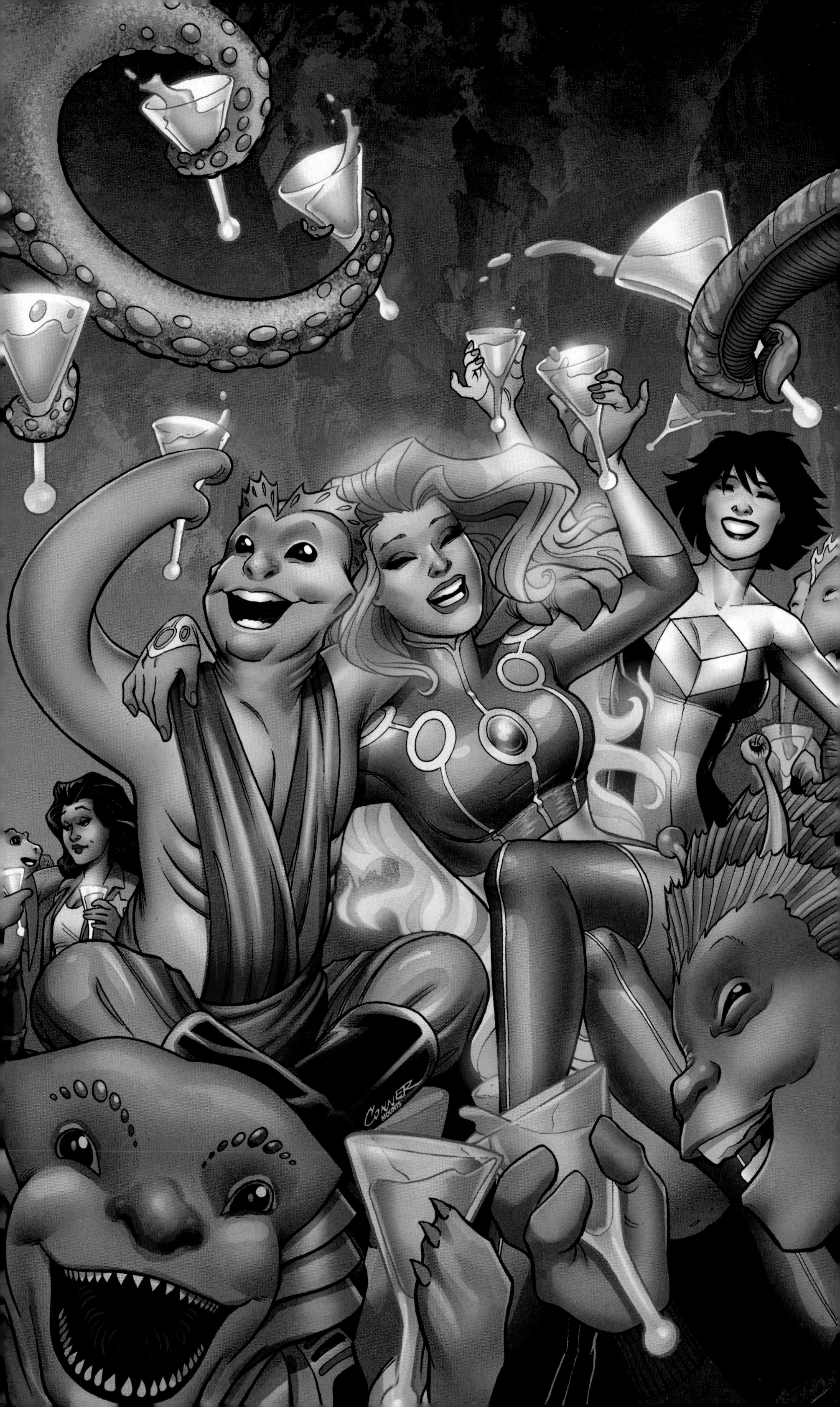
CONNER
MOUNTS

RUMBLE DOWN BELOW

AMANDA CONNER & JIMMY PALMIOTTI writers ELSA CHARRETIER art HI-FI colors ROB LEIGH letters

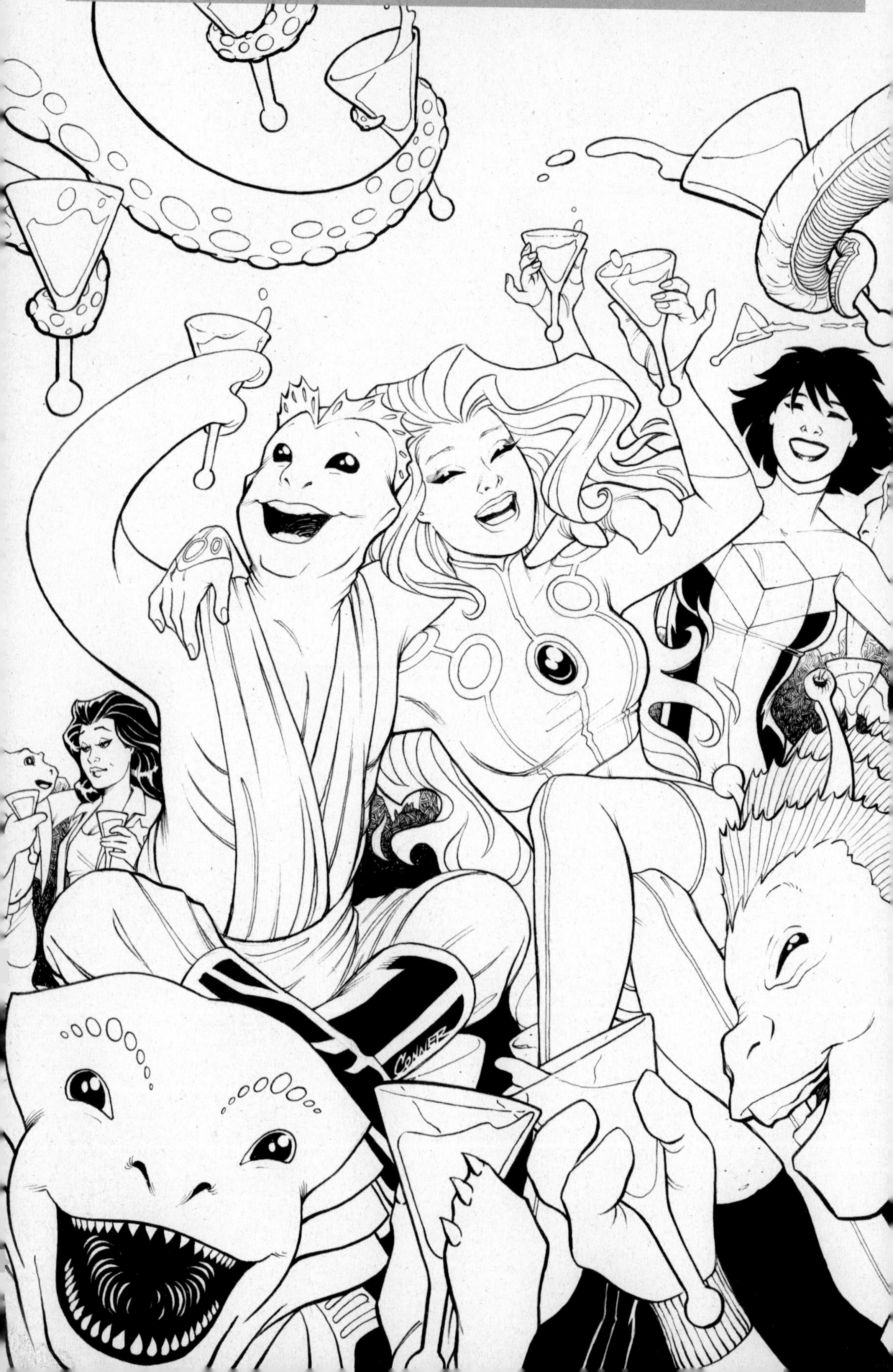

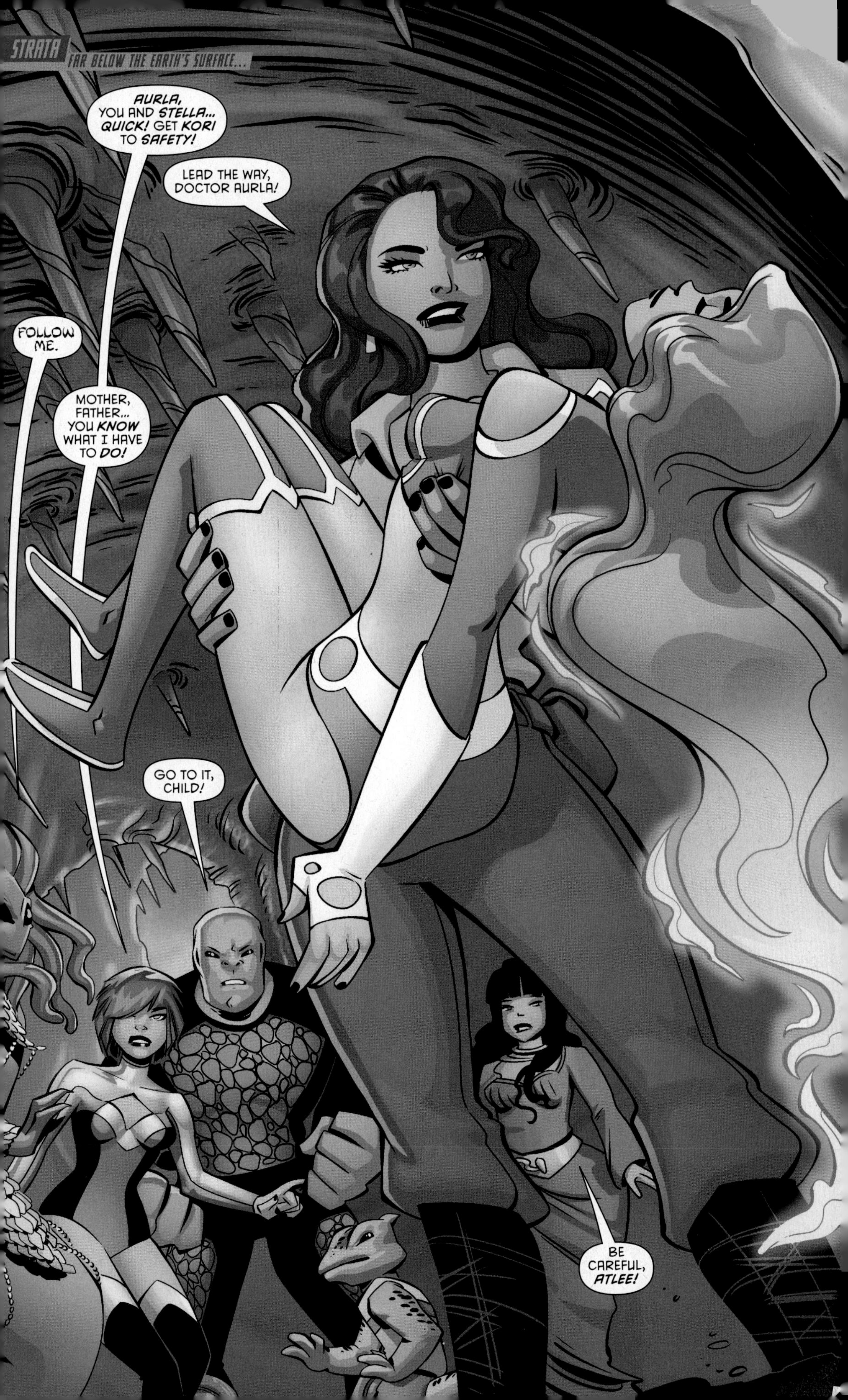
STRATA
FAR BELOW THE EARTH'S SURFACE...
AURLA, YOU AND STELLA... QUICK! GET KORI TO SAFETY!
LEAD THE WAY, DOCTOR AURLA!
FOLLOW ME.
MOTHER, FATHER... YOU KNOW WHAT I HAVE TO DO!
GO TO IT, CHILD!
BE CAREFUL, ATLEE!

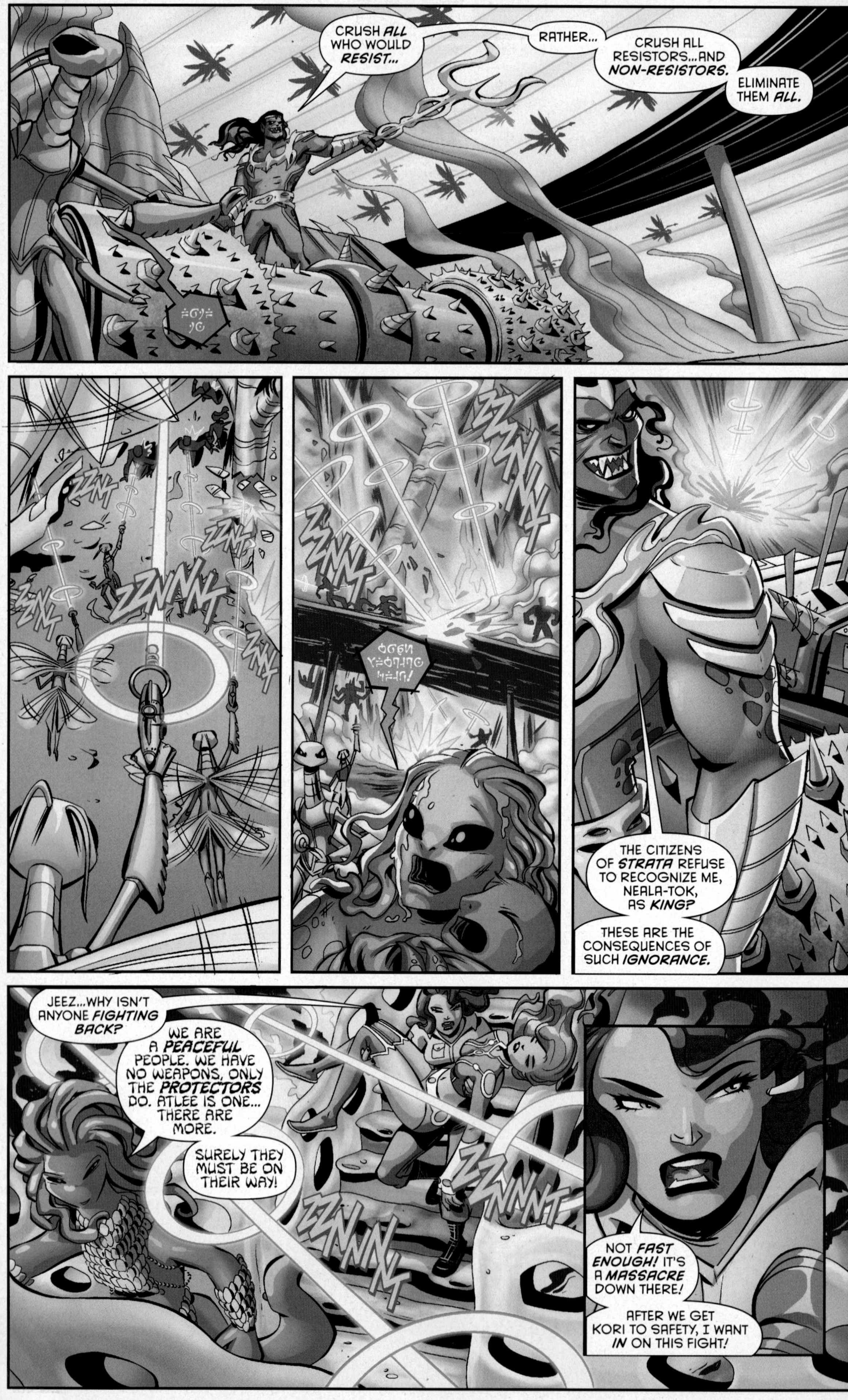
CRUSH ALL WHO WOULD RESIST...
RATHER...
CRUSH ALL RESISTORS...AND NON-RESISTORS.
ELIMINATE THEM ALL.
ZZNNT
ZZNNNT
ZZNNNT
ZZNNNT
ZZNNNT
ZZNNNT
ZZNNNT
THE CITIZENS OF STRATA REFUSE TO RECOGNIZE ME, NEALA-TOK, AS KING?
THESE ARE THE CONSEQUENCES OF SUCH IGNORANCE.
JEEZ...WHY ISN'T ANYONE FIGHTING BACK?
WE ARE A PEACEFUL PEOPLE. WE HAVE NO WEAPONS, ONLY THE PROTECTORS DO. ATLEE IS ONE... THERE ARE MORE.
SURELY THEY MUST BE ON THEIR WAY!
ZZNNNT
ZZNNNNT
NOT FAST ENOUGH! IT'S A MASSACRE DOWN THERE!
AFTER WE GET KORI TO SAFETY, I WANT IN ON THIS FIGHT!

WATCHING THE DEVASTATION OF THE INSOLENT STRATANS BRINGS GREAT JOY TO MY HEARTS!

NEALA-TOK, WE HAVE TRIED, REPEATEDLY, TO *PEACEFULLY NEGOTIATE* WITH YOU.

YET YOU ALWAYS SLINK OFF, AMASSING *ARMY* AFTER *ARMY* TO BATTLE THE PROTECTORS OF STRATA, *TIME* AND *TIME AGAIN.*

WHAT?

WE'LL STOP YOU. WE *ALWAYS* DO.

BUT... *THIS* TIME...

THIS TIME YOU HAVE GONE *TOO FAR.*

YOU HAVE NOW *FORCED* MY *HAND*, NEALA-TOK.

YOU HAVE BROKEN ONE OF OUR MOST *SACRED* LAWS.

YOU HAVE *MURDERED* OUR *CITIZENS.*

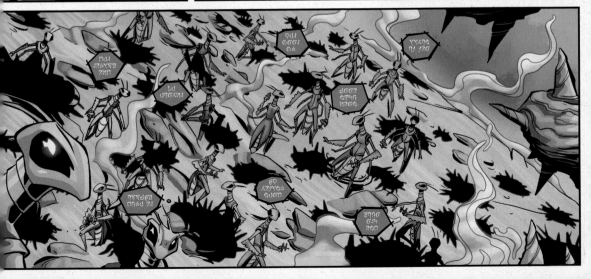

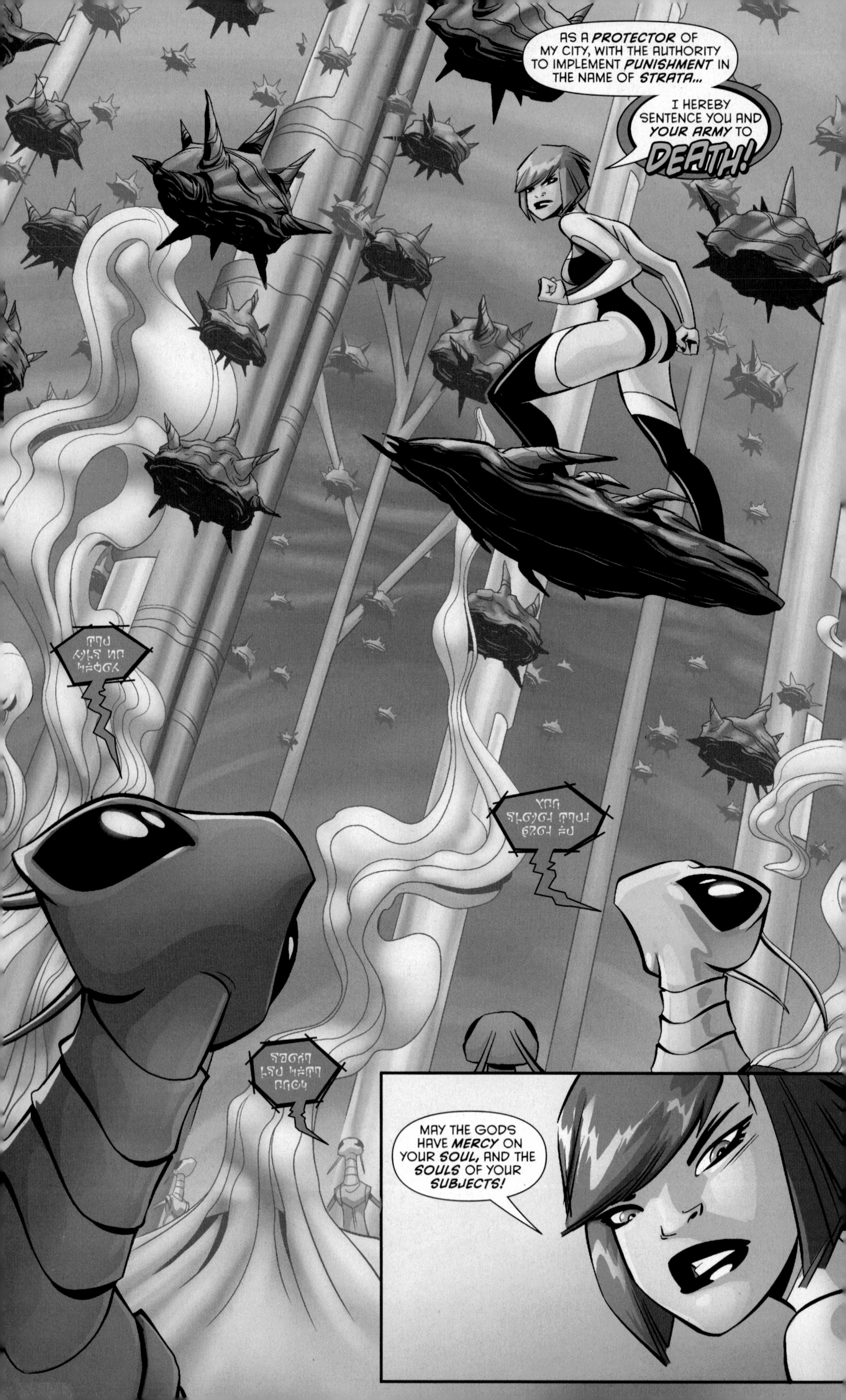
AS A PROTECTOR OF MY CITY, WITH THE AUTHORITY TO IMPLEMENT PUNISHMENT IN THE NAME OF STRATA...
I HEREBY SENTENCE YOU AND YOUR ARMY TO DEATH!
MAY THE GODS HAVE MERCY ON YOUR SOUL, AND THE SOULS OF YOUR SUBJECTS!

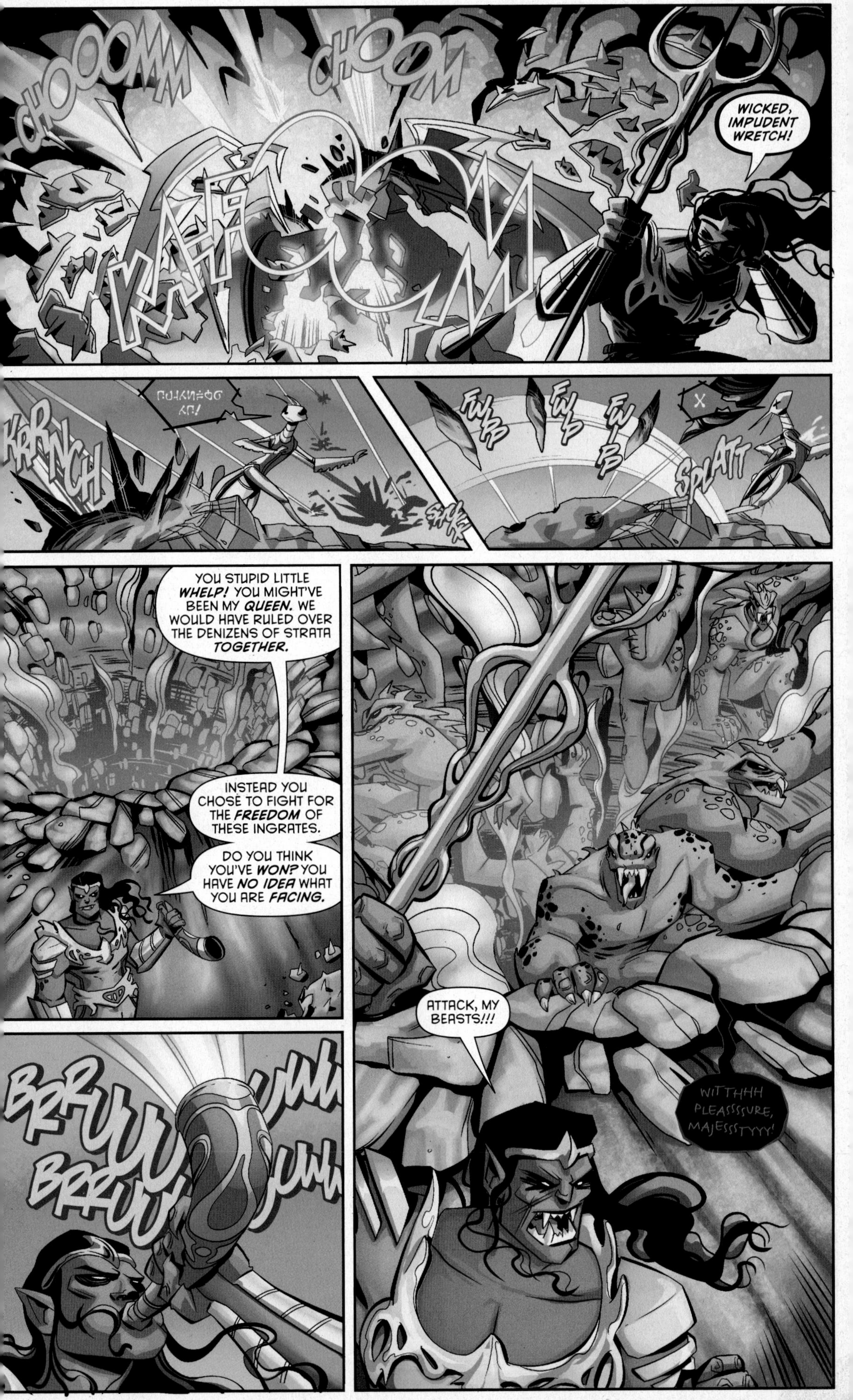
CHOOOMM
CHOOM
KAHOOOM
WICKED, IMPUDENT WRETCH!
KRRNCH
SHUK
FWIPP
FWIP
FWIPP
SPLATT
YOU STUPID LITTLE WHELP! YOU MIGHT'VE BEEN MY QUEEN. WE WOULD HAVE RULED OVER THE DENIZENS OF STRATA TOGETHER.
INSTEAD YOU CHOSE TO FIGHT FOR THE FREEDOM OF THESE INGRATES.
DO YOU THINK YOU'VE WON? YOU HAVE NO IDEA WHAT YOU ARE FACING.
BRRUUUMMM
BRRUUUMMM
ATTACK, MY BEASTS!!!
WITTHHH PLEASSSSURE, MAJESSSTYYY!

Up and at 'em!

ANYTHING?

THIS WOMAN... SHE IS LIKE *NOTHING* I HAVE EVER *SEEN*. APPARENTLY, SHE METABOLIZES LAMBENT RADIATION.

MY *FIRST* CONCERN WAS THAT SHE WAS NOT GETTING ENOUGH *LIGHT* TO CONVERT TO ENERGY.

HOWEVER, IT SEEMS THE VERY *OPPOSITE* IS HAPPENING.

THE ENERGY FROM OUR SUBTERRANEAN LIGHT SOURCE HAS *OVERLOADED* HER.

AT FIRST, HER BODY FOUGHT IT, AS AN INFECTION...

...BUT ACCORDING TO THE READINGS, SHE'S *ADAPTING* AND *PROCESSING* IT.

SO, SHE'LL BE *ALL RIGHT?*

YES, AND *MORE*. I HAVE NO IDEA HOW LONG IT WILL TAKE, THOUGH. I CAN'T SEEM TO *INTERPRET* SOME OF THE READINGS.

AURLA! WE HAVE *BIG PROBLEMS* APPROACHING.

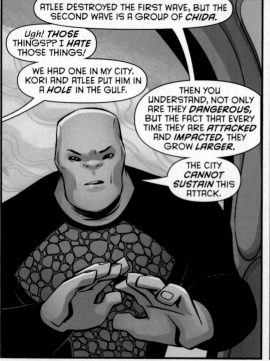

ATLEE DESTROYED THE FIRST WAVE, BUT THE SECOND WAVE IS A GROUP OF *CHIDA.*

Ugh! *THOSE* THINGS?? I *HATE* THOSE THINGS!

WE HAD ONE IN MY CITY. KORI AND ATLEE PUT HIM IN A *HOLE* IN THE GULF.

THEN YOU UNDERSTAND, NOT ONLY ARE THEY *DANGEROUS*, BUT THE FACT THAT EVERY TIME THEY ARE *ATTACKED* AND *IMPACTED*, THEY GROW *LARGER*.

THE CITY *CANNOT* SUSTAIN THIS ATTACK.

ARE THE *OTHER PROTECTORS* ON THEIR WAY?

ONLY *ATLEE* IS HERE. THE OTHER TWO ARE ON A SEPARATE MISSION, AND TOO FAR TO GET HERE IN TIME.

I'M AFRAID IT MAY BE *TOO MUCH* FOR ATLEE TO *DEAL* WITH.

OH NO.

GIVE ME A *WEAPON* AND *POINT THE WAY.*

STELLA...

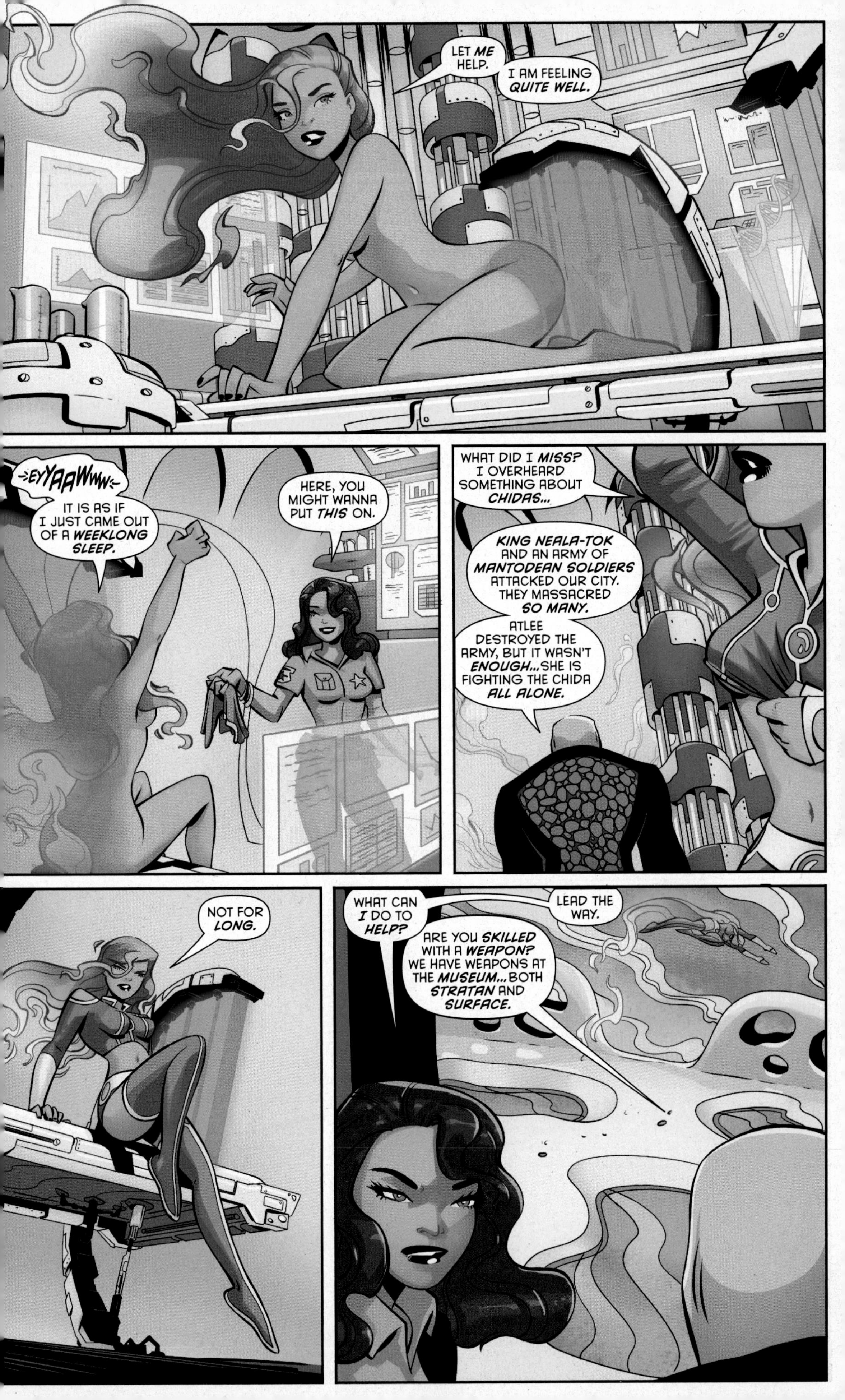
LET ME HELP.
I AM FEELING QUITE WELL.
EYYAAWWW
IT IS AS IF I JUST CAME OUT OF A WEEKLONG SLEEP.
HERE, YOU MIGHT WANNA PUT THIS ON.
WHAT DID I MISS? I OVERHEARD SOMETHING ABOUT CHIDAS...
KING NEALA-TOK AND AN ARMY OF MANTODEAN SOLDIERS ATTACKED OUR CITY. THEY MASSACRED SO MANY.
ATLEE DESTROYED THE ARMY, BUT IT WASN'T ENOUGH...SHE IS FIGHTING THE CHIDA ALL ALONE.
NOT FOR LONG.
WHAT CAN I DO TO HELP?
LEAD THE WAY.
ARE YOU SKILLED WITH A WEAPON? WE HAVE WEAPONS AT THE MUSEUM... BOTH STRATAN AND SURFACE.

Pet Sounds.

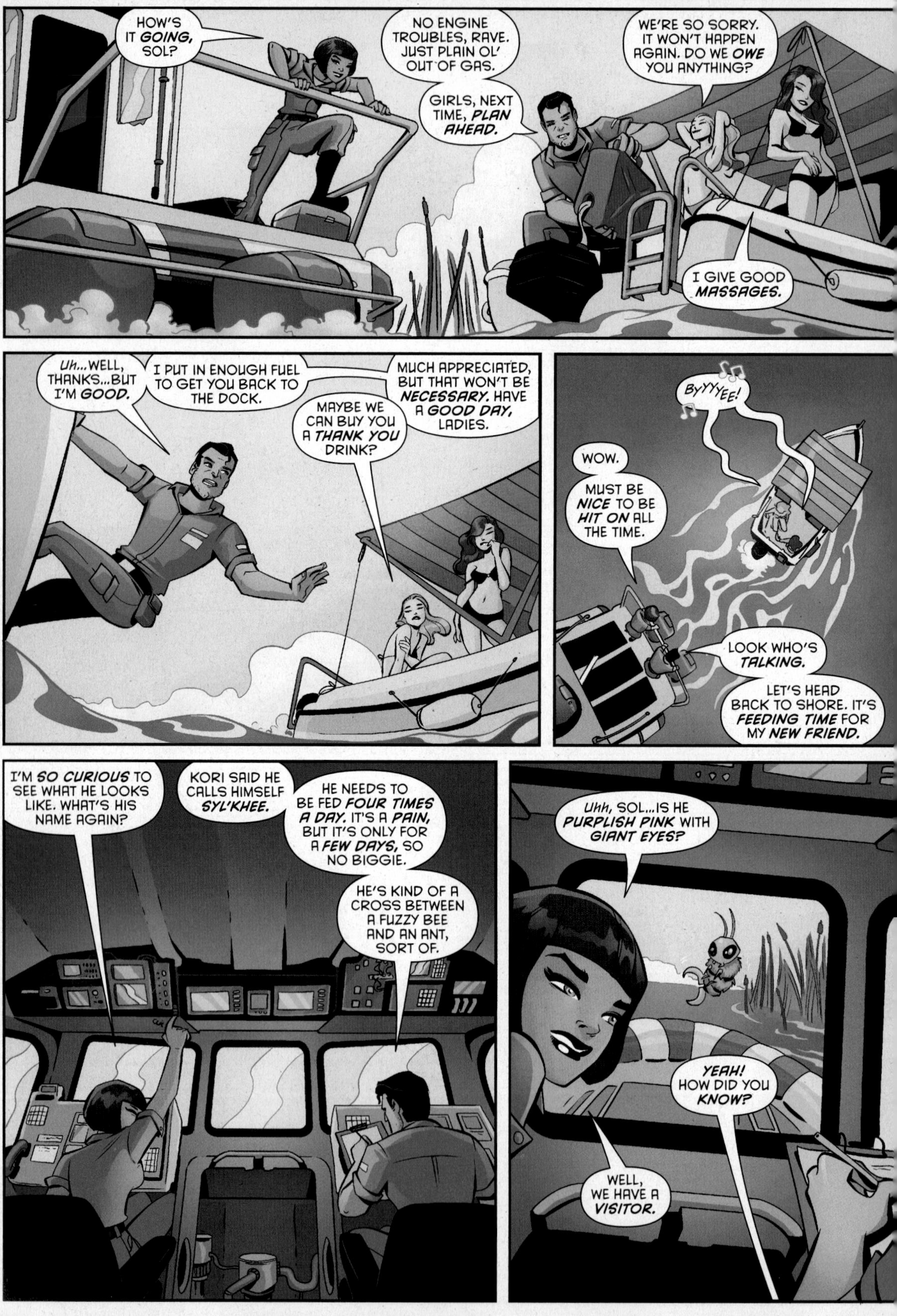
HOW'S IT GOING, SOL?
NO ENGINE TROUBLES, RAVE. JUST PLAIN OL' OUT OF GAS.
GIRLS, NEXT TIME, PLAN AHEAD.
WE'RE SO SORRY. IT WON'T HAPPEN AGAIN. DO WE OWE YOU ANYTHING?
I GIVE GOOD MASSAGES.
Uh...WELL, THANKS...BUT I'M GOOD.
I PUT IN ENOUGH FUEL TO GET YOU BACK TO THE DOCK.
MUCH APPRECIATED, BUT THAT WON'T BE NECESSARY. HAVE A GOOD DAY, LADIES.
MAYBE WE CAN BUY YOU A THANK YOU DRINK?
ByYYYEE!
WOW.
MUST BE NICE TO BE HIT ON ALL THE TIME.
LOOK WHO'S TALKING.
LET'S HEAD BACK TO SHORE. IT'S FEEDING TIME FOR MY NEW FRIEND.
I'M SO CURIOUS TO SEE WHAT HE LOOKS LIKE. WHAT'S HIS NAME AGAIN?
KORI SAID HE CALLS HIMSELF SYL'KHEE.
HE NEEDS TO BE FED FOUR TIMES A DAY. IT'S A PAIN, BUT IT'S ONLY FOR A FEW DAYS, SO NO BIGGIE.
HE'S KIND OF A CROSS BETWEEN A FUZZY BEE AND AN ANT, SORT OF.
Uhh, SOL...IS HE PURPLISH PINK WITH GIANT EYES?
YEAH! HOW DID YOU KNOW?
WELL, WE HAVE A VISITOR.

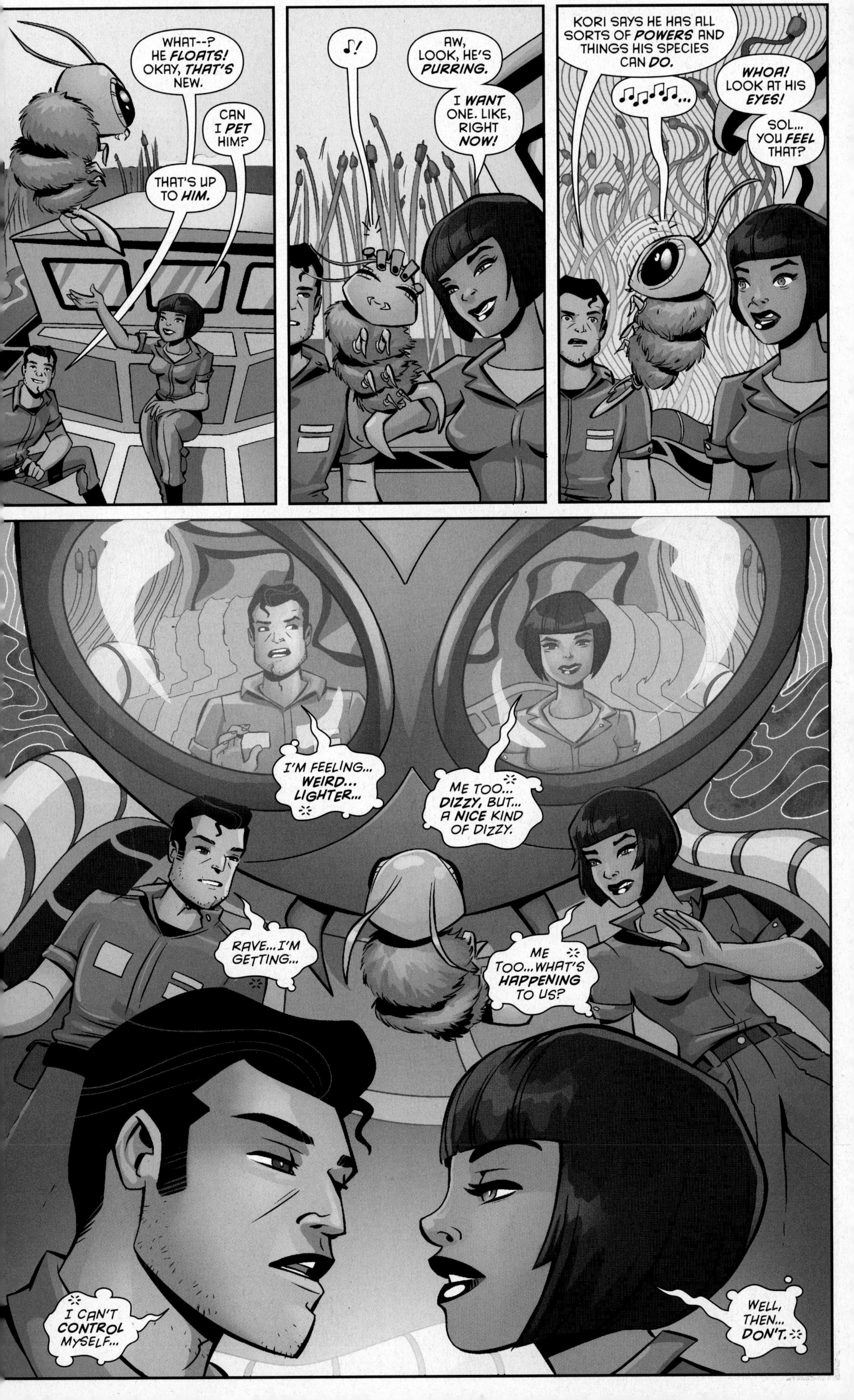
WHAT--? HE *FLOATS!* OKAY, *THAT'S* NEW.
CAN I *PET* HIM?
THAT'S UP TO *HIM.*
♪!
AW, LOOK, HE'S *PURRING.*
I *WANT* ONE. LIKE, RIGHT *NOW!*
KORI SAYS HE HAS ALL SORTS OF *POWERS* AND THINGS HIS SPECIES CAN *DO.*
♪♪♪♪...
WHOA! LOOK AT HIS *EYES!*
SOL... YOU *FEEL* THAT?
I'M FEELING... *WEIRD... LIGHTER...*
ME TOO... *DIZZY,* BUT... A *NICE* KIND OF DIZZY.
RAVE... I'M GETTING...
ME TOO... WHAT'S *HAPPENING* TO US?
I CAN'T *CONTROL* MYSELF...
WELL, THEN... *DON'T.*

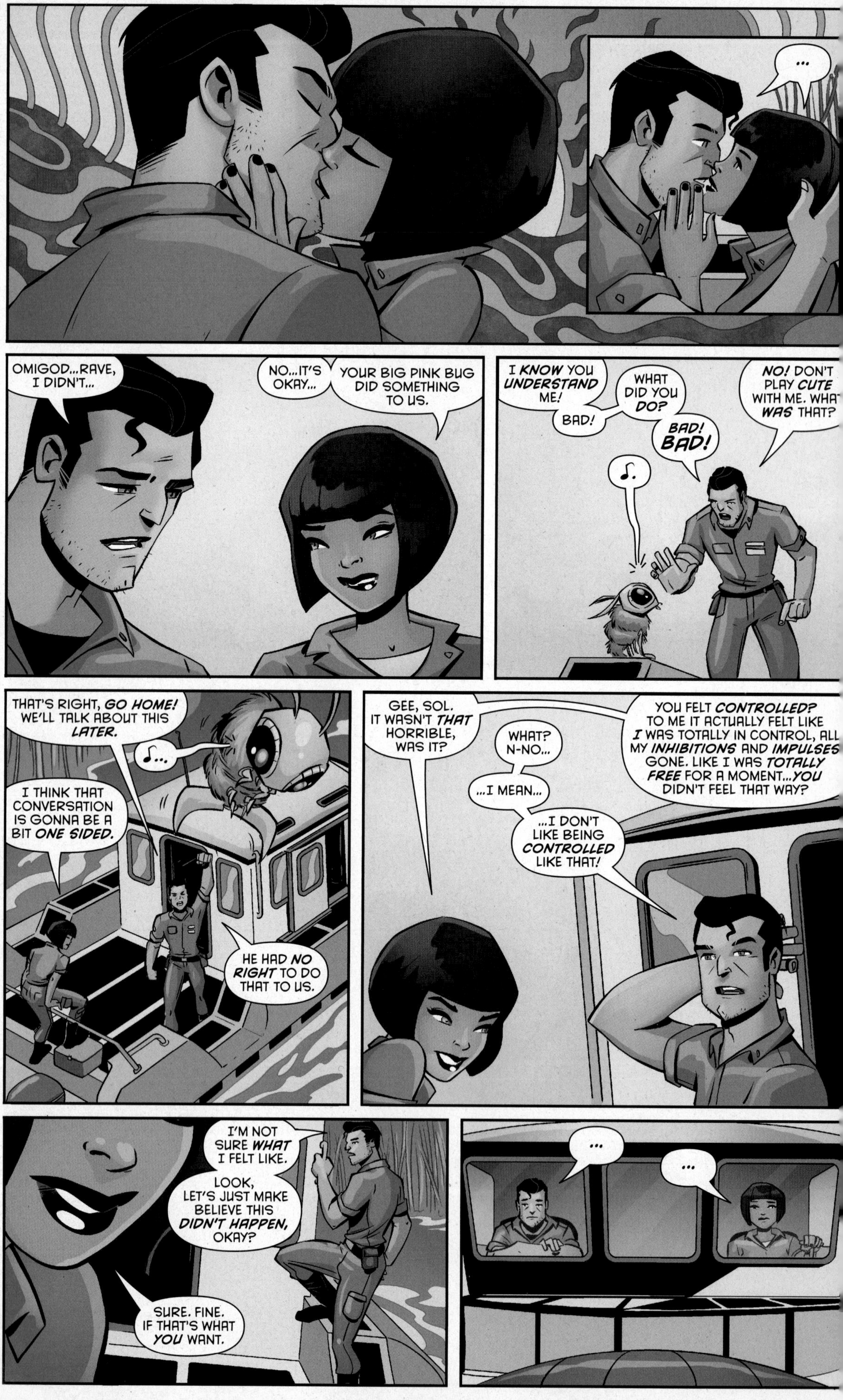
...
OMIGOD...RAVE, I DIDN'T...
NO...IT'S OKAY...
YOUR BIG PINK BUG DID SOMETHING TO US.
I KNOW YOU UNDERSTAND ME!
BAD!
WHAT DID YOU DO?
BAD! BAD!
NO! DON'T PLAY CUTE WITH ME. WHAT WAS THAT?
THAT'S RIGHT, GO HOME! WE'LL TALK ABOUT THIS LATER.
I THINK THAT CONVERSATION IS GONNA BE A BIT ONE SIDED.
HE HAD NO RIGHT TO DO THAT TO US.
GEE, SOL. IT WASN'T THAT HORRIBLE, WAS IT?
WHAT? N-NO...
...I MEAN...
...I DON'T LIKE BEING CONTROLLED LIKE THAT!
YOU FELT CONTROLLED? TO ME IT ACTUALLY FELT LIKE I WAS TOTALLY IN CONTROL, ALL MY INHIBITIONS AND IMPULSES GONE. LIKE I WAS TOTALLY FREE FOR A MOMENT...YOU DIDN'T FEEL THAT WAY?
I'M NOT SURE WHAT I FELT LIKE.
LOOK, LET'S JUST MAKE BELIEVE THIS DIDN'T HAPPEN, OKAY?
SURE. FINE. IF THAT'S WHAT YOU WANT.
...
...

Meanwhile, down below...

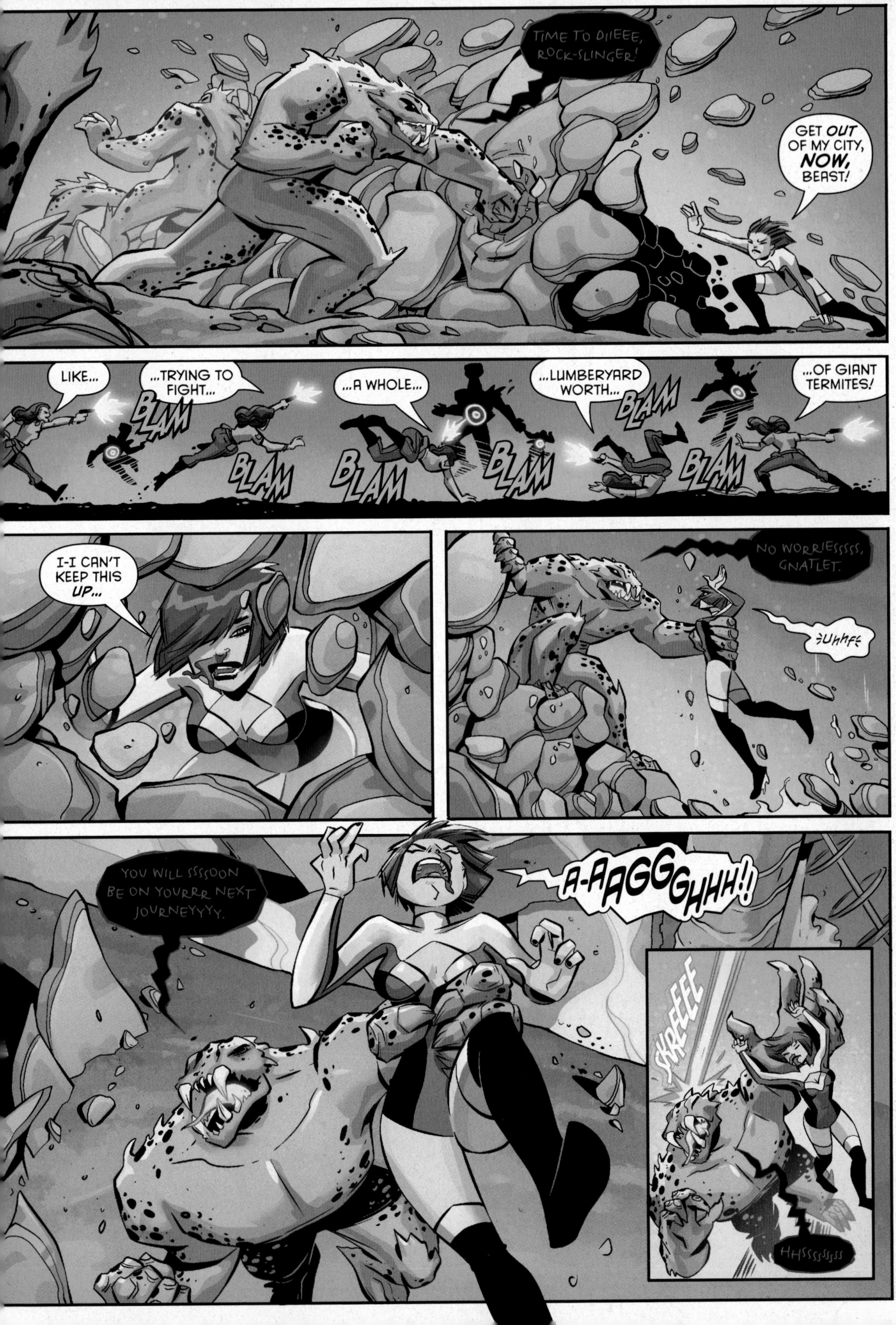

TIME TO DIIEEE, ROCK-SLINGER!
GET OUT OF MY CITY, NOW, BEAST!
LIKE...
...TRYING TO FIGHT...
BLAM
BLAM
...A WHOLE...
BLAM
...LUMBERYARD WORTH...
BLAM
BLAM
...OF GIANT TERMITES!
BLAM
I-I CAN'T KEEP THIS UP...
NO WORRIESSSSS, GNATLET.
UHHF
YOU WILL SSSSOON BE ON YOURRR NEXT JOURNEYYYY.
A-AAAGGGHHH!!
SKREEEEE
HHSSSSSSSS

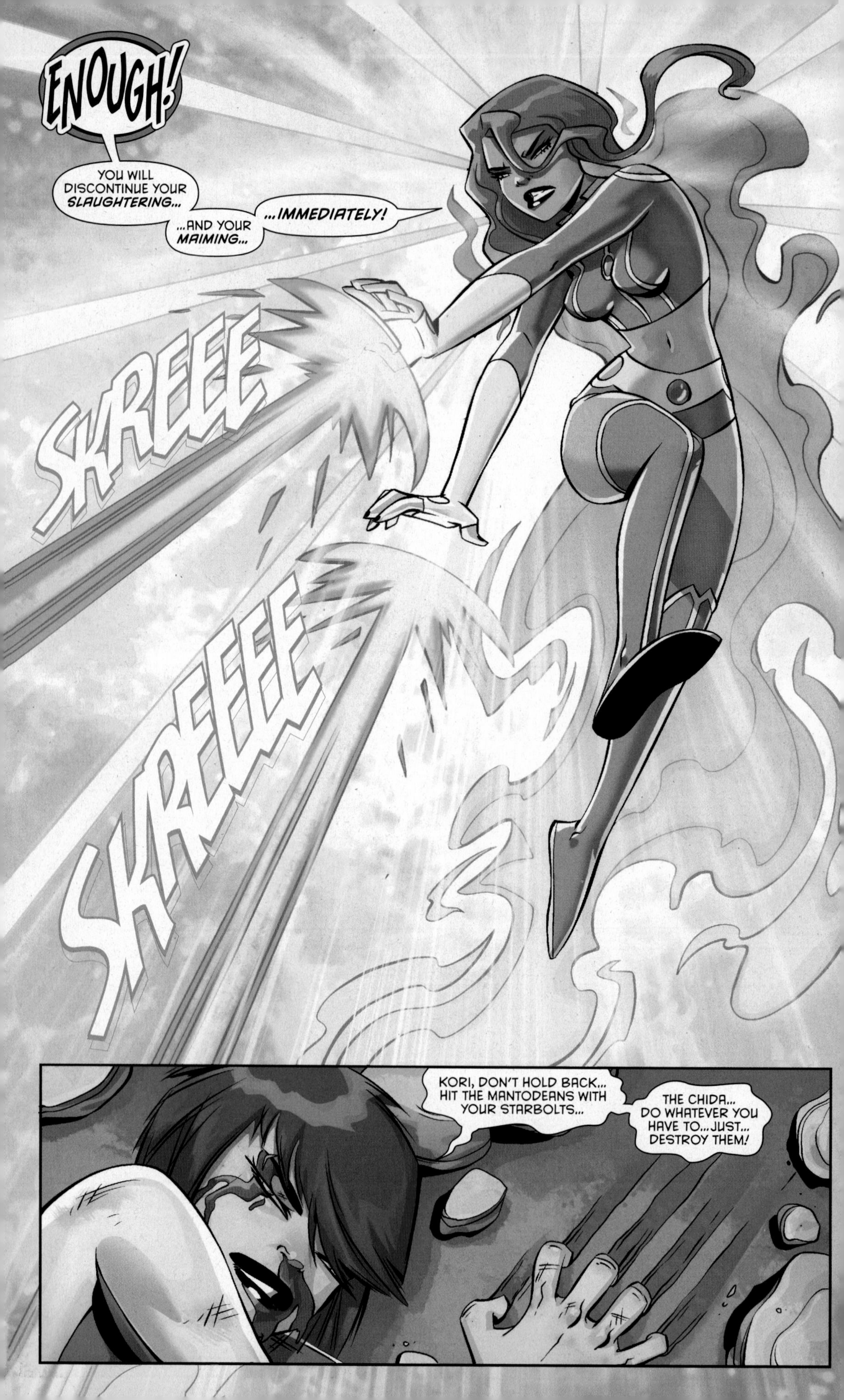
ENOUGH!
YOU WILL DISCONTINUE YOUR SLAUGHTERING...
...AND YOUR MAIMING...
...IMMEDIATELY!
SKREEE
SKREEEE
KORI, DON'T HOLD BACK... HIT THE MANTODEANS WITH YOUR STARBOLTS...
THE CHIDA... DO WHATEVER YOU HAVE TO... JUST... DESTROY THEM!

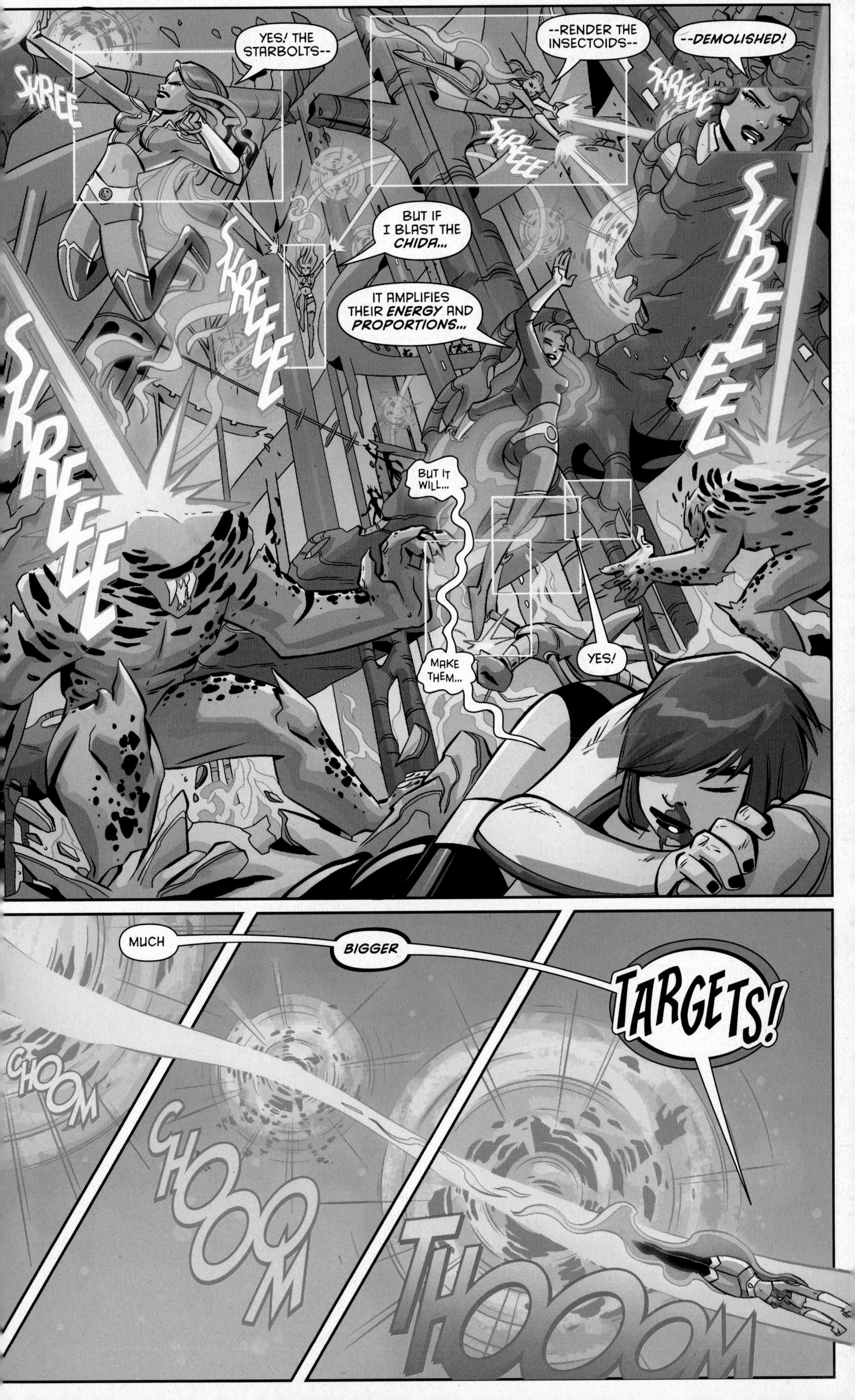
SKREE
YES! THE STARBOLTS--
--RENDER THE INSECTOIDS--
--DEMOLISHED!
SKREEE
SKREEE
SKREEEE
BUT IF I BLAST THE CHIDA...
IT AMPLIFIES THEIR ENERGY AND PROPORTIONS...
SKREEEE
SKREEEE
BUT IT WILL...
MAKE THEM...
YES!
MUCH
BIGGER
TARGETS!
CHOOM
CHOOM
THOOOM

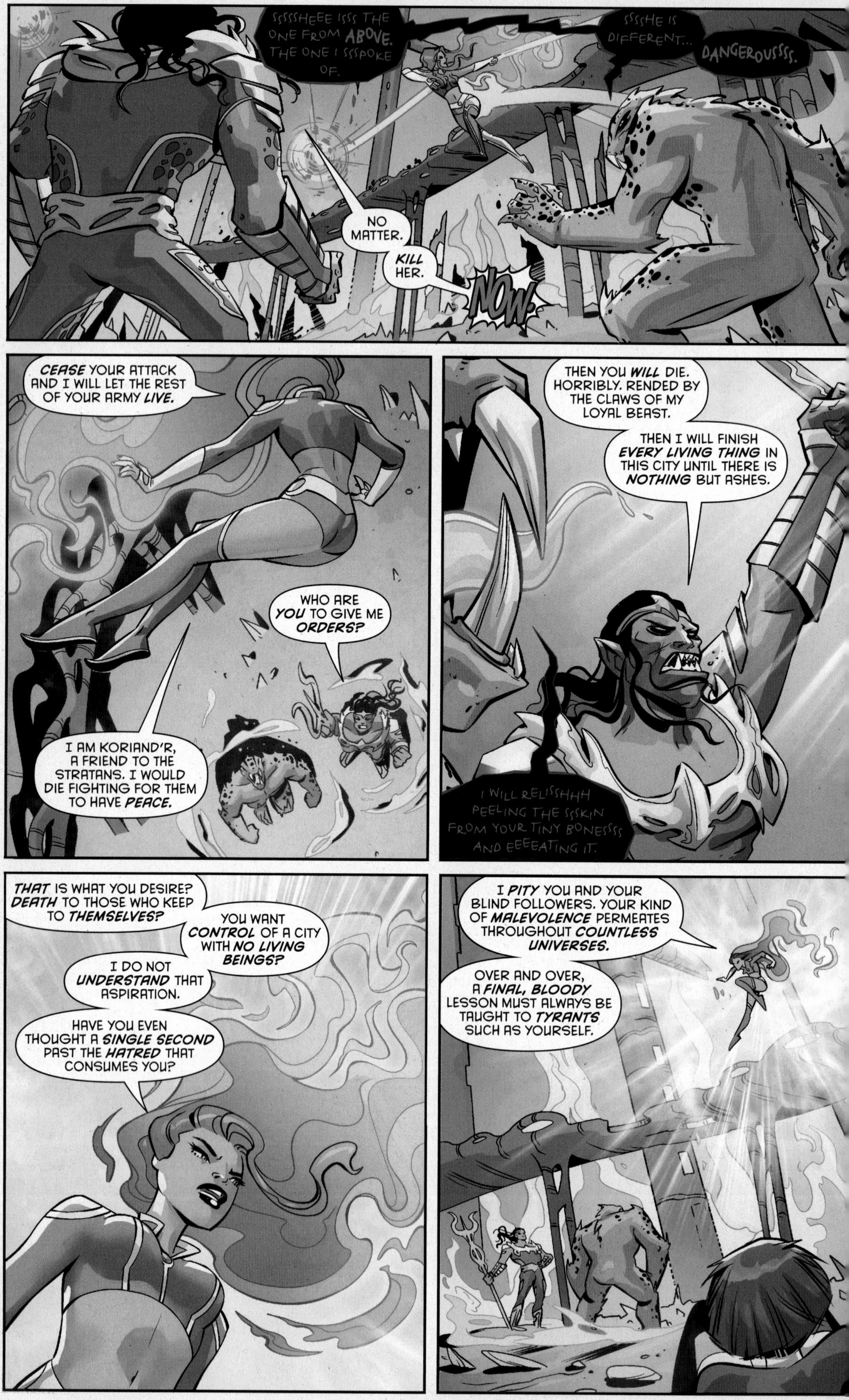
SSSSSHEEE ISSS THE ONE FROM ABOVE. THE ONE I SSSPOKE OF.
SSSSHE IS DIFFERENT...
DANGEROUSSSS.
NO MATTER.
KILL HER.
NOW.
CEASE YOUR ATTACK AND I WILL LET THE REST OF YOUR ARMY LIVE.
WHO ARE YOU TO GIVE ME ORDERS?
I AM KORIAND'R, A FRIEND TO THE STRATANS. I WOULD DIE FIGHTING FOR THEM TO HAVE PEACE.
THEN YOU WILL DIE. HORRIBLY. RENDED BY THE CLAWS OF MY LOYAL BEAST.
THEN I WILL FINISH EVERY LIVING THING IN THIS CITY UNTIL THERE IS NOTHING BUT ASHES.
I WILL RELISSHHH PEELING THE SSSKIN FROM YOUR TINY BONESSSS AND EEEEATING IT.
THAT IS WHAT YOU DESIRE? DEATH TO THOSE WHO KEEP TO THEMSELVES?
YOU WANT CONTROL OF A CITY WITH NO LIVING BEINGS?
I DO NOT UNDERSTAND THAT ASPIRATION.
HAVE YOU EVEN THOUGHT A SINGLE SECOND PAST THE HATRED THAT CONSUMES YOU?
I PITY YOU AND YOUR BLIND FOLLOWERS. YOUR KIND OF MALEVOLENCE PERMEATES THROUGHOUT COUNTLESS UNIVERSES.
OVER AND OVER, A FINAL, BLOODY LESSON MUST ALWAYS BE TAUGHT TO TYRANTS SUCH AS YOURSELF.

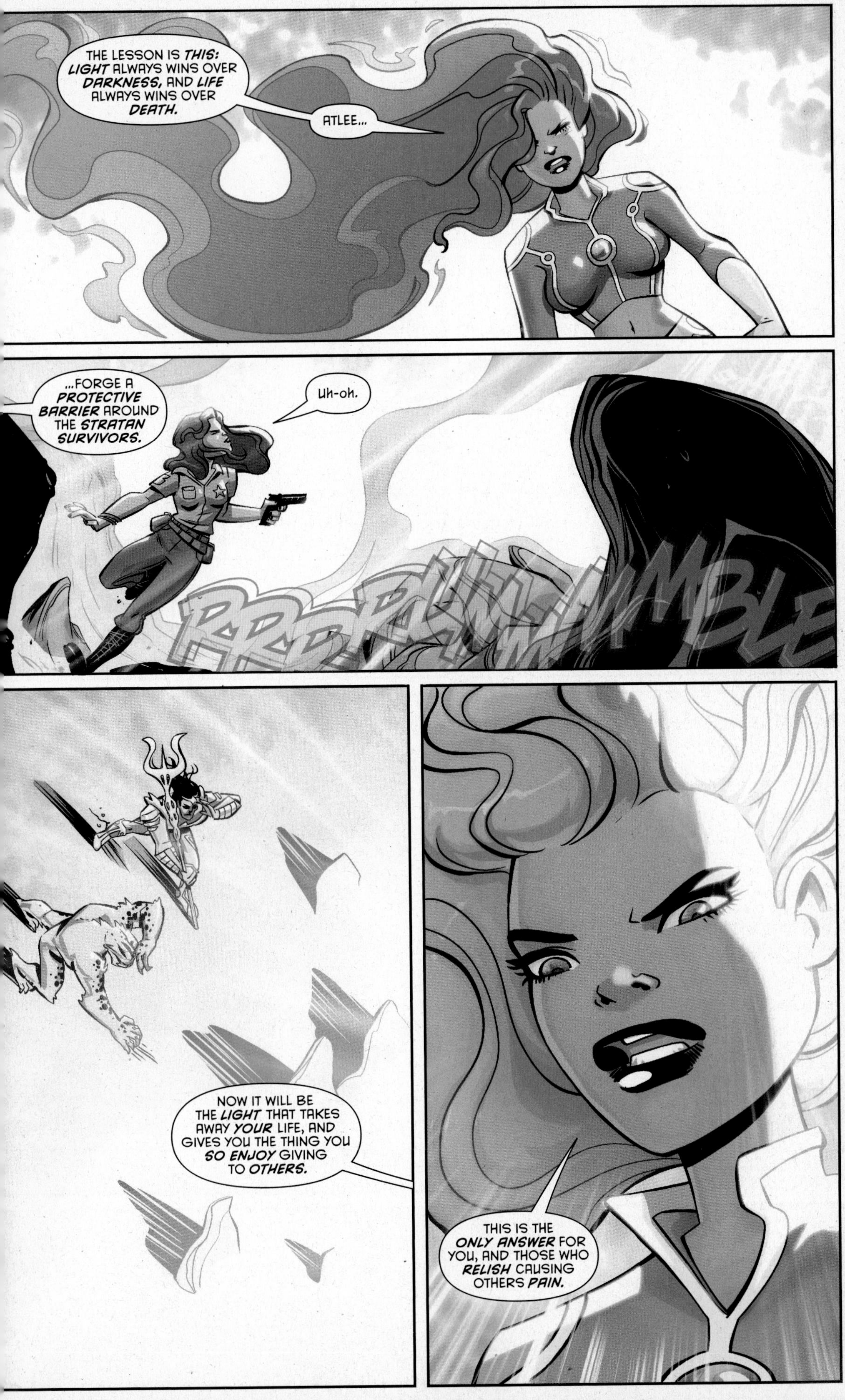
THE LESSON IS THIS: LIGHT ALWAYS WINS OVER DARKNESS, AND LIFE ALWAYS WINS OVER DEATH.
ATLEE...
...FORGE A PROTECTIVE BARRIER AROUND THE STRATAN SURVIVORS.
Uh-oh.
RRRRRUMMMMMBLE
NOW IT WILL BE THE LIGHT THAT TAKES AWAY YOUR LIFE, AND GIVES YOU THE THING YOU SO ENJOY GIVING TO OTHERS.
THIS IS THE ONLY ANSWER FOR YOU, AND THOSE WHO RELISH CAUSING OTHERS PAIN.

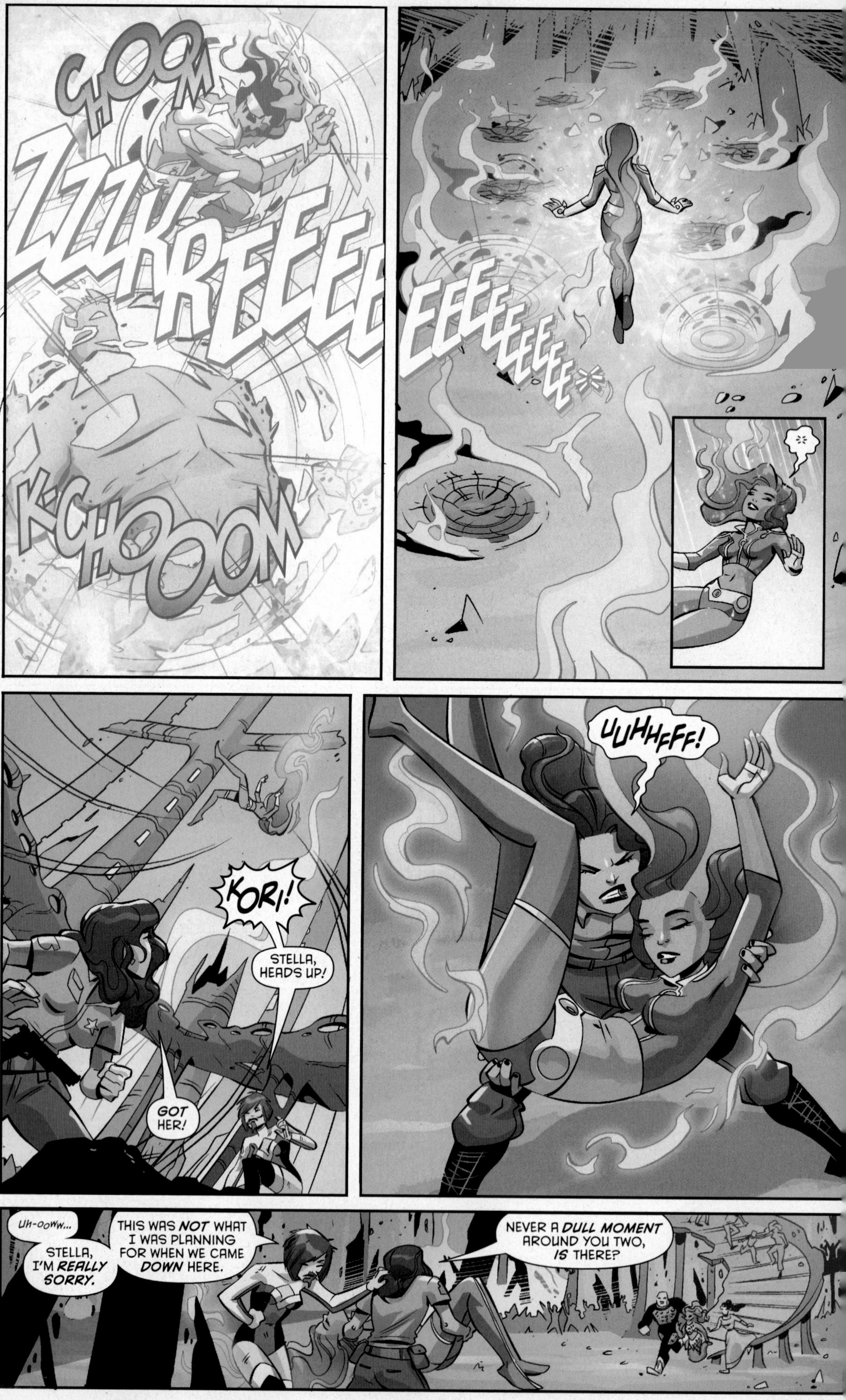

CHOOOM
ZZZKREEEEEEEEEEEEEEE*
K-CHOOOOM
KORI!
STELLA, HEADS UP!
GOT HER!
UUHHFFF!
UH-OOWW...
STELLA, I'M REALLY SORRY.
THIS WAS NOT WHAT I WAS PLANNING FOR WHEN WE CAME DOWN HERE.
NEVER A DULL MOMENT AROUND YOU TWO, IS THERE?

Sedation and celebration.

AURLA...THIS EVIVOSPHERE... FEEL SO MUCH **BETTER.**

I'VE NEVER SEEN KORI DO THAT BLINDING LIGHT THING.

ME NEITHER. WHAT'S THE DIAGNOSIS?

MY POSTULATION IS THAT YOUR FRIEND IS IN A **DEEP SLEEP.** HER MIND AND BODY HAVE SHIFTED HER INTO THIS STAGE.

ARE YOU TELLING ME SHE'S IN A **COMA?**

I AM **UNSURE** WHAT THAT **IS.**

ᚱᛁᛏᛏ ᛏᚱᛀᚲ ᚤᛒᚷ ᚲᚺᛈ?

ᛈᚢᛀᚷ ᛆᛗᚤᚢ ᛆᚷᚷᛈᛏ ᚤᚤ ᛏᚺᛆ ᚲᛏᛗᛆ. YES, THIS **WOULD** BE CONSIDERED A COMA. I ESTIMATE SHE WILL BE LIKE THIS FOR A WHILE. SHE WILL RECOVER **FULLY,** GIVEN TIME.

DO YOU HAVE ANY IDEA **HOW LONG?**

MY READINGS SAY APPROXIMATELY **SIXTEEN** CYCLES...ABOUT **THIRTY-TWO** OF YOUR SURFACE YEARS.

OH MY GOD... **THIRTY-TWO YEARS?** ARE YOU **SERIOUS?**

STAY **POSITIVE,** STELLA. WE KNOW SO **LITTLE** ABOUT HOW HER PHYSIOLOGY WORKS...IT COULD BE A **LOT LESS.**

OR **MORE!** THIS IS A NIGHTMARE.

ATLEE, THE REBIRTH IS ABOUT TO **BEGIN.** WE MUST JOIN THE OTHERS.

WE CANNOT HELP KORIAND'R AT THIS POINT. HER RECOVERY RELIES ON HER OWN **PHYSICAL PROCESS** NOW.

ATLEE, WHAT'S THE **REBIRTH?**

Umm... IT'S HARD TO **DESCRIBE...** IT'S MORE SOMETHING YOU HAVE TO **SEE.**

IT'S A **CEREMONY** AS OLD AS OUR PEOPLE.

OH?

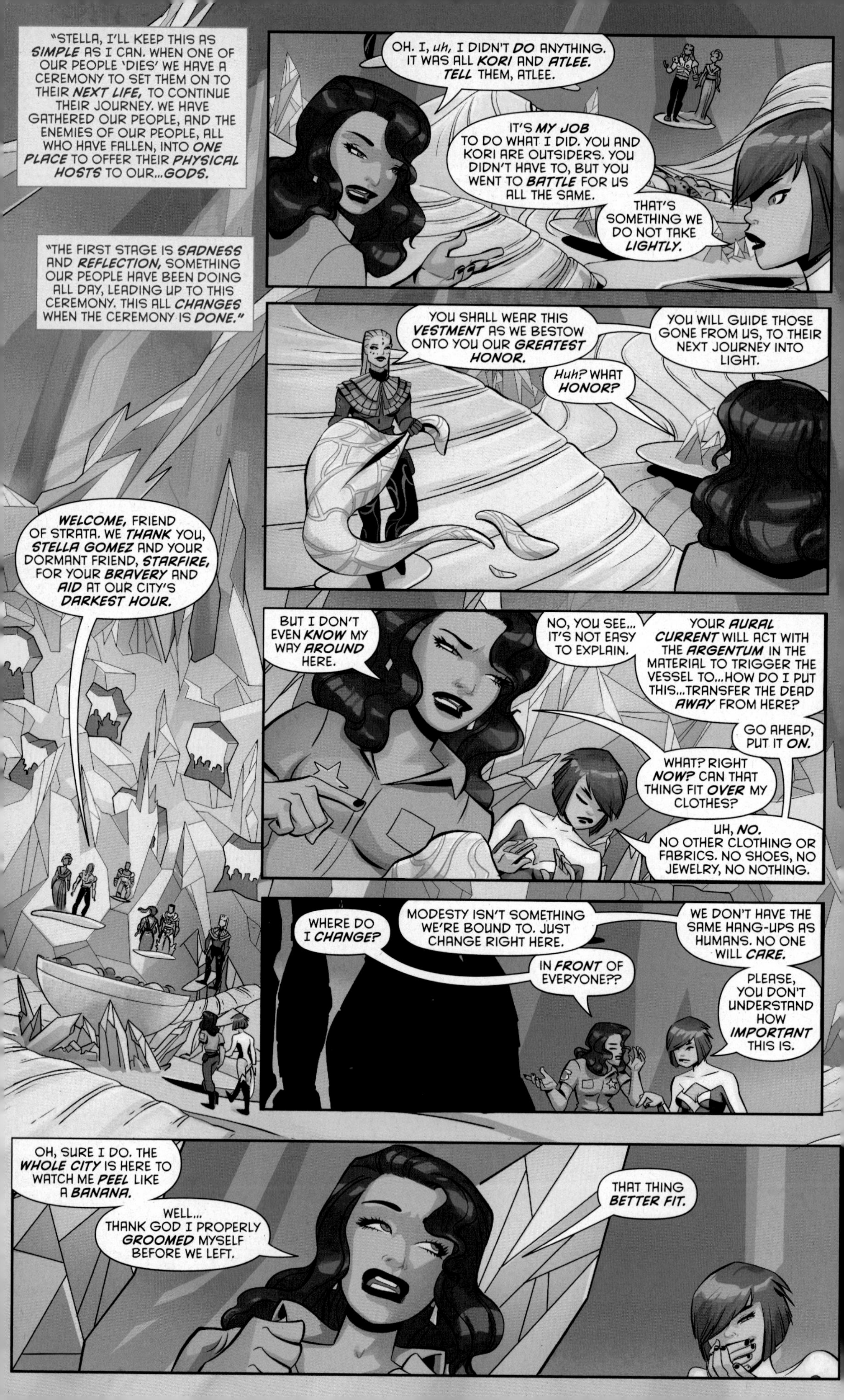
"STELLA, I'LL KEEP THIS AS SIMPLE AS I CAN. WHEN ONE OF OUR PEOPLE 'DIES' WE HAVE A CEREMONY TO SET THEM ON TO THEIR NEXT LIFE, TO CONTINUE THEIR JOURNEY. WE HAVE GATHERED OUR PEOPLE, AND THE ENEMIES OF OUR PEOPLE, ALL WHO HAVE FALLEN, INTO ONE PLACE TO OFFER THEIR PHYSICAL HOSTS TO OUR...GODS.
OH. I, uh, I DIDN'T DO ANYTHING. IT WAS ALL KORI AND ATLEE. TELL THEM, ATLEE.
IT'S MY JOB TO DO WHAT I DID. YOU AND KORI ARE OUTSIDERS. YOU DIDN'T HAVE TO, BUT YOU WENT TO BATTLE FOR US ALL THE SAME.
THAT'S SOMETHING WE DO NOT TAKE LIGHTLY.
"THE FIRST STAGE IS SADNESS AND REFLECTION, SOMETHING OUR PEOPLE HAVE BEEN DOING ALL DAY, LEADING UP TO THIS CEREMONY. THIS ALL CHANGES WHEN THE CEREMONY IS DONE."
YOU SHALL WEAR THIS VESTMENT AS WE BESTOW ONTO YOU OUR GREATEST HONOR.
YOU WILL GUIDE THOSE GONE FROM US, TO THEIR NEXT JOURNEY INTO LIGHT.
Huh? WHAT HONOR?
WELCOME, FRIEND OF STRATA. WE THANK YOU, STELLA GOMEZ AND YOUR DORMANT FRIEND, STARFIRE, FOR YOUR BRAVERY AND AID AT OUR CITY'S DARKEST HOUR.
BUT I DON'T EVEN KNOW MY WAY AROUND HERE.
NO, YOU SEE... IT'S NOT EASY TO EXPLAIN.
YOUR AURAL CURRENT WILL ACT WITH THE ARGENTUM IN THE MATERIAL TO TRIGGER THE VESSEL TO...HOW DO I PUT THIS...TRANSFER THE DEAD AWAY FROM HERE?
GO AHEAD, PUT IT ON.
WHAT? RIGHT NOW? CAN THAT THING FIT OVER MY CLOTHES?
UH, NO. NO OTHER CLOTHING OR FABRICS. NO SHOES, NO JEWELRY, NO NOTHING.
WHERE DO I CHANGE?
MODESTY ISN'T SOMETHING WE'RE BOUND TO. JUST CHANGE RIGHT HERE.
WE DON'T HAVE THE SAME HANG-UPS AS HUMANS. NO ONE WILL CARE.
IN FRONT OF EVERYONE??
PLEASE, YOU DON'T UNDERSTAND HOW IMPORTANT THIS IS.
OH, SURE I DO. THE WHOLE CITY IS HERE TO WATCH ME PEEL LIKE A BANANA.
WELL... THANK GOD I PROPERLY GROOMED MYSELF BEFORE WE LEFT.
THAT THING BETTER FIT.

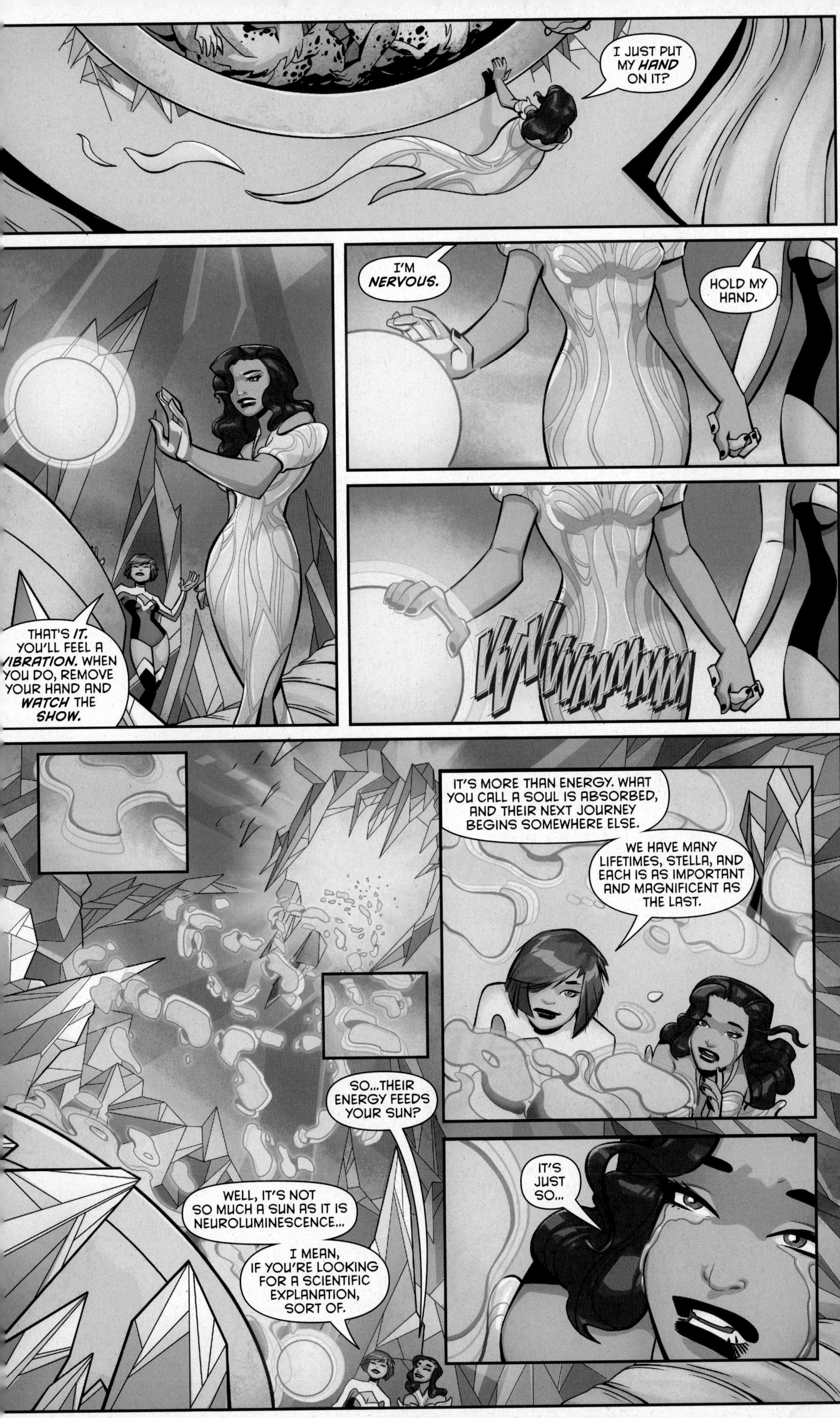
I JUST PUT MY *HAND* ON IT?
THAT'S *IT.* YOU'LL FEEL A *VIBRATION.* WHEN YOU DO, REMOVE YOUR HAND AND *WATCH* THE *SHOW.*
I'M *NERVOUS.*
HOLD MY HAND.
VVVVMMMMMM
SO...THEIR ENERGY FEEDS YOUR SUN?
WELL, IT'S NOT SO MUCH A SUN AS IT IS NEUROLUMINESCENCE...
I MEAN, IF YOU'RE LOOKING FOR A SCIENTIFIC EXPLANATION, SORT OF.
IT'S MORE THAN ENERGY. WHAT YOU CALL A SOUL IS ABSORBED, AND THEIR NEXT JOURNEY BEGINS SOMEWHERE ELSE.
WE HAVE MANY LIFETIMES, STELLA, AND EACH IS AS IMPORTANT AND MAGNIFICENT AS THE LAST.
IT'S JUST SO...

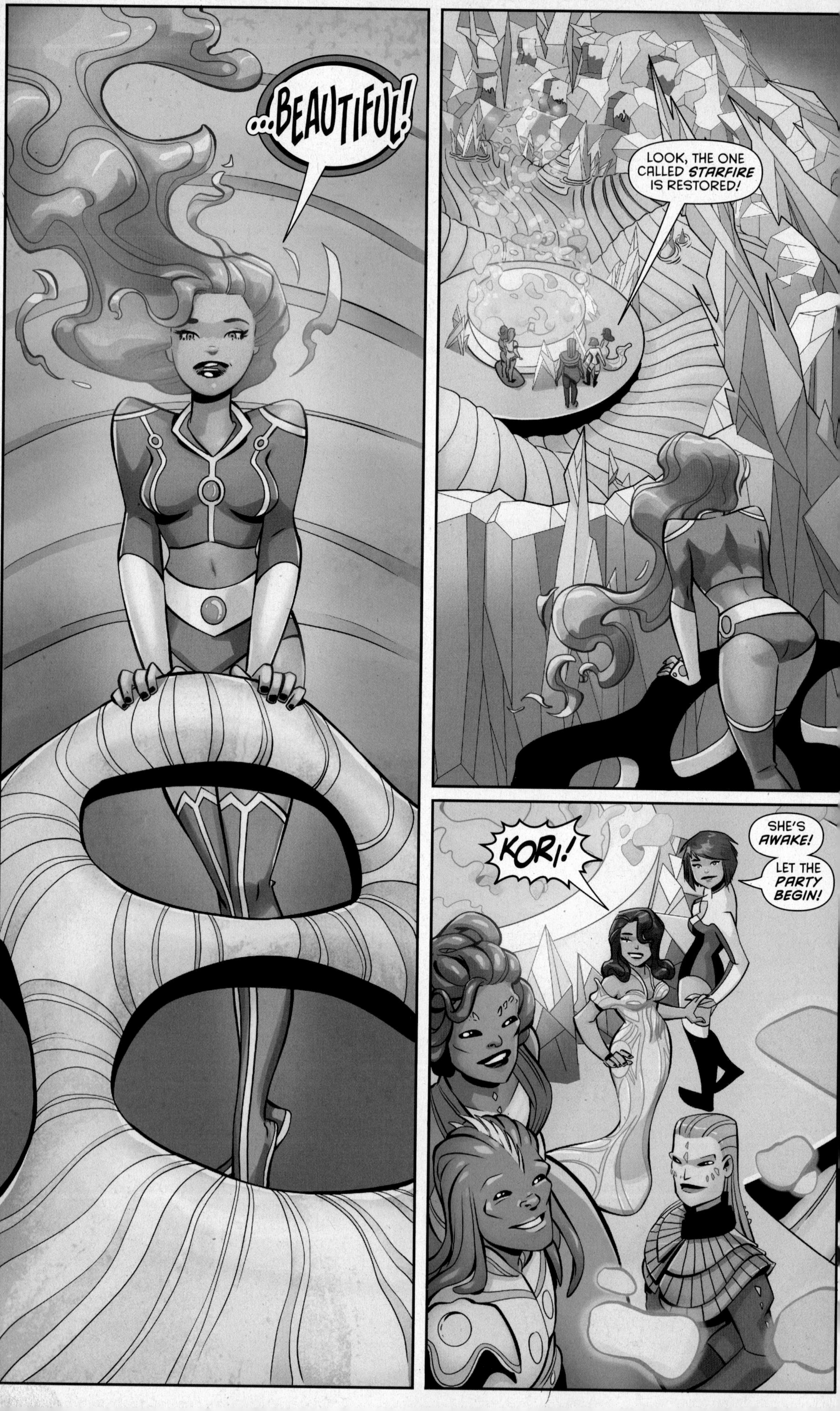
...BEAUTIFUL!
LOOK, THE ONE CALLED STARFIRE IS RESTORED!
KORI!
SHE'S AWAKE!
LET THE PARTY BEGIN!

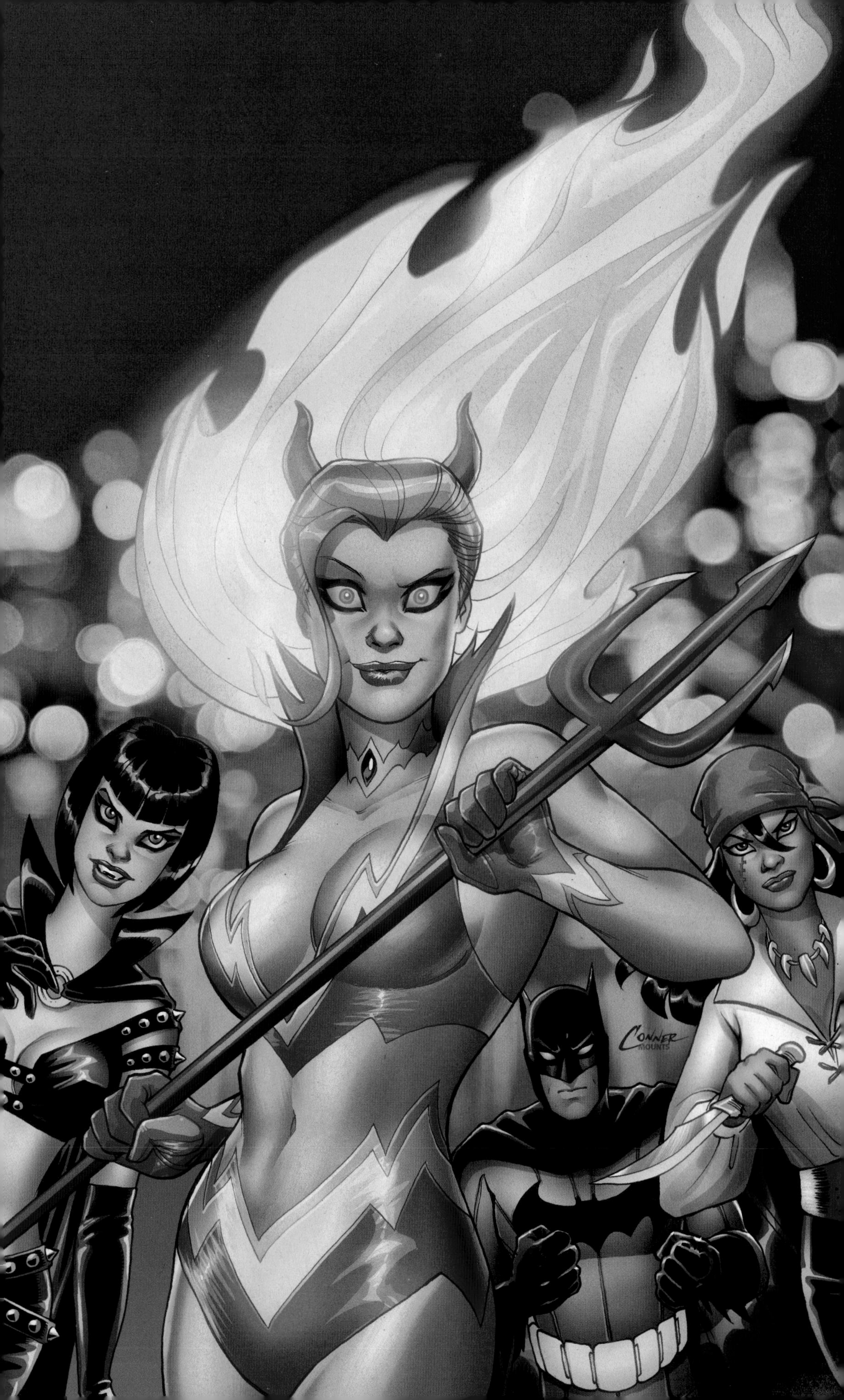
CONNER
MOUNTS

REVELRIES AND REVELATIONS

AMANDA CONNER & JIMMY PALMIOTTI writers ELSA CHARRETIER art HI-FI colors TOM NAPOLITANO letters

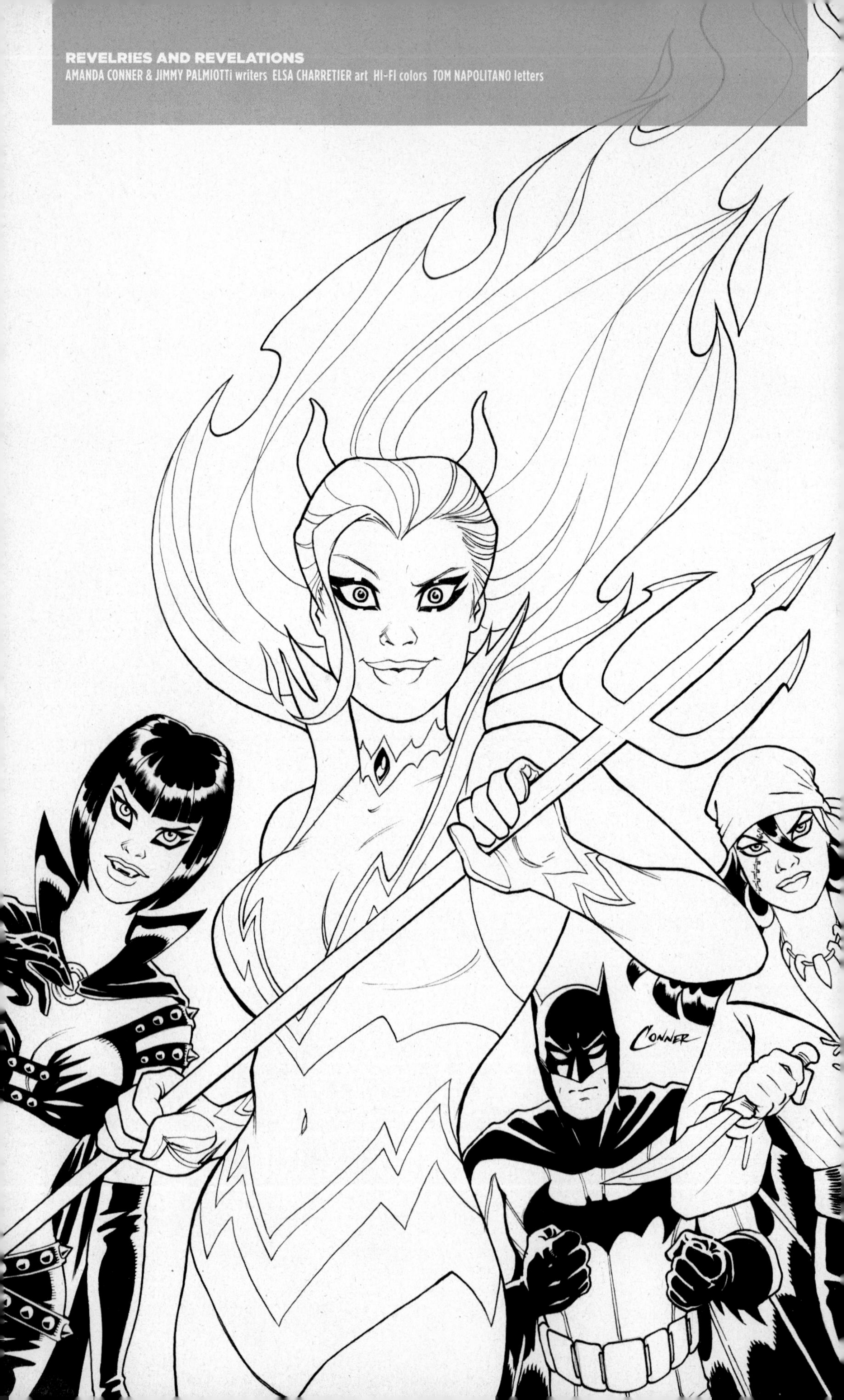
CONNER

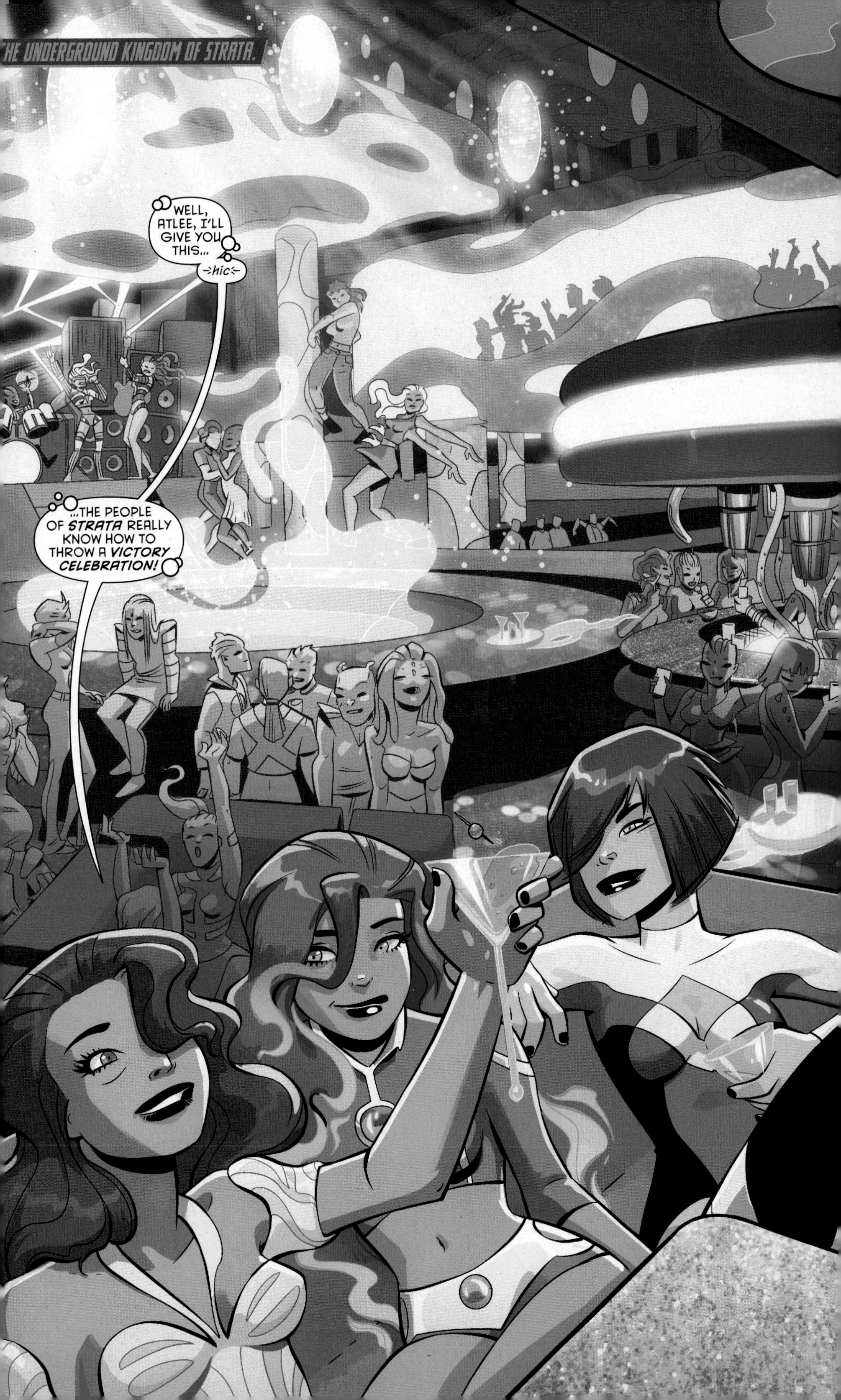
THE UNDERGROUND KINGDOM OF STRATA.
WELL, ATLEE, I'LL GIVE YOU THIS...
hic
...THE PEOPLE OF STRATA REALLY KNOW HOW TO THROW A VICTORY CELEBRATION!

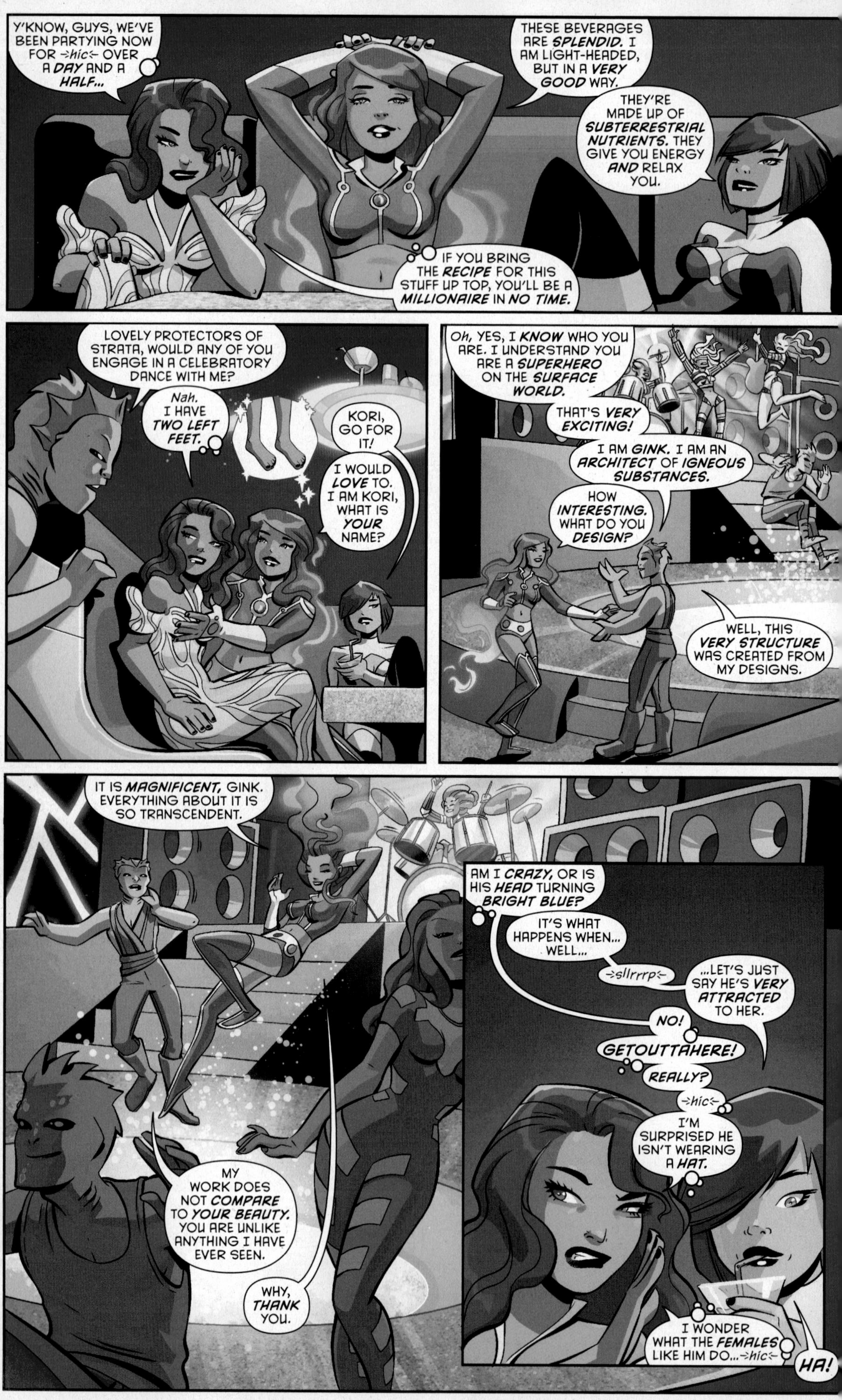

Y'KNOW, GUYS, WE'VE BEEN PARTYING NOW FOR ⇢hic⇠ OVER A DAY AND A HALF...
THESE BEVERAGES ARE SPLENDID. I AM LIGHT-HEADED, BUT IN A VERY GOOD WAY.
THEY'RE MADE UP OF SUBTERRESTRIAL NUTRIENTS. THEY GIVE YOU ENERGY AND RELAX YOU.
IF YOU BRING THE RECIPE FOR THIS STUFF UP TOP, YOU'LL BE A MILLIONAIRE IN NO TIME.
LOVELY PROTECTORS OF STRATA, WOULD ANY OF YOU ENGAGE IN A CELEBRATORY DANCE WITH ME?
Nah. I HAVE TWO LEFT FEET.
KORI, GO FOR IT!
I WOULD LOVE TO. I AM KORI, WHAT IS YOUR NAME?
Oh, YES, I KNOW WHO YOU ARE. I UNDERSTAND YOU ARE A SUPERHERO ON THE SURFACE WORLD.
THAT'S VERY EXCITING!
I AM GINK. I AM AN ARCHITECT OF IGNEOUS SUBSTANCES.
HOW INTERESTING. WHAT DO YOU DESIGN?
WELL, THIS VERY STRUCTURE WAS CREATED FROM MY DESIGNS.
IT IS MAGNIFICENT, GINK. EVERYTHING ABOUT IT IS SO TRANSCENDENT.
MY WORK DOES NOT COMPARE TO YOUR BEAUTY. YOU ARE UNLIKE ANYTHING I HAVE EVER SEEN.
WHY, THANK YOU.
AM I CRAZY, OR IS HIS HEAD TURNING BRIGHT BLUE?
IT'S WHAT HAPPENS WHEN... WELL...
⇢sllrrrp⇠
...LET'S JUST SAY HE'S VERY ATTRACTED TO HER.
NO!
GETOUTTAHERE!
REALLY?
⇢hic⇠
I'M SURPRISED HE ISN'T WEARING A HAT.
I WONDER WHAT THE FEMALES LIKE HIM DO...⇢hic⇠
HA!

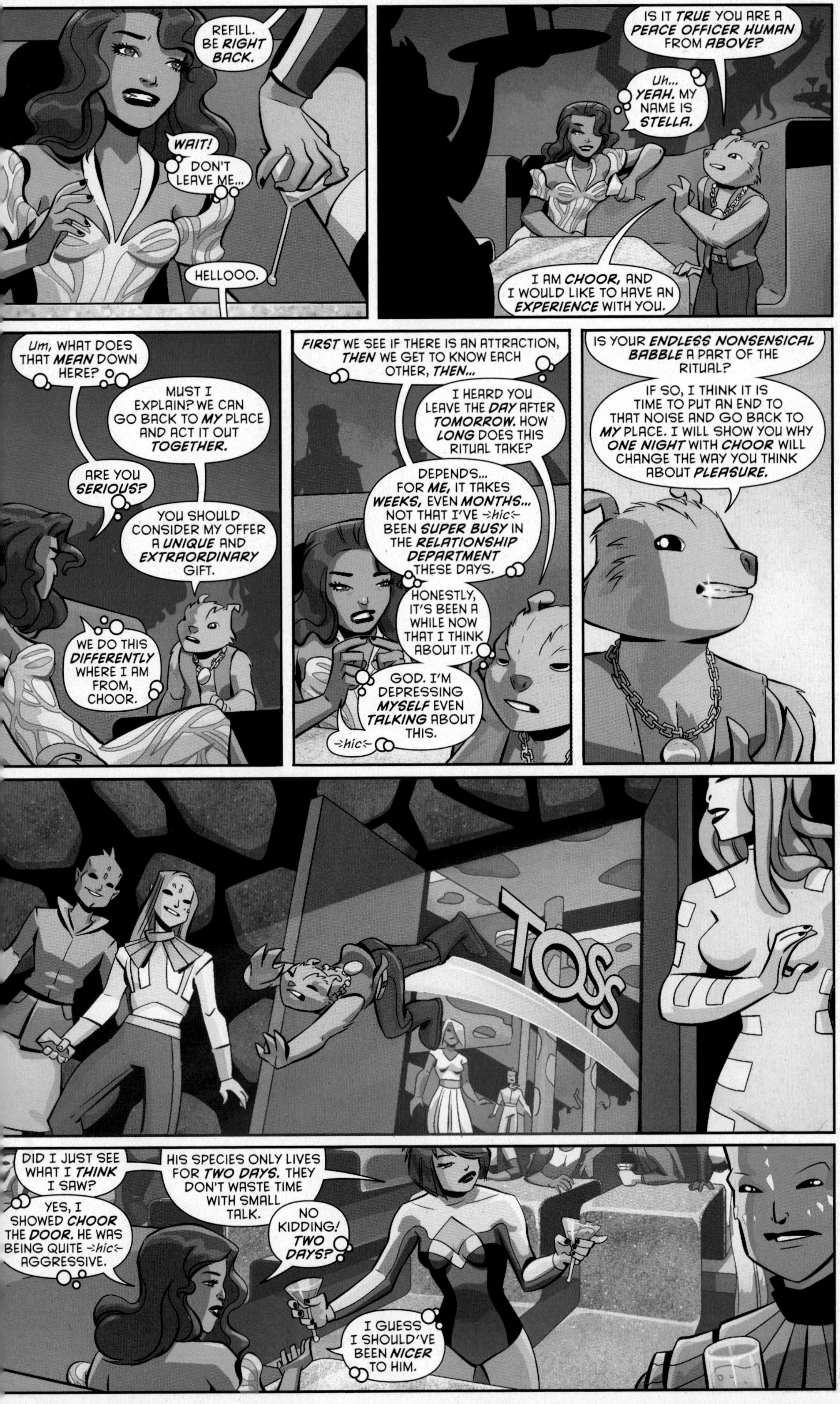
REFILL. BE RIGHT BACK.
WAIT!
DON'T LEAVE ME...
HELLOOO.
IS IT TRUE YOU ARE A PEACE OFFICER HUMAN FROM ABOVE?
Uh... YEAH. MY NAME IS STELLA.
I AM CHOOR, AND I WOULD LIKE TO HAVE AN EXPERIENCE WITH YOU.
Um, WHAT DOES THAT MEAN DOWN HERE?
MUST I EXPLAIN? WE CAN GO BACK TO MY PLACE AND ACT IT OUT TOGETHER.
ARE YOU SERIOUS?
YOU SHOULD CONSIDER MY OFFER A UNIQUE AND EXTRAORDINARY GIFT.
WE DO THIS DIFFERENTLY WHERE I AM FROM, CHOOR.
FIRST WE SEE IF THERE IS AN ATTRACTION, THEN WE GET TO KNOW EACH OTHER, THEN...
I HEARD YOU LEAVE THE DAY AFTER TOMORROW. HOW LONG DOES THIS RITUAL TAKE?
DEPENDS... FOR ME, IT TAKES WEEKS, EVEN MONTHS... NOT THAT I'VE ->hic<- BEEN SUPER BUSY IN THE RELATIONSHIP DEPARTMENT THESE DAYS.
HONESTLY, IT'S BEEN A WHILE NOW THAT I THINK ABOUT IT.
GOD. I'M DEPRESSING MYSELF EVEN TALKING ABOUT THIS.
->hic<-
IS YOUR ENDLESS NONSENSICAL BABBLE A PART OF THE RITUAL?
IF SO, I THINK IT IS TIME TO PUT AN END TO THAT NOISE AND GO BACK TO MY PLACE. I WILL SHOW YOU WHY ONE NIGHT WITH CHOOR WILL CHANGE THE WAY YOU THINK ABOUT PLEASURE.
TOSS
DID I JUST SEE WHAT I THINK I SAW?
YES, I SHOWED CHOOR THE DOOR. HE WAS BEING QUITE ->hic<- AGGRESSIVE.
HIS SPECIES ONLY LIVES FOR TWO DAYS. THEY DON'T WASTE TIME WITH SMALL TALK.
NO KIDDING! TWO DAYS?
I GUESS I SHOULD'VE BEEN NICER TO HIM.

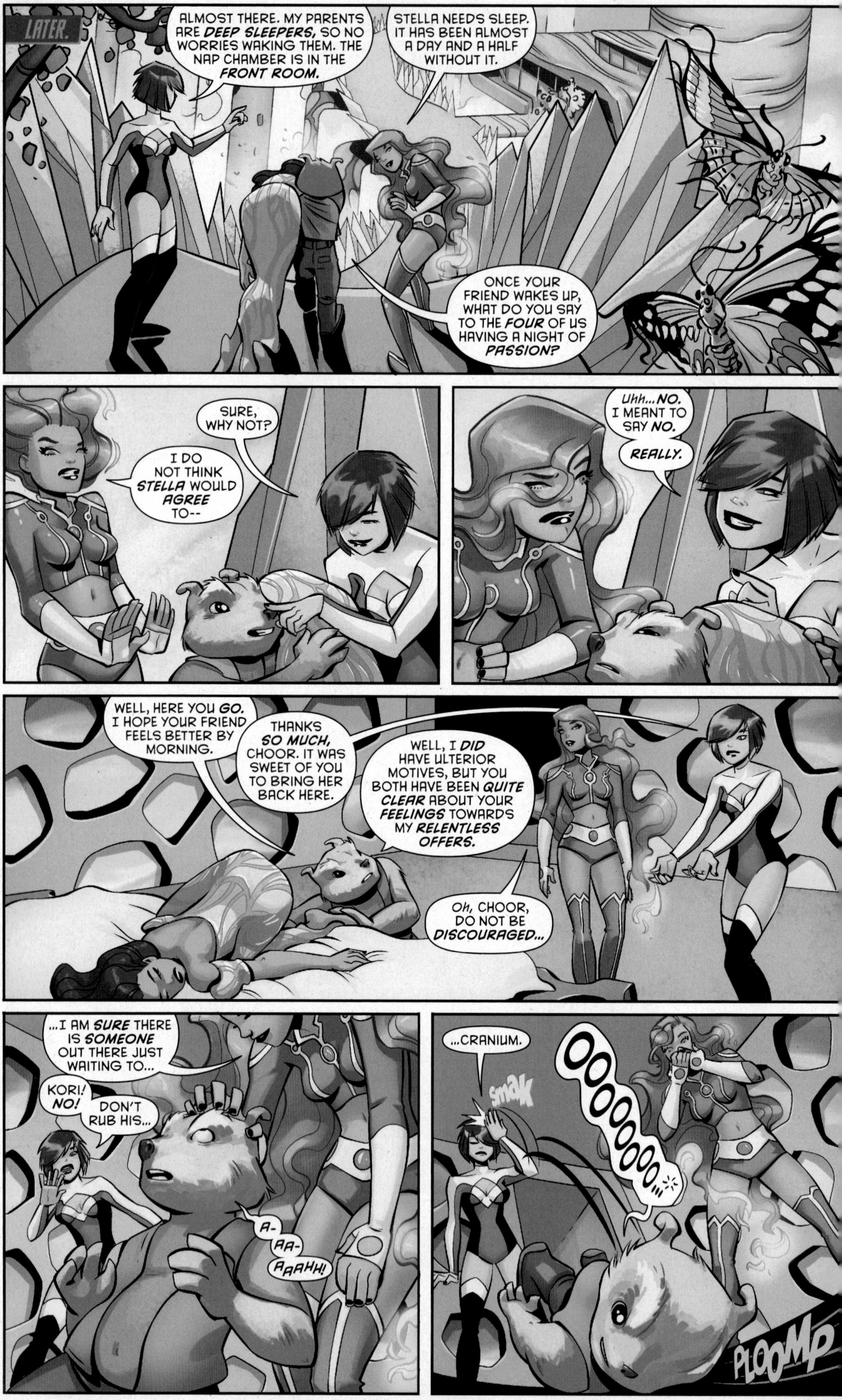
LATER.
ALMOST THERE. MY PARENTS ARE DEEP SLEEPERS, SO NO WORRIES WAKING THEM. THE NAP CHAMBER IS IN THE FRONT ROOM.
STELLA NEEDS SLEEP. IT HAS BEEN ALMOST A DAY AND A HALF WITHOUT IT.
ONCE YOUR FRIEND WAKES UP, WHAT DO YOU SAY TO THE FOUR OF US HAVING A NIGHT OF PASSION?
SURE, WHY NOT?
I DO NOT THINK STELLA WOULD AGREE TO--
UHH...NO. I MEANT TO SAY NO.
REALLY.
WELL, HERE YOU GO. I HOPE YOUR FRIEND FEELS BETTER BY MORNING.
THANKS SO MUCH, CHOOR. IT WAS SWEET OF YOU TO BRING HER BACK HERE.
WELL, I DID HAVE ULTERIOR MOTIVES, BUT YOU BOTH HAVE BEEN QUITE CLEAR ABOUT YOUR FEELINGS TOWARDS MY RELENTLESS OFFERS.
OH, CHOOR, DO NOT BE DISCOURAGED...
...I AM SURE THERE IS SOMEONE OUT THERE JUST WAITING TO...
KORI! NO!
DON'T RUB HIS...
A- AA- AAAHH!
...CRANIUM.
SMAK
OOOOOOO...!
PLOOMP

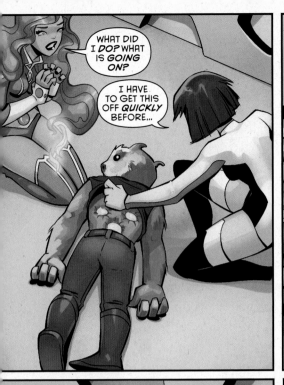

WHAT DID I *DO*? WHAT IS *GOING ON*?

I HAVE TO GET THIS OFF *QUICKLY* BEFORE...

???

DON'T LET THEM HIT THE GROUND! THEY'RE *DELICATE*!

POP! POP! POIT! POP! POIT!

ATLEE, WHAT JUST *HAPPENED*?

WAIT FOR IT...

mama mama mama mama mama

HAHAHAAHAHAHA

mama mama mama mama mama

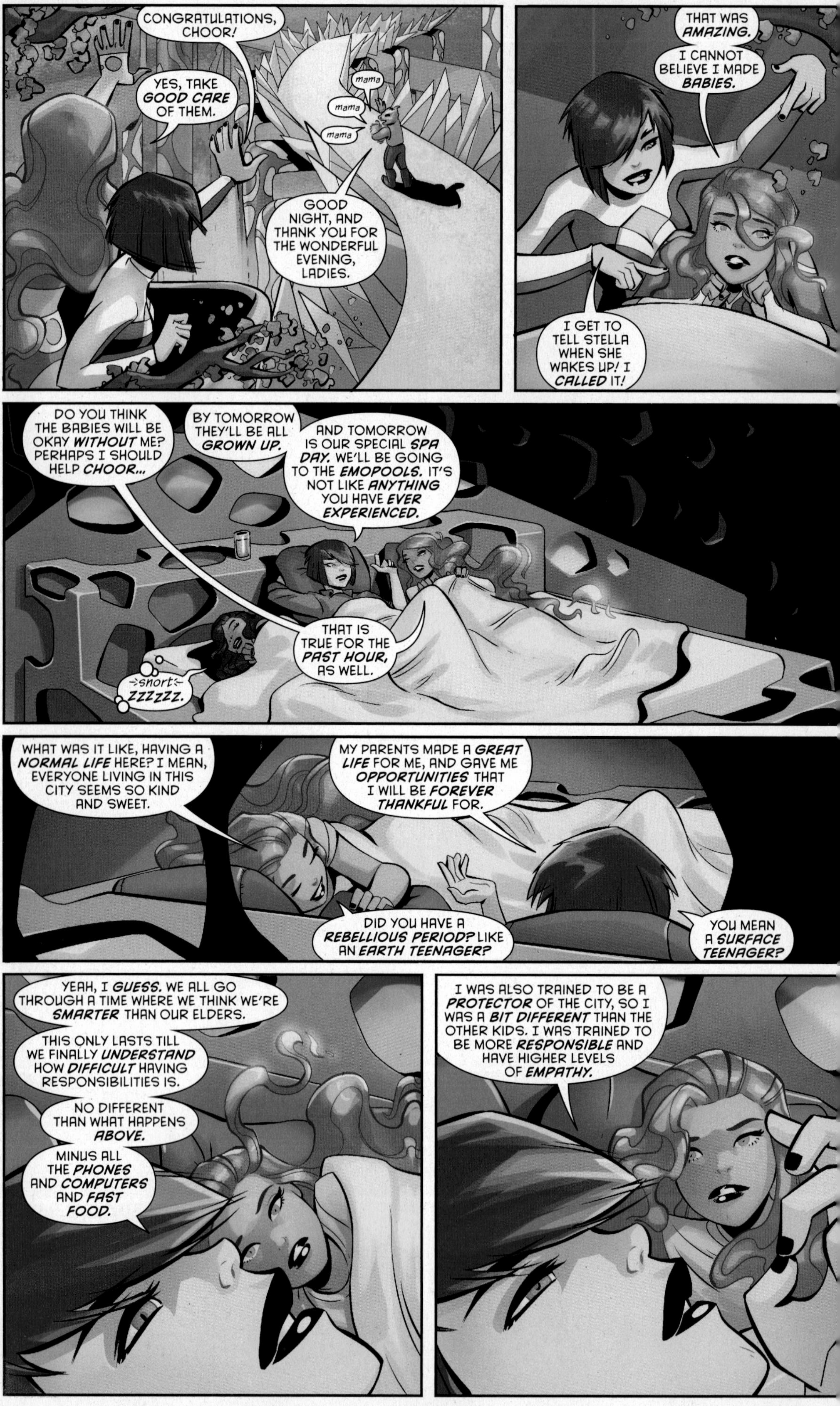

CONGRATULATIONS, CHOOR!
YES, TAKE GOOD CARE OF THEM.
mama
mama
mama
GOOD NIGHT, AND THANK YOU FOR THE WONDERFUL EVENING, LADIES.
THAT WAS AMAZING.
I CANNOT BELIEVE I MADE BABIES.
I GET TO TELL STELLA WHEN SHE WAKES UP! I CALLED IT!
DO YOU THINK THE BABIES WILL BE OKAY WITHOUT ME? PERHAPS I SHOULD HELP CHOOR...
BY TOMORROW THEY'LL BE ALL GROWN UP.
AND TOMORROW IS OUR SPECIAL SPA DAY. WE'LL BE GOING TO THE EMOPOOLS. IT'S NOT LIKE ANYTHING YOU HAVE EVER EXPERIENCED.
THAT IS TRUE FOR THE PAST HOUR, AS WELL.
snort ZZZZZZ.
WHAT WAS IT LIKE, HAVING A NORMAL LIFE HERE? I MEAN, EVERYONE LIVING IN THIS CITY SEEMS SO KIND AND SWEET.
MY PARENTS MADE A GREAT LIFE FOR ME, AND GAVE ME OPPORTUNITIES THAT I WILL BE FOREVER THANKFUL FOR.
DID YOU HAVE A REBELLIOUS PERIOD? LIKE AN EARTH TEENAGER?
YOU MEAN A SURFACE TEENAGER?
YEAH, I GUESS. WE ALL GO THROUGH A TIME WHERE WE THINK WE'RE SMARTER THAN OUR ELDERS.
THIS ONLY LASTS TILL WE FINALLY UNDERSTAND HOW DIFFICULT HAVING RESPONSIBILITIES IS.
NO DIFFERENT THAN WHAT HAPPENS ABOVE.
MINUS ALL THE PHONES AND COMPUTERS AND FAST FOOD.
I WAS ALSO TRAINED TO BE A PROTECTOR OF THE CITY, SO I WAS A BIT DIFFERENT THAN THE OTHER KIDS. I WAS TRAINED TO BE MORE RESPONSIBLE AND HAVE HIGHER LEVELS OF EMPATHY.

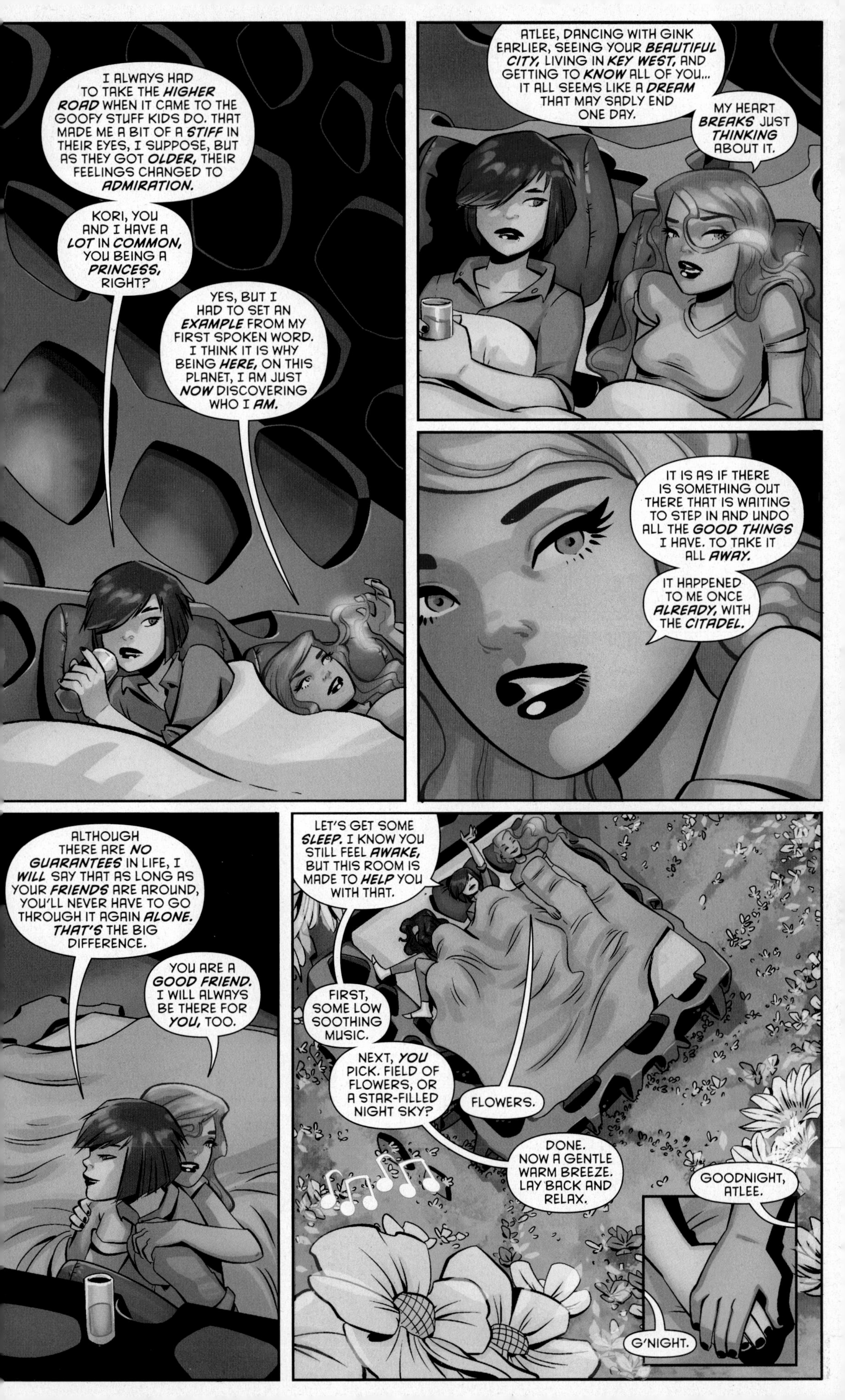
I ALWAYS HAD TO TAKE THE HIGHER ROAD WHEN IT CAME TO THE GOOFY STUFF KIDS DO. THAT MADE ME A BIT OF A STIFF IN THEIR EYES, I SUPPOSE, BUT AS THEY GOT OLDER, THEIR FEELINGS CHANGED TO ADMIRATION.
KORI, YOU AND I HAVE A LOT IN COMMON, YOU BEING A PRINCESS, RIGHT?
YES, BUT I HAD TO SET AN EXAMPLE FROM MY FIRST SPOKEN WORD. I THINK IT IS WHY BEING HERE, ON THIS PLANET, I AM JUST NOW DISCOVERING WHO I AM.
ATLEE, DANCING WITH GINK EARLIER, SEEING YOUR BEAUTIFUL CITY, LIVING IN KEY WEST, AND GETTING TO KNOW ALL OF YOU... IT ALL SEEMS LIKE A DREAM THAT MAY SADLY END ONE DAY.
MY HEART BREAKS JUST THINKING ABOUT IT.
IT IS AS IF THERE IS SOMETHING OUT THERE THAT IS WAITING TO STEP IN AND UNDO ALL THE GOOD THINGS I HAVE. TO TAKE IT ALL AWAY.
IT HAPPENED TO ME ONCE ALREADY, WITH THE CITADEL.
ALTHOUGH THERE ARE NO GUARANTEES IN LIFE, I WILL SAY THAT AS LONG AS YOUR FRIENDS ARE AROUND, YOU'LL NEVER HAVE TO GO THROUGH IT AGAIN ALONE. THAT'S THE BIG DIFFERENCE.
YOU ARE A GOOD FRIEND. I WILL ALWAYS BE THERE FOR YOU, TOO.
LET'S GET SOME SLEEP. I KNOW YOU STILL FEEL AWAKE, BUT THIS ROOM IS MADE TO HELP YOU WITH THAT.
FIRST, SOME LOW SOOTHING MUSIC.
NEXT, YOU PICK. FIELD OF FLOWERS, OR A STAR-FILLED NIGHT SKY?
FLOWERS.
DONE. NOW A GENTLE WARM BREEZE. LAY BACK AND RELAX.
GOODNIGHT, ATLEE.
G'NIGHT.

Friendly Abduction.

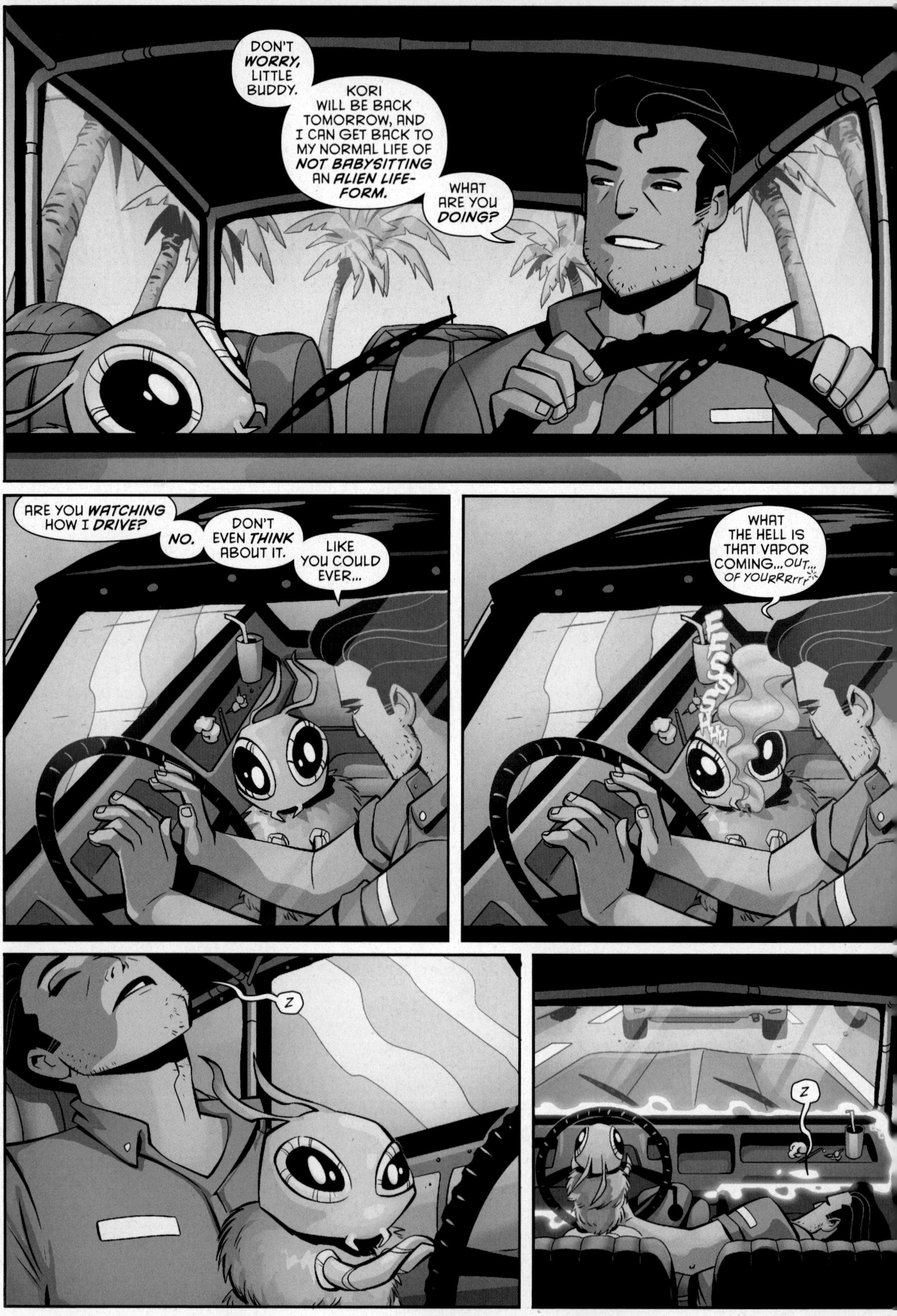

DON'T WORRY, LITTLE BUDDY.
KORI WILL BE BACK TOMORROW, AND I CAN GET BACK TO MY NORMAL LIFE OF NOT BABYSITTING AN ALIEN LIFE-FORM.
WHAT ARE YOU DOING?
ARE YOU WATCHING HOW I DRIVE?
NO.
DON'T EVEN THINK ABOUT IT.
LIKE YOU COULD EVER...
WHAT THE HELL IS THAT VAPOR COMING...OUT... OF YOURRRrrr
Z
Z

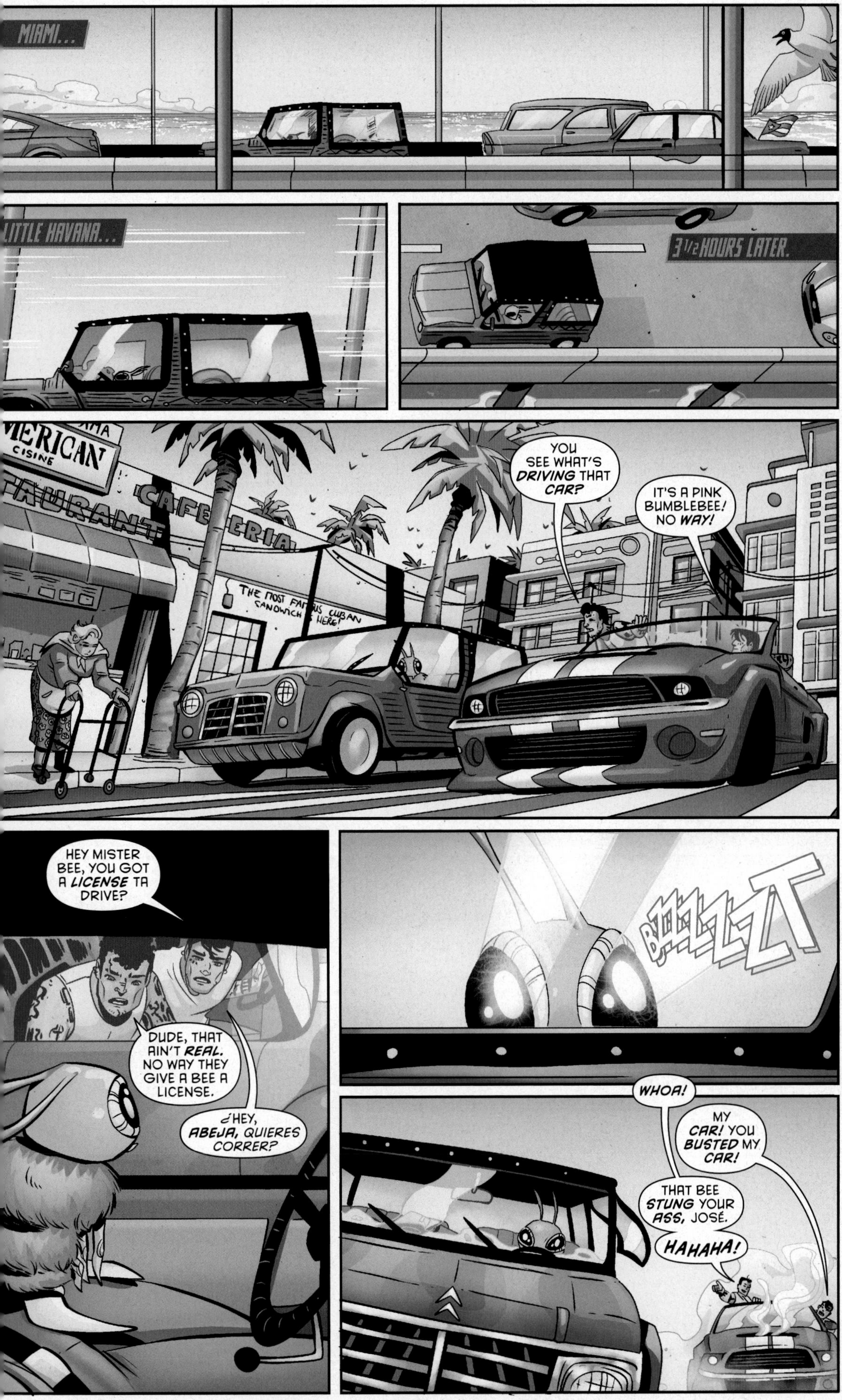

MIAMI...
LITTLE HAVANA...
3 1/2 HOURS LATER.
MERICAN
CISINE
CAFETERIA
THE MOST FAMOUS CUBAN SANDWICH IS HERE!
YOU SEE WHAT'S DRIVING THAT CAR?
IT'S A PINK BUMBLEBEE! NO WAY!
HEY MISTER BEE, YOU GOT A LICENSE TA DRIVE?
DUDE, THAT AIN'T REAL. NO WAY THEY GIVE A BEE A LICENSE.
¿HEY, ABEJA, QUIERES CORRER?
BZZZZT
WHOA!
MY CAR! YOU BUSTED MY CAR!
THAT BEE STUNG YOUR ASS, JOSÉ.
HAHAHA!

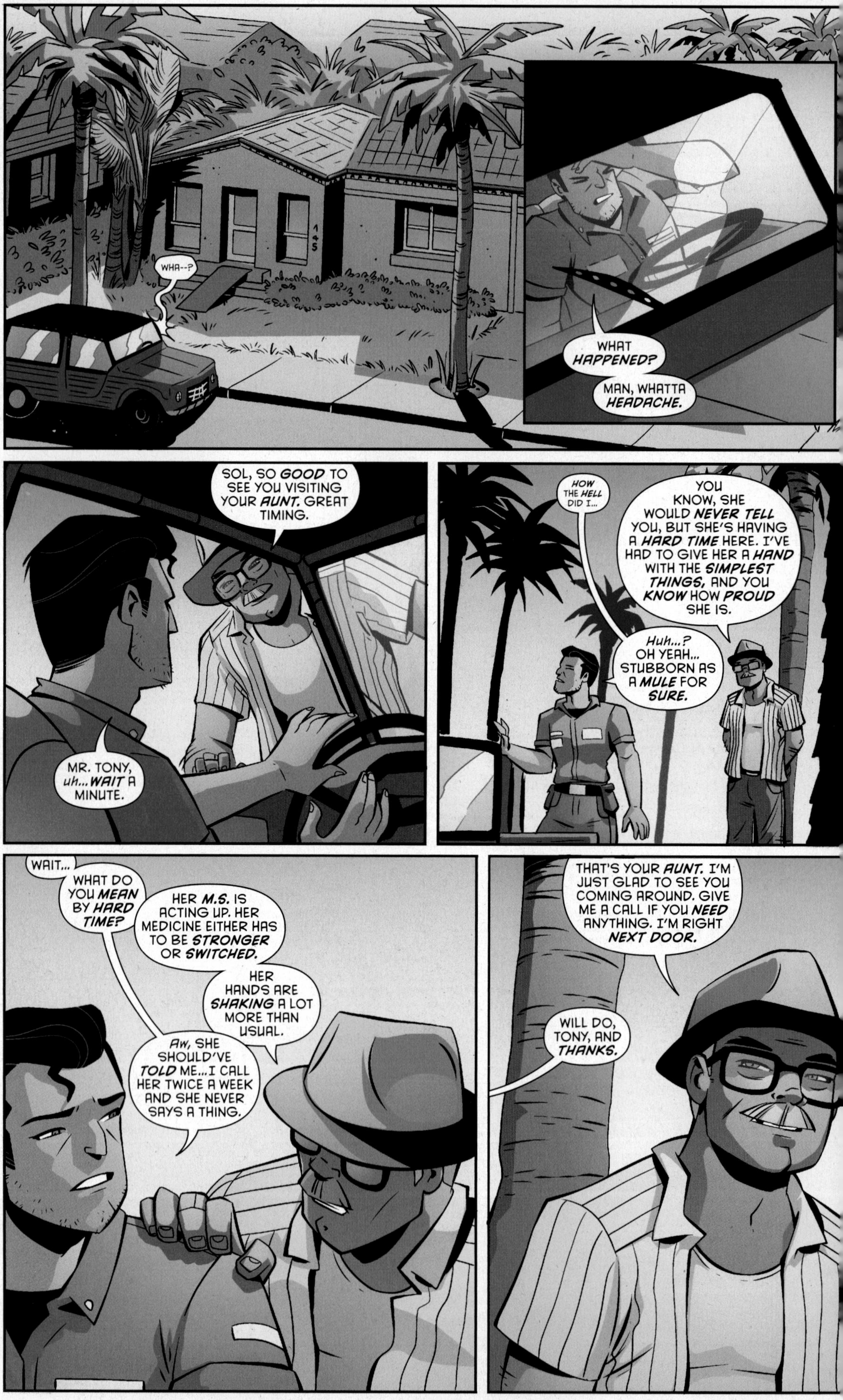
WHA--?
WHAT HAPPENED?
MAN, WHATTA HEADACHE.
SOL, SO GOOD TO SEE YOU VISITING YOUR AUNT. GREAT TIMING.
MR. TONY, uh...WAIT A MINUTE.
HOW THE HELL DID I...
YOU KNOW, SHE WOULD NEVER TELL YOU, BUT SHE'S HAVING A HARD TIME HERE. I'VE HAD TO GIVE HER A HAND WITH THE SIMPLEST THINGS, AND YOU KNOW HOW PROUD SHE IS.
Huh...? OH YEAH... STUBBORN AS A MULE FOR SURE.
WAIT...
WHAT DO YOU MEAN BY HARD TIME?
HER M.S. IS ACTING UP. HER MEDICINE EITHER HAS TO BE STRONGER OR SWITCHED.
HER HANDS ARE SHAKING A LOT MORE THAN USUAL.
Aw, SHE SHOULD'VE TOLD ME...I CALL HER TWICE A WEEK AND SHE NEVER SAYS A THING.
THAT'S YOUR AUNT. I'M JUST GLAD TO SEE YOU COMING AROUND. GIVE ME A CALL IF YOU NEED ANYTHING. I'M RIGHT NEXT DOOR.
WILL DO, TONY, AND THANKS.

Support Spa.

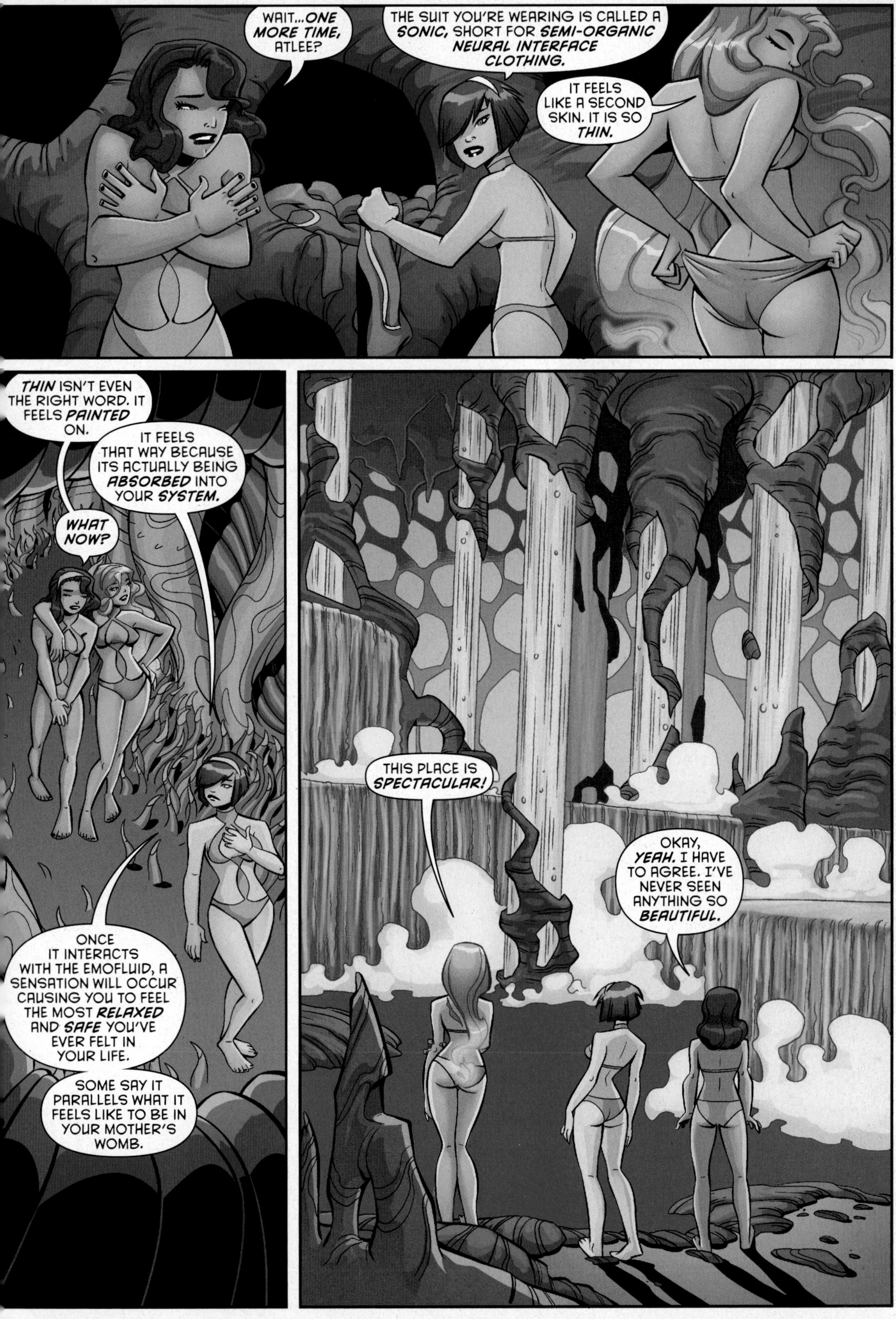
WAIT...ONE MORE TIME, ATLEE?
THE SUIT YOU'RE WEARING IS CALLED A SONIC, SHORT FOR SEMI-ORGANIC NEURAL INTERFACE CLOTHING.
IT FEELS LIKE A SECOND SKIN. IT IS SO THIN.
THIN ISN'T EVEN THE RIGHT WORD. IT FEELS PAINTED ON.
IT FEELS THAT WAY BECAUSE ITS ACTUALLY BEING ABSORBED INTO YOUR SYSTEM.
WHAT NOW?
ONCE IT INTERACTS WITH THE EMOFLUID, A SENSATION WILL OCCUR CAUSING YOU TO FEEL THE MOST RELAXED AND SAFE YOU'VE EVER FELT IN YOUR LIFE.
SOME SAY IT PARALLELS WHAT IT FEELS LIKE TO BE IN YOUR MOTHER'S WOMB.
THIS PLACE IS SPECTACULAR!
OKAY, YEAH. I HAVE TO AGREE. I'VE NEVER SEEN ANYTHING SO BEAUTIFUL.

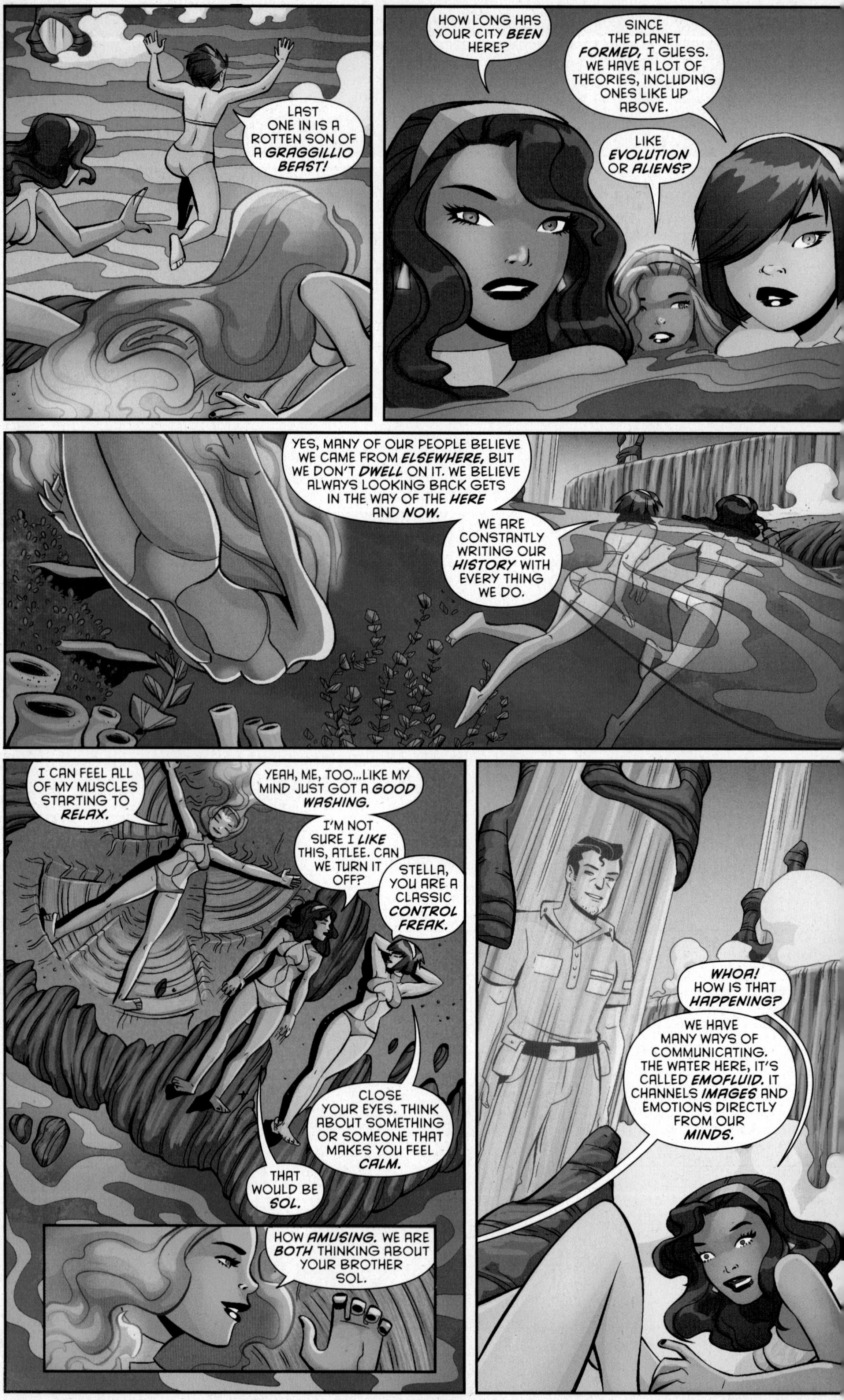
LAST ONE IN IS A ROTTEN SON OF A GRAGGILLIO BEAST!
HOW LONG HAS YOUR CITY BEEN HERE?
SINCE THE PLANET FORMED, I GUESS. WE HAVE A LOT OF THEORIES, INCLUDING ONES LIKE UP ABOVE.
LIKE EVOLUTION OR ALIENS?
YES, MANY OF OUR PEOPLE BELIEVE WE CAME FROM ELSEWHERE, BUT WE DON'T DWELL ON IT. WE BELIEVE ALWAYS LOOKING BACK GETS IN THE WAY OF THE HERE AND NOW.
WE ARE CONSTANTLY WRITING OUR HISTORY WITH EVERY THING WE DO.
I CAN FEEL ALL OF MY MUSCLES STARTING TO RELAX.
YEAH, ME, TOO...LIKE MY MIND JUST GOT A GOOD WASHING.
I'M NOT SURE I LIKE THIS, ATLEE. CAN WE TURN IT OFF?
STELLA, YOU ARE A CLASSIC CONTROL FREAK.
CLOSE YOUR EYES. THINK ABOUT SOMETHING OR SOMEONE THAT MAKES YOU FEEL CALM.
THAT WOULD BE SOL.
HOW AMUSING. WE ARE BOTH THINKING ABOUT YOUR BROTHER SOL.
WHOA! HOW IS THAT HAPPENING?
WE HAVE MANY WAYS OF COMMUNICATING. THE WATER HERE, IT'S CALLED EMOFLUID. IT CHANNELS IMAGES AND EMOTIONS DIRECTLY FROM OUR MINDS.

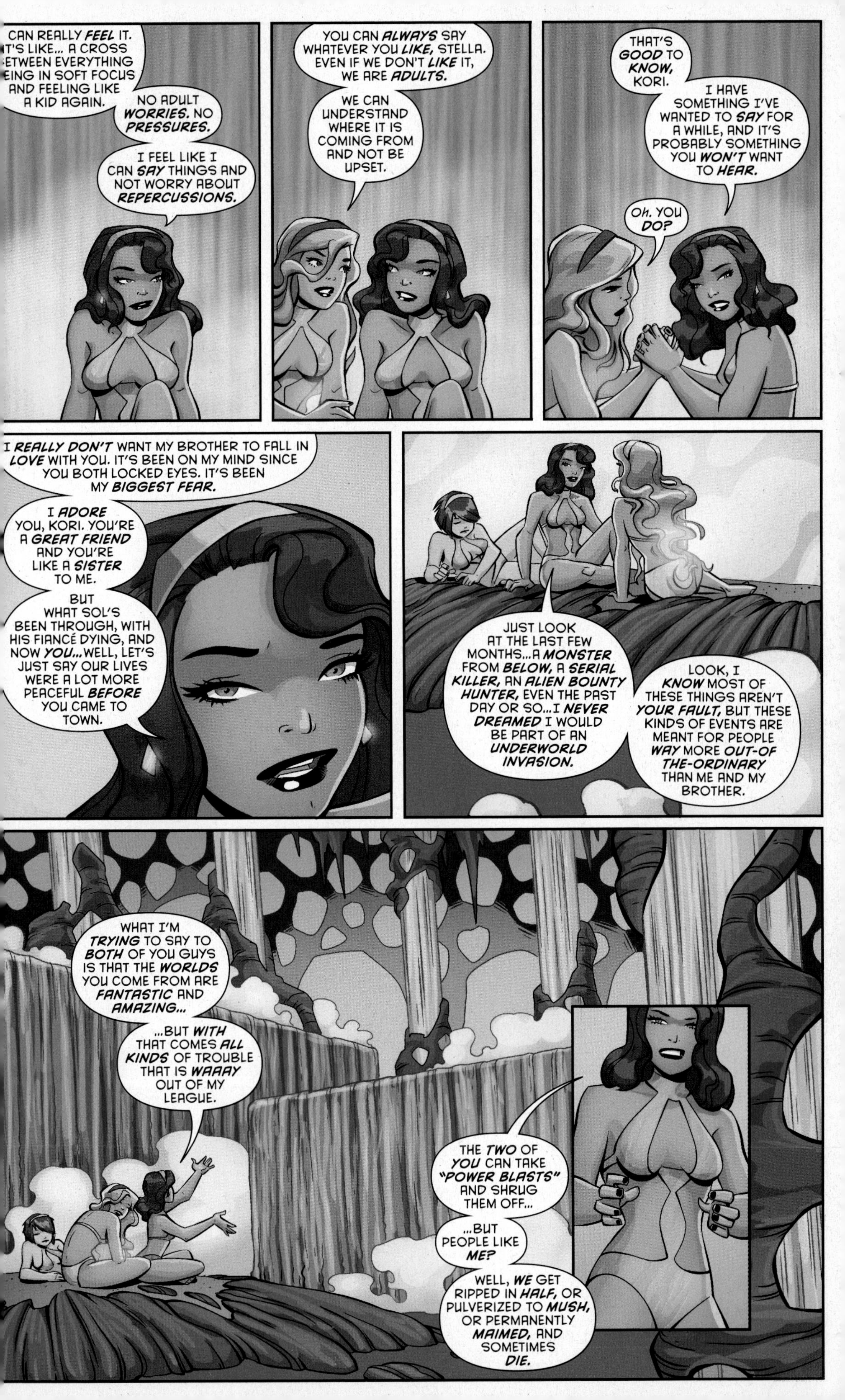

CAN REALLY FEEL IT. IT'S LIKE... A CROSS BETWEEN EVERYTHING BEING IN SOFT FOCUS AND FEELING LIKE A KID AGAIN.
NO ADULT WORRIES. NO PRESSURES.
I FEEL LIKE I CAN SAY THINGS AND NOT WORRY ABOUT REPERCUSSIONS.
YOU CAN ALWAYS SAY WHATEVER YOU LIKE, STELLA. EVEN IF WE DON'T LIKE IT, WE ARE ADULTS.
WE CAN UNDERSTAND WHERE IT IS COMING FROM AND NOT BE UPSET.
THAT'S GOOD TO KNOW, KORI.
I HAVE SOMETHING I'VE WANTED TO SAY FOR A WHILE, AND IT'S PROBABLY SOMETHING YOU WON'T WANT TO HEAR.
Oh. YOU DO?
I REALLY DON'T WANT MY BROTHER TO FALL IN LOVE WITH YOU. IT'S BEEN ON MY MIND SINCE YOU BOTH LOCKED EYES. IT'S BEEN MY BIGGEST FEAR.
I ADORE YOU, KORI. YOU'RE A GREAT FRIEND AND YOU'RE LIKE A SISTER TO ME.
BUT WHAT SOL'S BEEN THROUGH, WITH HIS FIANCÉ DYING, AND NOW YOU... WELL, LET'S JUST SAY OUR LIVES WERE A LOT MORE PEACEFUL BEFORE YOU CAME TO TOWN.
JUST LOOK AT THE LAST FEW MONTHS... A MONSTER FROM BELOW, A SERIAL KILLER, AN ALIEN BOUNTY HUNTER, EVEN THE PAST DAY OR SO... I NEVER DREAMED I WOULD BE PART OF AN UNDERWORLD INVASION.
LOOK, I KNOW MOST OF THESE THINGS AREN'T YOUR FAULT, BUT THESE KINDS OF EVENTS ARE MEANT FOR PEOPLE WAY MORE OUT-OF THE-ORDINARY THAN ME AND MY BROTHER.
WHAT I'M TRYING TO SAY TO BOTH OF YOU GUYS IS THAT THE WORLDS YOU COME FROM ARE FANTASTIC AND AMAZING...
...BUT WITH THAT COMES ALL KINDS OF TROUBLE THAT IS WAAAY OUT OF MY LEAGUE.
THE TWO OF YOU CAN TAKE "POWER BLASTS" AND SHRUG THEM OFF...
...BUT PEOPLE LIKE ME?
WELL, WE GET RIPPED IN HALF, OR PULVERIZED TO MUSH, OR PERMANENTLY MAIMED, AND SOMETIMES DIE.

I HONESTLY THOUGHT I COULD FIND A PLACE TO JUST BE *MYSELF,* AND PUT THE SUPERHERO CONCERNS *BEHIND* ME.

NOW I REALIZE THE *DANGER* I HAVE PUT EVERYONE IN.

OH, NO. HAVING ME *AROUND* YOU BOTH, *LIVING* WITH YOU, IT PUTS YOU IN *DANGER.*

I FEEL *TERRIBLE* TO HAVE DONE THIS.

HOWEVER, IT IS A VERY RELAXED KIND OF TERRIBLE FEELING.

I'M NOT ASKING YOU TO *LEAVE* AND *FORGET* US, KORI. I'M JUST ASKING THAT MAYBE YOU RECONSIDER YOUR *RELATIONSHIP* WITH MY *BROTHER.*

UNDERSTAND, *YOUR* LIFE IS, WELL...IT'S *EXTRAORDINARY.*

I WOULD *NEVER* ASK YOU TO *STOP* BEING *YOU,* BUT JUST CONSIDER THE *FALLOUT* OF THIS *ONE RELATIONSHIP.*

I KNOW YOU SEE ME AS A *TOUGH, STRONG WOMAN,* BUT IN MY HEART, I'M A SCARED OLDER SISTER TRYING TO HOLD ON TO THE MOST *IMPORTANT PERSON* IN MY *LIFE.*

THE IDEA THAT HE CAN BE PHYSICALLY HURT, OR EVEN *HEARTBROKEN* AGAIN IS *TOO MUCH* FOR ME TO BEAR.

SADLY, I SEE *BOTH* HAPPENING IF HE CONTINUES WITH YOU IN A RELATIONSHIP.

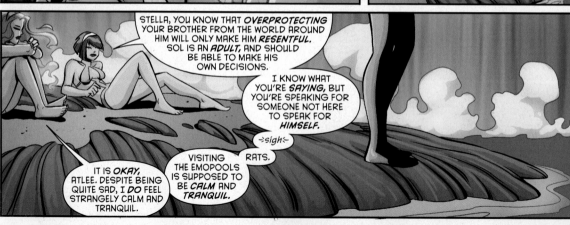

STELLA, YOU KNOW THAT *OVERPROTECTING* YOUR BROTHER FROM THE WORLD AROUND HIM WILL ONLY MAKE HIM *RESENTFUL.* SOL IS AN *ADULT,* AND SHOULD BE ABLE TO MAKE HIS OWN DECISIONS.

I KNOW WHAT YOU'RE *SAYING,* BUT YOU'RE SPEAKING FOR SOMEONE NOT HERE TO SPEAK FOR *HIMSELF.*

-›sigh‹-

RATS.

VISITING THE EMOPOOLS IS SUPPOSED TO BE *CALM* AND *TRANQUIL.*

IT IS *OKAY,* ATLEE. DESPITE BEING QUITE SAD, I *DO* FEEL STRANGELY CALM AND TRANQUIL.

STELLA HAS A *REASON* TO BE WORRIED. IF *ONE* BOUNTY HUNTER FOUND ME, IT IS REALISTIC TO ASSUME *MORE* WILL.

THEY ARE *KILLERS*, NOT CARING *WHO* GETS IN THE WAY TO GET THEIR BUSINESS DONE.

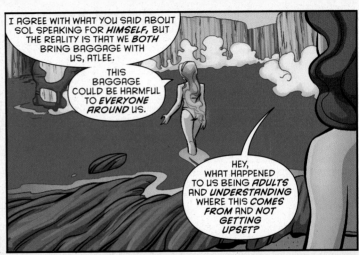

I AGREE WITH WHAT YOU SAID ABOUT SOL SPEAKING FOR *HIMSELF*, BUT THE REALITY IS THAT WE *BOTH* BRING BAGGAGE WITH US, ATLEE.

THIS BAGGAGE COULD BE HARMFUL TO *EVERYONE* AROUND US.

HEY, WHAT HAPPENED TO US BEING *ADULTS* AND *UNDERSTANDING* WHERE THIS *COMES FROM* AND *NOT* GETTING UPSET?

Oh, IT IS OKAY. I AM ONLY A *LITTLE* UPSET, BUT ODDLY IN A VERY *DELIGHTFUL* WAY.

THAT IS BIZZARE, IS IT NOT?

X'HAL, WHAT--?

-glrrrbb-

DID I JUST SEE A *GIANT OCTOPUS THING* GRAB KORI, OR IS THIS CRAZY PLACE CAUSING *HALLUCINATIONS?*

Uh-oh.

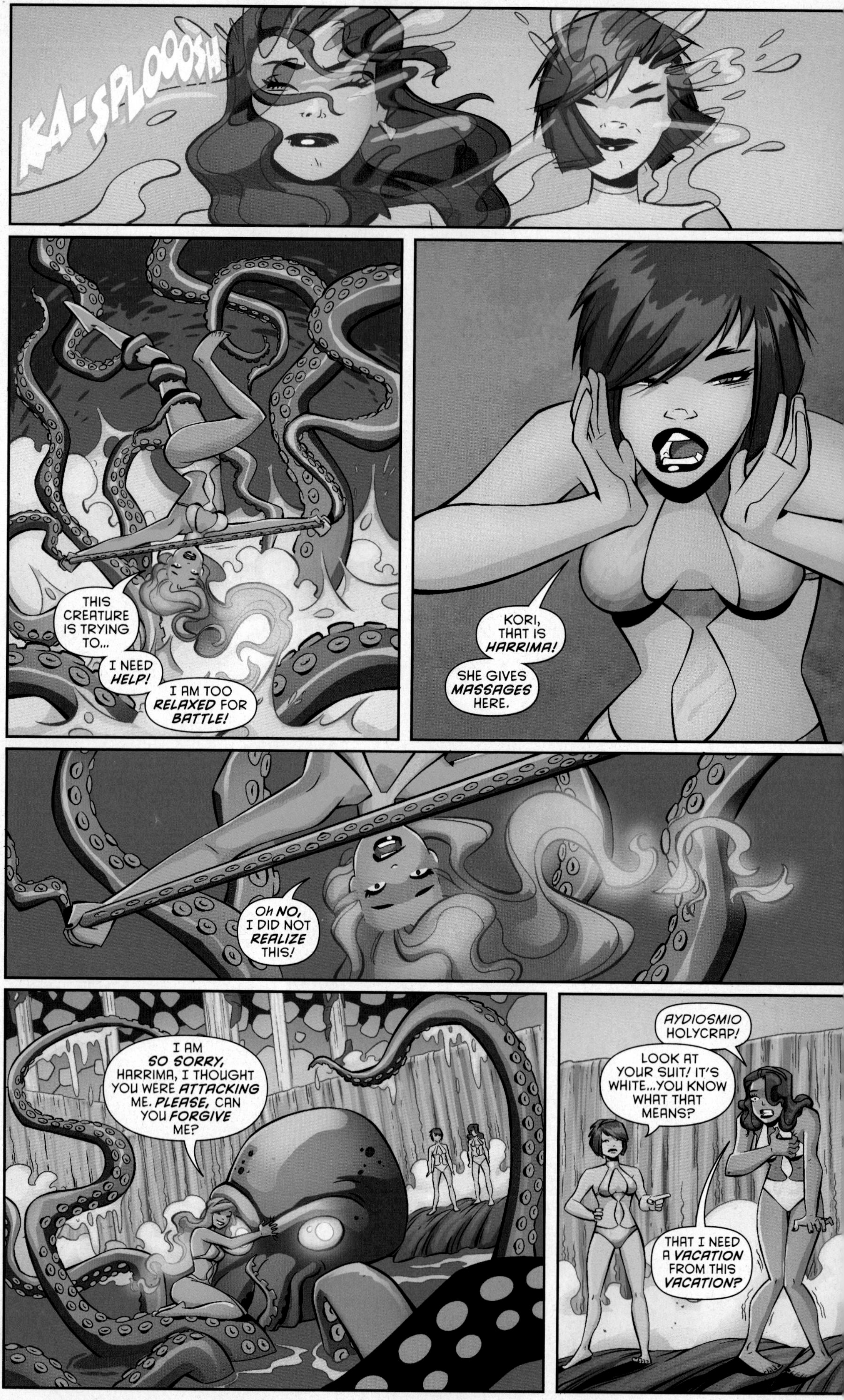
KA-SPLOOOSH!
THIS CREATURE IS TRYING TO...
I NEED HELP!
I AM TOO RELAXED FOR BATTLE!
KORI, THAT IS HARRIMA!
SHE GIVES MASSAGES HERE.
Oh NO, I DID NOT REALIZE THIS!
I AM SO SORRY, HARRIMA, I THOUGHT YOU WERE ATTACKING ME. PLEASE, CAN YOU FORGIVE ME?
AYDIOSMIO HOLYCRAP!
LOOK AT YOUR SUIT! IT'S WHITE...YOU KNOW WHAT THAT MEANS?
THAT I NEED A VACATION FROM THIS VACATION?

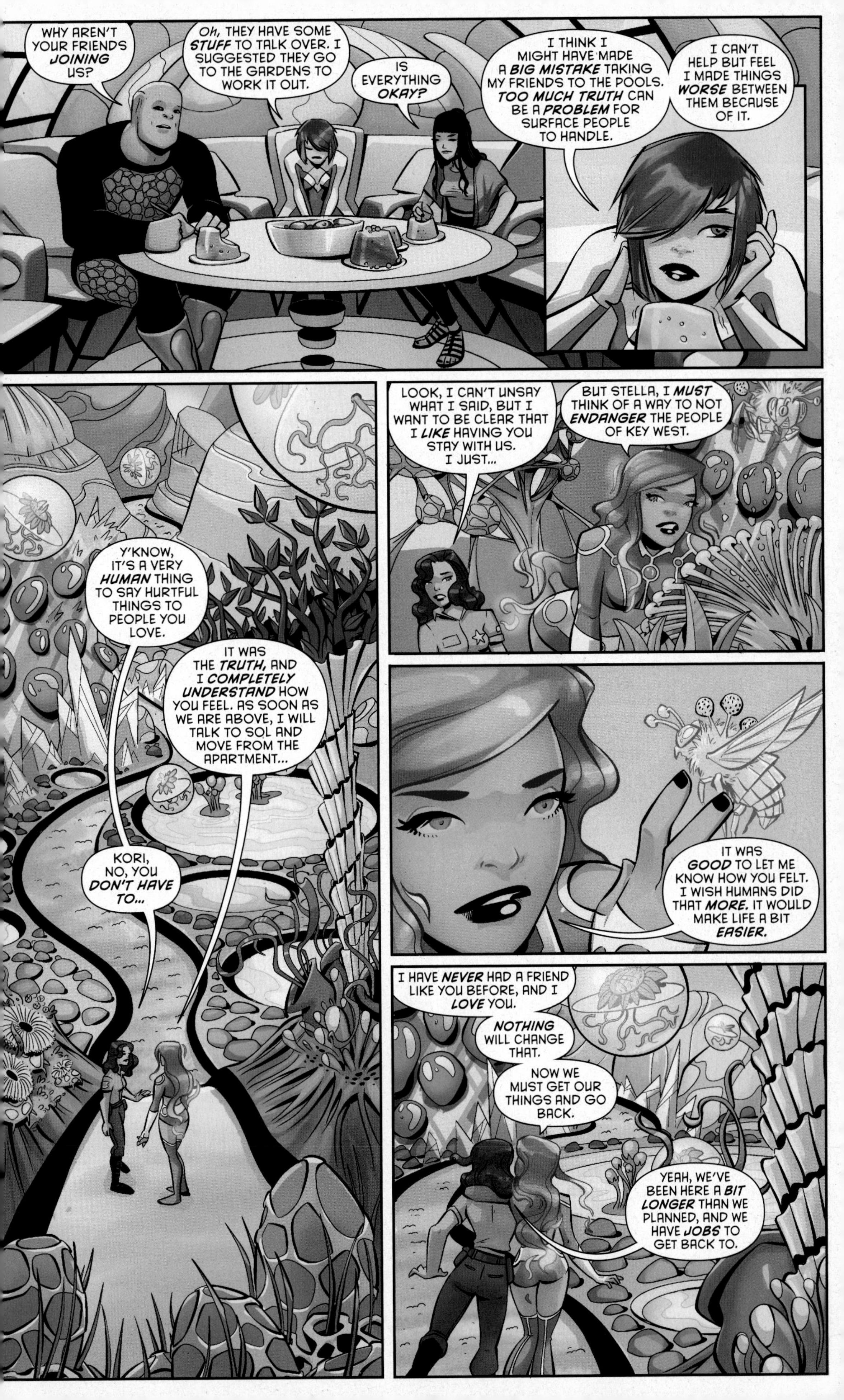
WHY AREN'T YOUR FRIENDS *JOINING* US?
Oh, THEY HAVE SOME *STUFF* TO TALK OVER. I SUGGESTED THEY GO TO THE GARDENS TO WORK IT OUT.
IS EVERYTHING *OKAY?*
I THINK I MIGHT HAVE MADE A *BIG MISTAKE* TAKING MY FRIENDS TO THE POOLS. *TOO MUCH TRUTH* CAN BE A *PROBLEM* FOR SURFACE PEOPLE TO HANDLE.
I CAN'T HELP BUT FEEL I MADE THINGS *WORSE* BETWEEN THEM BECAUSE OF IT.
Y'KNOW, IT'S A VERY *HUMAN* THING TO SAY HURTFUL THINGS TO PEOPLE YOU LOVE.
IT WAS THE *TRUTH,* AND I *COMPLETELY UNDERSTAND* HOW YOU FEEL. AS SOON AS WE ARE ABOVE, I WILL TALK TO SOL AND MOVE FROM THE APARTMENT...
KORI, NO, YOU *DON'T HAVE TO...*
LOOK, I CAN'T UNSAY WHAT I SAID, BUT I WANT TO BE CLEAR THAT I *LIKE* HAVING YOU STAY WITH US. I JUST...
BUT STELLA, I *MUST* THINK OF A WAY TO NOT *ENDANGER* THE PEOPLE OF KEY WEST.
IT WAS *GOOD* TO LET ME KNOW HOW YOU FELT. I WISH HUMANS DID THAT *MORE.* IT WOULD MAKE LIFE A BIT *EASIER.*
I HAVE *NEVER* HAD A FRIEND LIKE YOU BEFORE, AND I *LOVE* YOU.
NOTHING WILL CHANGE THAT.
NOW WE MUST GET OUR THINGS AND GO BACK.
YEAH, WE'VE BEEN HERE A *BIT LONGER* THAN WE PLANNED, AND WE HAVE *JOBS* TO GET BACK TO.

Contrition Expedition.

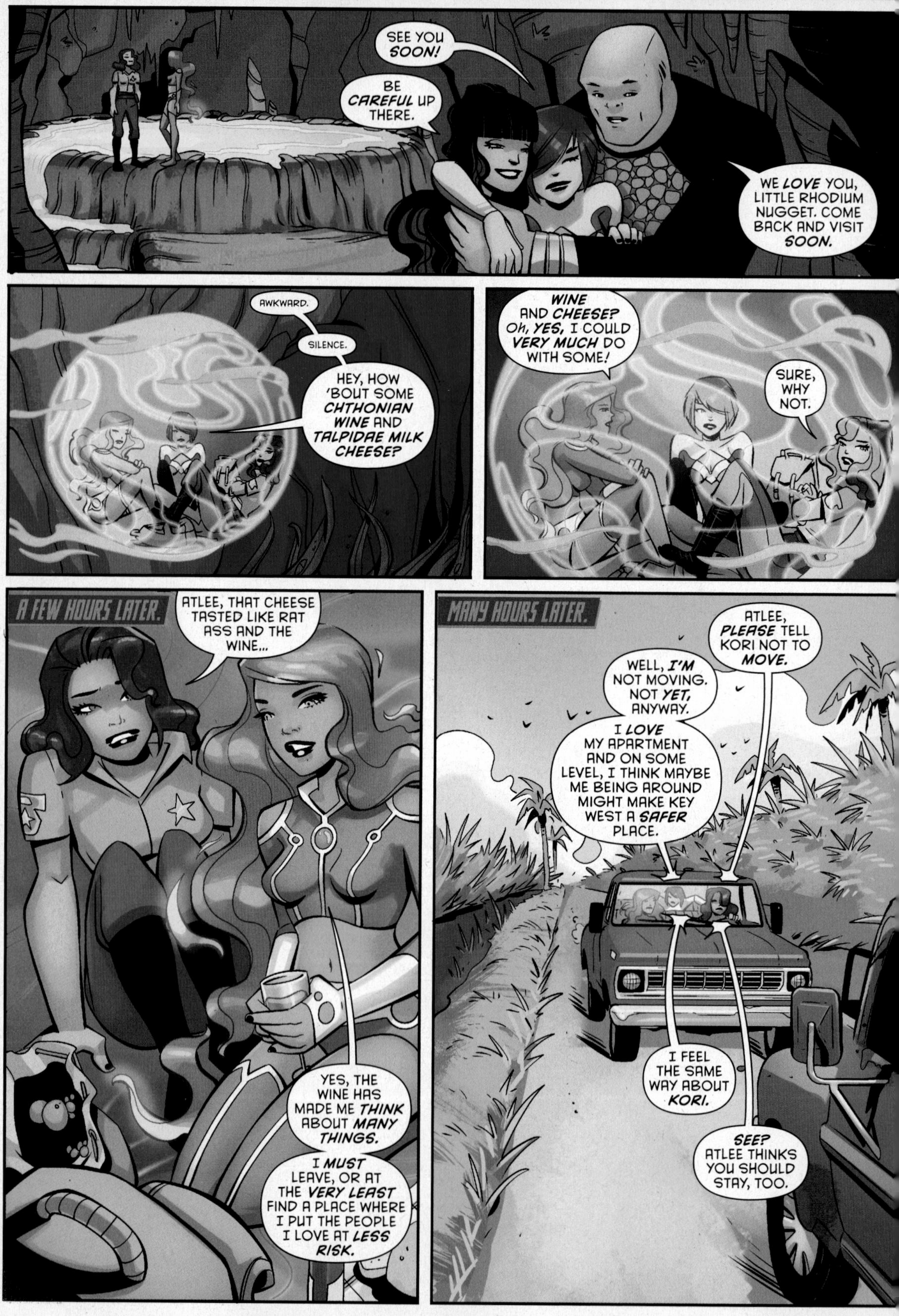
SEE YOU SOON!
BE CAREFUL UP THERE.
WE LOVE YOU, LITTLE RHODIUM NUGGET. COME BACK AND VISIT SOON.
AWKWARD.
SILENCE.
HEY, HOW 'BOUT SOME CHTHONIAN WINE AND TALPIDAE MILK CHEESE?
WINE AND CHEESE? Oh, YES, I COULD VERY MUCH DO WITH SOME!
SURE, WHY NOT.
A FEW HOURS LATER.
ATLEE, THAT CHEESE TASTED LIKE RAT ASS AND THE WINE...
YES, THE WINE HAS MADE ME THINK ABOUT MANY THINGS.
I MUST LEAVE, OR AT THE VERY LEAST FIND A PLACE WHERE I PUT THE PEOPLE I LOVE AT LESS RISK.
MANY HOURS LATER.
WELL, I'M NOT MOVING. NOT YET, ANYWAY.
I LOVE MY APARTMENT AND ON SOME LEVEL, I THINK MAYBE ME BEING AROUND MIGHT MAKE KEY WEST A SAFER PLACE.
ATLEE, PLEASE TELL KORI NOT TO MOVE.
I FEEL THE SAME WAY ABOUT KORI.
SEE? ATLEE THINKS YOU SHOULD STAY, TOO.

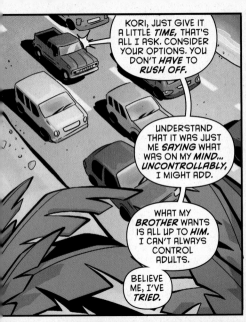

KORI, JUST GIVE IT A LITTLE *TIME*, THAT'S ALL I ASK. CONSIDER YOUR OPTIONS. YOU DON'T *HAVE* TO *RUSH OFF*.

UNDERSTAND THAT IT WAS JUST ME *SAYING* WHAT WAS ON MY *MIND*... *UNCONTROLLABLY*, I MIGHT ADD.

WHAT MY *BROTHER* WANTS IS ALL UP TO *HIM*. I CAN'T ALWAYS CONTROL ADULTS.

BELIEVE ME, I'VE *TRIED*.

Jeez, THERE'S *SO MUCH TRAFFIC*. THERE MUST BE AN *ACCIDENT* UP AHEAD. LEMME CHECK IN AND SEE WHAT'S GOING ON.

HEY, PAPO, IT'S *ME*.

WHAT DO YOU *MEAN* WHERE HAVE I BEEN?

WHAT?

ARE YOU *PULLING* MY LEG?

NO, I HAD *NO* IDEA.

YEAH, SEE YOU *SOON*, I HOPE.

ATLEE, DO YOU WANT TO *TELL ME* SOMETHING?

Uhh... DO I?

THE *TIME RATIO* THING UP *HERE*, VERSUS THE *TIME RATIO* THING *DOWN BELOW*?

Oh. OH! WHOOPS.

WHAT IS THE "WHOOPS"?

THE *TIME*. Oh *NO*. I MISCALCULATED THE *TIME* WE WOULD BE *AWAY*.

SO WE WERE *NOT AWAY* FOR A FEW DAYS?

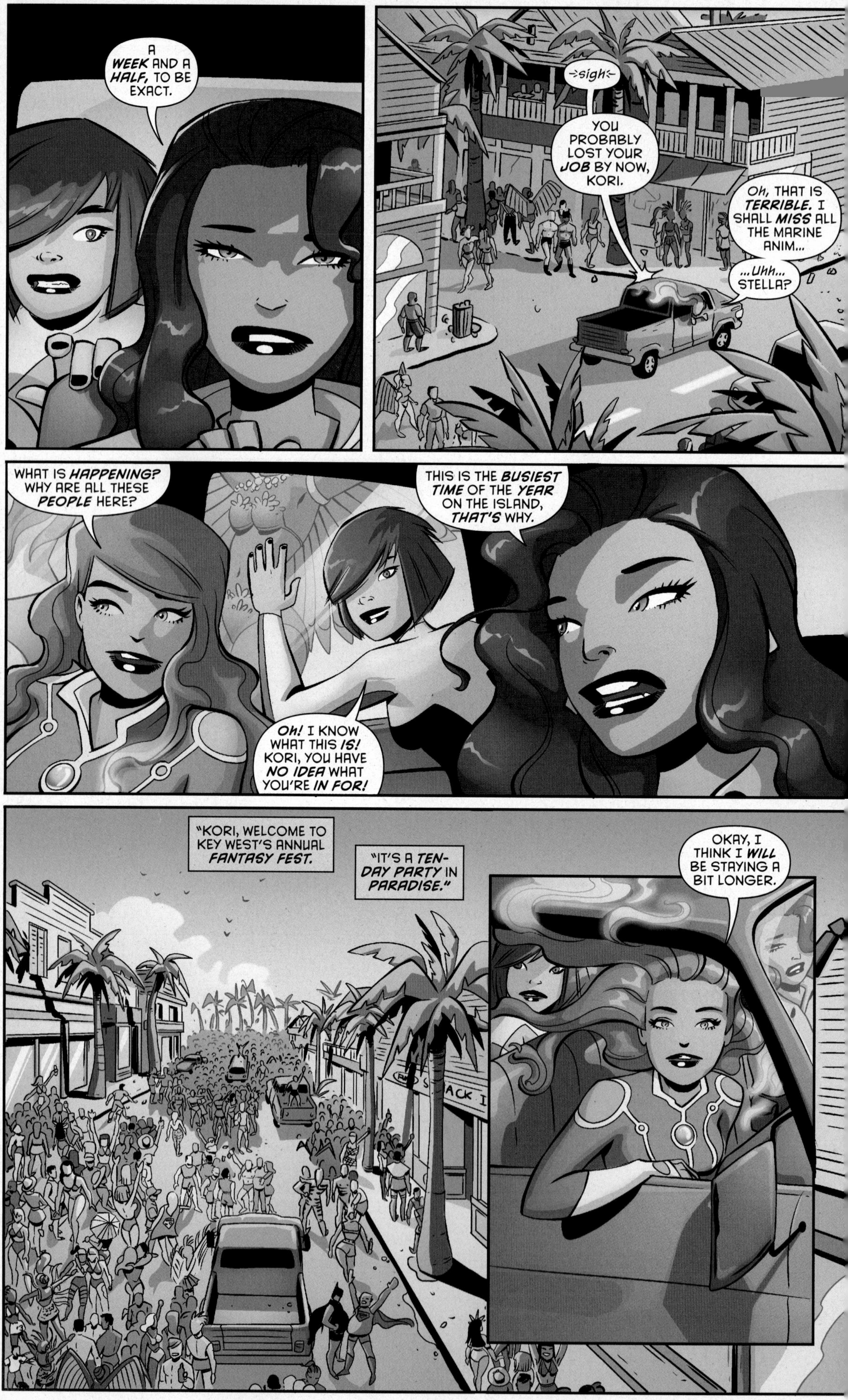
A WEEK AND A HALF, TO BE EXACT.
~sigh~
YOU PROBABLY LOST YOUR JOB BY NOW, KORI.
Oh, THAT IS TERRIBLE. I SHALL MISS ALL THE MARINE ANIM...
...Uhh... STELLA?
WHAT IS HAPPENING? WHY ARE ALL THESE PEOPLE HERE?
THIS IS THE BUSIEST TIME OF THE YEAR ON THE ISLAND, THAT'S WHY.
Oh! I KNOW WHAT THIS IS! KORI, YOU HAVE NO IDEA WHAT YOU'RE IN FOR!
"KORI, WELCOME TO KEY WEST'S ANNUAL FANTASY FEST.
"IT'S A TEN-DAY PARTY IN PARADISE."
OKAY, I THINK I WILL BE STAYING A BIT LONGER.

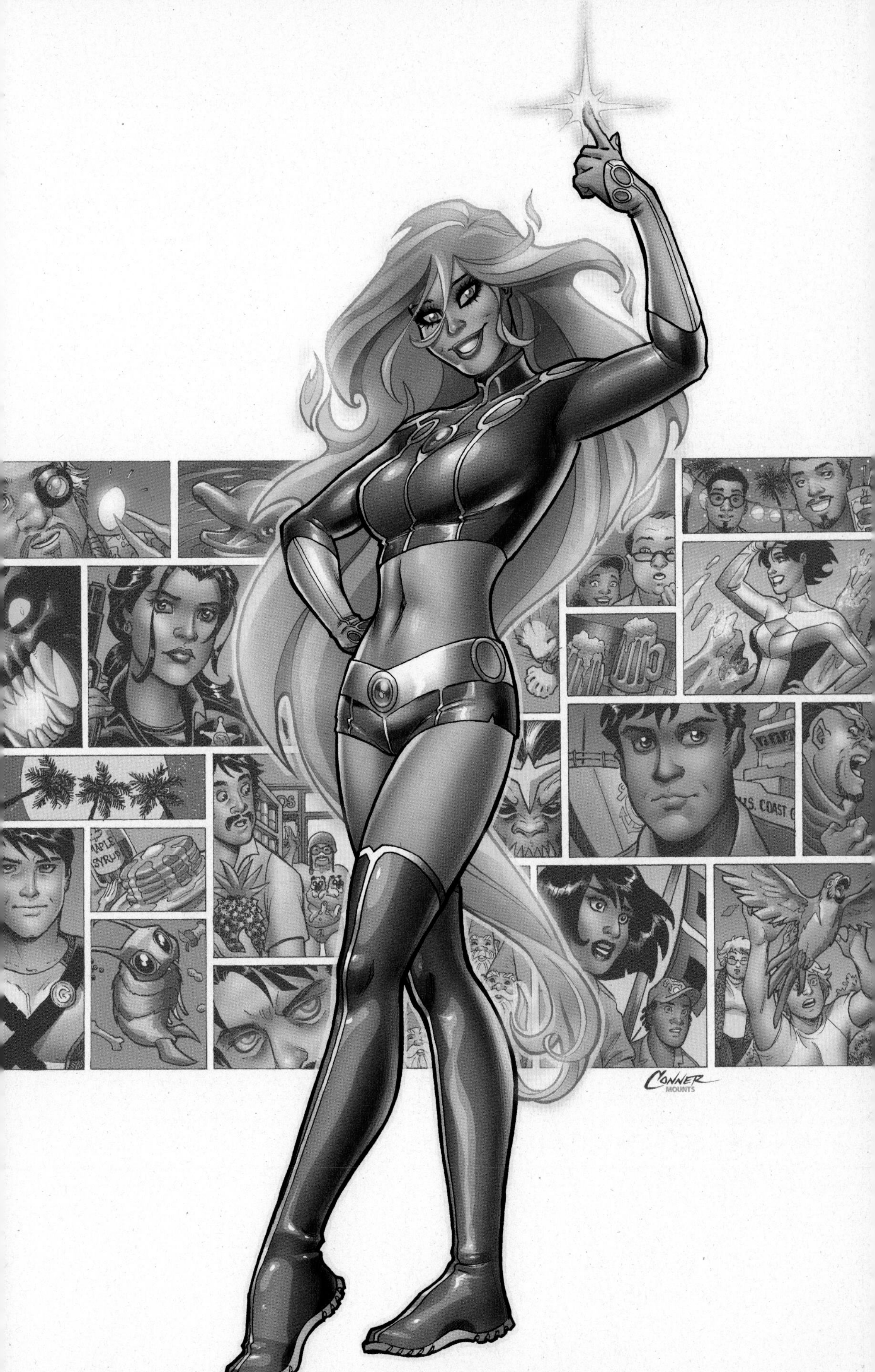
CONNER
MOUNTS

CLOSE FRIENDS, DISTANT ADVENTURES

AMANDA CONNER & JIMMY PALMIOTTI writers ELSA CHARRETIER art HI-FI colors COREY BREEN letters

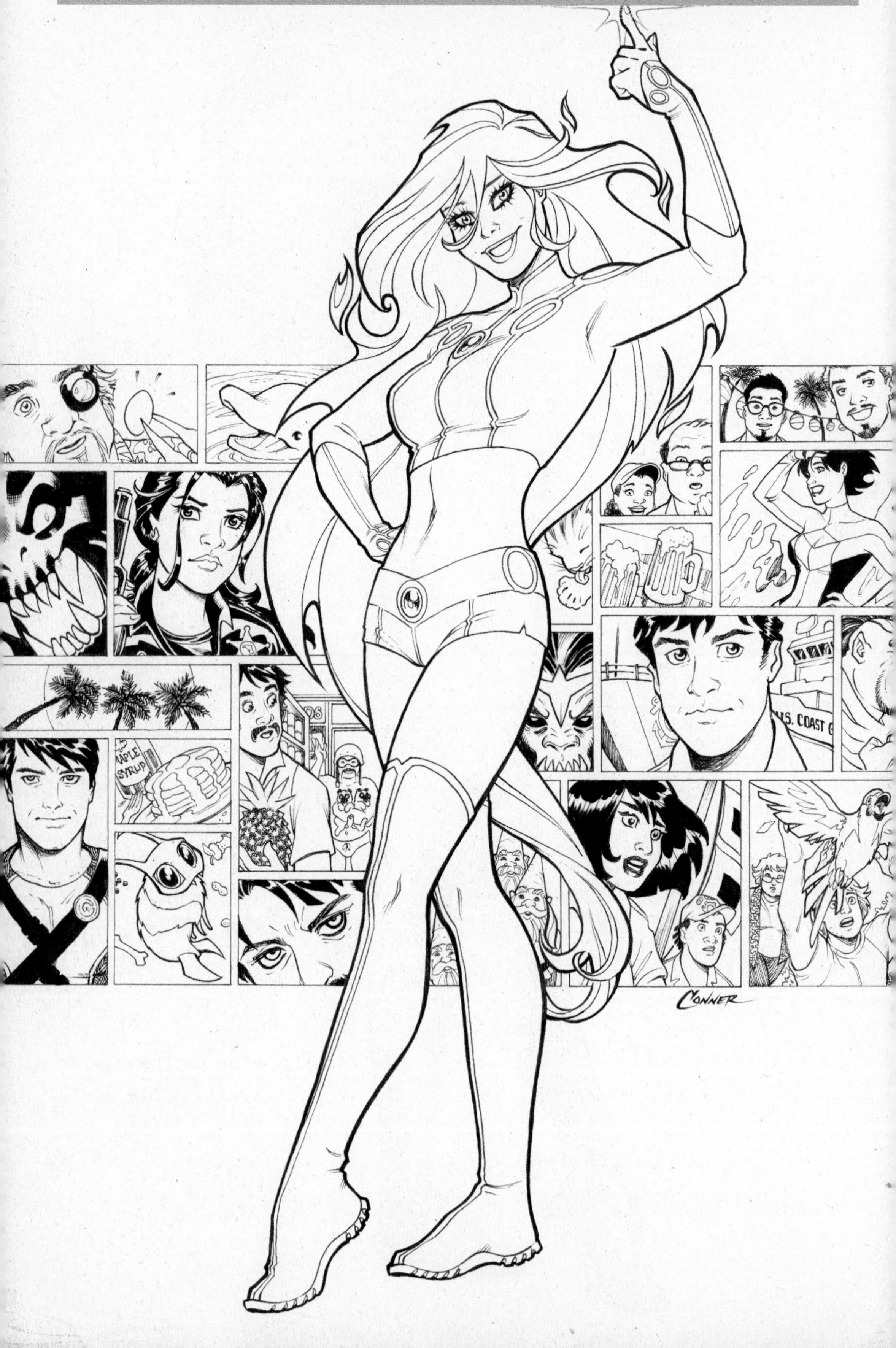

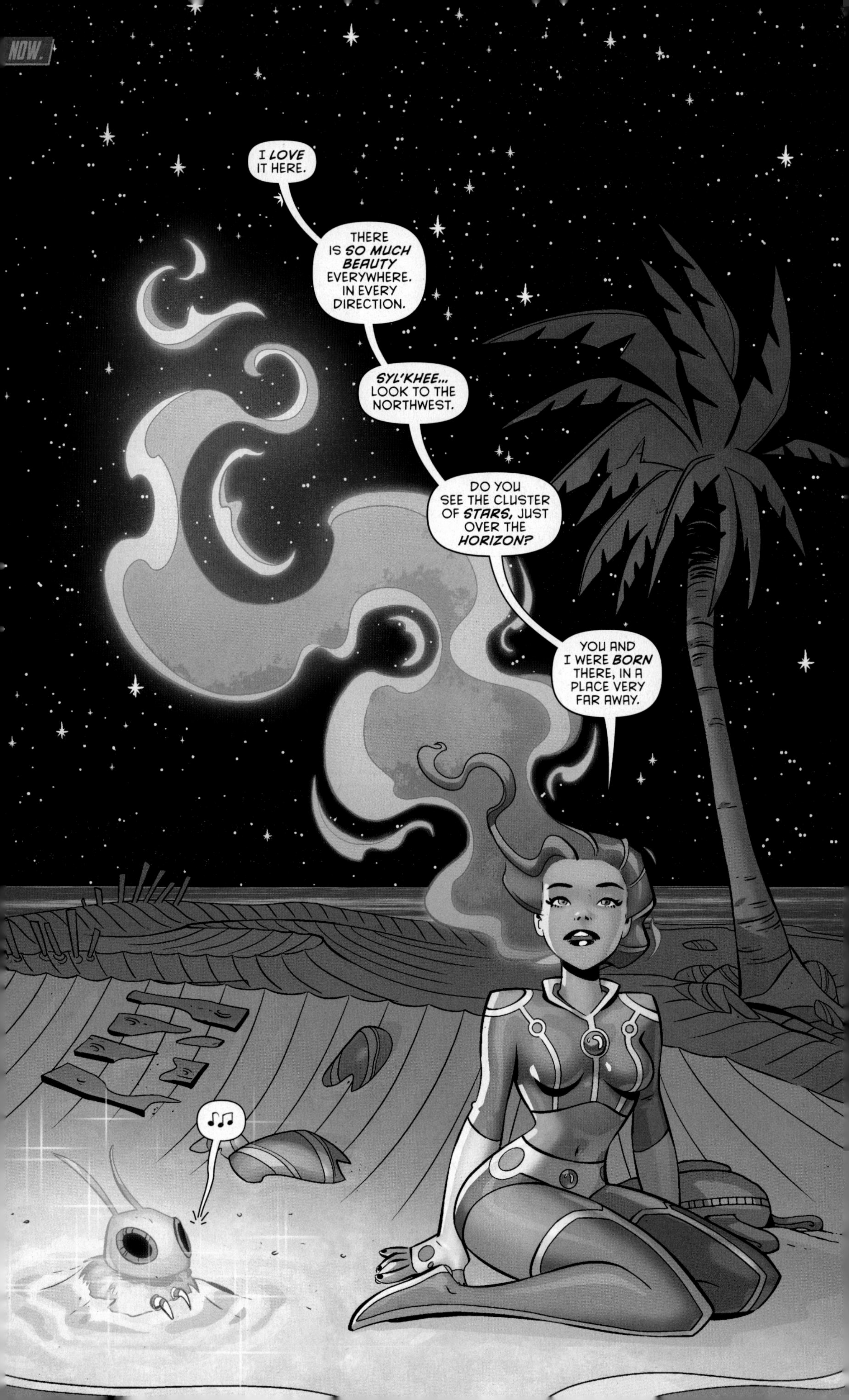
NOW.
I LOVE IT HERE.
THERE IS SO MUCH BEAUTY EVERYWHERE. IN EVERY DIRECTION.
SYL'KHEE... LOOK TO THE NORTHWEST.
DO YOU SEE THE CLUSTER OF STARS, JUST OVER THE HORIZON?
YOU AND I WERE BORN THERE, IN A PLACE VERY FAR AWAY.
♫

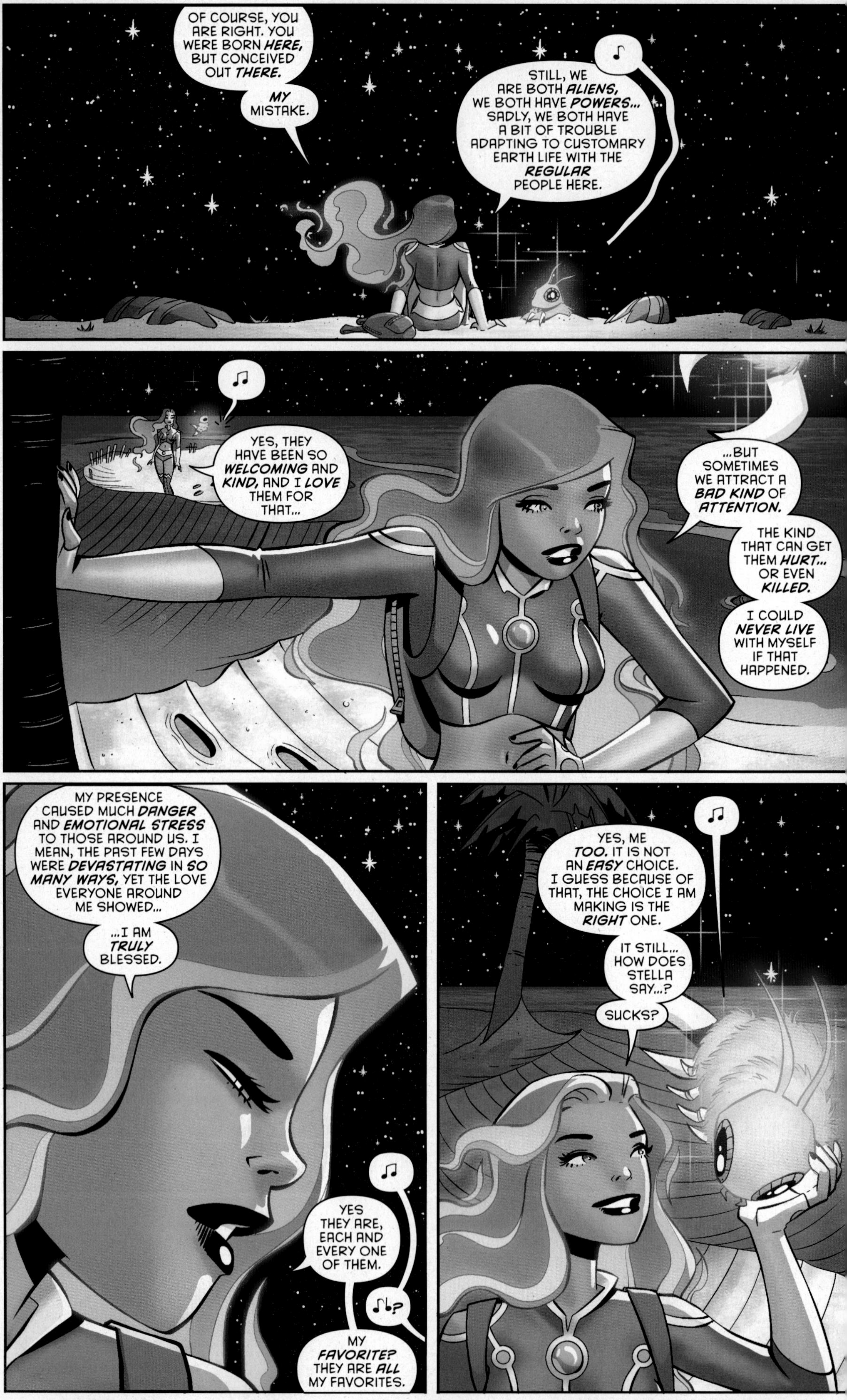
OF COURSE, YOU ARE RIGHT. YOU WERE BORN HERE, BUT CONCEIVED OUT THERE.
MY MISTAKE.
♪
STILL, WE ARE BOTH ALIENS, WE BOTH HAVE POWERS... SADLY, WE BOTH HAVE A BIT OF TROUBLE ADAPTING TO CUSTOMARY EARTH LIFE WITH THE REGULAR PEOPLE HERE.
♫
YES, THEY HAVE BEEN SO WELCOMING AND KIND, AND I LOVE THEM FOR THAT...
...BUT SOMETIMES WE ATTRACT A BAD KIND OF ATTENTION.
THE KIND THAT CAN GET THEM HURT... OR EVEN KILLED.
I COULD NEVER LIVE WITH MYSELF IF THAT HAPPENED.
MY PRESENCE CAUSED MUCH DANGER AND EMOTIONAL STRESS TO THOSE AROUND US. I MEAN, THE PAST FEW DAYS WERE DEVASTATING IN SO MANY WAYS, YET THE LOVE EVERYONE AROUND ME SHOWED...
...I AM TRULY BLESSED.
♫
YES THEY ARE, EACH AND EVERY ONE OF THEM.
♪♭?
MY FAVORITE? THEY ARE ALL MY FAVORITES.
♫
YES, ME TOO. IT IS NOT AN EASY CHOICE. I GUESS BECAUSE OF THAT, THE CHOICE I AM MAKING IS THE RIGHT ONE.
IT STILL... HOW DOES STELLA SAY...?
SUCKS?

Hard day on the planet.

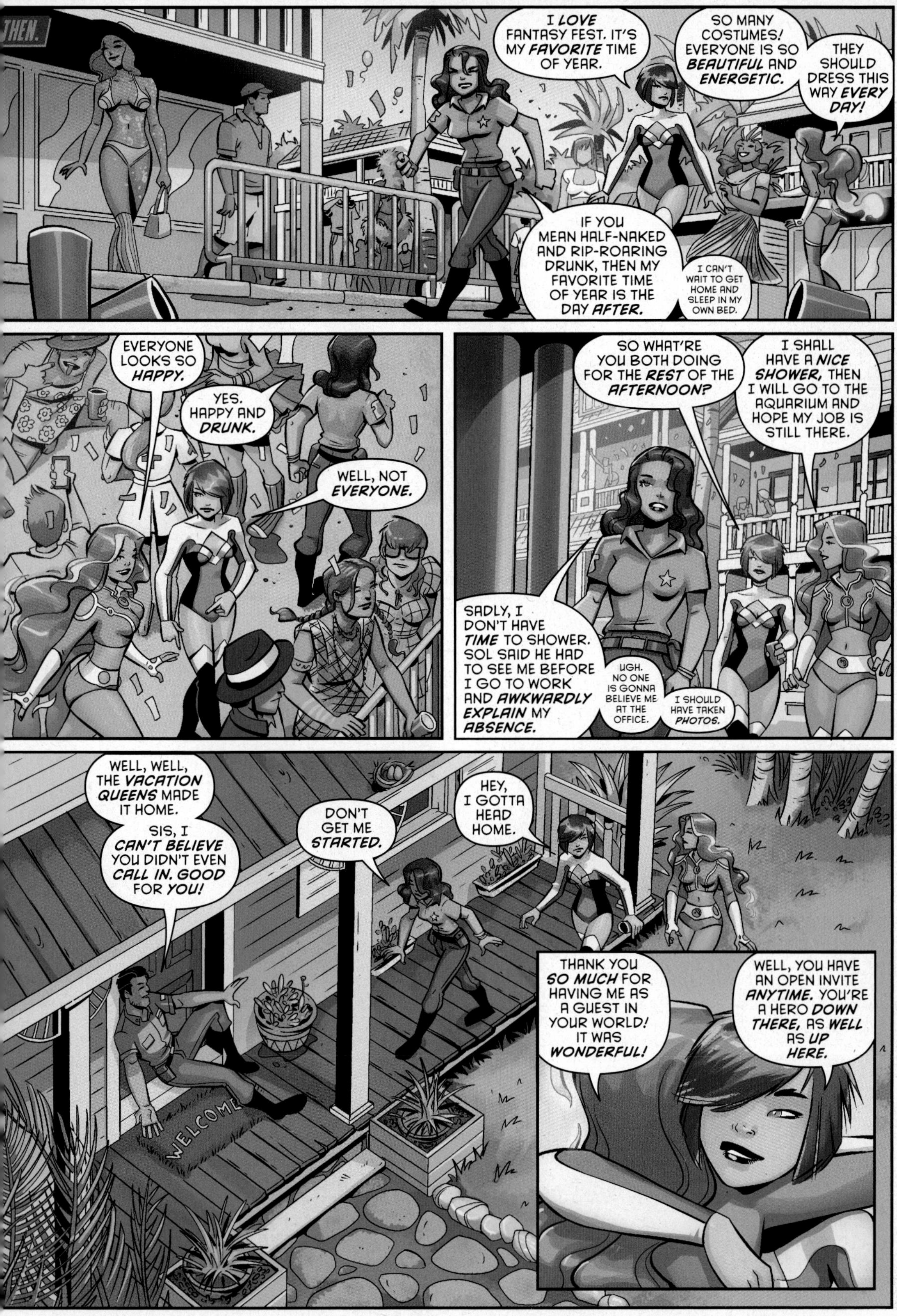
THEN.
I LOVE FANTASY FEST. IT'S MY FAVORITE TIME OF YEAR.
SO MANY COSTUMES! EVERYONE IS SO BEAUTIFUL AND ENERGETIC.
THEY SHOULD DRESS THIS WAY EVERY DAY!
IF YOU MEAN HALF-NAKED AND RIP-ROARING DRUNK, THEN MY FAVORITE TIME OF YEAR IS THE DAY AFTER.
I CAN'T WAIT TO GET HOME AND SLEEP IN MY OWN BED.
EVERYONE LOOKS SO HAPPY.
YES. HAPPY AND DRUNK.
WELL, NOT EVERYONE.
SO WHAT'RE YOU BOTH DOING FOR THE REST OF THE AFTERNOON?
I SHALL HAVE A NICE SHOWER, THEN I WILL GO TO THE AQUARIUM AND HOPE MY JOB IS STILL THERE.
SADLY, I DON'T HAVE TIME TO SHOWER. SOL SAID HE HAD TO SEE ME BEFORE I GO TO WORK AND AWKWARDLY EXPLAIN MY ABSENCE.
UGH. NO ONE IS GONNA BELIEVE ME AT THE OFFICE.
I SHOULD HAVE TAKEN PHOTOS.
WELL, WELL, THE VACATION QUEENS MADE IT HOME.
SIS, I CAN'T BELIEVE YOU DIDN'T EVEN CALL IN. GOOD FOR YOU!
DON'T GET ME STARTED.
HEY, I GOTTA HEAD HOME.
WELCOME
THANK YOU SO MUCH FOR HAVING ME AS A GUEST IN YOUR WORLD! IT WAS WONDERFUL!
WELL, YOU HAVE AN OPEN INVITE ANYTIME. YOU'RE A HERO DOWN THERE, AS WELL AS UP HERE.

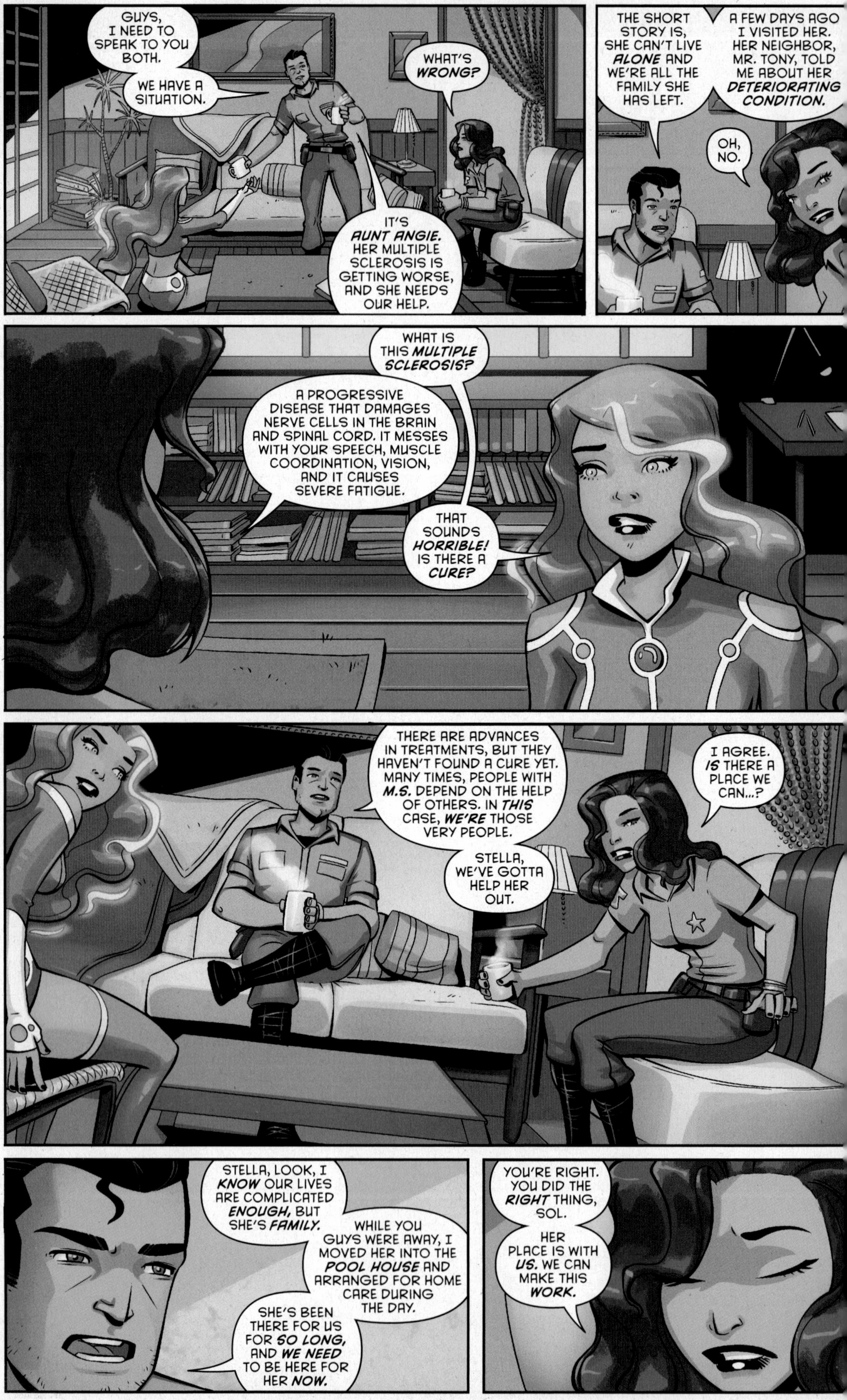
GUYS, I NEED TO SPEAK TO YOU BOTH.
WE HAVE A SITUATION.
WHAT'S *WRONG?*
IT'S *AUNT ANGIE.* HER MULTIPLE SCLEROSIS IS GETTING WORSE, AND SHE NEEDS OUR HELP.
THE SHORT STORY IS, SHE CAN'T LIVE *ALONE* AND WE'RE ALL THE FAMILY SHE HAS LEFT.
A FEW DAYS AGO I VISITED HER. HER NEIGHBOR, MR. TONY, TOLD ME ABOUT HER *DETERIORATING CONDITION.*
OH, NO.
WHAT IS THIS *MULTIPLE SCLEROSIS?*
A PROGRESSIVE DISEASE THAT DAMAGES NERVE CELLS IN THE BRAIN AND SPINAL CORD. IT MESSES WITH YOUR SPEECH, MUSCLE COORDINATION, VISION, AND IT CAUSES SEVERE FATIGUE.
THAT SOUNDS *HORRIBLE!* IS THERE A *CURE?*
THERE ARE ADVANCES IN TREATMENTS, BUT THEY HAVEN'T FOUND A CURE YET. MANY TIMES, PEOPLE WITH *M.S.* DEPEND ON THE HELP OF OTHERS. IN *THIS* CASE, *WE'RE* THOSE VERY PEOPLE.
STELLA, WE'VE GOTTA HELP HER OUT.
I AGREE. *IS* THERE A PLACE WE CAN...?
STELLA, LOOK, I *KNOW* OUR LIVES ARE COMPLICATED *ENOUGH,* BUT SHE'S *FAMILY.*
WHILE YOU GUYS WERE AWAY, I MOVED HER INTO THE *POOL HOUSE* AND ARRANGED FOR HOME CARE DURING THE DAY.
SHE'S BEEN THERE FOR US FOR *SO LONG,* AND *WE NEED* TO BE HERE FOR HER *NOW.*
YOU'RE RIGHT. YOU DID THE *RIGHT* THING, SOL.
HER PLACE IS WITH *US.* WE CAN MAKE THIS *WORK.*

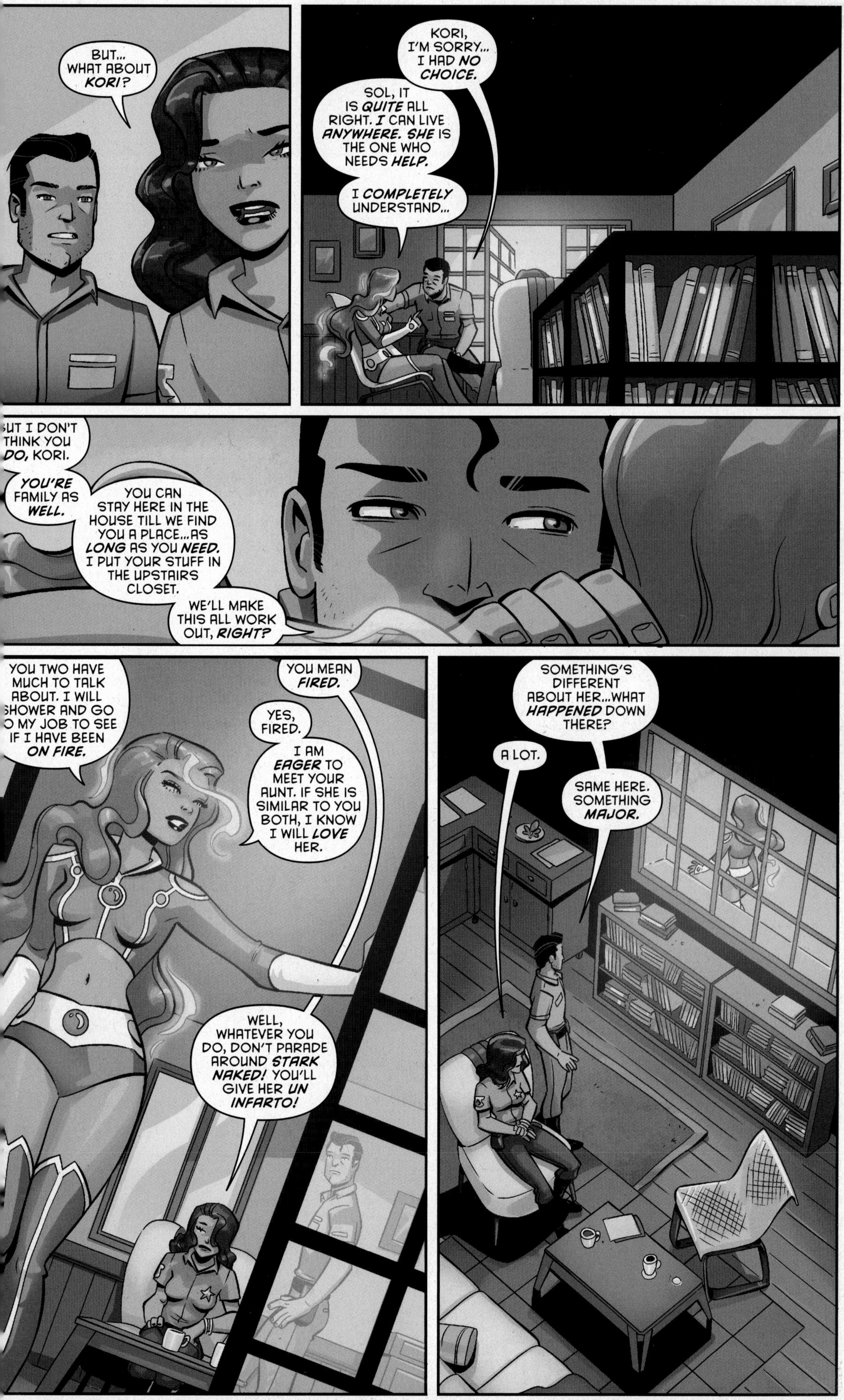

BUT... WHAT ABOUT *KORI*?
KORI, I'M SORRY... I HAD *NO CHOICE.*
SOL, IT IS *QUITE* ALL RIGHT. *I* CAN LIVE *ANYWHERE. SHE* IS THE ONE WHO NEEDS *HELP.*
I *COMPLETELY* UNDERSTAND...
BUT I DON'T THINK YOU *DO,* KORI.
YOU'RE FAMILY AS *WELL.*
YOU CAN STAY HERE IN THE HOUSE TILL WE FIND YOU A PLACE...AS *LONG* AS YOU *NEED.* I PUT YOUR STUFF IN THE UPSTAIRS CLOSET.
WE'LL MAKE THIS ALL WORK OUT, *RIGHT?*
YOU TWO HAVE MUCH TO TALK ABOUT. I WILL SHOWER AND GO TO MY JOB TO SEE IF I HAVE BEEN *ON FIRE.*
YOU MEAN *FIRED.*
YES, FIRED.
I AM *EAGER* TO MEET YOUR AUNT. IF SHE IS SIMILAR TO YOU BOTH, I KNOW I WILL *LOVE* HER.
WELL, WHATEVER YOU DO, DON'T PARADE AROUND *STARK NAKED!* YOU'LL GIVE HER *UN INFARTO!*
SOMETHING'S DIFFERENT ABOUT HER...WHAT *HAPPENED* DOWN THERE?
A LOT.
SAME HERE. SOMETHING *MAJOR.*

Freedom of choice.

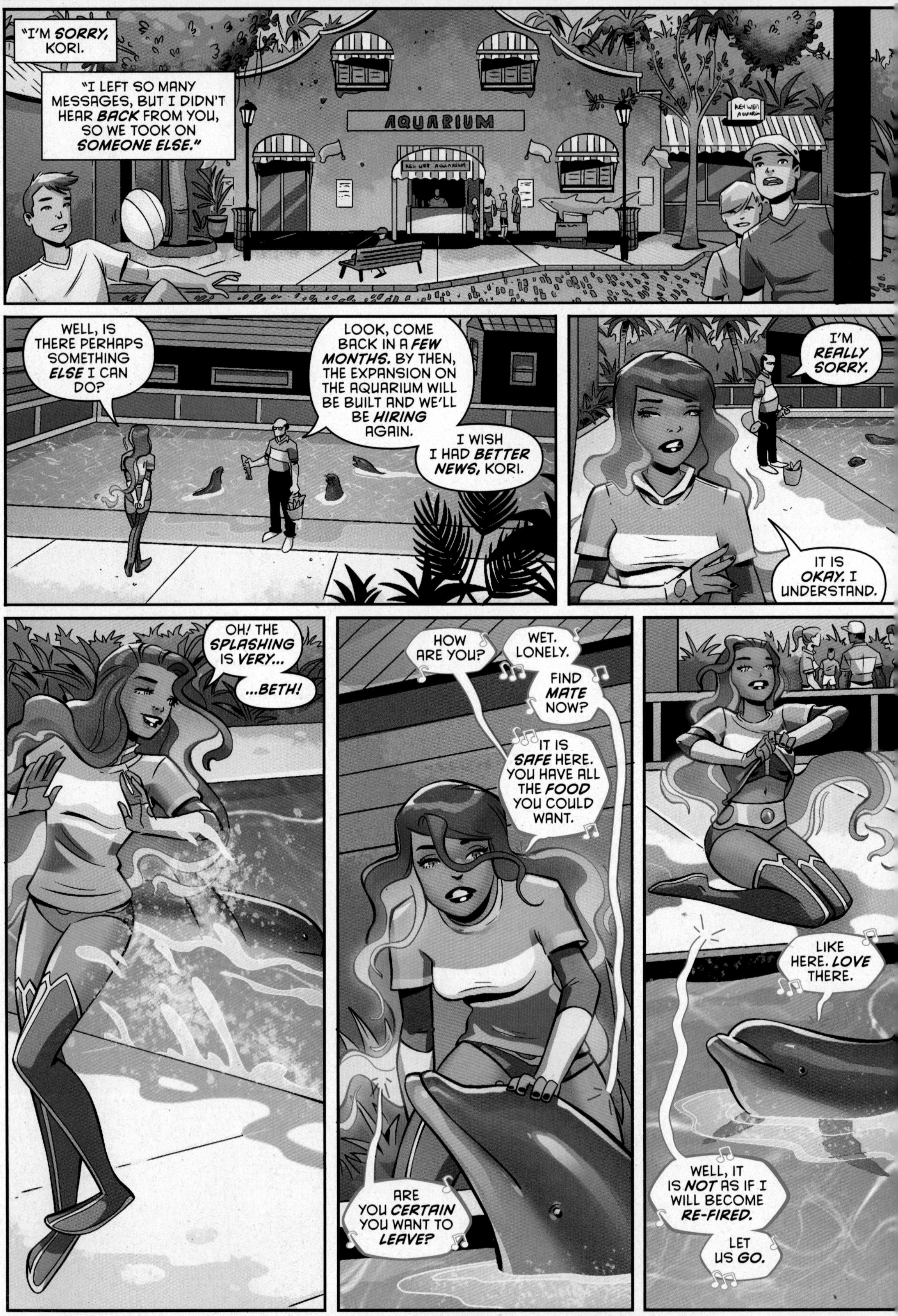

"I'M SORRY, KORI.
"I LEFT SO MANY MESSAGES, BUT I DIDN'T HEAR BACK FROM YOU, SO WE TOOK ON SOMEONE ELSE."
AQUARIUM
WELL, IS THERE PERHAPS SOMETHING ELSE I CAN DO?
LOOK, COME BACK IN A FEW MONTHS. BY THEN, THE EXPANSION ON THE AQUARIUM WILL BE BUILT AND WE'LL BE HIRING AGAIN.
I WISH I HAD BETTER NEWS, KORI.
I'M REALLY SORRY.
IT IS OKAY. I UNDERSTAND.
OH! THE SPLASHING IS VERY...
...BETH!
HOW ARE YOU?
WET. LONELY.
FIND MATE NOW?
IT IS SAFE HERE. YOU HAVE ALL THE FOOD YOU COULD WANT.
ARE YOU CERTAIN YOU WANT TO LEAVE?
LIKE HERE. LOVE THERE.
WELL, IT IS NOT AS IF I WILL BECOME RE-FIRED.
LET US GO.

The happy song.

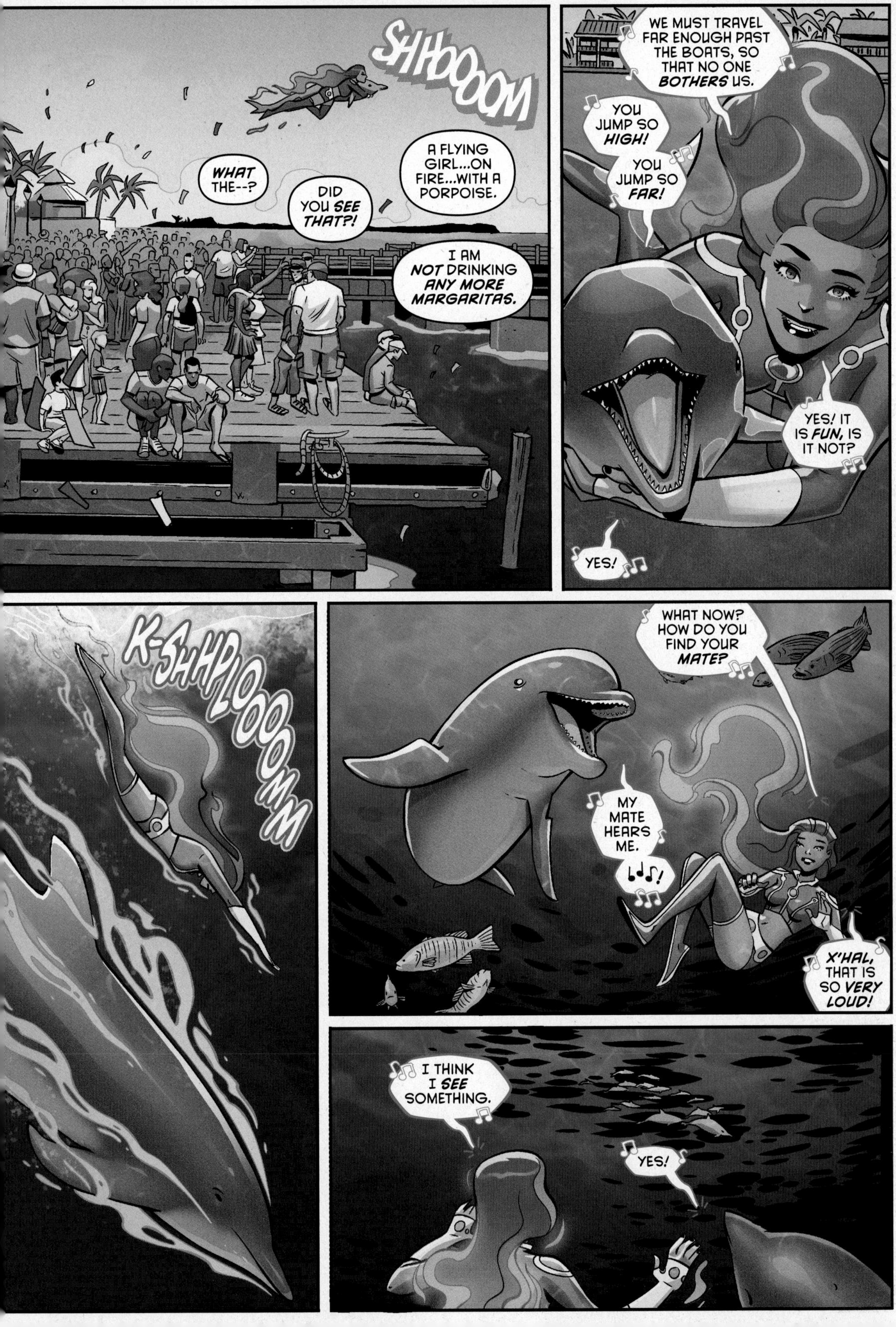

SHHOOOOM
WHAT THE--?
DID YOU SEE THAT?!
A FLYING GIRL...ON FIRE...WITH A PORPOISE.
I AM NOT DRINKING ANY MORE MARGARITAS.
WE MUST TRAVEL FAR ENOUGH PAST THE BOATS, SO THAT NO ONE BOTHERS US.
YOU JUMP SO HIGH!
YOU JUMP SO FAR!
YES! IT IS FUN, IS IT NOT?
YES!
K-SHHPLOOOOMM
WHAT NOW? HOW DO YOU FIND YOUR MATE?
MY MATE HEARS ME.
X'HAL, THAT IS SO VERY LOUD!
I THINK I SEE SOMETHING.
YES!

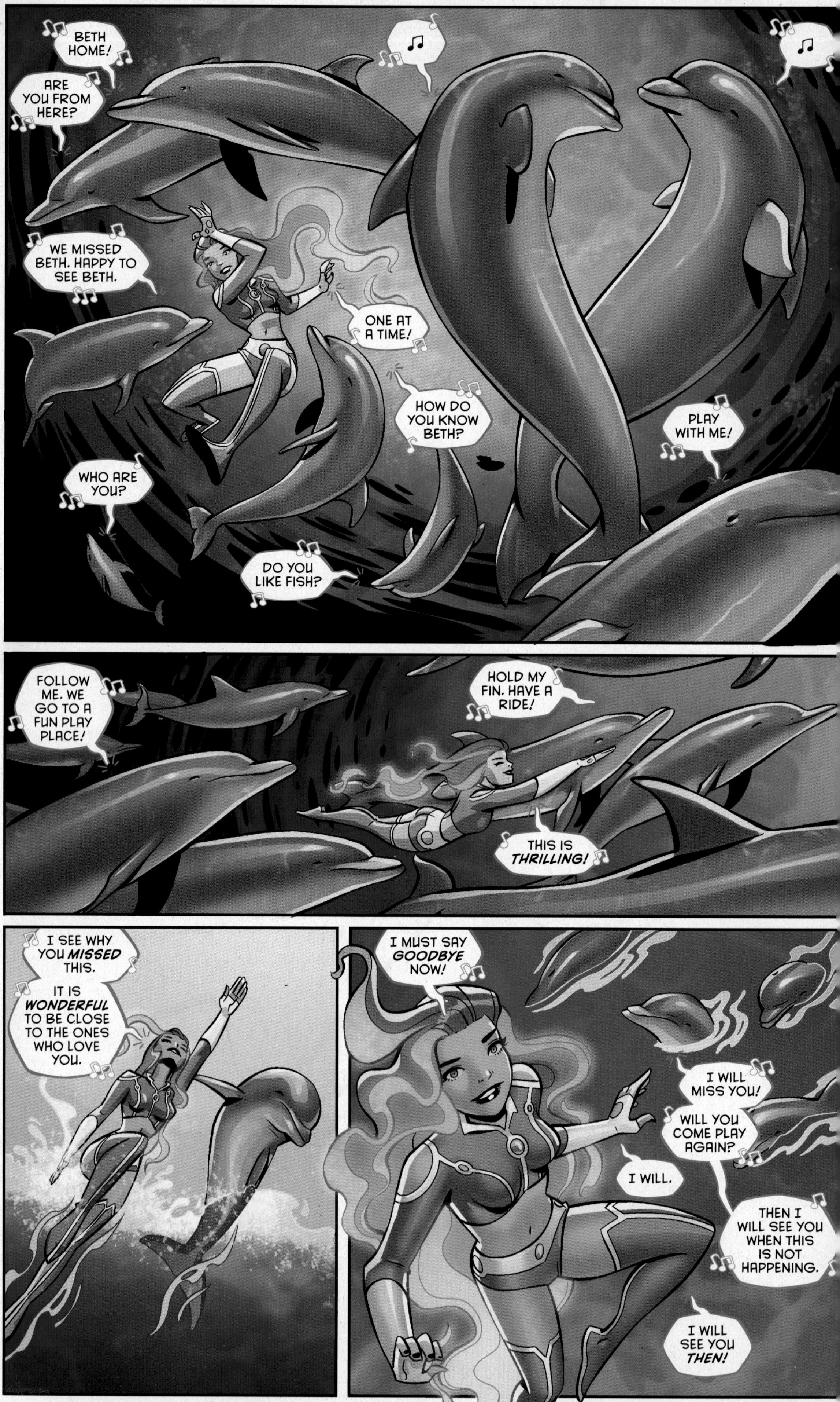
BETH HOME!
ARE YOU FROM HERE?
WE MISSED BETH. HAPPY TO SEE BETH.
ONE AT A TIME!
HOW DO YOU KNOW BETH?
PLAY WITH ME!
WHO ARE YOU?
DO YOU LIKE FISH?
FOLLOW ME. WE GO TO A FUN PLAY PLACE!
HOLD MY FIN. HAVE A RIDE!
THIS IS *THRILLING!*
I SEE WHY YOU *MISSED* THIS.
IT IS *WONDERFUL* TO BE CLOSE TO THE ONES WHO LOVE YOU.
I MUST SAY *GOODBYE* NOW!
I WILL MISS YOU!
WILL YOU COME PLAY AGAIN?
I WILL.
THEN I WILL SEE YOU WHEN THIS IS NOT HAPPENING.
I WILL SEE YOU *THEN!*

I GOTTA SAY...I'M KIND OF *JEALOUS* SHE CAN SLEEP SO *SOUNDLY* LIKE THIS.

IT'S BEEN A GOOD *FIFTEEN HOURS.* SHOULD WE WAKE HER *UP?*

LET'S *TALK* FIRST. COME OUTSIDE.

SO, TELL ME, WHAT *HAPPENED* WHILE I WAS AWAY?

RAVENA HAPPENED.

WHAT? EXPLAIN.

WELL...*RAVE* AND *I* WERE *WORKING* WHEN *KORI'S* PET *SYL' KHEE* APPEARED AND STARTED...I DUNNO... *SINGING.*

IT WAS *HYPNOTIC,* AND WE BOTH HAD THIS CRAZY OUT-OF-BODY *EXPERIENCE.*

LONG STORY SHORT, WE WOUND UP *KISSING* EACH OTHER. WE WERE *BOTH* TOTALLY THROWN OFF GUARD.

THE KISS *STARTED* SOMETHING I COULDN'T *STOP.*

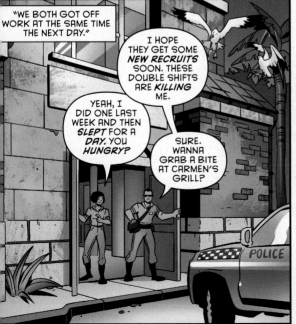

"WE BOTH GOT OFF WORK AT THE SAME TIME THE NEXT DAY."

I HOPE THEY GET SOME *NEW RECRUITS* SOON. THESE DOUBLE SHIFTS ARE *KILLING* ME.

YEAH, I DID ONE LAST WEEK AND THEN *SLEPT* FOR A *DAY.* YOU *HUNGRY?*

SURE. WANNA GRAB A BITE AT CARMEN'S GRILL?

POLICE

"WE DIDN'T SPEAK ABOUT WHAT *HAPPENED* THE DAY BEFORE UNTIL THE END OF THE MEAL. THEN RAVE HIT ME WITH A BOMB."

SOL, I HAVE SOMETHING TO *TELL* YOU, AND YOU PROBABLY DON'T WANNA *HEAR* IT.

IF IT WAS ABOUT THAT *KISS* YESTERDAY...

SOL, *PLEASE* LET ME SPEAK BEFORE I LOSE MY *DUTCH COURAGE.*

SORRY.

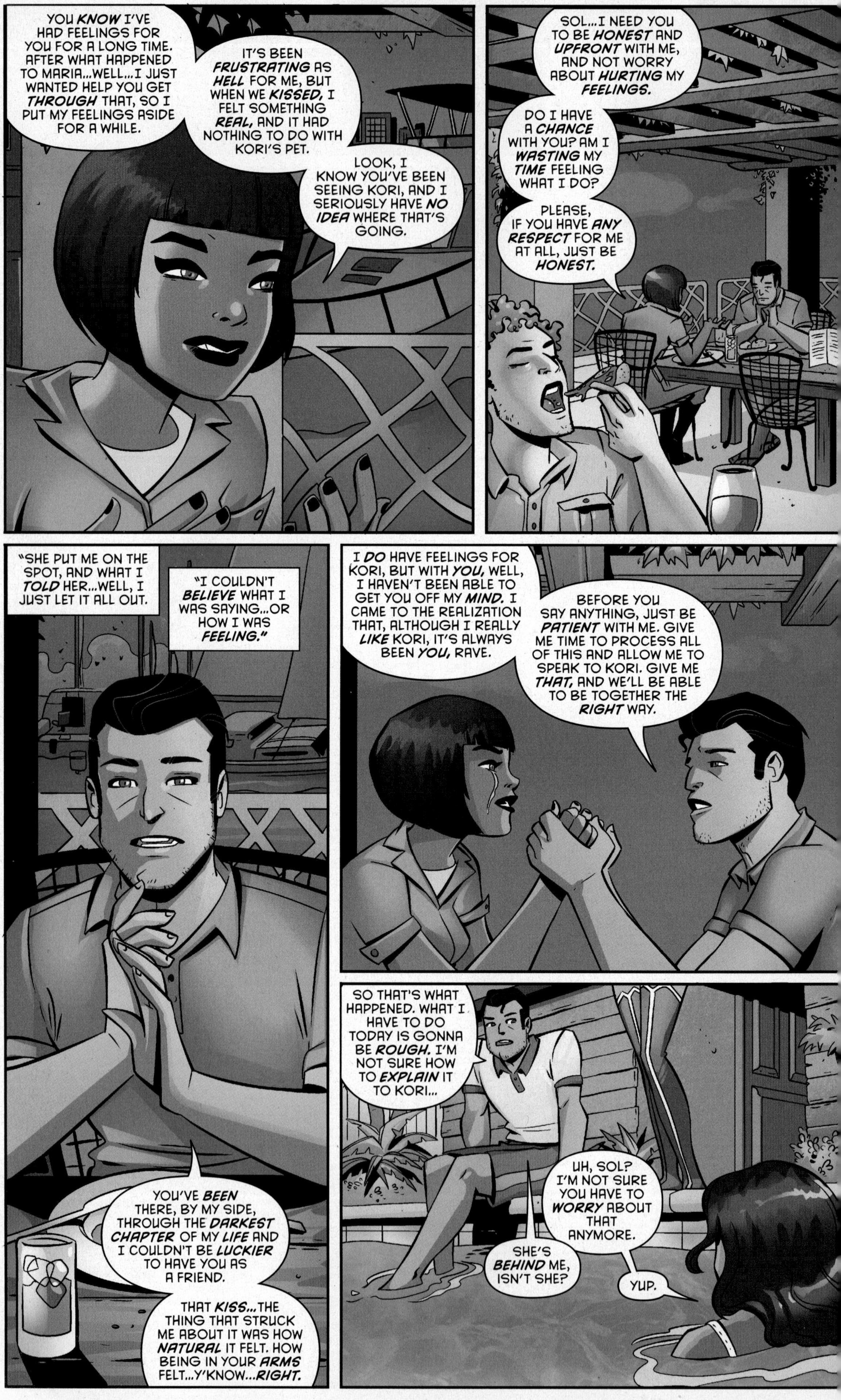
YOU KNOW I'VE HAD FEELINGS FOR YOU FOR A LONG TIME. AFTER WHAT HAPPENED TO MARIA...WELL...I JUST WANTED HELP YOU GET THROUGH THAT, SO I PUT MY FEELINGS ASIDE FOR A WHILE.
IT'S BEEN FRUSTRATING AS HELL FOR ME, BUT WHEN WE KISSED, I FELT SOMETHING REAL, AND IT HAD NOTHING TO DO WITH KORI'S PET.
LOOK, I KNOW YOU'VE BEEN SEEING KORI, AND I SERIOUSLY HAVE NO IDEA WHERE THAT'S GOING.
SOL...I NEED YOU TO BE HONEST AND UPFRONT WITH ME, AND NOT WORRY ABOUT HURTING MY FEELINGS.
DO I HAVE A CHANCE WITH YOU? AM I WASTING MY TIME FEELING WHAT I DO?
PLEASE, IF YOU HAVE ANY RESPECT FOR ME AT ALL, JUST BE HONEST.
"SHE PUT ME ON THE SPOT, AND WHAT I TOLD HER...WELL, I JUST LET IT ALL OUT.
"I COULDN'T BELIEVE WHAT I WAS SAYING...OR HOW I WAS FEELING."
YOU'VE BEEN THERE, BY MY SIDE, THROUGH THE DARKEST CHAPTER OF MY LIFE AND I COULDN'T BE LUCKIER TO HAVE YOU AS A FRIEND.
THAT KISS...THE THING THAT STRUCK ME ABOUT IT WAS HOW NATURAL IT FELT. HOW BEING IN YOUR ARMS FELT...Y'KNOW...RIGHT.
I DO HAVE FEELINGS FOR KORI, BUT WITH YOU, WELL, I HAVEN'T BEEN ABLE TO GET YOU OFF MY MIND. I CAME TO THE REALIZATION THAT, ALTHOUGH I REALLY LIKE KORI, IT'S ALWAYS BEEN YOU, RAVE.
BEFORE YOU SAY ANYTHING, JUST BE PATIENT WITH ME. GIVE ME TIME TO PROCESS ALL OF THIS AND ALLOW ME TO SPEAK TO KORI. GIVE ME THAT, AND WE'LL BE ABLE TO BE TOGETHER THE RIGHT WAY.
SO THAT'S WHAT HAPPENED. WHAT I HAVE TO DO TODAY IS GONNA BE ROUGH. I'M NOT SURE HOW TO EXPLAIN IT TO KORI...
UH, SOL? I'M NOT SURE YOU HAVE TO WORRY ABOUT THAT ANYMORE.
SHE'S BEHIND ME, ISN'T SHE?
YUP.

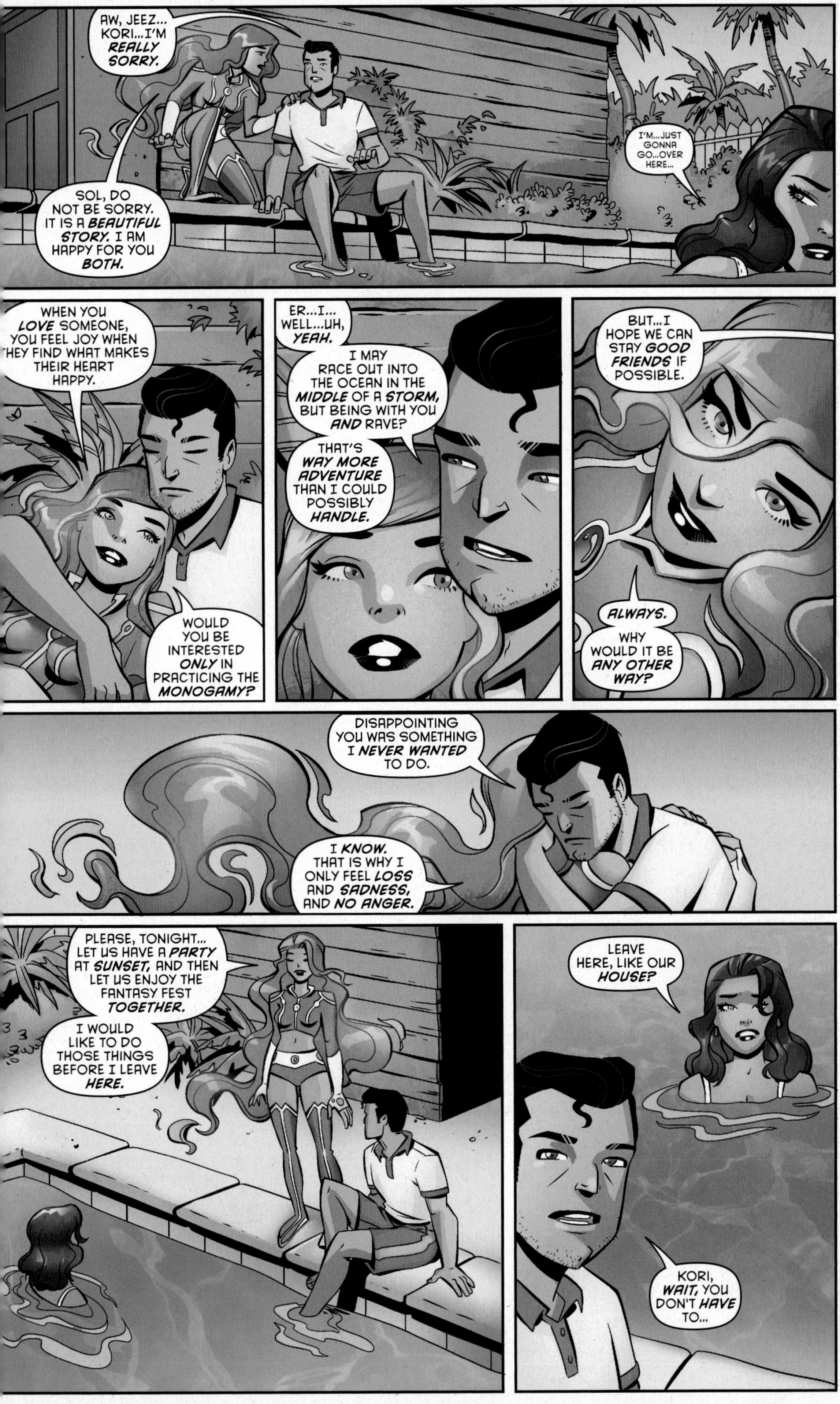
AW, JEEZ... KORI...I'M REALLY SORRY.
SOL, DO NOT BE SORRY. IT IS A BEAUTIFUL STORY. I AM HAPPY FOR YOU BOTH.
I'M...JUST GONNA GO...OVER HERE...
WHEN YOU LOVE SOMEONE, YOU FEEL JOY WHEN THEY FIND WHAT MAKES THEIR HEART HAPPY.
WOULD YOU BE INTERESTED ONLY IN PRACTICING THE MONOGAMY?
ER...I... WELL...UH, YEAH.
I MAY RACE OUT INTO THE OCEAN IN THE MIDDLE OF A STORM, BUT BEING WITH YOU AND RAVE?
THAT'S WAY MORE ADVENTURE THAN I COULD POSSIBLY HANDLE.
BUT...I HOPE WE CAN STAY GOOD FRIENDS IF POSSIBLE.
ALWAYS.
WHY WOULD IT BE ANY OTHER WAY?
DISAPPOINTING YOU WAS SOMETHING I NEVER WANTED TO DO.
I KNOW. THAT IS WHY I ONLY FEEL LOSS AND SADNESS, AND NO ANGER.
PLEASE, TONIGHT... LET US HAVE A PARTY AT SUNSET, AND THEN LET US ENJOY THE FANTASY FEST TOGETHER.
I WOULD LIKE TO DO THOSE THINGS BEFORE I LEAVE HERE.
LEAVE HERE, LIKE OUR HOUSE?
KORI, WAIT, YOU DON'T HAVE TO...

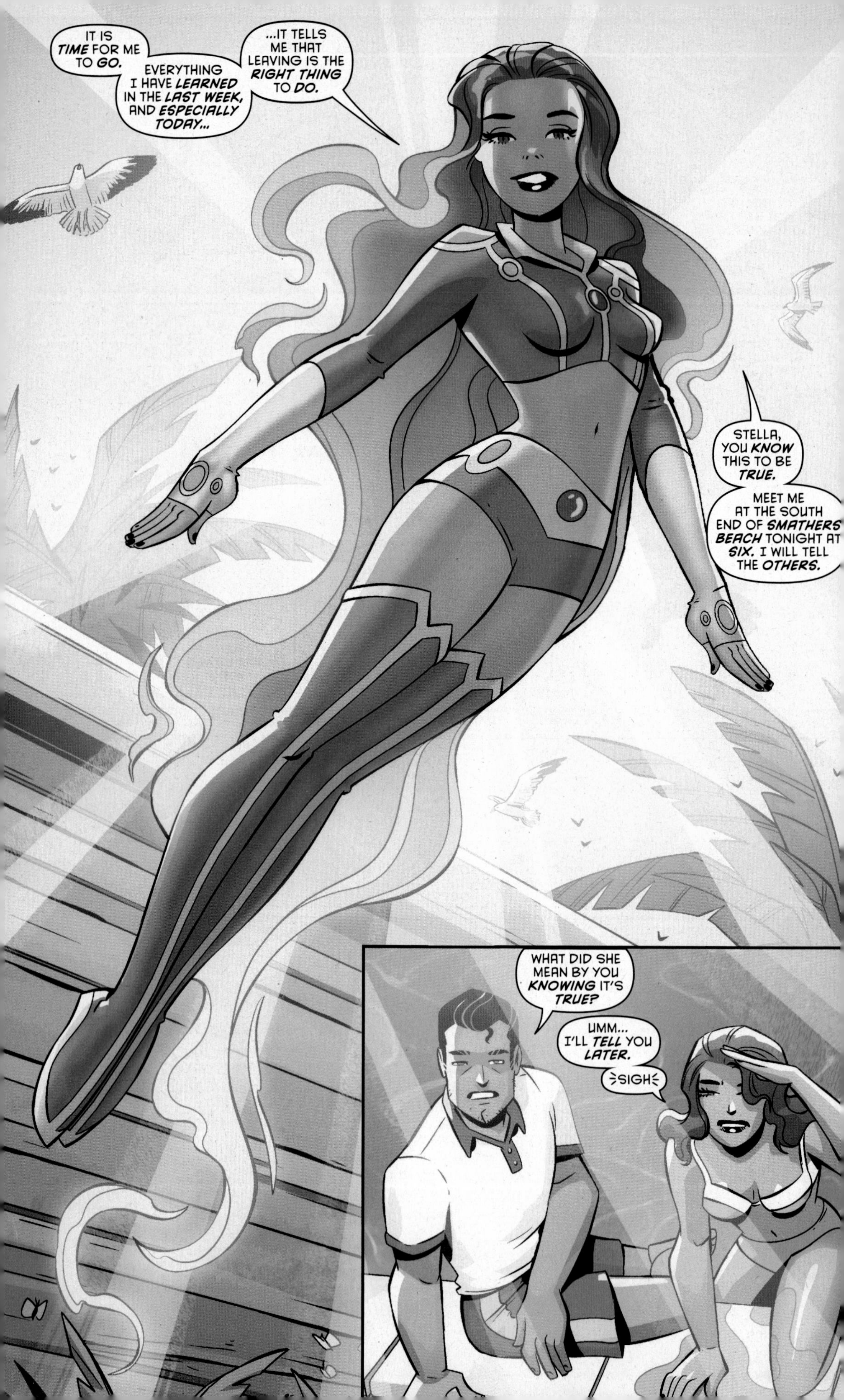
IT IS TIME FOR ME TO GO.
EVERYTHING I HAVE LEARNED IN THE LAST WEEK, AND ESPECIALLY TODAY...
...IT TELLS ME THAT LEAVING IS THE RIGHT THING TO DO.
STELLA, YOU KNOW THIS TO BE TRUE.
MEET ME AT THE SOUTH END OF SMATHERS BEACH TONIGHT AT SIX. I WILL TELL THE OTHERS.
WHAT DID SHE MEAN BY YOU KNOWING IT'S TRUE?
UMM... I'LL TELL YOU LATER.
SIGH

Farewell food fest.

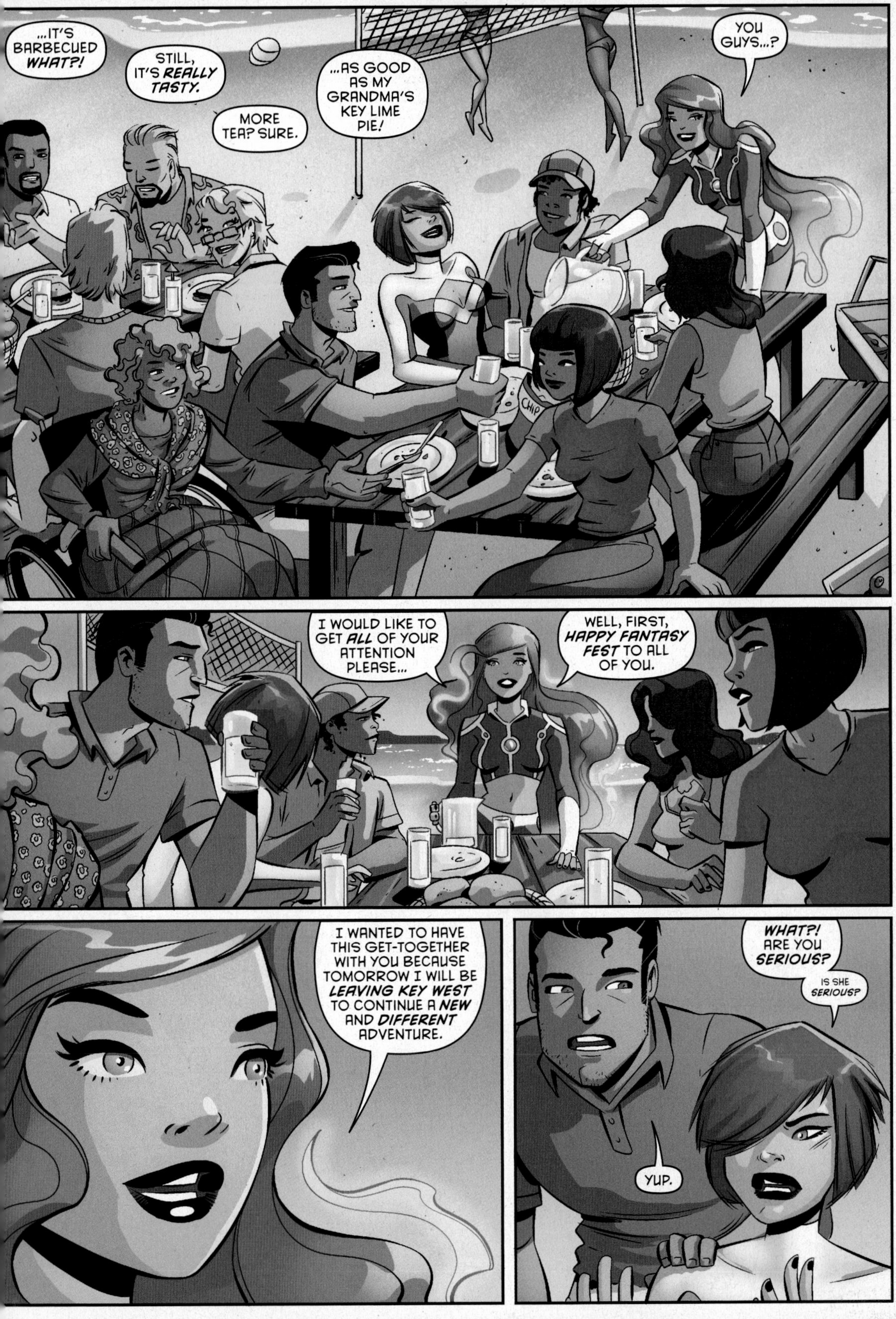
...IT'S BARBECUED WHAT?!
STILL, IT'S REALLY TASTY.
MORE TEA? SURE.
...AS GOOD AS MY GRANDMA'S KEY LIME PIE!
YOU GUYS...?
CHIP
I WOULD LIKE TO GET ALL OF YOUR ATTENTION PLEASE...
WELL, FIRST, HAPPY FANTASY FEST TO ALL OF YOU.
I WANTED TO HAVE THIS GET-TOGETHER WITH YOU BECAUSE TOMORROW I WILL BE LEAVING KEY WEST TO CONTINUE A NEW AND DIFFERENT ADVENTURE.
WHAT?! ARE YOU SERIOUS?
IS SHE SERIOUS?
YUP.

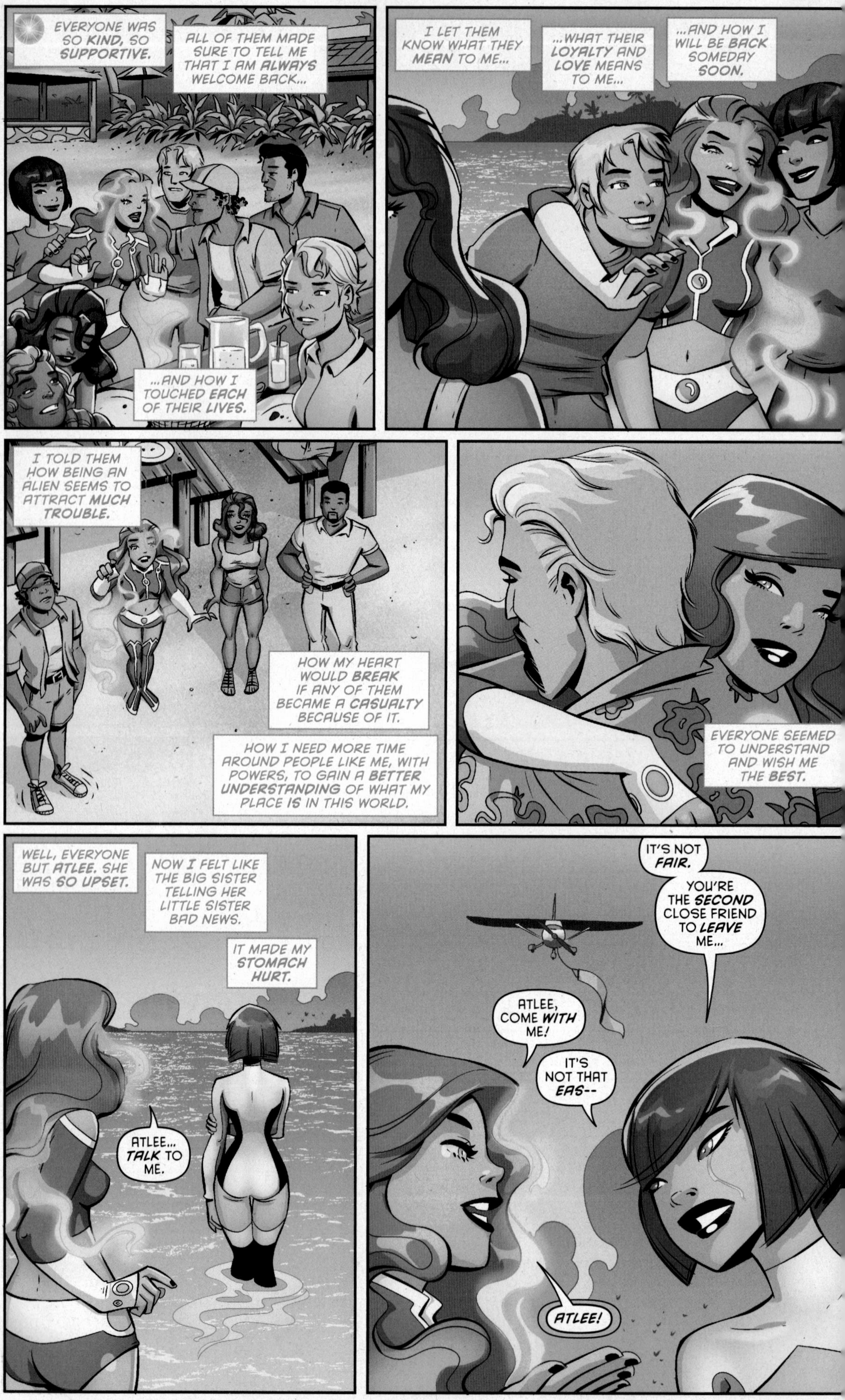
EVERYONE WAS SO KIND, SO SUPPORTIVE.
ALL OF THEM MADE SURE TO TELL ME THAT I AM ALWAYS WELCOME BACK...
...AND HOW I TOUCHED EACH OF THEIR LIVES.
I LET THEM KNOW WHAT THEY MEAN TO ME...
...WHAT THEIR LOYALTY AND LOVE MEANS TO ME...
...AND HOW I WILL BE BACK SOMEDAY SOON.
I TOLD THEM HOW BEING AN ALIEN SEEMS TO ATTRACT MUCH TROUBLE.
HOW MY HEART WOULD BREAK IF ANY OF THEM BECAME A CASUALTY BECAUSE OF IT.
HOW I NEED MORE TIME AROUND PEOPLE LIKE ME, WITH POWERS, TO GAIN A BETTER UNDERSTANDING OF WHAT MY PLACE IS IN THIS WORLD.
EVERYONE SEEMED TO UNDERSTAND AND WISH ME THE BEST.
WELL, EVERYONE BUT ATLEE. SHE WAS SO UPSET.
NOW I FELT LIKE THE BIG SISTER TELLING HER LITTLE SISTER BAD NEWS.
IT MADE MY STOMACH HURT.
ATLEE... TALK TO ME.
IT'S NOT FAIR.
YOU'RE THE SECOND CLOSE FRIEND TO LEAVE ME...
ATLEE, COME WITH ME!
IT'S NOT THAT EAS--
ATLEE!

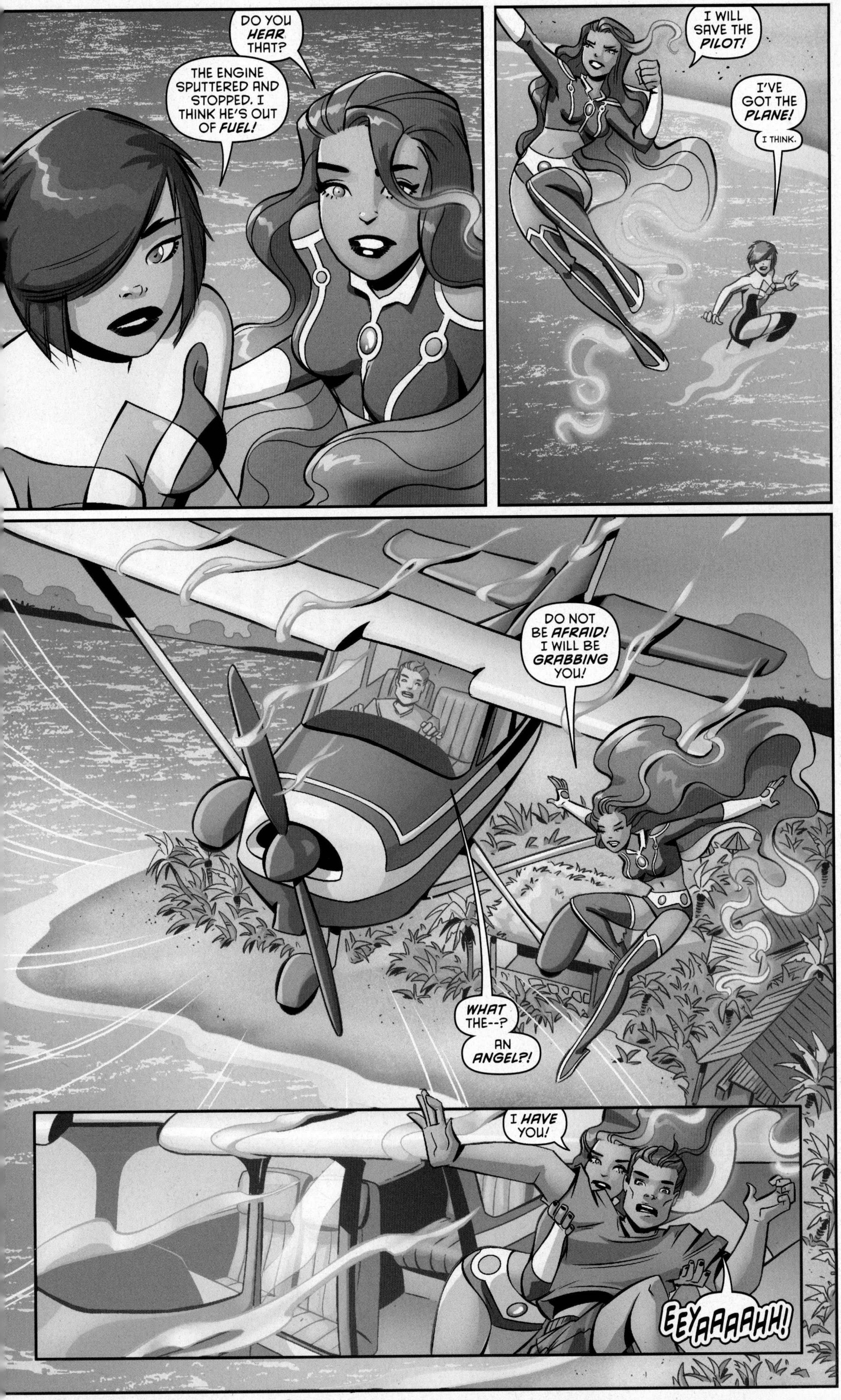
DO YOU HEAR THAT?
THE ENGINE SPUTTERED AND STOPPED. I THINK HE'S OUT OF FUEL!
I WILL SAVE THE PILOT!
I'VE GOT THE PLANE!
I THINK.
DO NOT BE AFRAID! I WILL BE GRABBING YOU!
WHAT THE--?
AN ANGEL?!
I HAVE YOU!
EEYAAAAHH!

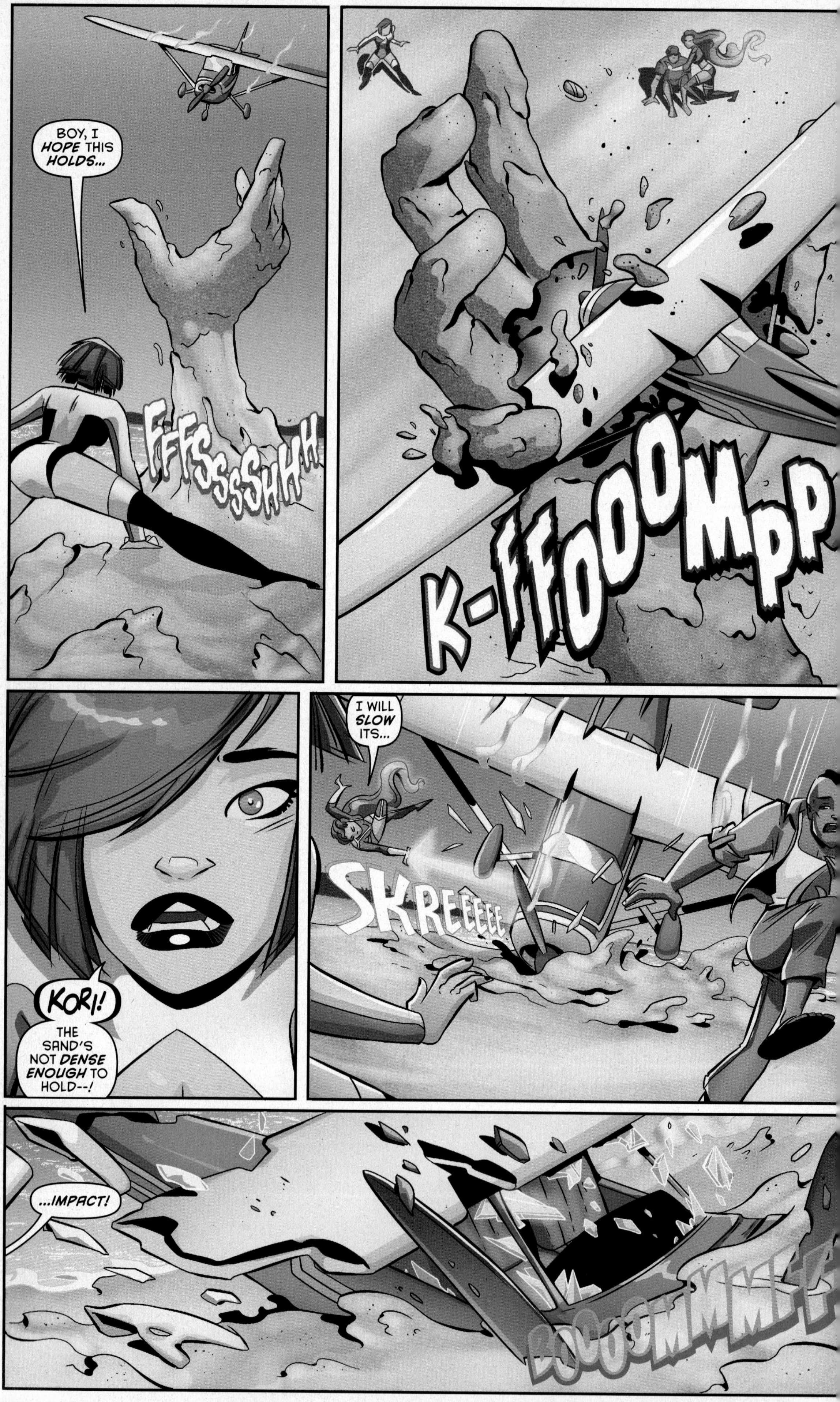

BOY, I HOPE THIS HOLDS...
FFFSSSSHHH
K-FFOOOMPP
KORI!
THE SAND'S NOT DENSE ENOUGH TO HOLD--!
I WILL SLOW ITS...
SKREEEEE
...IMPACT!
BOOOOMMMFF

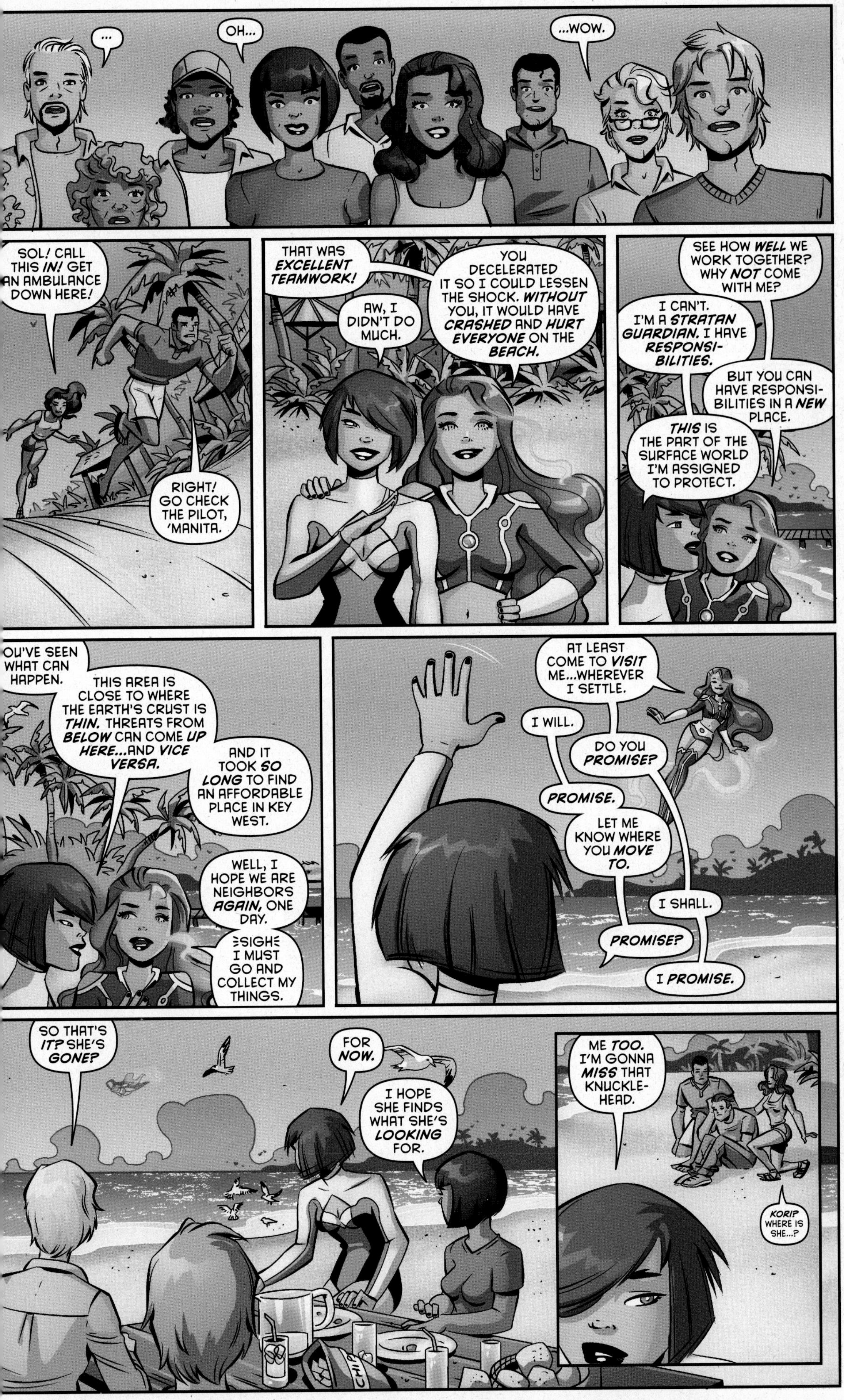
...
OH...
...WOW.
SOL! CALL THIS IN! GET AN AMBULANCE DOWN HERE!
RIGHT! GO CHECK THE PILOT, 'MANITA.
THAT WAS EXCELLENT TEAMWORK!
AW, I DIDN'T DO MUCH.
YOU DECELERATED IT SO I COULD LESSEN THE SHOCK. WITHOUT YOU, IT WOULD HAVE CRASHED AND HURT EVERYONE ON THE BEACH.
SEE HOW WELL WE WORK TOGETHER? WHY NOT COME WITH ME?
I CAN'T. I'M A STRATAN GUARDIAN. I HAVE RESPONSI-BILITIES.
BUT YOU CAN HAVE RESPONSI-BILITIES IN A NEW PLACE.
THIS IS THE PART OF THE SURFACE WORLD I'M ASSIGNED TO PROTECT.
OU'VE SEEN WHAT CAN HAPPEN.
THIS AREA IS CLOSE TO WHERE THE EARTH'S CRUST IS THIN. THREATS FROM BELOW CAN COME UP HERE...AND VICE VERSA.
AND IT TOOK SO LONG TO FIND AN AFFORDABLE PLACE IN KEY WEST.
WELL, I HOPE WE ARE NEIGHBORS AGAIN, ONE DAY.
SIGH I MUST GO AND COLLECT MY THINGS.
AT LEAST COME TO VISIT ME...WHEREVER I SETTLE.
I WILL.
DO YOU PROMISE?
PROMISE.
LET ME KNOW WHERE YOU MOVE TO.
I SHALL.
PROMISE?
I PROMISE.
SO THAT'S IT? SHE'S GONE?
FOR NOW.
I HOPE SHE FINDS WHAT SHE'S LOOKING FOR.
ME TOO. I'M GONNA MISS THAT KNUCKLE-HEAD.
KORI? WHERE IS SHE...?
CHIP

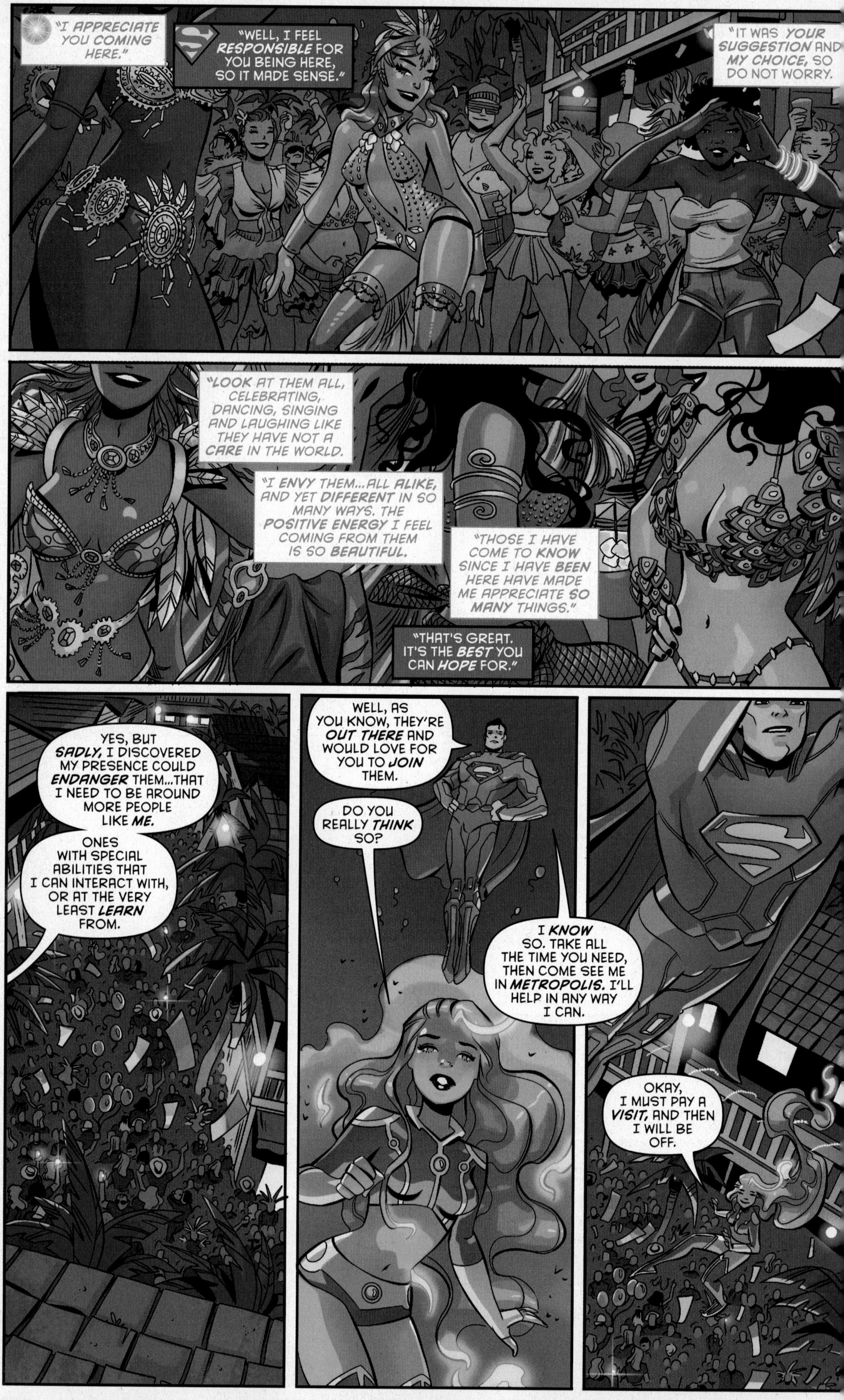
"I APPRECIATE YOU COMING HERE."
"WELL, I FEEL RESPONSIBLE FOR YOU BEING HERE, SO IT MADE SENSE."
"IT WAS YOUR SUGGESTION AND MY CHOICE, SO DO NOT WORRY.
"LOOK AT THEM ALL, CELEBRATING, DANCING, SINGING AND LAUGHING LIKE THEY HAVE NOT A CARE IN THE WORLD.
"I ENVY THEM...ALL ALIKE, AND YET DIFFERENT IN SO MANY WAYS. THE POSITIVE ENERGY I FEEL COMING FROM THEM IS SO BEAUTIFUL.
"THOSE I HAVE COME TO KNOW SINCE I HAVE BEEN HERE HAVE MADE ME APPRECIATE SO MANY THINGS."
"THAT'S GREAT. IT'S THE BEST YOU CAN HOPE FOR."
YES, BUT SADLY, I DISCOVERED MY PRESENCE COULD ENDANGER THEM...THAT I NEED TO BE AROUND MORE PEOPLE LIKE ME.
ONES WITH SPECIAL ABILITIES THAT I CAN INTERACT WITH, OR AT THE VERY LEAST LEARN FROM.
WELL, AS YOU KNOW, THEY'RE OUT THERE AND WOULD LOVE FOR YOU TO JOIN THEM.
DO YOU REALLY THINK SO?
I KNOW SO. TAKE ALL THE TIME YOU NEED, THEN COME SEE ME IN METROPOLIS. I'LL HELP IN ANY WAY I CAN.
OKAY, I MUST PAY A VISIT, AND THEN I WILL BE OFF.

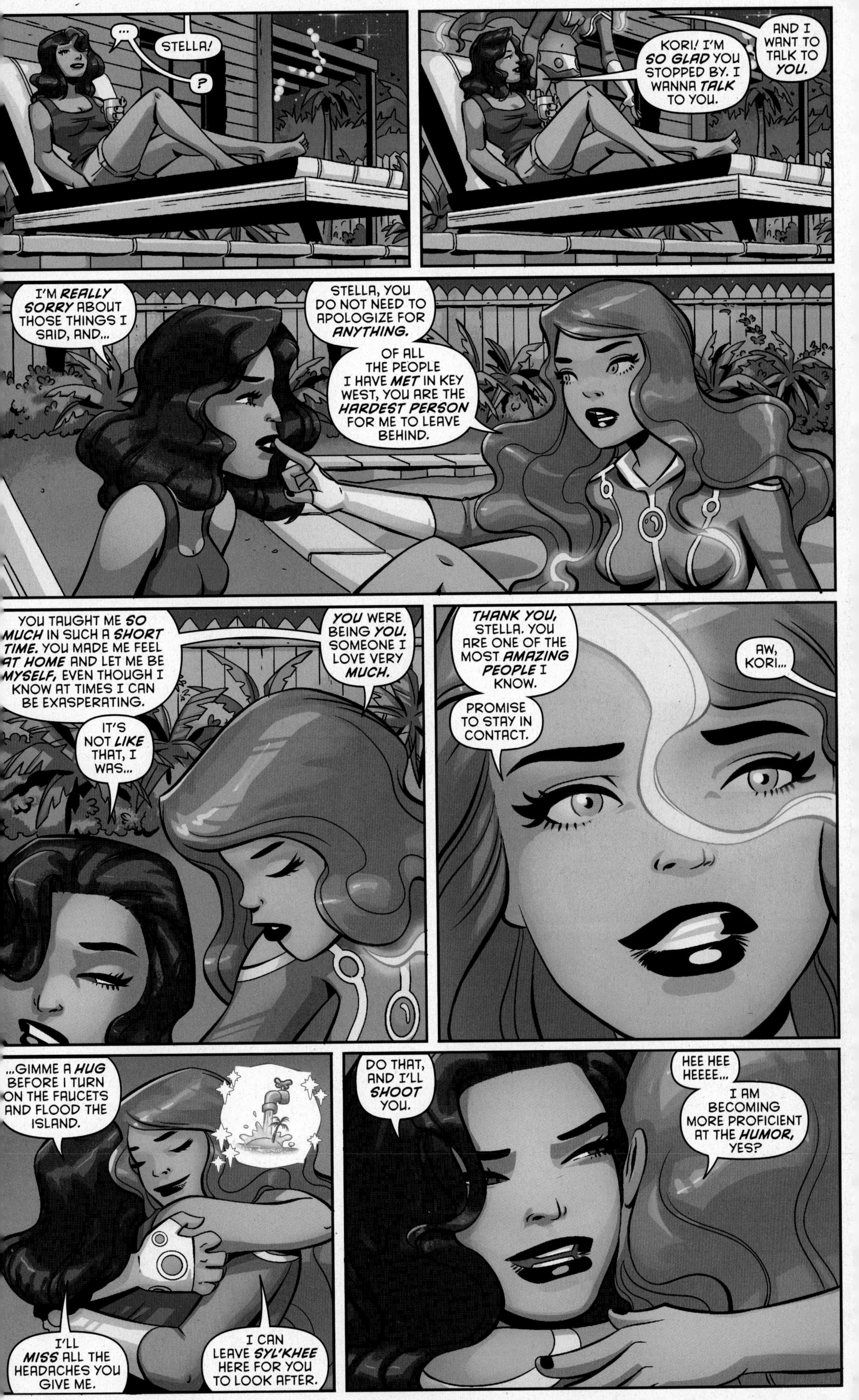
...
STELLA!
?
KORI! I'M SO GLAD YOU STOPPED BY. I WANNA TALK TO YOU.
AND I WANT TO TALK TO YOU.
I'M REALLY SORRY ABOUT THOSE THINGS I SAID, AND...
STELLA, YOU DO NOT NEED TO APOLOGIZE FOR ANYTHING.
OF ALL THE PEOPLE I HAVE MET IN KEY WEST, YOU ARE THE HARDEST PERSON FOR ME TO LEAVE BEHIND.
YOU TAUGHT ME SO MUCH IN SUCH A SHORT TIME. YOU MADE ME FEEL AT HOME AND LET ME BE MYSELF, EVEN THOUGH I KNOW AT TIMES I CAN BE EXASPERATING.
IT'S NOT LIKE THAT, I WAS...
YOU WERE BEING YOU. SOMEONE I LOVE VERY MUCH.
THANK YOU, STELLA. YOU ARE ONE OF THE MOST AMAZING PEOPLE I KNOW.
PROMISE TO STAY IN CONTACT.
AW, KORI...
...GIMME A HUG BEFORE I TURN ON THE FAUCETS AND FLOOD THE ISLAND.
I'LL MISS ALL THE HEADACHES YOU GIVE ME.
I CAN LEAVE SYL'KHEE HERE FOR YOU TO LOOK AFTER.
DO THAT, AND I'LL SHOOT YOU.
HEE HEE HEEEE...
I AM BECOMING MORE PROFICIENT AT THE HUMOR, YES?

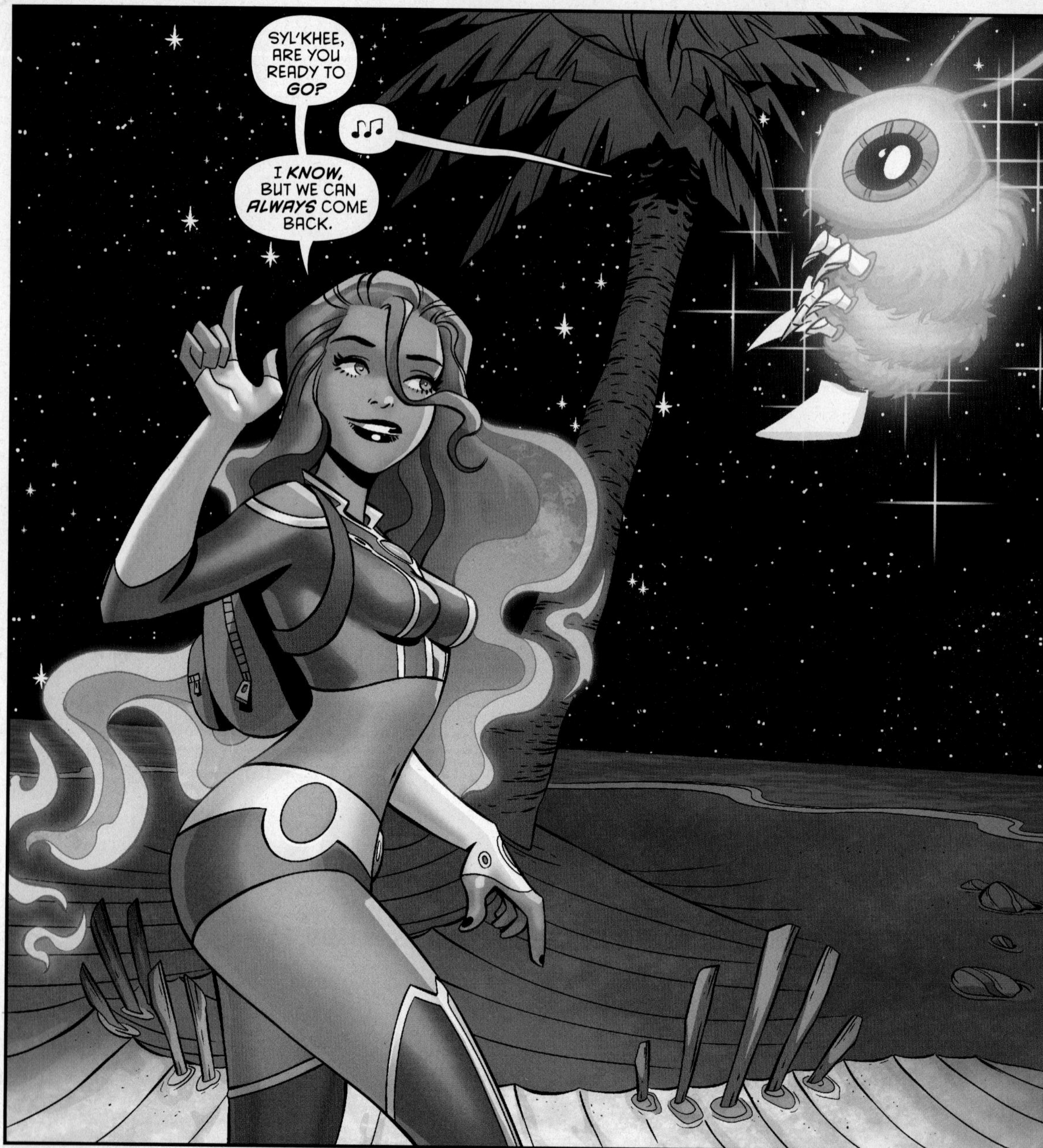
SYL'KHEE, ARE YOU READY TO GO?
I KNOW, BUT WE CAN ALWAYS COME BACK.

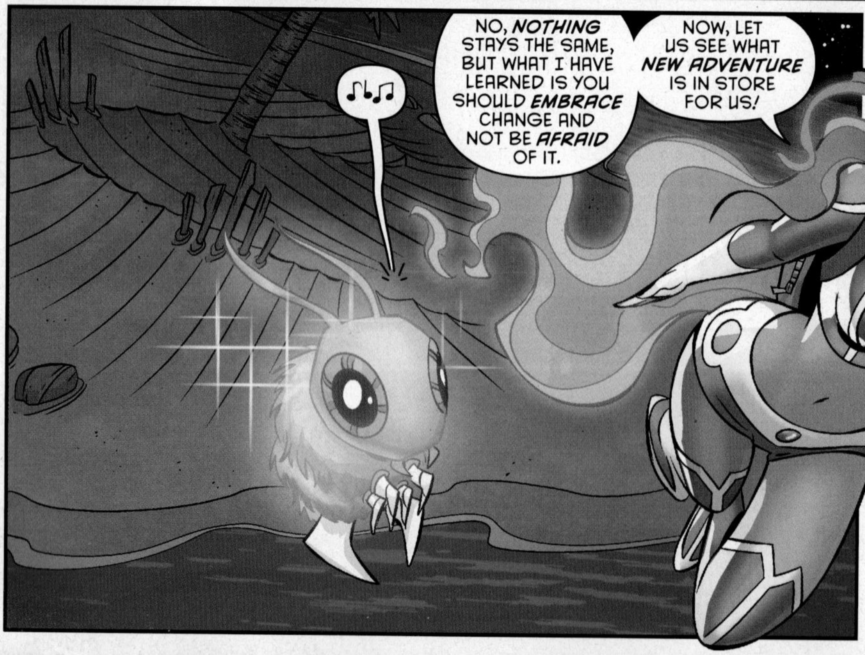
NO, NOTHING STAYS THE SAME, BUT WHAT I HAVE LEARNED IS YOU SHOULD EMBRACE CHANGE AND NOT BE AFRAID OF IT.
NOW, LET US SEE WHAT NEW ADVENTURE IS IN STORE FOR US!

THE END

Special thanks to all of you wonderful readers. Your support has meant the world to us...and remember, in comics, nothing goes away forever.

STARFIRE #8

ADULT COLORING BOOK VARIANT COVER BY DAVE JOHNSON

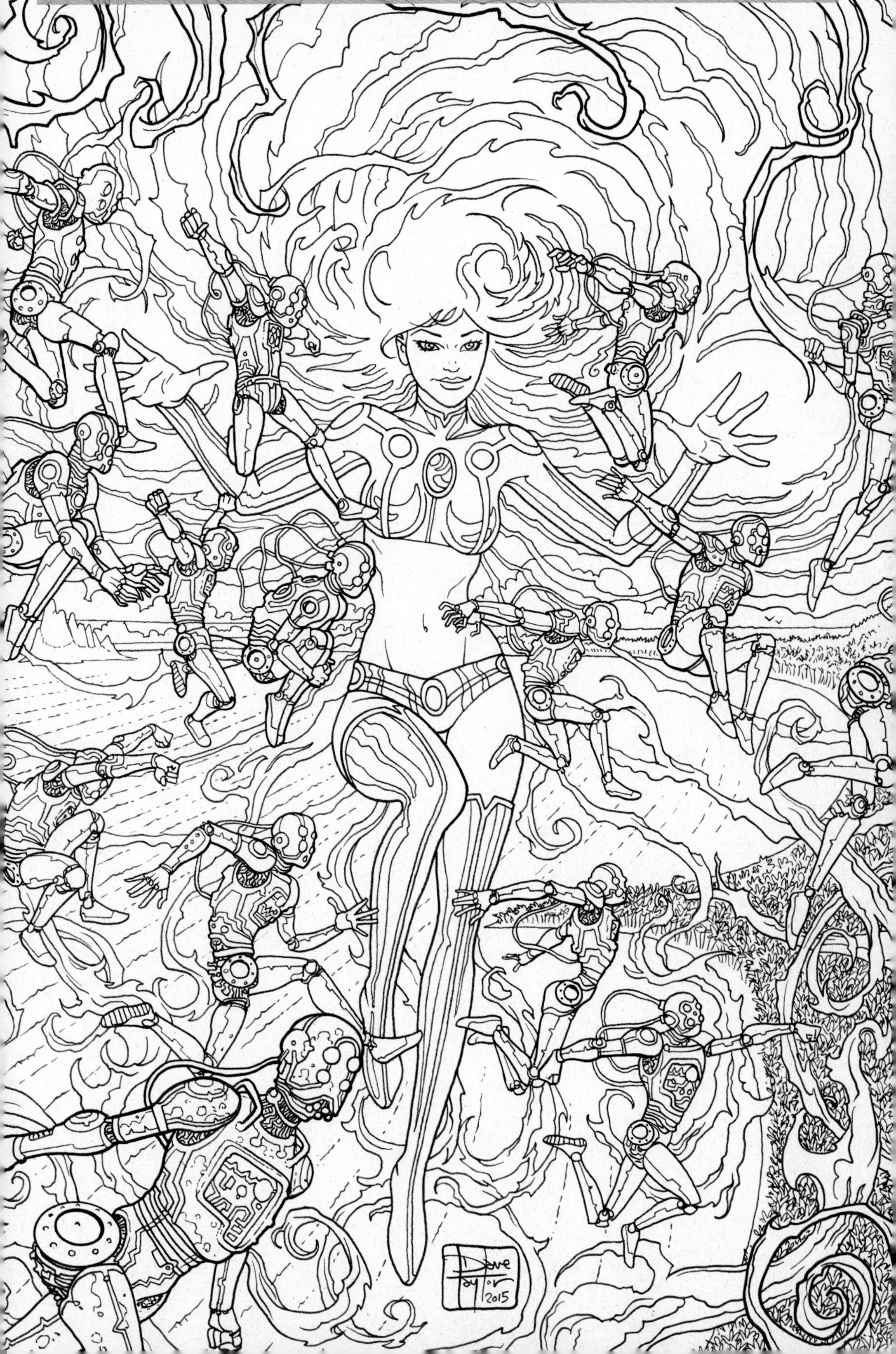

STARFIRE #9
VARIANT COVER BY NEAL ADAMS, SCOTT WILLIAMS & ALEX SINCLAIR

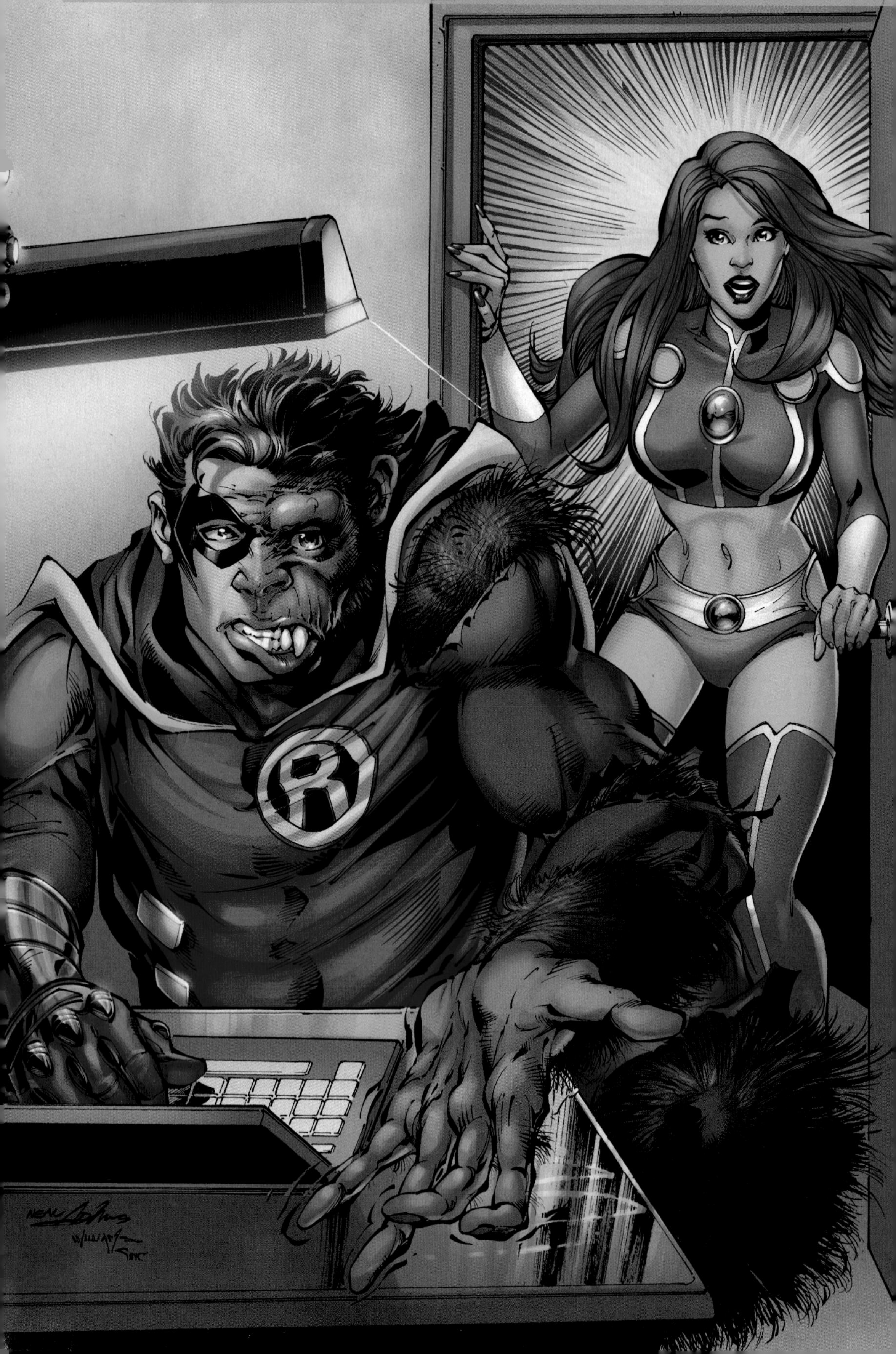

STARFIRE #11

VARIANT COVER BY JOHN ROMITA JR., SCOTT HANNA & BRAD ANDERSON

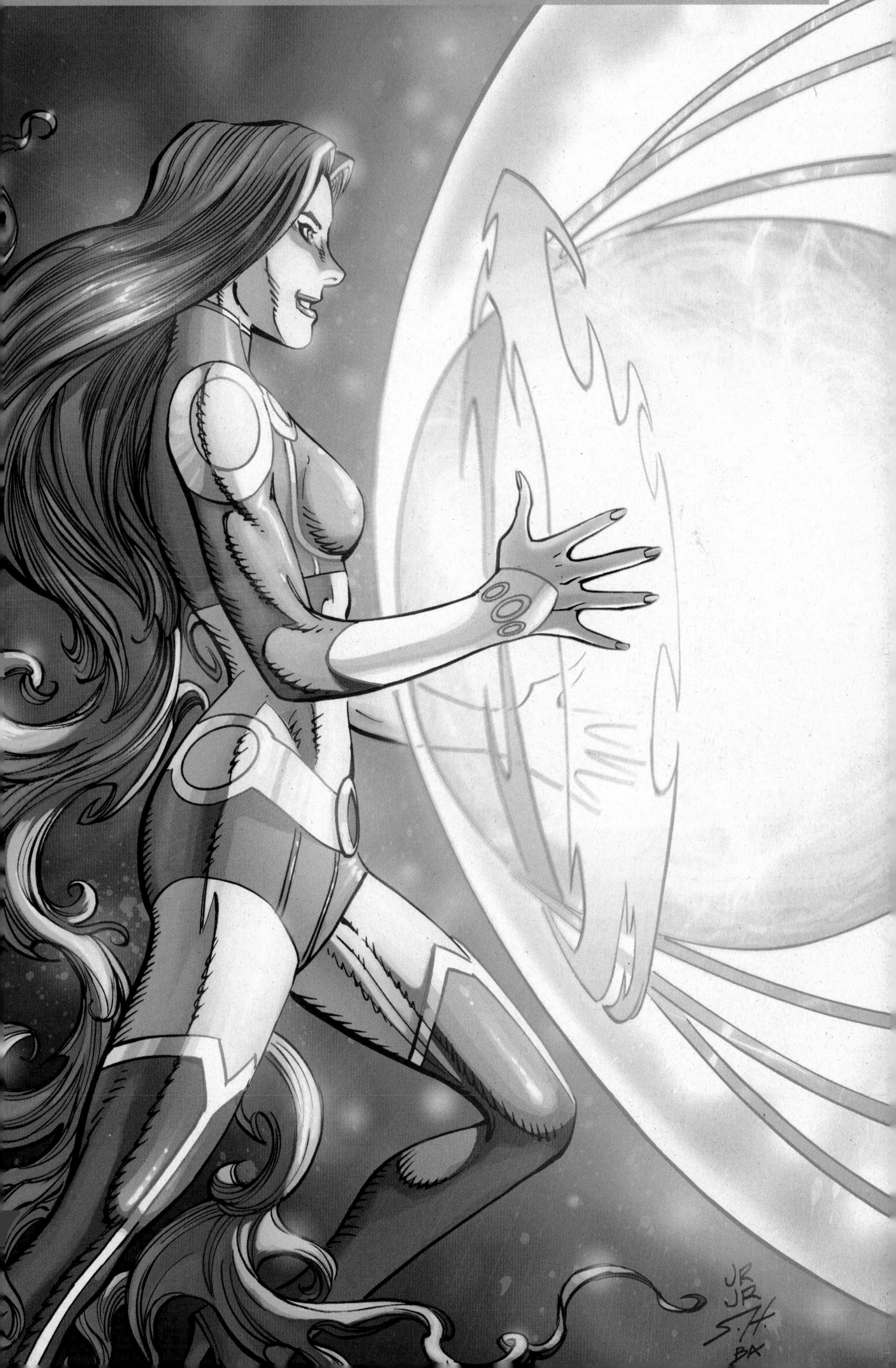

UNUSED INVENTORY COVER BY EMANUELA LUPACCHINO & HI-FI

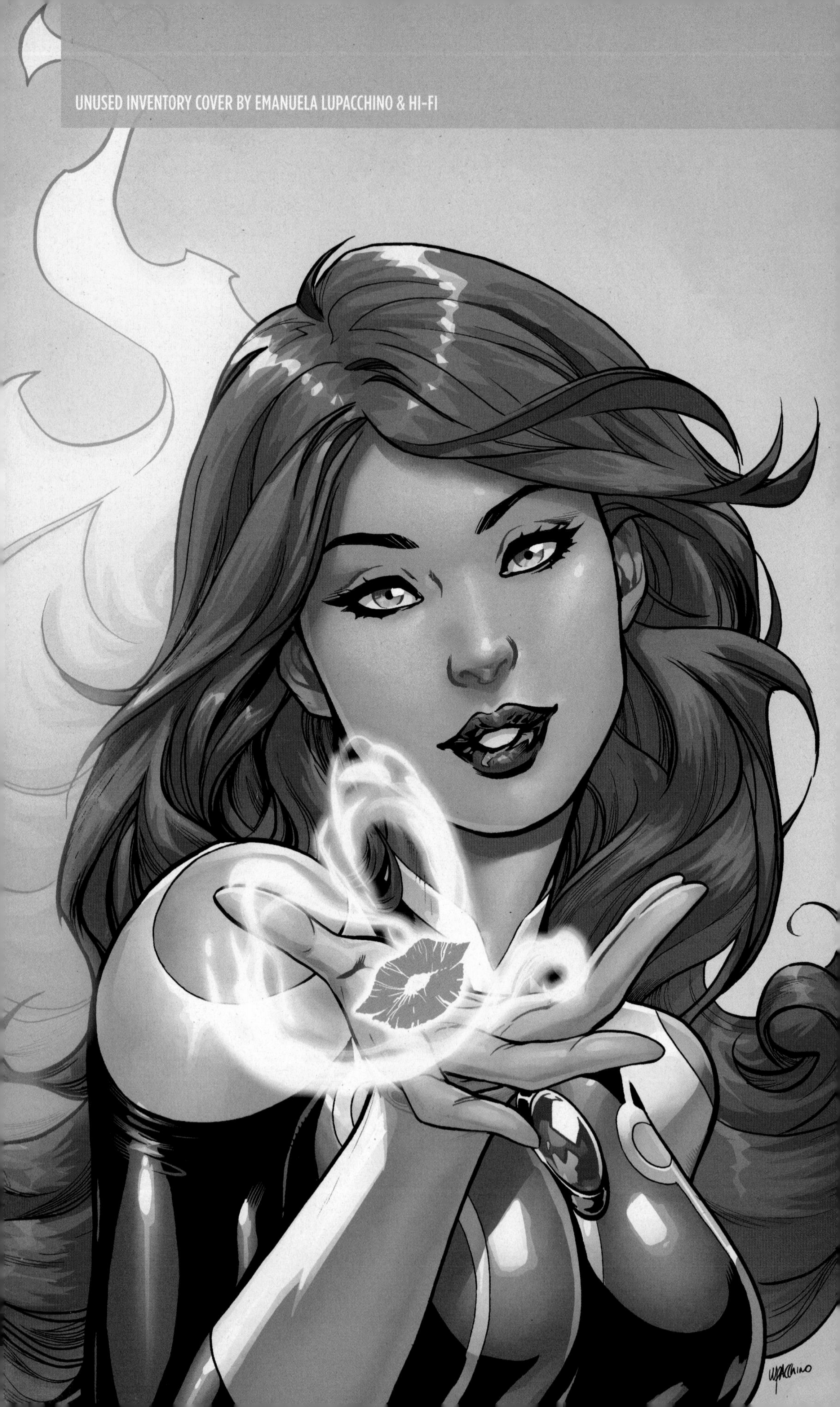

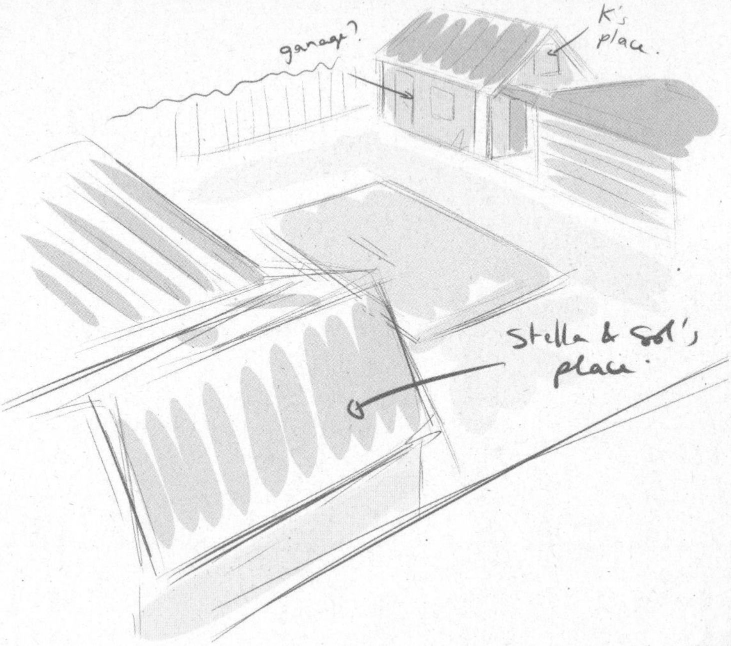
garage?
K's place.
Stella & Sol's place.

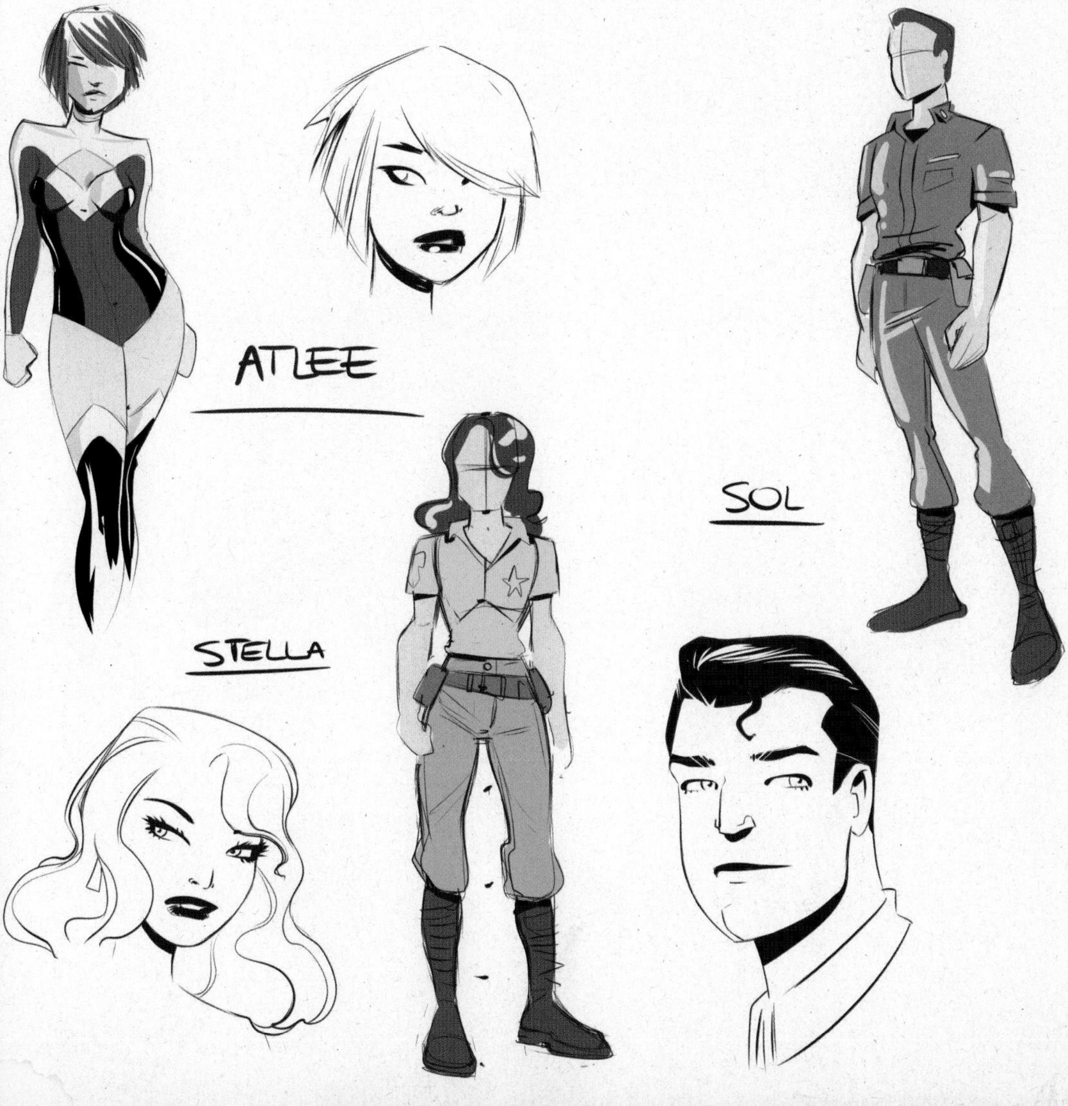
ATLEE
SOL
STELLA

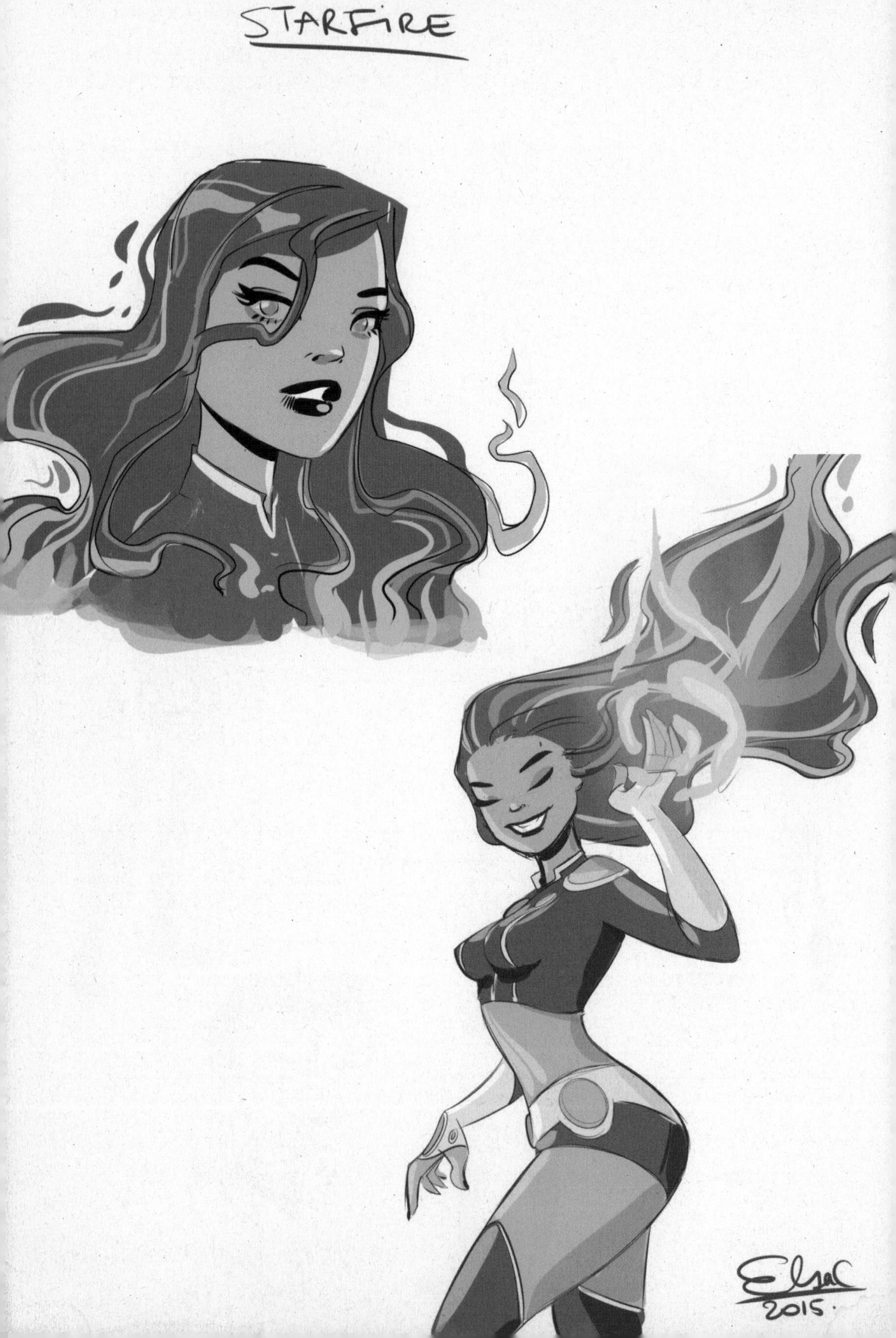
STARFIRE
Elsa C
2015.

HARLEY QUINN
VOLUME 1: HOT IN THE CITY

AMANDA **CONNER** JIMMY **PALMIOTTI** CHAD **HARDIN**
STEPHANE **ROUX** ALEX **SINCLAIR** PAUL **MOUNTS**

DC COMICS™

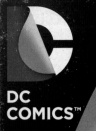

"Simone and artist Ardian Syaf not only do justice to Babs' legacy, but build in a new complexity that is the starting point for a future full of new storytelling possibilities. A hell of a ride."
—IGN

START AT THE BEGINNING!

BATGIRL VOLUME 1: THE DARKEST REFLECTION

BATWOMAN VOLUME 1: HYDROLOGY

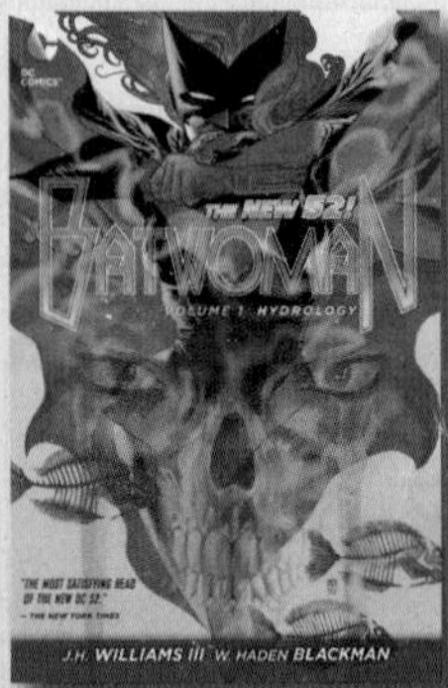
THE NEW 52!
BATWOMAN
VOLUME 1: HYDROLOGY
J.H. WILLIAMS III W. HADEN BLACKMAN

RED HOOD AND THE OUTLAWS VOLUME 1: REDEMPTION

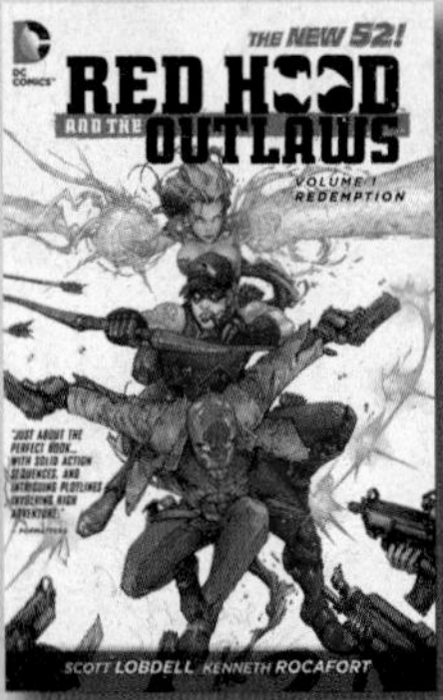
THE NEW 52!
RED HOOD AND THE OUTLAWS
VOLUME 1 REDEMPTION
SCOTT LOBDELL KENNETH ROCAFORT

BATWING VOLUME 1: THE LOST KINGDOM

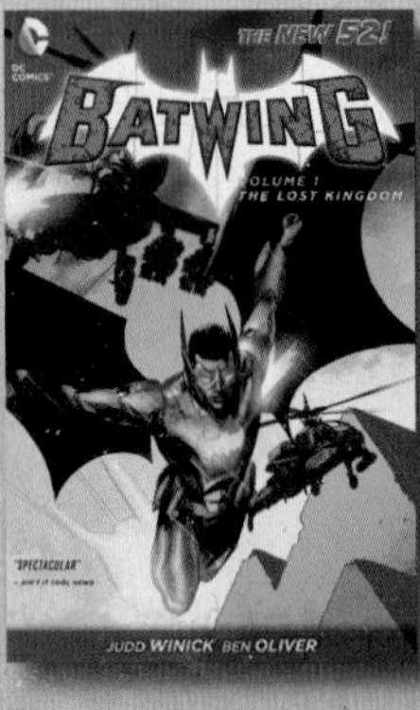
THE NEW 52!
BATWING
VOLUME 1 THE LOST KINGDOM
JUDD WINICK BEN OLIVER

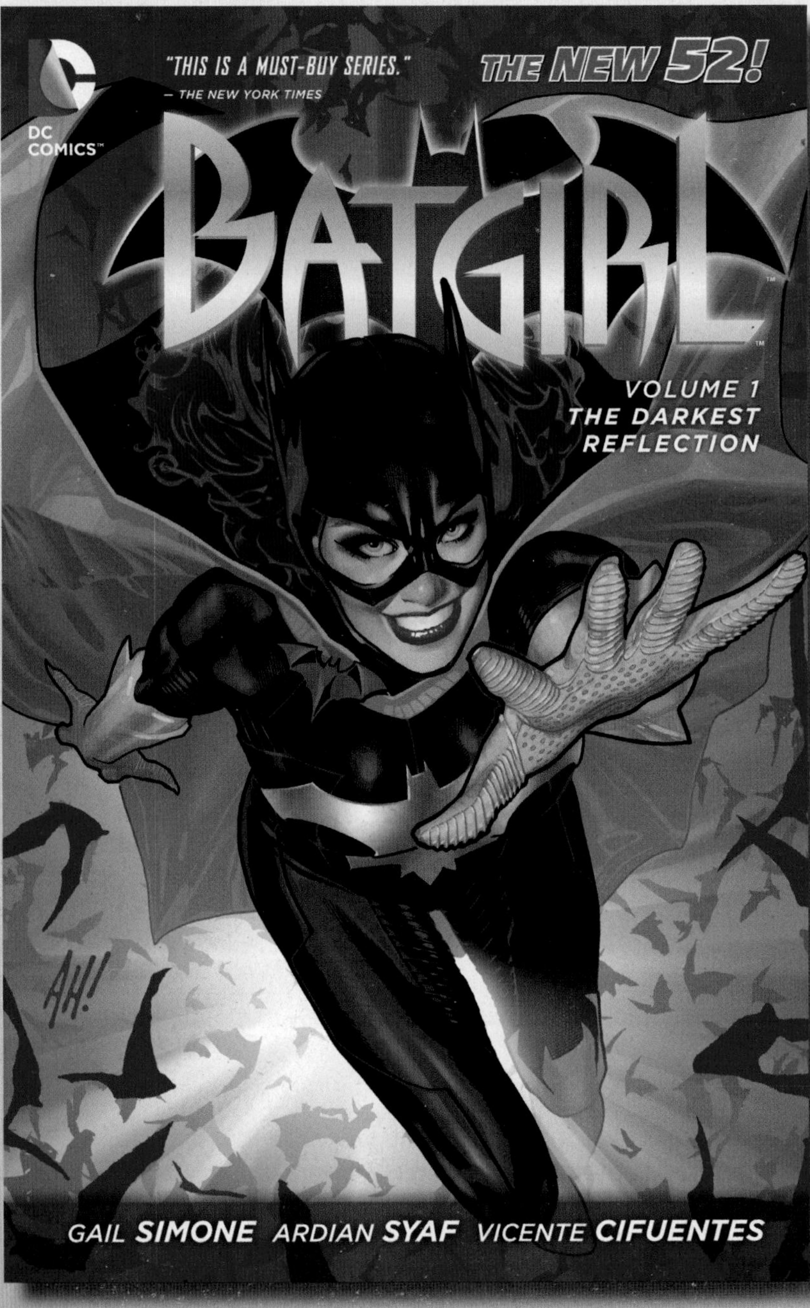
DC COMICS™
"THIS IS A MUST-BUY SERIES."
— THE NEW YORK TIMES
THE NEW 52!
BATGIRL
VOLUME 1 THE DARKEST REFLECTION
GAIL SIMONE ARDIAN SYAF VICENTE CIFUENTES